POLICY PARADOX

POLICY PARADOX:
THE ART OF POLITICAL
DECISION MAKING

DEBORAH STONE
Brandeis University

W · W · NORTON & COMPANY · NEW YORK · LONDON

Library of Congress Cataloging-in-Publication Data

Stone, Deborah A.
    Policy paradox : the art of political decision making / Deborah
Stone.
        p.   cm.
    Rev. ed. of: Policy paradox and political reason, c1988.
    Includes bibliographical references and index.
    ISBN 0-393-96857-X (pbk.)
    1. Policy science—Economic aspects. 2. Political planning—
Economic aspects. I. Stone, Deborah A. Policy paradox and
political reason. II. Title.
H97.S83   1996   96-52119
320′.6—dc21

W. W. Norton & Company, Inc., 500 Fifth Avenue, New York, N.Y. 10110
                    http://www.wwnorton.com
W. W. Norton & Company Ltd., 10 Coptic Street, London WC1A 1PU

    3 4 5 6 7 8 9 0

For Jim

somewhere always,
alone among the noise and policies of summer

Contents

Preface to the New Edition

If we're lucky, our affection for our books grows as our books grow older. And if we're lucky in this way, it's very hard to write a new edition, because you can't revise a book without rejecting and abandoning something of its first incarnation. *Policy Paradox and Political Reason* brought me many friends and loyal fans, so I was all the more reluctant to squeeze the scissors.

Thanks to three editors who each had a hand in *Policy Paradox*, I overcame my trepidations and squeezed. (All hands were safely out of the way, I hasten to add, and besides, I didn't really squeeze the scissors; I clicked on them. But if I follow that linguistic turn very far, you and I will be on a different voyage, one even more fantastic than the one we're about to take into politics.) Backspace. Up Arrow. As I was saying, I revised. How much? Enough to make the book up-to-date and even clearer for students, but not so much that my colleagues (as one of them bluntly requested) would need to reorganize their syllabi.

Before I say more about changes to the book, though, let me say something about you. Some of you (mostly professors) have read the earlier book, and some of you (mostly students) haven't. Students and other new readers might wonder why they should care what's different about this edition. Truth to tell, you shouldn't, but you should read the preface anyway because it will tell you quickly what the book is about or at least what the author thinks it's about. And for that matter, if you read the preface again once you've finished the book, you'll get an aerial perspective, a view of the forest for the trees.

Back to the changes. Let's take what's unchanged, first. This book grew out of my dissatisfaction with the fields of public policy and policy analysis. As far as I can tell, my four critiques of the standard policy literature are as necessary today as they were when I first conceived the book. So *Policy Paradox* remains deeply imbued with these critiques and is still structured as a counterpoint to the dominant policy thinking. Here are the critiques in a nutshell.

First, if one reads or talks very much about policy in academic settings, one can't help but notice a profound rejection of politics in favor of rational analysis. By and large, academic writing disparages politics as an unfortunate obstacle to good policy. Many political scientists have contributed to this literature of disparagement by demonstrating how actual policy making "deviates" from pure rational analysis. I believe we are all political creatures, in our daily lives as well as in our governance, and I wanted to construct a mode of policy analysis that accepts politics as a creative and valuable feature of social existence.

Second, the field of policy analysis is dominated by economics and its model of society as a market. A market, as conceived in classical microeconomics, is a collection of atomized individuals who have no community life. They have independent preferences, and their relationships consist entirely of trading with one another to maximize their individual well-being. Like many social scientists, I do not find the market model a convincing description of the world I know or, for that matter, any world I would want to live in. I wanted a kind of analysis that began with a model of political community, where individuals live in a web of dependencies, loyalties, and associations, and where they envision and fight for a public interest as well as their individual interests. This kind of analysis could not take individual preferences as "given," as most economists do, but would instead have to account for where people get their images of the world and how those images shape their preferences.

Third, the study of public policy, as it is conveyed in much of the political science literature, is remarkably devoid of theory. In trying to understand how policy gets made, political scientists have come up with an unrealistic "production" model of policy, according to which policy is assembled in stages, as if on a conveyer belt. They have written ten volumes describing particular controversies in different "issue areas" such as welfare policy or defense policy. They have offered case studies demonstrating the hopeless complexity and serendipity of policy making. And, when they have generalized from case studies, the generalizations are often fatuous: "Implementation is more likely to be successful when the program enjoys a high degree of political support. . . ." (This piece of wisdom is from a leading textbook on implementation, and you and I both know you didn't need to pay tuition to arrive at this conclusion. Surely you didn't believe implementation is more likely to be successful when a program has little political support.) Since I've always thought there are generic arguments in public policy that cut across issue areas and stages of policy making, I wanted a mode of analysis that equipped me to recognize and formulate recurring arguments and counterarguments—in short, a rhetoric of policy argument.

Lastly, the fields of public policy and policy analysis largely worship objectivity and determinate rules. They aim to derive rules of behavior that will automatically lead to the objectively "best" results. I do not believe there are objective principles of goodness or rules for human behavior that can ever work automatically. I wanted a kind of analysis that recognizes analytical concepts, problem statements, and policy instruments as being political claims themselves, instead of granting them privileged status as universal truths.

In these ways, *Policy Paradox* has changed very little. Both its purpose and its central argument remain the same. The book still aims to craft and teach a kind of political analysis that values politics and community, and that renders more visible the arguments and political claims underlying what is usually passed off as scientific truth, beyond dispute. It still argues that each of the analytic standards we use to set goals, define problems, and judge policy solutions is politically constructed. There is no "gold standard" of equality, efficiency, social measurement, causation, effectiveness, or anything else.

Here's what *has* changed. In this edition, I've updated the illustrations to include such contemporary controversies as affirmative action, welfare reform, national health insurance, voting rights, and criminal justice policy. I've added review boxes to each chapter to highlight the main points. I've also shortened the title—no one, not even I, could remember the title of the first version. Most importantly, I tried to clarify and correct what came across as a kind of agnosticism, or even, some said, amoralism. Although I do believe there is no objective standard of equity, one that everyone in a society accepts and one that affects everyone in a community in the same way, neither do I believe that all distributions are morally equivalent. The book does not argue that values don't matter. Quite the contrary—I try to show, in every chapter, why the policy analyst or decision maker MUST bring his or

i.e.: positivist / postpositivist

her values into the picture, precisely because all the king's concepts and techniques cannot yield definitive answers about the One Best Way.

Just because rewards, penalties, rules, and other policy instruments do not work with automatic and predictable mechanical regularity, as rational choice models would usually have it, it does not follow that all means of making policy decisions or getting people to change their behavior are equally consistent with democracy, justice, or community cohesion. Some kinds of inducement systems, for example, create more autonomy and self-determination for individuals, and some lead to more cohesiveness and cooperation than do others. In Part IV, I aim to demonstrate that every conceivable policy "instrument" or "solution" has broad effects on values, such as equity, democracy, or liberty, and that neglecting these effects leads to a pinched, distorted, ultimately unpolitical political analysis.

Even though, as I argue, the broad goals and principles at the heart of political conflict—things such as equity, efficiency, liberty, and security—can never be reduced to simple deterministic criteria and, therefore, cannot tell us how we should best decide policy questions, broad goals and principles can serve a crucial purpose. As aspirations for a society, they stand as ideals and promises for ourselves and future generations. They can unite people in striving for a better world, merely by forcing us to talk about what we mean by these vague words.

In arguing about the meaning of ideals, we are required to justify our own political wishes as something more than self-interest, and we must be open to seeing alternative points of view if we hope to persuade those who disagree. The capacity to imagine a better world, one more just or harmonious or liberating, and the capacity to reenvision problems and solutions continuously are qualities that make us human and give us a fighting chance at improving our lot. For all the trouble caused by vague goals, imprecise definitions of problems, and unruly policy instruments, we would be fools to trade them in for a calculator.

If this is your first encounter with *Policy Paradox*, I assure you the edition in your hands is much better than the one you missed. At any rate, it has more cartoons. But if you are one of the book's loyal fans, you can thank (or blame) John Covell, who bought the original concept for Little Brown, and Leo Wiegman, who found the book in a stack on his floor when he got to HarperCollins and rescued a difficult situation with grace and generosity. When you're done with this version, you can thank (or blame) Roby Harrington of W. W. Norton & Company, whose editorial wisdom, enthusiasm for his work, and knack for author T.L.C. breathed life into this version. All three editors have kept watch over *Policy Paradox*, no matter that they have all changed desks during the life of the book. I thank each of them for a kind of loyalty and nurturing that is ever more rare in publishing.

Former colleagues at the Institute of Policy Sciences of Duke University provoked and stimulated this project. Robert Behn's essay "Policy Analysts and Policy Politicians" (in the *Journal of Policy Analysis and Management*) first set me to thinking about the differences between analytical and political logic. His and James Vaupel's work on decision analysis and our numerous discussions pushed me to articulate dissatisfactions that were at first only vague mental itches. Carol Stack's ethnography and friendship kept me grounded in the real world. While I taught at M.I.T., I drew particularly from the work of Donald Schoen and Martin Rein on problem framing and from the work of Suzanne Berger on interests. Carl Kaysen first suggested starting with a political analogue of the economists' Robinson Crusoe society. The initial version benefited from the thoughtful and helpful advice of James Anderson, Donald Blackmer, Roger Cobb, Joshua Cohen, Andrew Dunham, Steven Erie, Michael Lipsky, John Kingdon, Lynn Mather, Martha Minow, James Morone, Marian Palley, and the late Aaron Wildavsky.

If you like this version, you've got still more people to thank. Thank Marion Smiley, Bob Kuttner, several anonymous reviewers, umpteen cohorts of students, and my Reader of First Resort, Jim Morone. Thank my parents, Sybil and Steve Stone, who requisition, dote on, and correct most everything I write, and who still hold me to the acid test: "Are you happy?" While you're at it, thank Bob Kuttner and Paul Starr for whatever political insight and stylistic verve I've absorbed by hanging around *The American Prospect*, the magazine they cofounded. (Better yet, subscribe.) Thank Rich Rivellese at Norton, who tuned into the manuscript and lavished it with smarts, time, and a wicked sense of humor. Last but not least, thank Andy Dunham of Colorado College because he had more influence on this version than anyone. He is paradoxically my most challenging yet most gentle critic, and in hours of conversation about politics, paradoxes, and life, everywhere from sea level to five thousand feet, he has always managed to keep me feeling precariously safe.

Writers live with their own special paradoxes. One that has always fascinated me is that, to be able to write, an author has to create an imaginary audience for the piece not yet written. I summoned innumerable audiences to my study for the writing of this book—students, colleagues, former teachers, intellectual and political adversaries, and even, I confess, the MacArthur Foundation talent scouts. I thank them all for their eager ears, in absentia. None of them, however, was as impressed and enthusiastic as my grandmother, Celia E. Stone, who died long before I began *Policy Paradox*. She used to read my school and college papers and talk with me about them, and she was a fabulous audience. She made me want to write for people like her. She was intelligent, and, though unable to continue her schooling beyond high school, keenly interested in ideas. Whenever I write, I always put her in front row center.

As for thanking Jim Morone, leave that to me. (I can't let you disturb him anyway, since he's either writing *Sin*, or sleeping it off, or virtuously laying in our wood supply for next winter.) We have been privileged to share the writing life as precious few people ever do, and though *Policy Paradox* is no doubt better as a result, the whys and ways of my thanks to him are best reserved for a private realm, one where the scissors are real and their main job is creating bouquets for him.

Lempster, New Hampshire
July 1996

The visual paradox on the cover is from a lithograph by Josef Albers. In this and other works in the series, Albers uses nothing but straight lines to create illusions of volume and space. In his own words,

> Solid volume shifts to open space and open space to volume. Masses moving at first to one side may suddenly appear to be moving to the opposite side, or in another direction. Likewise, upward acts also as downward, forward as backward, and verticals function as horizontals. . . . Black lines produce gray tones, and, for sensitive eyes, even color.

> Thus we cannot remain in a single viewpoint, we need more for the sake of free vision.
> —from *Despite Straight Lines*

I can't imagine a better metaphor for *Policy Paradox* and give my thanks to the Josef and Anni Albers Foundation for permission to reproduce the print.

Introduction

Paradoxes are nothing but trouble. They violate the most elementary principle of logic: Something cannot be two different things at once. Two contradictory interpretations cannot both be true. A paradox is just such an impossible situation, and political life is full of them. Consider some examples.

LOSING IS WINNING

When the Republicans gained control of the House of Representatives after the 1994 midterm elections, passing a balanced-budget amendment to the U.S. Constitution was tops on their legislative agenda. Republicans had long criticized Democrats for profligate government spending and high deficits. Getting a constitutional amendment to require a balanced budget would be a powerful legal weapon they could use to cut government programs drastically. Early in 1995, it looked like both houses of Congress would pass the budget amendment easily. As time got closer to a Senate vote in March, however, the Republicans didn't seem to have the 67 votes necessary to pass a constitutional amendment. Senator Bob Dole, the Republican majority leader, kept postponing the vote, hoping to pick up more support, but eventually he brought the bill to a vote without having 67 votes lined up. Why would he bring the matter to a vote, knowing that the Republicans would fail to pass it? On the eve of the vote, he explained:

"We really win if we win, but we may also win if we lose."[1]

After the vote, the headlines were unanimous: "Senate Rejects Amendment on Balancing the Budget; Close Vote is Blow to GOP," went the *New York Times'* verdict. "GOP is Loser on Budget Amendment," echoed the *Boston Globe*.[2] What did Dole mean by claiming that a loss could be a victory?

Politicians always have at least two goals. First is a policy goal—whatever program or proposal they would like to see accomplished or defeated, whatever problem they would like to see solved. Perhaps even more important, though, is a political goal. Politicians always want to preserve their power, or gain enough power, to be able to accomplish their policy goals. Even though a defeat of the balanced budget amendment was a loss for Republicans' policy goal, Dole thought it might be a gain for Republicans' political strength. (So, apparently, did the *New York Times*, whose sub-headline read "Risk to Democrats.") Republican leaders acknowledged that they had lost a constitutional device that would have helped them immensely in redeeming their campaign pledge to enact the "Contract with America." But they also saw some important political gains. Senator Orrin Hatch, the chief sponsor of the amendment, called the vote "a clear delineation between the parties." A Republican pollster explained how the vote might help Republican candidates in the next Congressional election: "It lays out the differences as sharply as we could want them: We want to cut spending, and they don't."[3] Dole, already campaigning for the Presidency, used the occasion to lambaste President Clinton for "abdicating his responsibility" to control federal deficits, while Republicans in both houses talked about making Democrats pay at the polls in the next election. "As far as I'm concerned," Newt Gingrich crowed, "it's like a fork in chess. They can give us a victory today; they can give us a victory in November '96."[4]

[1] Quoted in Jill Zuckman, "No Voting, More Anger on Budget," *Boston Globe*, March 2, 1995, p. 1.

[2] Both headlines on front page, *New York Times*, March 3, 1995; *Boston Globe*, March 5, 1995.

[3] Quotations in "GOP Is Loser on Budget Amendment," *Boston Globe*, March 5, 1995, p. 1.

[4] Quotation from "Senate Rejects Amendment on Balanced Budget," *New York Times*, March 3, 1995, p. A1.

Parades: Recreation or Speech?

An Irish gay and lesbian group wanted to march in Boston's annual Saint Patrick's day parade. The organizers of the parade wanted to stop them. The gay and lesbian group said a parade is a public recreational event, and therefore, civil rights law protected them against discrimination in public accommodations. The parade organizers claimed a parade is an expression of beliefs, really an act of speech. Their right to say what they wanted—by excluding from the parade those with a different message—should be protected by the First Amendment. Is a parade a public recreational event or an act of self-expression? Might it be both? What would you do if you were a justice on the Supreme Court and had to decide one way or the other?[5]

For or against Welfare?

When asked about public spending on welfare, 48 percent of Americans say it should be cut. But when asked about spending on programs for poor children, 47 percent say it should be increased, and only 9 percent want cuts.[6]

Do Americans want to enlarge or curtail welfare spending? It all depends on how the question is framed.

Enemies or Allies?

The Food and Drug Administration (FDA) regulates the testing and marketing of new pharmaceutical drugs. For decades, drug manufacturers have complained that the regulations make developing new drugs excessively costly and painfully slow. Thanks to the FDA, they have argued, the pharmaceutical industry is hardly profitable anymore, and the U.S. has lost its lead as the world's innovator of medical miracles. Drug companies have consistently wanted the FDA off their backs. When, however, the Republican party finally took control of the

[5]Linda Greenhouse, "High Court Lets Parade in Boston Bar Homosexuals," *New York Times,* June 20, 1995, p. A1.

[6]Jason DeParle, "Despising Welfare, Pitying Its Young," *New York Times,* December 18, 1994, p. E5.

House in 1995 and prepared to privatize most of the functions of the FDA, the pharmaceutical manufacturers were the first to rush to the FDA's defense.

Why the sudden turnabout? At one level, an industry and its regulatory agency are adversaries. One is a watchdog for the other, a guardian of the public interest against exploitation by those with more narrow self-interests. At another level, though, regulators and the regulated always have a symbiotic relationship. They depend on each other. Without an industry to regulate, the regulatory agency would be out of business. And, in the case of drug manufacturing, without the seal of government approval for its drugs, the industry would lose the "world's confidence in the superiority of American drugs," and the American public's confidence in the safety and efficacy of drugs. "We are for a strong F.D.A.," said the head of the Health Industry Manufacturers' Association. "They are our credibility."[7]

In politics, as in life, many relationships are simultaneously adversarial and symbiotic.

WHICH CAME FIRST—THE PROBLEM OR THE SOLUTION?

In the 1950s, a federal program for mass transit was proposed as a solution to urban congestion. Subways and buses were presented as a more efficient means of transportation than private cars. In the late 1960s, environmental protection was the word of the day, and mass transit advocates peddled subways and buses as a way to reduce automobile pollution. Then with the OPEC oil embargo of 1972, Washington's attention was riveted by the energy crisis, and mass transit was sold as an energy-saving alternative to private automobiles. Was this a case of three problems for which mass transit just happened to be a solution, or a constant solution adapting to a changing problem?[8]

BABIES: PRODUCT OR SERVICE?

New reproductive technologies have fundamentally changed the way people can have babies and create families. "Baby M" was born in

[7]Philip J. Hilts, "FDA Becomes Target of Empowered Groups," *New York Times*, Feb. 12, 1995, p. 24.

[8]John Kingdon, *Agendas, Alternatives and Public Policies* (Boston: Little Brown, 1984), p. 181.

1986 as the result of a contract between William Stern and Marybeth Whitehead, both married, though not to each other. The contract provided for Mrs. Whitehead to be artificially inseminated with Mr. Stern's sperm, to bring the baby to term in her womb, and then to give the baby to Mr. and Mrs. Stern to raise as their child. In return, Mr. Stern would pay Mrs. Whitehead $10,000, plus expenses.

After the birth, Mrs. Whitehead decided she wanted to keep the baby, who was, after all, her biological daughter. The case went to court. Although the immediate issue was who would win the right to raise "Baby M," the policy question on everybody's mind was whether the courts should recognize and enforce surrogate motherhood contracts. Most states prohibit the sale of babies in their adoption laws. So the question of paramount importance was whether a surrogate motherhood contract is a contract for the sale of a baby or for a socially useful service.

On the one hand, Mrs. Whitehead could be seen as renting her womb. Like any professional service provider, she agreed to observe high standards of practice—in this case, prenatal care. According to the contract, she would not drink, smoke, or take drugs, and she would follow medical advice. Like any physical laborer, she was selling the use of her body for a productive purpose. By her own and the Sterns' account, she was altruistically helping to create a child for a couple who could not have their own.

On the other hand, Mrs. Whitehead could be seen as producing and selling a baby. She underwent artificial insemination in anticipation of a fee—no fee, no baby. She agreed to have amniocentesis and to have an abortion if the test showed any defects not acceptable to Mr. Stern. She agreed to accept a lower fee if the baby were born with any mental or physical handicaps—low-value baby, low price.

Is a surrogate motherhood contract for a service or for a baby?

How can we make sense of a world where such paradoxes occur? In an age of science, of human mastery over the innermost and outermost realms, how are we to deal with situations that will not observe the elementary rules of scientific decorum? Can we make public policy behave?

The fields of political science, public administration, law, and policy analysis have shared a common mission of rescuing public policy from the irrationalities and indignities of politics, hoping to make policy instead with rational, analytical, and scientific methods. This endeavor is what I call "the rationality project," and it has been a core part of

American political culture almost since the beginning. The project began with James Madison's effort to "cure the mischiefs of faction" with proper constitutional design, thereby assuring that government policy would be protected from the self-interested motives of tyrannous majorities.[9] In the 1870s, Christopher Columbus Langdell, dean of the Harvard Law School, undertook to take the politics out of law by reforming legal training. Law was a science, he proclaimed, to be studied by examining appellate court decisions as specimens and distilling their common essence into a system of principles. There was no need for either students or professors to gain practical experience.

At the turn of the twentieth century, the rationality project was taken up in spades by the Progressive reformers, who removed policy-making authority from elected bodies and gave it to expert regulatory commissions and professional city managers, in an effort to render policy making more scientific and less political. The quest for an apolitical science of government continues in the twentieth century with Herbert Simon's search for a "science of administration," Harold Lasswell's dream of a "science of policy forming and execution," and the current effort of universities, foundations, and government to foster a profession of policy scientists.

This book has two aims. First, I argue that the rationality project misses the point of politics. Moreover, it is an impossible dream. From inside the rationality project, politics looks messy, foolish, erratic, and inexplicable. Events, actions, and ideas in the political world seem to leap outside the categories that logic and rationality offer. In the rationality project, the categories of analysis are somehow above politics or outside it. Rationality purports to offer a correct vantage point, from which we can judge the goodness of the real world.

I argue, instead, that the very categories of thought underlying rational analysis are themselves a kind of paradox, defined in political struggle. They do not exist before or without politics, and because they are necessarily abstract (they are categories of *thought*, after all), they can have multiple meanings. Thus, analysis is itself a creature of politics; it is strategically crafted argument, designed to create ambiguities and paradoxes and to resolve them in a particular direction. (This much is certainly awfully abstract for now, but each of the subsequent chapters is designed to show very concretely how one analytic category of politics and policy is a constantly evolving political creation.)

Beyond demonstrating this central misconception of the rationality

[9]This was the argument of his *Federalist Paper No. 10*, about which more is said in Chapters 10 and 15.

project, my second aim is to derive a kind of political analysis that makes sense of policy paradoxes such as the ones depicted above. I seek to create a framework in which such phenomena, the ordinary situations of politics, do not have to be explained away as extraordinary, written off as irrational, dismissed as folly, or disparaged as "pure politics." Unfortunately, much of the literature about public policy proceeds from the idea that policy making in practice deviates from some hypothetical standards of good policy making, and that there is thus something fundamentally wrong with politics. In creating an alternative mode of political analysis, I start from the belief that politics is a creative and valuable feature of social existence.

The project of making public policy rational rests on three pillars: a model of reasoning, a model of society, and a model of policy making. The *model of reasoning* is rational decision making. In this model, decisions are or should be made in a series of well-defined steps:

1. Identify objectives.
2. Identify alternative courses of action for achieving objectives.
3. Predict the possible consequences of each alternative.
4. Evaluate the possible consequences of each alternative.
5. Select the alternative that maximizes the attainment of objectives.

This model of rational behavior is so pervasive it is a staple of checkout-counter magazines and self-help books. For all of its intuitive appeal, however, the rational decision-making model utterly fails to explain Bob Dole's thinking or behavior at the time of the balanced budget amendment vote. Did he attain his objective or didn't he? Did he win or lose? Worse, the model could not help formulate political advice for Dole beforehand, for if we accept his reasoning that he wins either way, then it doesn't matter which way the vote goes and he should just sit back and enjoy the play. Of course, Dole was not only reasoning when he claimed that losing was winning. He was also trying to manipulate how the outcome of the vote would be perceived and how it would influence future political contests between the Republicans and the Democrats. In fact, all the Republican credit-claiming and victory speeches upon losing the vote suggest that politicians have a great deal of control over interpretations of events, and that the political analyst who wants to choose a wise course of action should focus less on assessing the objective consequences of actions and more on how the interpretations will go. If politicians can attain their objectives by portraying themselves as having attained them, then they should be studying portraiture, not cost-benefit analysis.

A model of political reason ought to account for the possibilities of changing one's objectives, of pursuing contradictory objectives simultaneously, of winning by appearing to lose and turning loss into an appearance of victory, and most unusual, of attaining objectives by portraying oneself as having attained them. Throughout this book, I develop a model of political reasoning quite different from the model of rational decision making. Political reasoning is reasoning by metaphor and analogy. It is trying to get others to see a situation as one thing rather than another. For example, parades can be seen as public recreational events, or as collective marches to express an idea. Each vision constructs a different political contest, and invokes a different set of rules for resolving the conflict. Babies created under surrogate motherhood contracts are a phenomenon quite unlike anything we already know. The situation is not exactly like professional service, not exactly like wage labor, not exactly like a contract for pork bellies, not exactly like a custody dispute between divorced parents, and not exactly like an adoption contract. Legislatures and courts deal with the issue by asking, "Of the things that surrogate motherhood isn't, which is it most like?"

Political reasoning is metaphor-making and category-making, but not just for beauty's sake or for insight's sake. It is strategic portrayal for persuasion's sake, and ultimately for policy's sake. This concept of political reason is developed and illustrated throughout the book, and I take up the idea directly again in the last chapter.

The *model of society* underlying the contemporary rationality project is the market. Society is viewed as a collection of autonomous, rational decision makers who have no community life. Their interactions consist entirely of trading with one another to maximize their individual well-being. They each have objectives or preferences, they each compare alternative ways of attaining their objectives, and they each choose the way that yields the most satisfaction. They maximize their self-interest through rational calculation. The market model and the rational decision-making model are thus very closely related.

The market model is not restricted to things we usually consider markets, that is, to systems where goods and services are bought and sold. Electoral voting, the behavior of legislators, political leadership, the size of the welfare rolls, and even marriage have all been explained in terms of the maximization of self-interest through rational calculation. The market model posits that individuals have relatively fixed, independent preferences for goods, services, and policies. In real societies, where people are psychologically and materially dependent, where they are connected through emotional bonds, traditions, and social groups, their preferences are based on loyalties and comparisons of images. How people define their preferences depends to a large extent on how choices are presented to them and by whom. They want greater welfare spending when it is called helping poor children, but not when it is called welfare. Sometimes, as in the case of "Baby M," they are not quite sure what they are buying and selling, or whether they have engaged in a sale at all.

In place of the model of society as a market, I construct a model of society as a political community (Part I). Chapter 1, "The Market and the Polis," sets forth the fundamental elements of human behavior and social life that I take to be axiomatic, and contrasts them with the axioms of the market model. I start with a model of political community, or "polis," because I began my own intellectual odyssey in this territory with a simple reflection: Both policy and thinking about policy are produced in political communities.

The observation may be trite, but it has radical consequences for a field of inquiry that has been dominated by a conception of society as a market. To take just one example, the market model of society envisions societal welfare as the aggregate of individuals' situations. All behavior is explained as people striving to maximize their own self-interest. The market model therefore gives us no way to talk about how people fight over visions of the public interest or the nature of the community—the truly significant political questions underlying policy choices.

The *model of policy making* in the rationality project is a production model, where policy is created in a fairly orderly sequence of stages, almost as if on an assembly line. Many political scientists, in fact, speak of "assembling the elements" of policy. An issue is "placed on the agenda," and a problem gets defined. It moves through the legislative and executive branches of government, where alternative solutions are proposed, analyzed, legitimized, selected, and refined. A solution is implemented by the executive agencies and constantly challenged and revised by interested actors, perhaps using the judicial branch. And finally, if the policy-making process is managerially sophisticated, it provides a means of evaluating and revising implemented solutions.

So conceived, the policy-making process parallels the cognitive steps of the rational model of decision making . Government becomes a rational decision maker writ large—albeit not a very proficient one. Much of the political science literature in this genre is devoted to understanding where and how good policy gets derailed in the process of production. This model of policy making as rational problem solving cannot explain why sometimes policy solutions go looking for problems. It cannot tell us why solutions, such as privatizing the FDA's drug evaluation, turn into problems. It only tells us things are working "backward" or poorly.

The production model fails to capture what I see as the essence of policy making in political communities: the struggle over ideas. Ideas are a medium of exchange and a mode of influence even more powerful than money and votes and guns. Shared meanings motivate people to action and meld individual striving into collective action. Ideas are at the center of all political conflict. Policy making, in turn, is a constant struggle over the criteria for classification, the boundaries of categories, and the definition of ideals that guide the way people behave.

Chapters 2 through 15 examine the constituent ideas of policy and policy analysis in light of their construction in a political community. Each idea is an argument, or more accurately, a collection of arguments in favor of different ways of seeing the world. Every chapter is devoted to showing how there are multiple understandings of what appears to be a single concept, how these understandings are created, and how they are manipulated as part of political strategy. Revealing the hidden arguments embedded in each concept illuminates, and may help resolve, the surface conflicts.

The reader would certainly be justified in asking why I chose the particular set of ideas included here. The broad architecture of the book takes its shape from the notion of a policy issue implied in the rationality project: We have a goal; we have problem, which is a discrepancy between the goal and reality; and we seek a solution to erase the discrepancy. Parts II, III, and IV correspond to the three parts of this framework: goals, problems, and solutions.

As I demonstrate throughout the book, the political careers of most policy issues are not nearly so simple as this three-part formula would suggest. For example, people do not always perceive a goal first and then look for disparities between the goal and the status quo. Often, they see a problem first, which triggers a search for solutions and statement of goals. Or, they see a solution first, then formulate a problem that requires their solution (and their services). Nevertheless, I use this framework because it expresses a logic of problem solving that is widespread in the policy analysis literature and because it parallels the models of rational decision making and the policy-making process.

Part II is about goals—not the specific goals of particular policy issues, such as expanding health insurance coverage or lowering health care costs, but the enduring values of community life that give rise to controversy over particular policies: equity, efficiency, security, and liberty. These values are "motherhood issues": everyone is for them when they are stated abstractly, but the fight begins as soon as we ask what people mean by them. These values not only express goals, but also serve as the standards we use to evaluate existing situations and policy proposals.

One tenet of the rationality project is that there are objective and neutral standards of evaluation that can be applied to politics, but that come from a vantage point outside politics, untainted by the interests of political players. The theme of Part II is that behind every policy issue lurks a contest over conflicting, though equally plausible, conceptions of the same abstract goal or value. The abstractions are aspirations for a community, into which people read contradictory interpretations. It may not be possible to get everyone to agree on the same interpretation, but the first task of the political analyst is to reveal and clarify the underlying value disputes so that people can see where they differ and move toward some reconciliation.

There might well have been other ideas in the section on goals. Justice, privacy, social obligation, and democracy come to mind. Equity, efficiency, security, and liberty begged more insistently for political analysis only because, sadly, they are invoked more often as criteria in policy analysis. Once having read this book, the reader will have no trouble seeing some of the paradoxes in other criteria.

Part III is about problems and about how we know there is a disparity between social goals and the current state of affairs. There are many modes of defining problems in policy discourse, and each mode is like a language within which people offer and defend conflicting interpretations. "Symbols" and "Numbers" are about verbal and numerical languages, respectively, and both examine devices of symbolic representation within those languages. We also define problems in terms of what causes them ("Causes"), who is lined up on each side ("Interests"), or what kind of choice they pose ("Decisions"). Here, too, I might have chosen other categories; for example, one could examine problem formulation according to different disciplines, such as economics, law, political science, or ethics. I did not choose that framework because it would only perpetuate the somewhat artivicial divisions of academia, and the categories I did choose seem to me a better representation of modes of discourse in political life.

Part IV is about solutions, or more accurately, about the temporary resolutions of conflict. These chapters start from the assumption that all policies involve deliberate attempts to change people's behavior, and each chapter in this section deals with a mechanism for bringing about such change—creating incentives and penalties ("Inducements"), mandating rules ("Rules"), informing and persuading ("Facts"), stipulating rights and duties ("Rights"), and reorganizing authority ("Powers").

The common theme of this part is that policy instruments are not just tools, each with its own function and its own appropriateness for certain kinds of jobs. In the standard political science model of the policy-making process, policy solutions are decided upon and then implemented, though things usually go awry at the implementation stage. The task of the analyst is to figure out which is the right or best tool to use, and then to fix mistakes when things don't go as planned. I argue, instead, that each type of policy instrument is a kind of political arena, with its peculiar ground rules, within which political conflicts are continued. Each mode of social regulation draws lines around what people may and may not do and how they may or may not treat each other. But these boundaries are constantly contested, either because they are ambiguous and do not settle conflicts, or because they allocate benefits and burdens to the people on either side, or both. Boundaries become real and acquire their meaning in political struggles. The job of the analyst, in this view, is to understand the rules of the game well enough to know the standard moves and have a repertoire of effective countermoves.

If deep down inside, you are a rationalist, you might want to know whether the topics covered by the chapters are "exhaustive" and "mutually exclusive." They are most assuredly not. Our categories of thought and modes of argument are intertwined and not easily delineated. That is one reason, I shall argue, why we have and always will have politics. Then, too, I remind you that I am trying to demonstrate precisely that essential political concepts are paradoxes. They have contradictory meanings that by formal logic ought to be mutually exclusive but by political logic are not. I do hope, however, that my categories at least provide a useful way to divide up an intellectual territory for exploration, and at best provide a new way of seeing it.

As for whether my categories are exhaustive, I can only plead the quintessential political defense: I had to draw the line somewhere.

PART I

POLITICS

1

The Market and the Polis

A theory of policy politics must start with a model of political society, that is, a model of the simplest version of society that retains the essential elements of politics. *Polis,* the Greek word for city-state, seems a fitting name for the essential political society because it conjures up an entity small enough to have very simple forms of organization yet large enough to embody the elements of politics. In searching for the elements of politics, it is helpful to use the market model as a foil because of its predominance in contemporary policy discussions. The contrast between the models of political and market society will illuminate the ways the market model grossly distorts political life.

A market can be simply defined as a social system in which individuals pursue their own welfare by exchanging things with others whenever trades are mutually beneficial. Economists often begin their discussions of the market by conjuring up the Robinson Crusoe society, where two people on a lush tropical island swap coconuts and small game animals. They trade to make each person better off, but since each person always has the option of producing everything for himself, trading is never an absolute necessity for either one. (Economists usually neglect to mention that the "real" Crusoe was able to salvage a veritable microcosm of industrial society from his shipwrecked vessel—from gunpowder and muskets to cables and nails.) Participants in the market are in competition with each other for scarce resources; each person tries to acquire things at the least possible cost, and to convert raw materials into more valuable things that can be sold at the highest possible price.

In the market model, individuals act only to maximize their own self-interest. Here "self-interest" means their own welfare, however they define that for themselves. It does not mean that they act "selfishly"; their self-interest might include, for example, the well-being of their family and friends. The competitive drive to maximize one's own welfare stimulates people to be very resourceful, creative, clever, and productive, and ultimately raises the level of economic well-being of society as a whole. With this description of the essence of the market model, we can start to build an alternative model of the polis by contrasting more detailed features of the market model and a political community.

COMMUNITY

A model purporting to capture the essence of political life would have to be far more complex than the Robinson Crusoe society, with or without its industrial artifacts. Because politics and policy can happen only in communities, community must be the starting point of our polis. Public policy is about communities trying to achieve something as communities. This is true even though there is almost always conflict within a community over what its goals should be and who its members are, and even though every communal goal ultimately must be achieved through the behavior of individuals. Unlike the market, which starts with individuals and assumes no goals, preferences, or intentions other than those held by individuals, a model of the polis must assume both collective will and collective effort.

Untold volumes of political philosophy have tried to define and explain this phenomenon of collective intention. But even without being able to define it, we know intuitively that societies behave as if they had one. We can scarcely speak about societies without using the language of collective will ("Democrats want . . ."; "Farmers seek . . ."; "The administration is trying . . ."). Every child knows the feeling of being in a group and reaching consensus. We can argue about whether consensus implies unanimity or only majority, or whether apparent consensus masks suppressed dissension. But we know that consensus is a feeling of collective will, and we know when it exists and when it does not, just as surely (and sometimes mistakenly) as we know when we are hungry and when we are not.

A community must have a membership, and some way of defining who is a member of the community and who is not. Membership is in some sense the primary political issue, for membership definitions and rules determine who is allowed to participate in community activities, and who is governed by community rules and authority. Nation-states have rules for citizenship. Private clubs have qualifications for members and procedures by which people can join. Churches have formal rituals for new members to join. Neighborhoods may have no formal rules limiting who may become a member, but informal practices such as restrictive covenants on property deeds, bank redlining in mortgage lending, and sheer harassment may accomplish racial exclusion when formal rules cannot.

The most highly contested and passionate political fights are about membership. Mere physical residence in a place is not always the same thing as political membership. Proposition 187 in California, a provision that prohibits undocumented aliens from using public schools, Medicaid, and other social programs, is one of many immigration backlash movements that differentiates among residents, giving political benefits to some but not others. The distinction between residence and citizenship is only the beginning of conflicts over membership. In the United States, we have had a long tradition of multiple civic statuses among people who were nominally citizens: female and black citizens were not allowed to vote, own property, or serve on juries, for example, and Chinese-American citizens were subject to unique restrictions, such as having to carry proof of citizenship and being subject to deportation.[1]

A model of the polis must also include a distinction between political community and cultural community. A political community is a group of people who live under the same political rules and structure of governance and share status as citizens. A cultural community is a group of people who share a culture and draw their identities from a common language, history, and traditions.[2] In many nations, including the United States, the political community includes diverse cultural communities, and policy politics entails a profound dilemma: how to integrate several cultural communities into a single political community

---

[1] The concept and practice of multiple civic statuses is developed and documented by Rogers Smith, "Beyond Tocqueville, Myrdal, and Hartz: The Multiple Traditions in America," *American Political Science Review* 87, no. 3 (Sept. 1993): 549–66. An excellent meditation on membership is Chapter 2 of Michael Walzer's *Spheres of Justice* (Cambridge, Mass.: Harvard University Press, 1983).

[2] This distinction, as well as the whole issue of cultural pluralism within political communities, is clearly and richly explored in Will Kymlicka, *Liberalism, Community and Culture* (Oxford: Clarendon Press, 1989).

without destroying or sacrificing their identity and integrity. Issues such as bilingual education or interracial adoption simply cannot be understood in terms of individuals pursuing their self-interests. The arguments for permitting or encouraging bilingual education, or for prohibiting adoption of black and Native American children by parents of a different cultural community, are about defense of communities, and about the pitting of community interests against individual interests.

Membership in a community defines social and economic rights as well as political rights. What makes a collection of individuals a community is not only some definitional principles specifying who's in and who's out, but also mutual aid among members. Sharing burdens and bounty is the glue that holds people together. When immigrant groups have come to the U.S. (or elsewhere), they have tended to stick together in ethnic neighborhoods, and one of the first things they do is establish mutual aid societies to pool their resources. Through these associations, they provide each other with money for culturally acceptable funerals, for sickness and life insurance, and for credit to establish new businesses.[3] Pooling resources for redistribution to the needy is the essence of insurance, and in this sense of sharing and caring for each other, insurance is a characteristic feature of community.

In the market model, insurance is another financial product that firms sell in order to make a profit, and buyers buy in order to protect themselves against economic losses due to various risks, such as the risk of becoming unable to work. In the polis, mutual aid is a good in itself that people create, collectively, in order to foster and protect a community. Mutual aid is one bond among individuals that holds them together as a community. And in a larger sense, sharing, caring, and maintaining relationships is at least as strong a motivator of human behavior as competition, separation, and promotion of one's separate self-interests.

PUBLIC INTEREST

In the polis, there is a public interest. "Public interest" might mean any of several things. It could be individual interests held in common,

[3] See Lizabeth Cohen, *Making a New Deal: Industrial Workers in Chicago* (Cambridge, England: Cambridge University Press, 1991); and Scott Cummings, ed., *Self-Help in Urban America: Patterns of Minority Business Enterprise* (Port Washington, N.Y.: Kennikat Press, 1980).

things everyone wants for themselves, such as a high standard of living. ①
It could be individual goals for the community. Often people want ②
things for their community that conflict with what they want for themselves. They want good schools and clean air, perhaps, but also lower
taxes and the right to burn their trash. Citizens in this view have two
sides: a private, rather self-interested side and a more public-spirited
side, and we might think of the public interest as those things desired
by the public-spirited side of citizens.

Yet another interpretation of public interest is those goals on which ③
there is a consensus. Programs and policies favored by a majority of
citizens, for example, would comprise the public interest. In this interpretation, the public interest is not necessarily enduring. It is whatever
most people want at the moment, and so it changes over time. And of
course, this notion of public interest raises questions of what counts as
consensus and how we would know whether true consensus exists.

Finally, the public interest could mean things that are good for a ④
community as a community. Even the most minimally organized community has some stake in preserving its own sense of order and fair
play, whatever form that takes. All communities have a general interest
in having some governing processes and some means for resolving disputes without violence. The members of a community almost always
have an interest in its survival, and therefore in its perpetuation and its
defense against outsiders. This question of community survival is at
the heart of the debate over nuclear weapons. One side argues that
nuclear weapons are essential for survival because only they can provide sufficient national defense. The other side argues that nuclear
weapons are antithetical to survival because, if used, they will destroy
society and possibly annihilate mankind. Both sides agree that community survival is what is at stake.

There is virtually never full agreement on the public interest, yet we
need to make it a defining characteristic of the polis because so much
of politics is people fighting over what the public interest is and trying
to realize their own definitions of it. Let it be an empty box, but no
matter; in the polis, people expend a lot of energy trying to fill up that
box. The concept of public interest is to the polis what self-interest is
to the market. They are both abstractions whose specific contents we
do not need to know in order to use them to explain and predict people's behavior. We simply assume that people behave as if they were
trying to realize the public interest or maximize their self-interest.

This is not to deny that politics also includes people pursuing their
self-interest. But there is no society on earth in which people are

allowed to do that blatantly and exclusively, so that even if we only want to understand how people pursue their self-interest, we need to understand how conceptions of the public interest shape and constrain people's strategies for pursuing their own interests.

It would be as much a mistake to think that the market has no concept of public interest as to believe that the polis has no room for self-interest. But there is a world of difference between public interest in a market and a polis. In theory, the public interest or general welfare in a market society is the net result of all individuals pursuing their self-interest. In economic theory, given a well-functioning market and a fair initial income distribution, whatever happens is by definition the best result for society as a whole. In a market, in short, the empty box of public interest is filled as an afterthought with the side effects of other activities. In the polis, by contrast, people fill the box intentionally, with forethought, planning, and conscious effort.

[margin annotation: not mutually exclusive]

COMMONS PROBLEMS

Because people often pursue a conception of public interest that is different from their conception of self-interest, the polis is characterized by a special problem: how to combine self-interest and public interest, or, to put it another way, how to have both private benefits and collective benefits. Situations where self-interest and public interest work against each other are known as commons problems, and in the polis, commons problems are common. There are two types of commons problems. In one, actions with private benefits entail social costs; for example, discharging industrial wastes into a lake is a cheap method of disposal for a factory owner but ruins the water for everyone else. In the other, social benefits necessitate private sacrifices; for example, maintaining a school system requires individual tax payments. But note that any situation can be described both ways: clean lakes are a social benefit entailing the private costs of nonpolluting waste disposal, and a poor school system is the social cost of high private consumption. Whether we label a situation as "social benefits and private costs," or as "social costs and private benefits" is a matter of point of view. Commons problems are also called collective action problems because it is hard to motivate people to undertake private costs or forgo private benefits for the collective good.

In market theory, commons problems are thought to be the exception rather than the rule. Most actions in the market model do not have social consequences. In the polis, by contrast, commons problems are everything. Not only do they crop up frequently, but most significant policy problems are commons problems. It is rare in the polis that the benefits and costs of an action are entirely self-contained, affecting only one or two individuals. Actions have not only immediate effects, but side effects, unanticipated consequences, second- and third-order effects, long-term effects, and ripple effects. The language of policy is full of such metaphors recognizing the broad social consequences of individual actions. The major dilemma of policy in the polis is how to get people to give primacy to these broader consequences in their private calculus of choices, especially in an era when the dominant culture celebrates private consumption and personal gain.

INFLUENCE

Fortunately, the vast gap between self-interest and public interest is bridged in the polis by some potent forces: influence, cooperation, and loyalty. Influence is inherent in communities, even communities of two. People are not freewheeling, freethinking atoms whose desires arise from spontaneous generation. Our ideas about what we want and the choices we make are shaped by education, persuasion, and the general process of socialization. (Chapter 3 goes into more detail about how people's desires, or what economists call "preferences," are shaped by influences outside themselves.) Several studies of inner-city youths, for example, have shown how the desire for gold chains, expensive sneakers, and luxury cars is nothing but a reflection of mainstream consumer culture in which these things are heavily promoted as desirable. Yet according to some views, poor kids are supposed to ignore and resist the powerful messages around them, because they don't have enough (legitimately earned) money to afford these items.

Actions, no less than ideas, are influenced by others—by the choices other people have made and the ones we expect them to make, by what they want us to do, and by what we think they expect us to do. More often than not, our choices are conditional. A worker will go out on strike only if she thinks that enough of her fellow workers will join her. A citizen will complain about postal service only if he believes that the post office will take some action in response.

Influence works not simply by putting one individual under a figurative spell of another, but also in ways that lead to curious phenomena of collective behavior. "Bandwagon effects" in elections happen when a candidate's initial lead causes people to support him or her because they want to be on board with a winner. Panics happen when people fear an economic collapse, rush to cash out their bank accounts, and in so doing bring about the collapse they feared. Mobs often act with a peculiar sense of direction and purpose, as if coordinated by a leader, when in fact there is none. Fads for hula hoops or backward baseball caps are frivolous examples of collective behavior; prison riots and "white flight" from urban neighborhoods are more serious. Such things can happen only because people's choices are conditional. They want to do something only if most people will do it (say, go on strike), or to do something before most people do it (say, get their money out of the bank).

Influence sometimes spills over into coercion, and the line between them is fuzzy at best. In fact, one big difference between traditional conservatives and liberals is where they place that line. Liberals tend to see coercion in economic necessity, and the far Left is wont to see it in any kind of need, even that born of desire to "keep up with the Joneses." Conservatives have a more restricted view of coercion, seeing it only in physical force and commands backed up by the threat of force; but the far Right is wont to see coercion in any government rule or regulation, because all laws are backed by the government's monopoly on the legitimate use of force. There is no correct place to draw the line, because coercion is an idea about behavior, a label and an interpretation, rather than the behavior itself. In all its fuzziness, the influence-coercion boundary will be an aspect of many of the dilemmas developed in this book. For now, it is important to state that influence—in all its varieties and degrees of strength—is one of the central elements in politics.

COOPERATION

In the polis, cooperation is every bit as important as competition. This is true for two reasons. First, politics involves seeking allies and organizing cooperation in order to compete with opponents. Whenever there are two sides to an issue and more than two people involved, there must be alliances among the people on one side. Children usually learn this lesson when they play in threesomes. Every conflict unites some people as it divides others, and politics has as much to do with how alliances are made and held together as with how people are divided.[4] For this reason, the two-person models so prominent in the field of economics are politically empty: they have no possibility for strategic coalitions and shifting alliances, nor do they allow for joint effort, leadership, or coordination. For example, in one of the most popular textbooks on policy analysis, the chapter on "Public Choice," which deals with questions of the nature of society, how we should evaluate social welfare, and how we should make social choices, is developed entirely around a two-person model called "Bill-John City."[5]

The second reason cooperation must be central to a model of politics is that it is essential to power. Cooperation is often a more effective form of subordination than coercion. Authority that depends solely on coercion cannot extend very far. Even prison guards, with seemingly all the resources stacked on their side, need the cooperation of inmates to keep order in the prison. Despite bars, locks, and the guards' monopoly on weapons, prisoners outnumber the guards. So guards bargain with prisoners, offering them favors and privileges to gain their cooperation.[6] One of the most chilling aspects of accounts of Nazi concentration camps is how the camp commanders obtained the cooperation and participation of inmates in running the camps. Under threat of imminent death, prisoners were willing to conduct massacres and handle the bodies, while Nazi soldiers had often balked at the same tasks.[7] Accounts of extreme terrorism such as this illustrate another way that cooperation and coercion can become intertwined.

In the ideal market of textbooks, there is nothing but pure competition, which means no cooperation among either buyers or sellers. Sellers compete with each other to obtain raw materials at the lowest prices and to sell their products at the highest profit. They compete with perspicacious buyers, who shop around for the best deals and thereby force the sellers to offer lower prices. Cooperation, when it occurs, is a deviation from the well-functioning market and most words to describe it in the market model are pejorative—collusion, oligarchy, price-fixing, insider trading. In the polis, cooperation is the norm. It is

---

[4] A wonderful treatise on this aspect of politics is E. E. Schattschneider, *The Semisovereign People* (Hinsdale, Ill.: Dryden Press, 1970), especially chap. 4.

[5] Edith Stokey and Richard Zeckhauser, *A Primer of Policy Analysis* (New York: Norton, 1978), chap. 9.

[6] Gresham Sykes, *Society of Captives* (Princeton, N.J.: Princeton University Press, 1958), chap. 5.

[7] Jean-Francois Steiner, *Treblinka* (New York: Simon and Schuster, 1967), especially pp. 55–75.

the inseparable other side of competition and a necessary ingredient of power. The words to describe it are decidedly more positive—coalition, alliance, union, party, support.

LOYALTY

Related to cooperation is loyalty. Cooperation entails alliances, and alliances are at least somewhat enduring. In the ideal market, a buyer will switch suppliers in response to a price or quality change, rather than stick with the previous supplier. There is no "glue" in buyer-seller relations. In politics, relationships are not so fluid. They involve gifts, favors, support, and, most of all, future obligations. Political alliances bind people over time. To paraphrase E. E. Schattschneider, politics is more like choosing a spouse than shopping in a five-and-ten-cent store.[8]

The differing views of loyalty in the market and polis models are evident from our language, also. In the market, people are "buyers" and "sellers." In politics, they are "enemies" and "friends." It is characteristic of friendships that we stick with our friends, even when they hurt us or do things not much to our liking. We honor friends more for what we have shared in the past than for what we expect them to do for us now and in the future. Friendships are forgiving in a way that pure commercial relationships are not (or should not be). The idea of a "pure" commercial relationship is precisely one not tainted by loyalty or sentiment. In the polis, history counts for a lot; in the market, it counts for nothing.

This does not mean that political alliances are perfectly stable or that people never abandon friends and join hands with former enemies. Children learn this lesson from their threesomes, too. But it does mean that in the polis there is a presumption of loyalty. The expectation is that people will normally stick by their friends and allies, and that it takes a major event—something that triggers a deep fear or offers a vast opportunity—to get them to switch their loyalties. There is risk to breaking old alliances, and people do not do it lightly.

GROUPS

Influence, cooperation, and loyalty are powerful forces, and the result is that groups and organizations, rather than individuals, are the building

"Where do consumers fit in?"

[8] Schattschneider, op. cit. (note 4), p. 66.

blocks of the polis.[9] Groups are important in three ways. First, people belong to institutions and organizations, even when they are not formal members. They are participants in organizations as citizens, employees, customers, students, taxpayers, voters, and potential recruits, if not as staff, managers, or leaders. Their opinions are shaped by organizations, their interests are profoundly affected by the behavior of organizations, and they depend on organizations to represent their interests.

Second, policy making is not only about solving public problems, but about how groups are formed, split, and re-formed to achieve public purposes. On policy issues of any significance, it is groups that confront each other, using individuals only as their spokesmen. Groups coalesce and divide over policy proposals, depending on how they expect the proposal to affect them. Injured war veterans are glad to have the support of the retarded citizen groups when they are trying to establish a National Institute of Handicapped Research, but eager to dissociate themselves when job rights for the handicapped are at issue.

Third, groups are important because decisions of the polis are collective. They are explicitly collective, through formal procedures such as voting, administrative rule-making, and bargaining, and through public bodies, such as courts, juries, legislatures, committees, or agencies. Beyond this formal sense, public decisions are implicitly collective in that even when officials have "sole authority," they are influenced by outside opinion and pressure. Policy decisions are not made by abstract people, but by people in social roles and organizations, addressing audiences of people in social roles and organizations, and using procedures that have been collectively approved. The roles, settings, procedures, and audiences exert their own influence, even on the most strong-willed and independent minds.

INFORMATION

In the ideal market, information is "perfect," meaning it is accurate, complete, and available to everyone at no cost. In the polis, by contrast,

---

[9]To make groups the building block of the polis is not to espouse a pluralist theory of politics. Central to pluralist theory is the belief that all important interests become organized in groups and thus are represented in the give-and-take of pressure group politics. Equally important is the belief that no group can consistently dominate politics. I insist on groups not to show that a political system is fair or representative or balanced, but rather to point out that politics is necessarily a system of alliances. If we look at people only as individuals, we will miss facets of their motivation and action essential to an understanding of policy; even worse, we will miss aspects of politics that cannot be captured simply by adding up individual actions.

information is interpretive, incomplete, and strategically withheld. Of course, it would be silly to say there is no such thing as correct information. Surely, when the newspaper reports that a share of IBM stock sold yesterday for $118, or that Senator Kennedy voted for a gun control bill, or that a police officer used the word "nigger" forty-one times in tape-recorded interviews, we are quite confident that the information is accurate and that it makes sense to think of that kind of information as being correct or incorrect. But in politics, the important thing is what people make of such reports. People act on what they believe to be the financial health of a company, whether they think their senator represents their interests, or what they think a policeman's use of racial epithets means for the possibility of fair trials for black citizens. Interpretations are more powerful than facts.

Much of what we "know" is what we believe to be true. And what we believe about information depends on who tells us (the source) and how it is presented (the medium, the choice of language, the context). Some people are more likely to believe medical information from a doctor than from a friend, whereas others are more likely to believe a friend than a doctor. Some people find print more convincing than television, and vice versa. The words, pictures, and imagery of information affect its very message as well as its persuasiveness. Both the timing of information with respect to related events and the juxtaposition of one set of ideas with another can change the way information is perceived.

Because politics is driven by how people interpret information, much political activity is an effort to control interpretations. Political candidates and their campaign advisors are notorious for their creative presentation of information, or "spin control." But strategic manipulation of information is by no means the preserve of shady politicians. We all do it, have done it, and will continue to do it. (Think about the last time you told your professor why your paper was late, your students why the exams weren't graded yet, your friendly IRS agent what your earnings were, or even yourself about your honesty.) Information in the polis is different from information in the market model, both because it depends so much on interpretation and because it is itself the object of strategic manipulation. Part III of this book is centrally concerned with how information about policy is strategically created in politics.

In the polis, information is never complete. We can never know all the possible means for achieving a goal or all the possible effects of an action, especially since all actions have side effects, unanticipated consequences, and long-term effects. Nor can we know for sure what other people will do in response to our actions, yet often we choose to act on the basis of what we expect others to do. If people act at all, they must necessarily act on guesses, hunches, expectations, hopes, and faith, as well as on facts.

Information is never fully and equally available to all participants in politics. There is a cost to acquiring information, if only the cost of *+ providing* spending one's own time. To the extent that information is compli- cated, sophisticated, or technical, it requires education to be under- stood, and education is not uniformly distributed. These are by now standard critiques of the market model.

But even more important for a model of the polis is that crucial infor- mation is very often *deliberately* kept secret. The ideas of inventors, the *eg patents* business plans of entrepreneurs, the decision of a government to devalue its currency, the number of seats American Airlines reserves for "Super Saver" fares, whether a putative candidate will in fact run for election, where the town fathers are thinking of locating a sewage treatment plant—every one of these things is kept secret because some- one expects someone else to behave differently once the information is made public. Secrecy and revelation are tools of political strategy, and we would grossly misunderstand the character of information in poli- tics if we thought of it as neutral facts, readily disclosed.

PASSION

In the market, economic resources are governed by the laws of matter. Resources are finite, scarce, and consumed upon use. Whatever is used for making guns cannot be used for making butter (a textbook example conceived by someone who surely never made either). People can do only one thing at a time (produce guns or butter) and material can be only one thing at a time (a gun or a stick of butter).

In the polis, there is another set of laws operating alongside the laws of matter that might be called laws of paradox if the phrase weren't paradoxical itself. Instead I'll call them the laws of passion, because they describe phenomena that behave more like emotions than like physical matter. One of these laws is that passion feeds on itself. Like passion, political resources are often enlarged or enhanced through use, rather than diminished. Channels of influence and political con- nections, for example, grow by being used. The more people work together and help each other, the more committed they become to each other and to their nominal goal. The more something is done—say, a regulatory agency consults with industry leaders on its proposals, or a school board negotiates with teachers on salaries—the more valuable the personal connections and organizational ties become, and the more people's expectations of "doing things the way they have always been done" grow.

Political skills and authority also grow with use, and it is no accident that we often use the metaphor of "exercise" when talking about them. That skills should grow with practice is not so surprising, but it is worth exploring why authority should work the same way. Precedent is important in authority. The more one makes certain types of decisions, the easier it is to continue in the same path, in part because repeated decisions require no new thought, and in part because people are less likely to resist or even question orders and requests they have obeyed before. How often have we justified our own begrudging compliance by telling ourselves, "I've never protested all the other times I've been asked to do this, so how can I refuse now?" Or, on the other side, "I've let them get away with it many times before, so it is hardly fair to punish them now." In short, the more often an order is issued and obeyed, the stronger the presumption of compliance.

This phenomenon of resource expansion through exercise, use, practice, and expression is ignored in the market model. A distinguished former chairman of the Council of Economic Advisors once

"Closing averages on the human scene were mixed today. Brotherly love was down two points, while enlightened self-interest gained a half. Vanity showed no movement, and guarded optimism slipped a point in sluggish trading. Over all, the status quo remained unchanged."

wrote that market-like arrangements are good because they "reduce the need for compassion, patriotism, brotherly love and cultural solidarity as motivating forces behind social improvement. . . . However vital [these things] may be to a civilized society, [they] are in *too short supply* to serve as substitutes" for the more plentiful motive of self-interest.[10] To make such an analogy between compassion and widgets, to see them both as items with fixed quantities that are diminished by use, is to be blinded by the market model. Who but a die-hard economist would believe that people are born with a limited stockpile of sentiments and passions, to be hoarded through life lest they be spent too quickly? More often than not, waving the flag increases the feeling of patriotism, just as comforting a frightened child increases one's sense of compassion.

Some other laws of passion governing the polis can be mentioned briefly here and will be explored more fully in the rest of the book. One is that *the whole is greater than the sum of its parts*. A protest march, for example, means something more than a few thousand people walking down a street; the repeated refusal to sell houses to blacks in a neighborhood means something more than a series of unrelated seller decisions. Widgets may simply get cheaper through mass production— economists call that economies of scale—but most human actions change their meaning and impact when done in concert or in quantity.

Another law of passion is that *things can mean (and therefore be) more than one thing at once*. Conviction of white-collar criminals with nominal fines means both that the government condemns the activity and that it does not. Any expenditure is a debit to the spender, but income to somebody else. Thus, the growth of health care expenditures bemoaned by employers and taxpayers also means new professional opportunities and job growth, especially for women and minorities. Chapter 6 focuses on the role of ambiguity in politics. Here it is enough to note that ambiguity and symbolic meanings find no home in the market model of society, where everything has its precise value or cost.

POWER

Up to this point I have defined the polis by contrasting it with a market model of society. It is worth summarizing the characteristics here,

[10]Charles L. Schultze, *The Public Use of Private Interest* (Washington, D.C.: Brookings Institution, 1977), pp. 17–18, emphasis added.

Sum [handwritten annotation]

emphasizing what the polis is instead of what it is not:

1. It is a community, or perhaps multiple communities, with ideas, images, will, and effort quite apart from individual goals and behavior.

elf interests vs public [handwritten annotation]

2. It has a public interest, if only as an idea about which people fight.
3. Most of its policy problems are commons problems.
4. Influence is pervasive, and the boundary between influence and coercion is always contested.
5. Cooperation is as important as competition.
6. Loyalty is the norm.
7. Groups and organizations are the building blocks.
8. Information is interpretive, incomplete, and strategic.
9. It is governed by the laws of passion as well as the laws of matter.

Power [handwritten annotation]

By now, my readers must surely be wondering how a reputable political scientist could build a model of political society without making power a defining characteristic, let alone the primary one. I save power for last because it is derived from all the other elements. Power cannot be defined without reference to them. It is a phenomenon of communities. Its purpose is always to subordinate individual self-interest to other interests—sometimes to other individual or group interests, sometimes to the public interest. It operates through influence, cooperation, and loyalty. It is based also on the strategic control of information. And finally, it is a resource that obeys the laws of passion rather than the laws of matter.

Any model of society must specify its source of energy, the force or forces that drive change. In the market model, change is driven by exchange, which is in turn motivated by the individual quest to improve one's own welfare. Through exchanges, the use and distribution of resources is changed.

In the polis, change occurs through the interaction of mutually defining ideas and alliances. Ideas about politics shape political alliances, and strategic considerations of building and maintaining alliances in turn shape the ideas people espouse and seek to implement. In my model of the polis, I emphasize ideas and portrayals as key forms of power in policy making. This book is not so much about how people collect and deploy the "traditional" resources of power—money, votes, and offices—but how they use ideas to gather political support and diminish the support of opponents, all in order to control policy.

Ideas are the very stuff of politics. People fight about ideas, fight for them, and fight against them. Political conflict is never simply over

Concepts of Society

	Market Model	*Polis Model*
1. Unit of analysis	individual	community
2. Motivations	self-interest	public interest (as well as self-interest)
3. Chief conflict	self-interest vs. self-interest	self-interest vs. public interest (commons problems)
4. Source of people's ideas and preferences	self-generation within the individual	influences from outside
5. Nature of collective activity	competition	cooperation and competition
6. Criteria for individual decision-making	maximizing self-interest, minimizing cost	loyalty (to people, places, organizations, products), maximize self-interest, promote public interest
7. Building blocks of social action	individuals	groups and organizations
8. Nature of information	accurate, complete, fully available	ambiguous, interpretive, incomplete, strategically manipulated
9. How things work	laws of matter (eg., material resources are finite and diminish with use)	laws of passion (eg., human resources are renewable and expand with use)
10. Sources of change	material exchange	ideas, persuasion, alliances
	quest to maximize own welfare	pursuit of power, pursuit of own welfare, pursuit of public interest

material conditions and choices, but over what is legitimate. The passion in politics comes from conflicting senses of fairness, justice, rightness, and goodness. Moreover, people fight *with* ideas as well as about them. The different sides in a conflict create different portrayals of the battle—who is affected, how they are affected, and what is at stake. Political fights are conducted with money, with rules, with votes, and with favors, to be sure, but they are conducted above all with words and ideas.

Every idea about policy draws boundaries. It tells what or who is included or excluded in a category. These boundaries are more than intellectual—they define people in and out of a conflict or place them on different sides. In politics, the representation of issues is strategically designed to attract support to one's side, to forge some alliances and break others. Ideas and alliances are intimately connected.

Finally, the interaction between ideas and alliances is ever-changing and never-ending. Problems in the polis are never "solved" in the way that economic needs are met in the market model. It is not as though we can place an order for justice, and once the order is filled, the job is done. (Indeed, modern economists have had to wrestle with the problem of why even material needs seem to grow even as they are fulfilled.) As Plutarch wrote:

> They are wrong who think that politics is like an ocean voyage or a military campaign, something to be done with some end in view, or something which levels off as soon as that end is reached. It is not a public chore, to be got over with; it is a way of life.[11]

---

[11] Plutarch, cited in Jonathan Schell, *The Fate of the Earth* (New York: Avon Books, 1982), p. 109.

PART II

GOALS

This section is organized around five concepts that dominate the language of policy discourse. I call them goals because that term conveys the central tenet of modern policy analysis—namely, that policy is the rational attempt to attain objectives. But I would note at the outset that to call equity, efficiency, security, liberty, and community "goals" is to obscure some of the other functions these concepts serve. They are often invoked as justifications for a policy, for a government action, or for the government's not taking action. They are also used as criteria for evaluating public programs; in this way, they function as standards against which programs are assessed. They are often called values, suggesting a more complex array of considerations rather than a definitive endpoint.

What unites the extraordinary range of treatments of these goals in the policy analysis literature is the search for a single definition or single criterion. Each goal is associated with a general definition that is so much a part of our political culture that it appears to be common sense. Equity is defined as "treating likes alike." Efficiency is "getting the most output for a given input." Security is the "satisfaction of minimum human needs." Liberty is the ability to "do as you wish as long as you do not harm others."

None of these criteria in fact offers a simple or determinate rule. Each of them contains ambiguities and problems of interpretation that make them the object of political struggles. In each of the following chapters, I begin with the simple, commonsense definition of the concept and show the various intellectual strategies for challenging or expanding it. For each concept, there are several plausible but conflicting claims that can be made in its name.

In the polis, the concepts of equity, efficiency, security, and liberty are continuously constructed. Rather than giving a single answer to a policy problem, the general definitions provide a battleground for more particular fights. The simple definitions evoke a common goal, even if it cannot be made precise without sacrificing the commonality, and they provide a language with which the contestants in a political battle frame their positions. In a paradoxical way, the concepts unite people at the same time as they divide. Even though a political fight involves conflicting interpretations of one of these concepts, people aspire to convince others that their interpretation best fulfills the spirit of the larger concept to which everyone is presumed to subscribe.

Most important, these chapters are meant to demonstrate that there is an enormous range of choice in the interpretation of the criteria of policy analysis. Reigning interpretations vary from policy to policy, from time to time, and from place to place. Policy politics is the process of making these choices in interpretation.

2

Equity

The Dimensions of Equality

The most famous definition of political science says it is the study of "who gets what, when, and how."[1] Distributions—whether of goods and services, wealth and income, health and illness, or opportunity and disadvantage—are at the heart of public policy controversies. In this chapter we will describe issues as distributive conflicts in which equity is the goal. It is important to keep in mind from the outset that equity is the goal for all sides in a distributive conflict; the conflict comes over how the sides envision the distribution of whatever is at issue.

To see how it is possible to have competing visions of an equitable distribution, let's imagine we have a mouthwatering bittersweet chocolate cake to distribute in a public policy class.[2] We agree that the cake should be divided equally. The intuitively obvious solution is to count the number of people in the classroom, cut the cake into that number of equal-sized slices, and pass them out.

I've tried this solution in my classes, and believe me, my students always challenge my equitable solution. Here are some of the challenges:

[1] Harold Lasswell, *Politics: Who Gets What, When, How* (New York: McGraw-Hill, 1936; 2nd ed. with postscript, Cleveland: World Publishing, 1958).

[2] This analysis of equity is largely based on, and extends, the work of Douglas Rae and his coauthors. See Douglas Rae, "The Egalitarian State: Notes on a Contradictory System of Ideals," *Daedalus* 108, no. 4, (Fall 1979): 37–54; and Douglas Rae et al., *Equalities* (Cambridge, Mass.: Harvard University Press, 1981).

1. Some say my solution is unfair to the people left out of the class in the first place. "I wouldn't have skipped class last week if I had known you would be serving chocolate cake," says one. Students not even taking the course come up to me in the halls: "Unfair!" they protest. "We would have enrolled in your course if we had known about the cake." My cake is written up in *Gourmet Magazine* and students who applied to the university but did not get in write letters of protest. All these people describe my solution as *equal slices but unequal invitations.*

2. Some of my colleagues buttonhole me when I get back to my office. This is a Political Science Department course, they say, and your cake should have been shared in accordance with the structure of the department. The chairperson sends me a memo proposing the following division of any future cakes:

> Your undergraduates: crumbs
> Your graduate teaching assistant: mouthful
> All other grad students: work on our research while we eat cake
> Assistant professors: slivers
> Associate professors: wedges
> Full professors: wedges with extra frosting
> Chairperson: wedge with extra frosting, and a linen napkin

This solution might be described as *unequal slices for unequal ranks, but equal slices for equal ranks.*

3. A group of men's liberationists stages a protest. Women have always had greater access to chocolate cake, they claim, because girls are taught to bake while boys have to go outdoors and play football. Moreover, chocolate cake is more likely to be served in courses taught by females than males, and those courses draw proportionately more female students. In short, gender roles and gender divisions in social institutions combine to make gender the *de facto* determinant of cake distribution. The men insist that men as a group should get an equal share of the cake, and they propose that the cake be divided in two equal parts, with half going to the men (who comprise one-third of the students in the class) and half going to the women. *Unequal slices but equal blocs.*

4. One semester, all the students in my public policy class had just attended a three-course luncheon, which, mysteriously enough, did not include dessert. Several of them thought my chocolate cake should be treated as the last course of the luncheon. They pointed out that some students had managed to commandeer two

shrimp cocktails, pick all the artichoke hearts from the salad as it was passed around, and grab the rarest slices of roast beef from the platter. Shouldn't the other students—the ones who had only one shrimp cocktail, no artichoke hearts, and overcooked roast beef—get bigger slices of my chocolate cake? This solution, which I had to agree seemed fair, might be called *unequal slices but equal meals*.

5. Every year, a few students come forth, believe it or not, saying they hate the taste of chocolate. There's always someone who is allergic to chocolate. And another who says he was born without the crucial gene for chocolate digestion, and though it would do him no harm to eat my cake, he wouldn't derive any nutritional benefit from it either. These students think I might as well give them very, very small pieces (they want to be polite and sample my cake) and give bigger pieces to those who can truly appreciate the cake. Their solution might be called *unequal slices but equal value to recipients*.

6. The economics majors in the class want no part of these complicated solutions. Give everyone a fork, they yell, and let us go at it. *Unequal slices* (or perhaps I should say "hunks") *but equal starting resources*.

7. One semester I was caught with only enough chocolate to make a cupcake. It couldn't really be divided among the large number of people in my class. The math whizzes proposed an elegant solution: Put everyone's name in a hat, draw one ticket, and give the whole cupcake to the winner. They had a point: *unequal slices but equal statistical chances*.

8. Just when I thought I finally had an equitable solution, the student government activists jumped up. In a democracy, they said, the only fair way to decide who gets the cupcake is to give each person a vote and hold an election for the office of Cupcake Eater. Democracy, they implied, means *unequal slices but equal votes*.

Look carefully at what happened in the chocolate cake saga. We started with the simple idea that equality means the same-size slice for everyone. Then there were eight challenges to that idea, eight different visions of equality that would result in unequal slices but equality of something else. Here is the paradox in distributive problems: Equality may in fact mean inequality; equal treatment may require unequal treatment; and the same distribution may be seen as equal or unequal, depending on one's point of view. I have used the word "equality" to denote sameness and to signify the part of a distribution that contains uniformity—uniformity of slices, or of meals, or of voting power, for example. I have used "equity" to denote distributions regarded as fair, even though they contain both equalities and inequalities.

If we can get a systematic description of the challenges in the chocolate cake problem, we will have some tools we can apply in policy analysis. In any distribution, there are three important dimensions: the recipients (who gets something?), the item (what is being distributed?), and the process (how is the distribution to be decided upon and carried out?). Challenges 1, 2, and 3 are all based on a redefinition of the recipients. Challenges 4 and 5 redefine the item being distributed. And challenges 6, 7, and 8 focus on the process of distribution. The box below summarizes these concepts and the discussion to follow.

Challenge 1 is based on the definition of membership. It is all well and good to say that something should be divided equally, but the sticky question is, "Among whom?" Who should count as a member of the class of recipients? Sometimes this question seems straightforward, as when the state of New Hampshire says that all people who have purchased tickets to its lottery are eligible to win. But more often, defining the class of members entitled to "equal treatment," whatever that is, is the core of a political controversy.

Take the seemingly simple concept of citizenship. Who is to count as a citizen of the United States? On first thought, one might think a citizen is anyone born on American soil or born of American parents or legally naturalized. But once we think about the different purposes and policies for which we need a concept of citizenship, the definition becomes less obvious. When the right to vote is at issue, it is often believed that people should meet certain qualifications to be considered voting citizens. They should know how to read so that they can follow policy debates (literacy tests); they should own property so that they "have a stake in the system" (property qualification); or they should reside in the jurisdiction a certain length of time so that they "understand the issues" (residency requirements). In nineteenth-century England, citizens receiving public welfare were not allowed to vote, presumably because their need for assistance demonstrated their lack of civic responsibility. Or, to take some examples from our not-so-distant past, citizens, in order to vote, had to be white and male (for reasons I won't even try to justify).

Until recently, we took it for granted in the United States that voting citizens should be "adults"—that is, over the age of 21. Many people challenged that criterion, saying that if 18-year-olds are mature

CONCEPTS OF EQUALITY

Simple Definition: Same size share for everybody

Complications in the Polis:

Dimension	Issue	Dilemma
Recipients *who?*	1. Membership (the boundaries of community)	unequal invitations/ equal slices
	2. Rank-based distribution (internal subdivisions of society)	equal ranks/equal slices; unequal ranks/unequal slices
	3. Group-based distribution (major internal cleavages of society)	equal blocs/unequal slices
Items *what? Redefinition*	4. Boundaries of the item	equal meals/ unequal slices
	5. Value of the item	equal value/ unequal slices
Process *how? Distribution*	6. Competition (opportunity as starting resources)	equal forks/unequal slices
	7. Lottery (opportunity as statistical chance)	equal chances/ unequal slices
	8. Voting (opportunity as political participation)	equal votes/unequal slices

enough to defend their country, they are mature enough to vote. Then, too, if our foreign policy puts people at risk of losing their lives at the age of 18, they should have some say in making our foreign policy. The extension of voting rights to people between ages 18 and 21 (in 1971) exemplifies the redefinition of equality through the redefinition of membership.

Suppose now the question is not simply who should vote but who should vote in school board elections. One view is that all adult citizens should be entitled to vote because education of the next generation is a universal concern. Another is that only those affected by school board decisions should be able to vote. But then the tricky question is what we mean by "affected." Perhaps only adult citizens with school-age children, or better yet, only adult citizens with school-age children who actually attend public schools. Perhaps the children should be entitled to vote; they are, after all, the most affected by school board policy. Or, if we interpret "affected" in financial terms, perhaps only people who pay local property taxes should be entitled to vote, regardless of whether they have children. The point is not that any of these views is necessarily right, but that any of these groups could make an intellectually respectable claim that school board policy is inequitable on grounds that the "invitations" or rights to participate in elections were inequitably distributed.

Challenges 2 and 3 are both about how society is internally divided. Challenge 2 is a claim for distribution based on rank. It holds that there are relevant internal divisions for distributing something and that these divisions have been ignored. In economics, the conception of equity based on relevant internal subdivisions is called *horizontal and vertical equity*, with *horizontal equity* meaning equal treatment of people in the same rank and *vertical equity* meaning unequal treatment of people in different ranks. The two are obviously flip sides of the same coin.

If there is one central principle that legitimizes the idea of rank-based distribution, it is probably merit. Our fundamental belief that rewards such as jobs, places in universities, and pay should be distributed according to achievement, competence, and other measures of past performance goes hand in hand with a belief in the legitimacy of rank-based distribution. Military organizations and universities, factories and corporations, indeed government itself—all pay their employees according to rank, and rank is understood to be awarded according to some notion of individual merit.

Rank-based distribution is at the heart of the debate about pay equity for women. Advocates of "comparable worth" as a mode of determining wages and salaries do not want to eliminate rank-based pay, but seek instead to equalize pay for occupations requiring the same level of training, skill, and responsibility. They suggest, for example, that the jobs of food service workers, who are predominantly female, and truck drivers, who are predominantly male, entail equivalent levels of education, skill, and difficulty. Yet truck drivers receive about $970 per month compared with $640 for food service workers. Similarly, library work (primarily a female occupation) and carpentry (primarily a male occupation) are equivalent in skill and difficulty, but librarians receive $946 per month compared with carpenters' $1246 per month.[3] The comparable worth approach to equity would not pay library workers at the same rate as food service workers, but would pay them at the same rate as carpenters.

Advocates of comparable worth accept the idea of rank-based differentiation according to job characteristics, but believe that pay in the current system is in fact largely determined by gender rather than by skill, responsibility, difficulty, and other relevant criteria. Comparable worth would preserve unequal payment, but it would switch the basis of differentiation from a subdivision seen as invalid (gender) to one seen as valid (difficulty and skill levels of work).

Even within a framework of a rank- or merit-based distribution, there are many possible challenges to equity. One can ask whether the lines between ranks are correctly drawn or, put another way, whether the different ranks indeed represent different skills, knowledge, or other substantive factors bearing on distribution. Are the rewards given to each rank proportional to the differences between them? Are individuals correctly assigned to ranks? Does the system evaluate people fully and fairly? Are the criteria for differentiation the right ones at all? For example, do compensation systems based on seniority really reward the "right thing?"

Challenge 3 is a claim for group-based distribution. It holds that some major divisions in society are relevant to distributive equity and that membership in a group based on these divisions should sometimes outweigh individual characteristics in determining distribution. In societies with liberal individualist ideologies, group-based distribution is usually proposed as a remedy for previous violations of merit- or rank-based distribution. In the chocolate cake example, men proposed group-based distribution to compensate them for historical deprivations based on their gender.

The obvious analogue in contemporary politics is affirmative action, a policy of distributive preference to members of groups that have been

---

[3] These figures are from a 1978 study of jobs in the state of Washington, Helen Remick's "Beyond Equal Pay for Equal Work: Comparable Wroth in the State of Washington," in Ronnie Steinberg-Rattner, ed., *Equal Employment Policy Strategies for Implementation in the United States, Canada, and Europe* (Philadelphia: Temple University Press, 1980).

the victims of historical discrimination. Discussions of affirmative action usually conflate it with quotas, but affirmative action as it has been practiced in the U.S. has not always, or even mostly, involved quotas. Affirmative action is a loose term for various policies to give some group, primarily African Americans and women, an extra boost in distributive decisions. These policies include extra efforts to advertise job openings in outlets targeted to minority groups; extra steps in hiring to ensure that untraditional qualifications and career paths are not overlooked; special programs to enlarge the pool of qualified minority applicants (for example, summer enrichment programs at universities, or mentoring programs in businesses); altering the criteria for selection to give more weight to the special experiences (including discrimination) of members of minority groups. Affirmative action has been used primarily in education (distributing places in higher education), employment (distributing jobs and promotions), and business opportunities (distributing government contracts and financial credit).

Quotas are a means of reserving a certain portion of an item to be distributed for members of a group. Whether the items are places in a medical school class, positions in a firm, promotions to higher job categories, or government contracts for goods and services, quotas give weight to membership in a subgroup within the larger pool of potential recipients.

Quota systems can be designed so that members of a disadvantaged group receive a fixed number of places (or items), or so that they receive a share of the item proportional to their share in the applicant pool or in the entire population. Thus, for example, an affirmative action plan might call for an employer to hire blacks in 5 percent of all new positions if blacks constitute 5 percent of the applicant pool. Occasionally, however, affirmative action plans call for giving a group more than their proportionate share in the population (as the men's liberationists in my hypothetical class demanded). Federal court orders in 1983 and 1984, for example, required Alabama to promote one black state trooper for each white trooper promoted, even though blacks constituted only about one-quarter of the state's population and an even smaller proportion of state troopers. The U.S. Supreme Court, upholding these orders in a 1987 decision, recognized that racial classifications and preferences might sometimes be necessary to overcome pervasive and obstinate discrimination.[4] Typically U.S. courts have ordered the use of bloc-based distributive systems only when they have

[4] *U.S. v. Paradise* 480 U.S. 149; see also Stuart Taylor, Jr., "High Court Backs Basing Promotion on a Racial Quota," *New York Times*, February 26, 1987, p. 1.

seen evidence of egregious discrimination and flagrant violations of previous settlements or court orders.

How are group-based and rank-based distributions different? While rank-based distributions also divide people into groups, they assign people to those groups according to fairly fine-tuned individual measurements. The justification for assignment to ranks usually has something to do with individual history, performance, or achievement, even if actual assignment is influenced by other factors. Group-based distributions assign people to groups on the basis of simple demographic criteria, having more to do with ascriptive characteristics of identity rather than individual experience or performance. They tend to follow major social cleavages in society—divisions such as ethnicity, race, gender, or religion—that split a society into two or three large blocs and that have historically served as a basis for awarding privileges and disadvantages. In the U.S., we have based affirmative action primarily on race and gender, but other societies have recognized other social cleavages as critical in distributive equity. West Germany and Japan require employers to hire handicapped people in a certain percentage of jobs, and India has preferences for Untouchables, the lowest group in its historical caste system.

Just as there are challenges to the definition of equity from within the framework of rank-based distribution, there are similar challenges from within the framework of group-based distribution. One question is whether the definition of relevant groups makes sense and reflects some meaningful social reality. There are many questions about whether race and ethnicity are even coherent categories. How should we classify people who are of mixed-race parentage? (The very question presumes there is a something like "pure" racial identity, a very dubious assumption.[5]) Are race and national origin the same thing? Does it make sense to lump people from different Spanish-speaking cultures and nations together?

Another important challenge asserts that ascriptive identity characteristics such as race, gender, and nationality do not really capture or correspond to the actual experience of disadvantage or discrimination, yet the justification for group-based distribution is to compensate people for past disadvantage. Why should a wealthy, upper-class, highly educated, dark-skinned immigrant from the West Indies be given the same preferences as a poor, lower-class, unskilled dark-skinned American-born citizen? In this view, individual, merit-based distribu-

[5] See James F. Davis, *Who is Black?: One Nation's Definition* (Harrisburg: Pennsylvania State University Press, 1991).

tion should be the norm, and group-based distribution should be only a tool to correct deficiencies and restore distributive systems to a merit-based foundation. Demographic groupings are too "rough." They make unwarranted presumptions about individual cases, give compensatory preferences to people who never suffered any disadvantage, and thus continue to violate the norm of distribution according to personal merit instead of strengthening it.

These are precisely the kinds of challenges that inform the backlash against affirmative action in contemporary politics. One argument against affirmative action is essentially a call to replace group-based distribution with rank-based distribution. This view holds that race and gender are illegitimate criteria for distribution of anything, even if they are used in a compensatory fashion. It is impossible to use race or gender for the benefit of previously disadvantaged groups without also discriminating on the basis of race or gender *against* whites or men. Accordingly, private and public institutions should return to the use of individual merit, recognizing that a merit or competence criterion would likely result in smaller shares (of jobs, school places, construction contracts) for women and blacks. Note that this argument presumes a halcyon period in which individual merit was the sole distributive criterion for important opportunities. In practice, group-based distribution has often been used quietly while individual merit-based distribution was professed to be the norm. Colleges and universities, for example, commonly reserve places and/or bend the admissions criteria for students who fit particular categories they wish to represent—children of alumni, athletes, residents of states and countries that don't send many students to that school.

Another argument against affirmative action accepts the legitimacy of group-based distribution for compensatory purposes, but holds that we are using the wrong criteria to determine which groups deserve compensation. According to this view, public policy should try to compensate people when they personally have suffered social and economic disadvantage. Thus, some measure of need or of "disadvantaged background" should be the criterion on which special preferences are awarded, rather than simple membership in a race or gender category. Supporters of race- and gender-based affirmative action counter that, apart from the extraordinary difficulty of measuring need and disadvantage, such a shift in the bases of affirmative action would destroy its utility in eliminating race and gender discrimination per se, the very thing affirmative action was meant to undo. Moreover, discrimination against women and especially against blacks is so pervasive that even the most privileged among them cannot escape it or its hobbling effects.

Challenges 4 and 5 are based on redefining the item to be distributed. Challenge 4 redefines the boundaries of the item. Instead of seeing a cake as a thing in itself, it is viewed as part of a larger whole, a meal. To take something and make it part of a larger entity is to expand the boundaries of what is being distributed, to present a more global vision. Expansion might be across types of goods (from cake to meal), or across time (from what happens in the next hour to what has happened in the previous three hours as well).

Expanding the definitional boundaries of the item is always a redis- tributive strategy, because it calls for using the more narrowly defined item (in this case, the cake) to compensate for inequalities in a larger sphere (in this case, lunch). Challenges to the definition of an item are generally not either/or choices, but choices about how expansively to define the item along a continuum. The cake, for example, could be seen as part of today's lunch, part of today's meals, or part of this week's diet.

Student financial aid is an issue involving boundary challenges to the definition of an item. A few schools give aid strictly on the basis of students' academic merit. But most distribute aid at least in part on the basis of students' financial need. When a school considers financial need, it is looking at its financial aid—what it distributes—not as money in itself but as part of each student's total assets. It then has to decide what to count as a student's assets. Some schools look only at the student's current earnings and savings. Others take a more global view and include parents' earnings and savings. Law, medical, and business schools typically consider their students' high potential future earnings as part of their assets, and tend to offer loans rather than outright scholarships, on the theory that their students can easily pay back loans out of their future earnings. Thus, within the issue of financial aid, we have at least four possible definitions of what is being distributed: aid as money in itself, aid as part of a student's assets, aid as part of a family's assets, and aid as part of a student's lifetime earnings.

All explicitly redistributive policy, but especially welfare and tax policy, involves these questions of definition of assets. In setting levels of welfare grants, do we take into account people's cars and homes as part of their assets? Do we take into account their relatives' assets? In tax policy, the concept of deductions is used to take into account the fact that different people have different required expenses that should not be counted as part of their taxable income. The tax code in effect tries to tax people's disposable income more than their essential expenses. Thus, we allow deductions for support of dependents, for inescapable business expenses, and for medical expenses. Much of the controversy over tax reform has been about whether the existing deductions truly represent necessary and uncontrollable expenses, and therefore a diminution of disposable income, or whether they represent luxury items.

Many of the debates over arms control could be regarded as a conflict over the distribution of military strength between the United States and its enemies, with each side trying to achieve "at least equal strength." Here "strength" is the item being distributed, and the controversy is over how it should be defined. Is the relevant unit of comparison the sophistication of a country's best weapon, the kill potential of its total arsenal, the reliability of its weapons or of its control systems, or perhaps the level of its military expenditures?

Challenge 5 redefines the item in terms of its value to the individual. For lack of better terms, we might call this a switch from a more standardized value of the item (say, the weight of a slice of cake) to a more customized value (say, how much nutrition someone derives from cake). Clothing provides a somewhat less frivolous example than cake. No one would seriously argue that equality requires giving each person

"My body, being a bigger machine, requires more fuel."

a winter coat with the same amount of fabric. Even the Stalinist collective planners, who decried personal taste in fashion as a bourgeois foible, acknowledged that the essence of a coat is its fit rather than its fabric yardage.

Conflicts over this dimension of equality are especially intense in social policy. There, the services being distributed, such as education, medical care, and housing, derive their value from being tailored to the needs of the individual. Does equality in a multiethnic school district mean that every child should have the right to study in English (with appropriate remedial courses for non-English-speakers), or the right to study in one's native language (with all the advantages that confers)? Does equality in medical care mean that every person should have access to a physician, or to a physician of his or her own choosing? Does equality in housing mean every person should have a roof and indoor plumbing, or does it mean everyone should have housing in a place with enough privacy to suit his or her needs? These are all issues where one's judgment about the equity of the distribution turns on one's assessment of the importance of customized or individualized value.

Challenges 6, 7, and 8 all focus on the process of distribution. They are respectively calls for competition, lotteries, and elections. Process is important because our notion of fairness includes not only the end result but the sense of a fair process by which the results occurred. Thus, if after hearing testimony in a criminal case, the jury flipped a coin to decide whether to convict, we would think the trial unfair even if it resulted in a decision we believed was in accord with the evidence.[6] For many things in life—such as a prize lottery, an election, or an athletic competition—we are quite willing to accept unequal results so long as we know that the process is fair.

The process dimension of distribution is especially important in the polis because so many things of value, like cupcakes, are indivisible. Think of jobs, public offices, sites for "good" public facilities such as town offices or parks, and sites for necessary nuisances such as town dumps or noisy factories. Such things simply cannot be sliced up and parceled out; if they were, they would lose their value. Commons problems often require distributive solutions based on unequal slices but fair processes.

[6]For research showing that "people care more about how they are treated than what they get" from the criminal justice system, see Robert Lane, "Procedural Justice in a Democracy: How One Is Treated Versus What One Gets," *Social Justice Research* 2 (1988): 177–92.

Finally, process is important because in the polis, distributions do not happen by magic. They are carried out by real people taking real actions, not by invisible hands. Systems of distribution may be divisive and socially disruptive, as competition is often thought to be, or orderly and socially cohesive, as elections in a stable democracy are thought to be. They may inspire loyalty, as distribution of jobs by patronage is said to do, and bind people to one another, as elections bind an official to his or her constituency. Distribution of government jobs by lottery or even by examinations might inspire respect for the system's fairness, but probably not loyalty. Distributive systems may themselves provide employment. Witness our complicated tax system, which employs thousands in the Internal Revenue Service, thousands more as accountants, and still thousands more in seasonal tax preparation firms such as H & R Block. Or, distributive systems may provide little employment; for example, a flat-rate tax scheme would put a lot of people out of business. In short, the processes of distribution create or destroy things of value (such as loyalty, community spirit, or jobs) apart from the things they explicitly distribute.

We will return to the issue of social processes for collective choice. For now, it is enough to point out that one major class of challenges to the definition of equality is based on the notion of an equitable process. Instead of arguing about who the recipients are or what is being distributed, one can argue about whether the process of distribution is fair. Arguments for competition, lotteries, elections, bargaining, and adjudication are all of this nature.

In summary, then, every policy issue involves the distribution of something. There wouldn't be a policy conflict if there were not some advantage to protect or some loss to prevent. Sometimes the things being distributed are material and countable, such as money, taxes, or houses. Sometimes they are a bit less tangible, such as the chances of serving in the army, getting sick, being a victim of crime, or being selected for public office. But always, policy issues involve distribution.

Simple prescriptions such as "equal opportunity for all" or "treat like cases alike" are glib slogans that mask the dilemmas of distributive justice. The task for the analyst is to sort out three questions: First, who are the recipients and what are the many ways of defining them? Second, what is being distributed and what are the many ways of defining it? And third, what are the social processes by which distribution is determined? Ultimately, a policy argument must show a principled reason why it is proper to categorize cases as alike or different. As I will show throughout this book, many of the most profound political conflicts and strategic battles hinge on this seemingly mundane problem of classification.

THE ARGUMENTS FOR EQUALITY

Even when one is able to tease apart a political issue and see the dimensions of a distribution separately, there is still the question of where one stands. How does one decide whether to accept a challenge, or which concept of equity to use? Where one stands on issues of distribution is determined not so much by the specifics of any particular issue (say, tax policy or student financial aid) as by a more general world view. This world view includes assumptions about the meaning of community and the nature of property, assumptions that transcend particular issues.

One major divide in the great debate about equity is whether distributions should be judged by criteria of process or by criteria of recipients and items. Robert Nozick has written the most extensive defense of process criteria in *Anarchy, State and Utopia.*[7] He argues that a distribution is just if it came about by a voluntary and fair process. It is just if all the holdings in it—what people have—were acquired fairly.

How do we know whether things are "acquired fairly"? Nozick distinguishes two types of holdings and says we have to examine each to determine whether it was fairly acquired. First, anything newly created (such as an invention) or not formerly held as property (such as rights to own a taxicab in a city that just created a medallion system) must be acquired fairly. And second, anything acquired by transfer—say by sale, gift, or inheritance—must be acquired fairly. Thus, in order to judge whether a distribution is just, one needs historical evidence—perhaps records of how acquisitions took place, such as patent applications and property title histories.

Nozick contrasts his process or historical concept of justice with what he calls the *end-result concept.* In the end-result concept, one looks at characteristics of recipients or owners and characteristics of items, and asks whether there is an appropriate match. The first five challenges in the cake saga, he would say, are based on end-result thinking. They all assume that a just distribution is one in which both the recipients and items are correctly defined and each qualified recipient receives an equal share of each correctly defined item. Nozick calls this *end-*

[7] Robert Nozick, *Anarchy, State and Utopia* (New York: Basic Books, 1974).

result justice because in order to judge whether a distribution is fair, we look only at the end result and do not need any historical information as to how the distribution came about.

The other side of this theoretical divide is best represented by John Rawls in *A Theory of Justice.*[8] Rawls defines the relevant class of recipients as all citizens, and he defines the relevant items as social primary goods. Social primary goods are things that are very important to people (hence "primary") but are created, shaped, and affected by social structure and political institutions (hence "social"). Power, opportunity, wealth, income, civil rights, and liberties are things Rawls includes. He distinguishes them from natural primary goods—things very important to people but which, while affected by society, are less directly under its control. Here, Rawls includes intelligence, strength, imagination, talent, and good health.[9]

Rawls asks us to imagine ourselves designing rules for a society we are about to join. We are to put ourselves behind a "veil of ignorance": we know that the natural primary goods will be unequally distributed, but we do not know how much of each we individually will have. In those circumstances, what kind of rules would we want? Rawls says that most rational people would want social primary goods to be distributed equally, but we would allow social and economic inequalities if they worked to everyone's advantage and were attached to positions or offices open to everyone. For example, we might allow doctors to receive much higher pay than others if we thought high pay was necessary to motivate people to endure medical training, but we would insist that the opportunity to go to medical school be open to everyone.

Although Nozick calls Rawls's theory "end-result," Rawls's concept of justice is a process view in two important senses. First, he sees justice primarily as an attribute of the rules and institutions that govern society, and only secondarily as an attribute of the distributions which result from the rules. Rawls calls his view *justice as fairness.* Second, he develops his principles of justice through a process that is absolutely central to his theory: the formation of a hypothetical social contract

[8] John Rawls, *A Theory of Justice* (Cambridge, Mass.: Harvard University Press, 1971).

[9] We might quibble, as many have, with Rawls's list of natural primary goods. See, for example, Ronald Green's argument that good health should really be considered a social primary good because it is strongly affected by the social organization of insurance and medical care. Ronald Green, "Health Care and Justice in Contract Theory Perspective," in Robert Veatch and Roy Branson, Eds., *Ethics and Health Policy* (Cambridge, Mass.: Ballinger, 1976), pp. 111–26.

between free and equal people. Rawls's process is deliberation or "thought experiment." Though it is hypothetical rather than actual, such as Nozick's idea that we judge equity through the history of actual exchanges, it is a process nonetheless.

Each approach to distributive justice has its conceptual problems. The trickiest problem for Nozick's process concept of justice is defining "fairness" for original acquisitions and transfers. One could, of course, say that acquisitions and transfers are fair if they do not violate any legal rules of society—no fraudulent representations of merchandise, no stealing of other people's ideas in patent and copyright applications, no coercion in contract negotiations, and so forth. But that would be taking for granted the very thing we are trying to judge—the distributive rules of our society. If we were looking at the pre-Civil War United States, for example, when whites could own blacks as slaves and everything a single woman owned became her husband's property the day they married, Nozick's entitlement theory would still find the distribution of property just. Slaveholders and married men acquired their property fair and square, according to the law. So proponents of process concepts are left with the problem of where to find independent standards for judging distributive processes.

Similarly for end-result proponents. They must define what characteristics of recipients and items are relevant for justice. One approach is to look at society as it is and say that those characteristics people consider relevant are by definition relevant.[10] If people believe level of education is relevant in the distribution of wages and salaries, then education is important. If they think gender is not relevant, then a just distribution is one that is neutral toward gender.

The problem with this approach is that distributive conflicts arise precisely because people do not agree on the relevant characteristics of recipients and items. If people do not agree, then where should standards come from? Do we look to the majority, and dub their views correct because they have numerical superiority? And if so, how do we find the majority—through referenda, or public opinion polls, or in-depth surveys? How do we account for the fact that people seem to change their minds—that in one time and place, race is considered a relevant criterion for citizenship, but in another time and place it isn't? That in one era, education is thought to consist in the curriculum only, so that racially separate education could be equal education, but in another, education is thought to consist in the social and psychological

[10] This is Michael Walzer's approach in *Spheres of Justice* (New York: Basic Books, 1983).

experience as well as the curriculum, so that separate cannot be equal?[11] If we look to existing practices to find the correct definition of recipients and items, then we have no standards by which to criticize an existing distribution.

The other approach to defining recipients and items is to seek some universal standards not dependent on the norms of particular societies. This is John Rawls's approach. He looks to our innate sense of justice as well as our fundamental rationality and then derives principles of equity by asking us to deliberate about rules for a just society without being biased by knowing our own situation. But this solution works only if we believe that there is a universal logic about distributive justice to which all people would subscribe if stripped of their culture and their particular history.

In general, people who hold Nozick's process view of equity do not favor policies to effect redistribution directly, even when they think a current distribution is inequitable. If you believe that ultimately a distribution is to be judged by the process that created it, your prescription for injustice will be to correct any deficiencies in the process. Thus, if the rules of the game in marketplace competition give an unfair advantage to very large firms, the answer is to limit the behavior of large firms (say, through antitrust laws) rather than to take some of the resources of large firms and give them to small firms.

People who hold an end-result view of equity are more likely to favor direct redistribution. If you believe a distribution is to be judged by the standard of equal treatment of correctly defined recipients and items, your prescription for remedying injustice will be to correct incorrect definitions and redistribute the relevant items accordingly. Thus, in the school segregation issue, if blacks are receiving less than their share of education because education has been too narrowly defined as "curriculum only," the answer is to redefine education as "curriculum plus social integration" and redistribute the new item accordingly. In practice, however, the division between process and end-result solutions is not so clear. It is hard to redefine education without altering the whole institution and changing the process by which education is distributed.

A second major divide in the great debate is what kind of interference with liberty one finds acceptable as a price of distributive justice. Here, the difference between the two sides is in their conception of liberty. On the one side, liberty is freedom from constraints; on the

[11] This is the intellectual move made by the Supreme Court in *Brown v. Board of Education*, 347 U.S. 483 (1954).

other side, liberty is freedom to do what one wants to do.[12] People who hold a process view of equity usually also see liberty as freedom to use and dispose of one's resources as one wishes, without interference. If you hold that view, you will be very reluctant to sanction government redistribution, because any taxation or taking of property restricts people's freedom to use their resources as they wish. People who hold an end-result view are usually more wont to see liberty as having enough basic resources to choose out of desire rather than necessity. If you hold that view, you will spend a lot of time thinking about what resources are "basic" for human welfare and you will insist that government redistribute to ensure that everyone has the basic resources.

Nozick argues that in fact property and the constraint view of liberty are inextricably tied. What can a property right possibly mean, he asks, if not the right to use something without any restrictions? Any policy based on end-result distribution is self-contradictory, he believes, because what it gives with one hand it takes away with the other. In redistributing, it gives people entitlements to things—entitlements that can only mean the right to use the things as one wishes. Yet an end-result distribution can be maintained only by continuously interfering with people's rights to dispose of their property—by taxing and redistributing periodically to redress the unequal results of people's free choices.[13]

How do those who hold the other view of liberty get out of this box? One way is to distinguish between specific liberties and some abstract total liberty. It is possible to arrange for specific liberties, such as freedom from hunger, freedom of speech, or freedom to choose one's own doctor, without unduly constraining how people use their property. Another answer is that the amount of redistribution necessary to provide the basic resources for liberty is very limited, and need not interfere substantially with anyone's right to dispose of his or her resources. Equity, in this view, does not require uniform shares of something for everyone, but only adequate shares. End-result justice does not require the same amount of money for everyone, or the same size winter coat, but it does require a certain minimum income and wardrobe. Redistributive policy should ensure that everyone receives the basic minimum, and it should tax people only enough to give everyone the necessary minimum; it will not tax anyone so as to bring him or her below the minimum. This view of equity, sometimes called *fair*

---

[12]We'll have more to say about liberty in Chapter 5.
[13]Nozick, op. cit. (note 7) p. 171.

shares,[14] holds that property rights can still retain their essential meaning—the right to use one's property as one wishes—without these rights being absolutely unlimited.

A third divide is whether one sees property as an individual creation or a collective creation. In one view, things of value—the things worth having and fighting about—come into being and derive their value from individual effort. Even when something is created through cooperative efforts, such as an automobile or a space shuttle mission, it is still possible to identify individual contributions. For one thing, if cooperation is based on specialization and division of labor, then we can simply measure the value added by each person as the product passes through a sequential process of production.[15] Not surprisingly, this view of property usually goes with the process view of equity and the unconstrained-choice view of liberty. For without a concept of discrete, individually created units of value, it is impossible to evaluate distributions by examining discrete historical transactions.

In the other view, at least some very important things of value come into being through cooperation that yields a result greater—and qualitatively different—than the sum of its parts. Cooperation in the first view is like a relay race; the contributions of individual efforts to the victory are discrete and measurable. Cooperation in the second view is like a chamber music performance. The thing of value—the music as the audience hears it, as well as the experience of playing it—cannot possibly be described as the sum of individual voices. The music is the result of voices in tune with each other and in balance. To be sure, the music has its moments when one instrument comes forth to carry the theme or dress up a motif with ornaments, but even the quality and excitement of virtuoso playing depends on the quality and sensitivity of accompaniment.

Rawls's concept of social primary goods is one way of saying that important values are socially created. R. H. Tawney puts it another

---

[14] For the fair-shares view, see William Ryan, *Equality* (New York: Random House, 1981), especially chaps. 1–3.

[15] This argument is best defended by Nozick, op. cit. (note 7) pp. 186–87. He adds another defense of his notion that even cooperatively produced products have identifiable individual contributions, but I find it tautological. It runs like this: There must be an identifiable individual contribution because "people transfer their holdings and labor in free markets with prices determined in the usual manner. If marginal productivity theory is reasonably adequate, people will be receiving, in these voluntary transfers of holdings, roughly their marginal products." Essentially, this amounts to saying that since we can imagine a hypothetical discrete individual contribution (i.e., marginal product), there must be one.

way: "If each of the hundred thousand men who landed in France in 1914 had been presented with one-hundred-thousandth part of the cost of the first expeditionary force, and instructed to spend it, in the manner he thought best, in making the world safe for democracy, it is possible that the arrangement might have been welcomed by the keepers of the estaminets, but it is doubtful that the German advance would have stopped at the Marne."[16] It should be clear by now that if one conceives of property and value as individually created, then one is likely to favor policies that respect individual freedom to acquire and use things as one wishes. If one conceives of property and value as socially created, one is more likely to favor redistributive policies that guarantee everyone some access to socially created goods.

conception of property

The fourth great divide concerns human motivation. In one view, people are motivated to work, produce, and create primarily by need. They work to acquire the things they must have or would like to have. In the other view, people have a natural drive to work, produce, and create, and they are inhibited by need. In one view, deprivation is the chief stimulus to work; in the other, internal drive protected by security is the chief stimulus.

The connection between these views of motivation and stances on the equality debate is probably clear. If one believes that work is primarily the result of need, one will be loath to engage in distributive policies that guarantee the things people seek through work. Such policies can only reduce the productivity of society. This view does not preclude all social assistance; many people on this side of the divide favor redistribution of basic necessities (food, clothing, shelter) to those in dire need. If, on the other hand, one believes that people are more productive, creative, and energetic when they are secure, one will favor redistribution of a broader range of goods and services to a broader range of people.

By now it is certainly obvious that the two clusters of views described here are social conservatism and social liberalism. Conservatism includes beliefs in distributive justice as fair acquisitions, liberty as freedom to dispose of one's property, property as an individual creation, and work as motivated by financial need. Liberalism includes beliefs in distributive justice as fair shares of basic resources, liberty as freedom from dire necessity, property as a social creation, and productivity as stimulated by security. Each of these themes will be elaborated

---

[16] R. H. Tawney, *Equality*, 5th ed. (London: Unwin, 1964), pp. 122–23.

in the next few chapters, but I introduce them here because they all have a bearing on views of equity.

If all else fails, you can tell the players in the great debate about equity by where they put the burden of proof. On one side, differences among people—whether of income, wealth, education, or occupation—are to be considered the norm, and any deviation from these patterns must be justified. In the words of one player on this side, "To justify income redistribution, it is necessary to show that individuals somehow do not have a just title to the income they earned."[17] On the other side, equality in the distribution of certain crucial resources is considered the norm, and deviations from equality must be justified in terms of other social goals. To quote a player on this side, "All social values—liberty and opportunity, income and wealth and the bases of self-respect—are to be distributed equally unless an unequal distribution of any, or all, of these values is to everyone's advantage."[18]

Equity — who? what? how?
horizontal/vertical.
historical context
< worldviews >
|
meanings of comm^y, property, liberty ...
social conservativism vs. social liberalism

EVERY POLICY
ISSUE INVOLVES
DISTRIBUTION

---

[17] Mark Plattner, "The Welfare State vs. the Redistributive State," *The Public Interest* 55, (Spring 1979): 28–48; quotation is on p. 32.

[18] Rawls, op. cit. (note 8), p. 62.

3

Efficiency

"Getting the most out of a given input" or "achieving an objective for the lowest cost" are simple definitions of the goal of efficiency. But, as Aaron Wildavsky observed, technical efficiency does not tell you where to go, only that you should arrive there with the least possible effort.[1] Efficiency is thus not a goal in itself. It is not something we want for its own sake, but rather because it helps us attain more of the things we value. Still, I include it here in the section on goals because it is an idea that dominates contemporary American discourse about public policy.

Efficiency is a comparative idea. It is a way of judging the merits of different ways of doing things. It has come to mean the ratio between input and output, effort and results, expenditure and income, or cost and resulting benefit.[2] As a criterion for judging goodness, it has been applied to all manner of things. Efficient organizations are ones that get things done with a minimum of waste, duplication, and expenditure of resources. Efficient people are ones who get a lot done in a little time. Efficient allocations of resources are ones that yield the most total value for society from existing resources. Efficient choices are ones that result in the largest benefit for the same cost, or the least cost given the benefit.

All of these applications are variations on the theme of getting the

[1] Aaron Wildavsky, *Speaking Truth to Power: The Art and Craft of Policy Analysis* (Boston: Little, Brown, 1979), p. 131.

[2] Sumner H. Slichter, "Efficiency," in Edwin R. A. Seligman, ed., *Encyclopedia of Social Sciences*, (New York: Macmillan, 1947), vol. 5, pp. 437–39.

most out of something. Like the "equal slices" solution to the problem of dividing a cake, getting the most out of something is an intuitively appealing solution to the problems of how to choose between alternatives or how to organize purposeful activity. No one is opposed to efficiency any more than people are against equity. Everyone would like to attain something of value in the least costly way. The conflicts arise over three questions: Who gets the benefits and bears the burdens of a policy? How should we measure the values and costs of a policy? And what mode of organizing human activity is likely to yield the most efficient results?

WHAT IS EFFICIENCY?

In one of the classic essays on efficiency, Herbert Simon speculated on how an administrator might apply the criterion of efficiency to running a public library. He assumed that the resources at the disposal of the administrator were limited and that the governmental objectives for the library had been agreed upon. The administrator's job was to maximize these objectives with the available resources. Simon concluded: A "good" public library, from the administrative standpoint, is not one that owns all the books that have ever been published, but one that has used the limited funds which are allowed it to build up as good a collection as possible under the circumstances.[3] Building on the tradition of Simon's work, Aaron Wildavsky and his colleagues asked a similar question some 30 years later as they tried to evaluate the efficiency of a real library system in Oakland, California. They began with the idea that "an agency is inefficient if it can (but does not) produce more outputs for its budget."[4] Here is a summary of their analysis:

> One output of a library system is circulation. A key to circulation is a lively, up-to-date stock of books. New books cost money, which could be found by reallocating funds in the budget. Our analysis of library staffing showed significant overqualification among the personnel. Many branch libraries had a staff of two or more professionals where one professional

[3] Herbert Simon, *Administrative Behavior*, 2nd ed., (New York: Macmillian, 1947), pp. 186–87; emphasis added.

[4] The study of Oakland's services is reported by Frank Levy, Arnold Meltsner, and Aaron Wildavsky, in *Urban Outcomes* (Berkeley: University of California Press, 1974). The quotation here and the summary that follows are from Wildavsky's later reflections on the study in *Speaking Truth to Power*, op. cit. (note 1), p. 365.

with a paraprofessional could have handled the work. High-salaried professionals often did clerical tasks. If staffing policies were adjusted to the actual work load, the savings in salary could be put toward new books.[5]

All the scholars agree, then, that an efficiently run library is one that builds up a good collection of books, and the California team suggests that the Oakland library would be more efficient if it replaced some professionals with paraprofessionals, and spent the savings in salary on books.

We can imagine several plausible challenges to this solution.

1. Some citizens might ask whether the book collection is really what matters about a library after all. Maybe instead a library system should provide public lectures, discussion groups, storytelling for children, reference services, archives of community oral history, or summer and after-school jobs for local teenagers. Who set "building a book collection" as the objective? How should all the different possible functions of a library be weighed? In short, how do we know which objectives to use to judge the costs of attaining them?

2. Book lovers in the community might debate what kind of book collection would be "as good as possible." Should it emphasize books for kids or adults? Sci-fi buffs or history freaks? Entertainment or scholarly reference? Each type of book would benefit a different group of library users. What about the balance of out-of-print books, classics, and new releases? Different emphases might benefit respectively rare-book dealers, established publishers, and new authors and presses. What about stocking tape-recorded books, CDs, videos, and TV documentaries for people whose main form of entertainment and reference is not print media? Such a collection would create a new set of library users. These are all questions of constituency: whom does the library serve? And they arise even once we have assumed a fairly narrow definition of objectives: "Buy books."

3. The librarians who would be sacked by the professors' prescription for efficiency would be quick to point out that public libraries provide valuable employment for the community and avenues of

---

[5] Wildavsky, op. cit. (note 1), p. 365. Wildavsky and his colleagues would be quite sensitive to the kinds of challenges I am about to raise. I use this example not to criticize them, but to show that apparently clear-cut definitions and criteria become much more complex when we think politically.

upward mobility, especially for women. They would look at staffing as an output of libraries, not just an input. Staff salaries are not only an expenditure on one side of the ledger, but also income to members of the community on the other side. Because, as is so often true in the polis, inputs are simultaneously outputs, the arithmetic of the efficiency calculation is confused.

4. The librarians might go on to point out a variety of benefits deriving from their services, in addition to jobs. They read to kids in story hours, thus multiplying the impact of a single book. They effectively provide a few hours of day care for many parents, who can use the time to do other productive things. They do telephone reference work, saving other people time. They help school classes and community groups do research to plan programs, enhancing the value of these other activities. Maybe, the librarians might say, it's true that these functions don't require professionally trained librarians, but wouldn't Oakland get more output for its money if it took something from the book budget and put it into salaries for more paraprofessionals? There is no limit to the types of benefits one can imagine and impute to any input. How do we know when to stop counting benefits, and how do we put values on some of these benefits?

5. The costs of any activity, economists tell us, include not only the actual money outlays for it but the forgone opportunities. What else might we have accomplished with same expenditure? Here we come back to the first challenge: There are lots of other things the library administrator could have done with the budget besides either buying books or paying salaries. Which of all the possible forgone opportunities should count as costs in the efficiency calculus?

6. Some people think of an efficient library as one that would waste the least amount of time. Users would waste the least time looking for books if there were always a large staff on duty able to help locate books quickly. That would mean lots of librarians might be sitting around idle much of the time. Librarians would waste the least time if there were just enough librarians to do all the book searching. Every librarian would always be busy, but that would mean making the users wait in lines. One person's efficiency is another person's waste.

7. Some people think of an efficient library as one that is easy to use. A principal way I discover new material on a research topic is by

taking down a citation in a footnote, locating the book by its call number, and then browsing the books near it on the shelves. For me, the library would be much more efficient if it bought multiple copies of each book and placed them in different categories on the shelves, just as each book has several entries to be found under different topic headings in the catalog. That system would require duplication of books, and duplication is anathema to efficiency. Similarly, the people of Oakland might think that their library system would be easier to use if it had many small branches located within walking distance of every residential neighborhood. But the more branches, the more duplication of collections. The dilemma in both my ideal library and the multibranch system is that duplication can be seen either as waste or as enhancing ease of use.

Trying to measure efficiency is like trying to pull oneself out of quicksand without a rope. There is no firm ground. Objectives for public policy are forged in political conflict and are constantly changing, not handed down on a stone tablet. Even if we assume a very narrow objective, such as a good book collection, that objective is subject to competing interpretations. What kind of book collection? And good for whom? And even if we settle these questions, how do we measure the costs and benefits of any library policy, given that costs are simultaneously benefits to someone else, that benefits extend in an infinite chain, and that costs conceived as forgone opportunities are limited only by our imagination?

At the societal level, efficiency is an ideal meant to guide how society chooses to spend its money or allocate its resources in order to get the most value. As the library example illustrates, there are any number of possible paths to the goal of "most value for the money." These paths, and their results, cannot be scored on any *a priori* metric of efficiency. Efficiency is always a contestable concept. Everyone supports the general idea of getting the most out of something, but to go beyond the vague slogans and apply the concept to a concrete policy choice requires making assumptions about who and what counts as important. There are no correct answers to these questions to be found outside the political process. The answers built into supposedly technical analyses of efficiency are nothing more than political claims. By offering different assumptions, sides in a conflict can portray their preferred outcomes as being most efficient.

Concepts of Efficiency

Simple Definition   Getting the most output for a given input

Complications in the Polis

Output   1. Who determines what is the correct output goal, or objective of a program?

2. How should we value and compare multiple objectives?

3. How do different objectives or outputs benefit different constituencies or groups?

Input   4. How should we count inputs (e.g., labor costs) that are simultaneously outputs to somebody else (e.g., jobs for local community)?

5. How should we decide which of the many benefits/outputs of any input to count in the equation?

6. How should we count the virtually unlimited opportunity costs of resources used as inputs?

Markets and Efficiency

Beyond these contests over what kinds of policies are efficient, there is a larger intellectual debate about the best mode of organizing society to achieve the greatest social welfare. The idea that voluntary exchanges are the best way to achieve efficiency is the central tenet of the theory of markets. This idea is so important in contemporary policy discussions, and so central to most of economics, that it is worth taking some time to analyze it carefully.

mkt model.

Markets are networks of exchanges. In the simplest market model, the barter economy, two people exchange different goods, usually coconuts for pineapples or some other tropical fruit revealing our romantic fascination with the Robinson Crusoe tale. Once we move to an economy a bit larger than a two-person island society, contracts and governments to enforce them become essential to a market. Without government enforcement of contracts, people would be loath to trade with strangers. They would hesitate to make exchanges that could not be completed right on the spot. And they would not buy anything much more complicated than a banana, whose condition can be judged and whose durability is not a part of its value.

Another important function of government is to define rules of ownership. Ownership, in turn, is a right to use and trade something backed up by the state. The legal rules of ownership in a society serve to define what is ownable, by whom, and how. Virtually anything can be turned into an ownable commodity, and ownable commodities can swiftly be made unownable. In the United States, black people were ownable before the Civil War; now they are not. Beaches are ownable in the United States; on the island of Saint Maarten, they are not—anybody can use any beach. Lenin's government changed houses from something ownable to something not. The U.S. Environmental Protection Agency, with its creation of imaginary air bubbles and permits to pollute within them, converted air into something ownable for the purposes of discharging gases.

Although the things that are subject to exchange in a market are usually defined by governments, people sometimes engage in transactions of things the government expressly forbids as ownable property. They buy and sell the use of bodies in prostitution, and more recently in surrogate motherhood arrangements, where in effect, a couple who cannot have children rents the womb of another woman to produce a baby. People can also try to sell ownable things they do not happen to own, such as the Brooklyn Bridge or stolen goods, but communities move quickly to curtail such deals, precisely because they undermine the trust essential to a system of exchange.

Whether in legal markets or black markets, though, the rules of ownership are defined outside the market; that is, they are made prior to any exchange. People will not enter into exchanges until they can conceive of things—be they babies, bodies, beaches, bungalows, or bubbles—as ownable, and unless they have previously established some rules about what ownership means.

Exchanges themselves have two important characteristics that serve as defining assumptions of the market model and allow its adherents to claim that markets are the most efficient mode of social organization. First, the exchanges are voluntary. People engage in trades only if they want to, and they want to trade only when they believe a trade will make them better off. Second, people make their voluntary exchanges on the basis of two kinds of information—objective information about the price and quality of all alternatives available for trade, and subjective information about their own needs, desires, and abilities (or "preferences" in the language of economics).

The theory of markets says that as long as exchanges meet these conditions of being both voluntary and fully informed, plus a few other conditions to be discussed later, they lead to the goal of allocative efficiency: Resources always move in a direction that make people better off. This is because exchanges are choices. Individuals survey a variety of possible exchanges, match the two kinds of information—available alternatives and personal preferences—and select the exchange that yields the "best results." Since no one would voluntarily engage in a trade that made him or her worse off, and people would engage in trades only when at least one side was made better off, all voluntary exchanges must lead to situations where at least one person is better off and no one is worse off.

In the theory of markets, voluntary exchanges transform resources into something more valuable. One kind of transformation is very straightforward—the conversion of raw materials into finished goods or, put a bit more abstractly, the conversion of inputs into final outputs. This is the standard type of transformation familiar in economics textbooks, and it occurs over the course of several exchanges. An entrepreneur exchanges money for raw materials from raw materials suppliers, money for labor from employees, and perhaps money for equipment from capital goods suppliers. Workers and machines convert raw materials into finished goods, and the entrepreneur then exchanges goods for money from consumers.

But there is another, more mystical, sort of transformation in market theory, and that is the exchange itself. The paradox of markets is that all items have two values: their market price, or what we might call universal value, and their value to a particular individual or firm, or what we might call subjective value. My loaf of bread and your two dollars are equivalent in the first sense, but we engage in a trade only because they are unequal in the second sense. To me, two dollars is more valuable than a loaf of bread, and to you, a loaf of bread is more valuable than two dollars. Your need for food makes bread more valuable to you, and my ability to convert flour into bread makes the dollar more valuable to me.[6] We are both made better off by the exchange, even though our little economic system contains the same two dollars and loaf of bread before and after the exchange.

What goes on in a market is that both need and ability alter the universal values of things to individuals. That is the magic of voluntary exchanges: They convert universal or market value to a higher individual value, and thus produce efficiency. They make sure that resources and money are allocated to the people who get the most from them. "Get the most" might mean the most satisfaction of a need or desire, or it might mean the most potential for conversion to a more valuable good or service. Either way, voluntary exchanges are supposed to ensure getting the most for the least, because they leave decisions in the hands of the people who have the best information about subjective values as determined by needs and abilities—individuals themselves.

Market models, even though they are concerned with distribution of things to people, use the term *allocation* instead of *distribution*. *Allocation* emphasizes the production side of the economy, rather than the consumption side. The usual expressions in English are *resource allocation* but *income distribution*. Market models are concerned with whether resources (dollars, labor, raw materials, or finished goods) go to the people who can use them to greatest productive advantage or who will derive the greatest amount of welfare from them. Thus, when Milton Friedman says that the "function of payment in accordance with product in a market society is not primarily distributive, but allocative," he means that the purpose of payment is not to reward contribution or deservingness but to signal the direction of resources to their best use.[7]

Theories of distributive equity and the theory of allocative efficiency have very different perspectives on the nature of social welfare. In market theory, it is assumed that if all the exchanges in a system are efficient, the result will be efficiency at the societal level or "maximum social welfare." In fact, the discipline of economics is steadfast in its

---

[6]Adam Smith used the terms "value in exchange" for what I have called "universal value," and "value in use" for what I have called "subjective value." His famous example of the disparity between these two values is diamonds and water: "Nothing is more useful than water but it will purchase scarce anything. . . . A diamond, on the contrary, has scarce any value in use; but a very great quantity of other goods may be had in exchange for it." *The Wealth of Nations* (first published in 1776; Harmondsworth, England: Penguin Books, 1982), Book I, chap. 4, pp. 131–32.

[7]Milton Friedman, *Capitalism and Freedom* (Chicago: University of Chicago Press, 1962), p. 166.

assertions that only individuals can judge welfare, individuals can judge only their own welfare, and therefore, societal welfare can be defined only as the aggregate of individual situations.

The idea of allocative efficiency takes as a given the pre-existing income distribution. If a tycoon decides to spend lots of money on a gigantic statue of himself or on wrapping a building in tinsel and ribbon for a week, those decisions are deemed to be efficient. There is no place in the economic concept of efficiency for other people to make judgments about the value to society of the rich man's purchases.

By contrast, theories of distributive justice, not to mention real-world politics, require the analyst to make explicit comparisons between people and judgments about the value of items. To decide who should count as a recipient or whether particular subdivisions in society should determine the distribution of resources is to stand outside one-self and define welfare for society as a whole. Similarly, a societal perspective is required to decide whether an item should be interpreted as a thing in itself or as part of something larger; or to decide whether the important value of something is its objective content or its customized, individual value; or to decide whether one type of social decision-making process is better than another.

Let's recapitulate why voluntary exchanges are supposed to produce allocative efficiency. First, people do not engage in exchanges unless someone expects to be made better off by the exchange and no one expects to be harmed. Thus, barring incorrect information and unpredictable disasters (such as weather destroying a commodity after a deal has been struck), exchanges must necessarily lead to improvements in the welfare of individuals. Second, every exchange is, besides a physical exchange of resources, a conversion of market values into higher subjective values. Every exchange, in other words, should lead to a situation in which the new holders get more value out of the resources than the old holders. And finally, if exchanges make people better off as individuals, they necessarily make society as a whole better off. Since welfare (and the "best" use of resources) can be judged only subjectively by individuals, the only concept of social welfare that makes any sense is one that identifies societal welfare with the aggregate welfare of individuals.

Voluntary exchange as spelled out in the theory of markets has a certain intuitive appeal as a solution to the problem of efficiency, but here, too, there have been numerous challenges. And here, too, people tend to have a predisposition for or against markets as a mode of organization, apart from the specifics of particular policy issues. In fact, the challenges to voluntary exchange fall rather neatly into two groups:

ones that accept the basic premise that voluntary exchange leads to efficiency and ones that do not.

CHALLENGES FROM THE MARKET

The first type of challenge accepts the general argument that voluntary exchange leads to efficiency, but recognizes that unconstrained markets do not always work as they should. The gist of this type of challenge is to point out that some conditions of the market model do not hold in a particular situation and that it is possible to correct the conditions. Challenges in this vein arise from within the economics discipline and the market vision. The field of welfare economics focuses particularly on the problem of when markets fail—market failure— and how they can be restored or corrected.

In order for markets to yield efficiency, there must be numerous buyers and sellers of any resource, so that no person or firm can influence the market price. When this condition fails, there is monopoly if a seller can control price or monopsony if a buyer can control price. In welfare economics, monopolies are often called natural or technical, which are both ways of saying they are unavoidable. Something about the good or service itself renders multiple producers infeasible. Utilities—gas, electricity, and telephone service—are the most common examples. Because they involve digging up streets, laying networks of pipes, wires, or cables, and huge capital investments, they are best done by a single firm. Where there are natural monopolies, the argument goes, the best policy is to accept monopoly as a fact of life and control its harmful side effects through government regulation.[8]

A second condition for a well-functioning market is that there must be full information about the available alternatives, so that exchanges truly result in the best situation for everyone. For a variety of reasons, this condition is not always met. Providing full information (from the seller's side) or acquiring it (from the buyer's side) always entails some costs, which people may not be willing to bear. Sellers may conceal features of their products that would hurt sales. Buyers may not have sufficient knowledge to understand information about products or even to ask the right questions. When there is imperfect information, the best policy is to preserve voluntary exchanges but to improve infor-

---

[8]Not all economists accept the idea of natural or inevitable monopolies, and there is a lively debate about this type of market failure—as well as the others. For the classic challenge to the natural monopoly argument, see Harold Demsetz, "Why Regulate Utilities?" *Journal of Law and Economics* 11 (1968): 55–65.

mation. Depending on the nature of the problem, information might be improved by imposing disclosure requirements (such as food nutrition labeling or energy efficiency ratings for appliances); or by providing information about quality (such as licensing, accreditation, and certification schemes).

A third condition is that the decisions and actions of parties to an exchange must not affect the welfare of people who are not part of the exchange. Without this condition of independence, we could not be sure that exchanges—even voluntary and fully informed ones—make everyone better off. Situations in which there are effects on people outside an exchange are called externalities. In welfare economics, externalities are usually thought of as negative effects, or as the type of commons problem in which actions with private benefits entail social costs. In the theory of markets, externalities can be corrected in a variety of ways, but the essential problem is to force people to consider social costs and harmful effects on others when they engage in any exchange.[9]

A fourth condition is that the resources involved in exchanges must be used individually and used up if they are used at all (excludable and rival in the jargon of welfare economics). When this condition is not met, there is a type of market failure called collective goods. They are the type of commons problem described in Chapter 1 as social benefits entailing private sacrifices. National defense and lighthouses are the ubiquitous textbook examples, and the argument there is that voluntary exchanges will fail to produce collective goods in sufficient quantities because there is no way to harness individual willingness to pay for them. Collective goods are the one type of failure that market advocates acknowledge as not correctable within a system of voluntary exchange. For these situations, some kind of collective action is necessary.[10]

---

[9] A useful review of both the externalities and information types of market failure is Otto Davis and Morton Kamien, "Externalities, Information and Alternative Collection Action," in Robert Dorfman and Nancy Dorfman, eds., *Economics of the Environment* (New York: Norton, 1977).

[10] The classic definition of collective goods is Paul Samuelson's in "The Pure Theory of Public Expenditure," *Review of Economics and Statistics* 36 (1954): 387–89. An interesting essay on collective goods from a political perspective by an economist and lawyer is Peter Steiner, "The Public Sector and the Public Interest," in Robert Haveman and Julian Margolis, eds., *Public Expenditure and Policy Analysis* (Chicago: Rand McNally College Publishers, 1977), pp. 21–58. Steiner defines public goods as anything the public wants in different quantity or quality than the market would provide, and for which there is a viable public demand (p. 25).

CHALLENGES FROM THE POLIS

A vastly different type of challenge questions whether a society organized entirely as a system of voluntary exchanges can really produce efficiency. Do markets really produce maximum social welfare? Challenges in this vein arise from a fuller understanding of human psychology and a wider vision of society as polity.

One important line of critique questions the whole idea of welfare, happiness, and satisfaction implicit in market theory. There are many activities people undertake for their intrinsic rewards. Often, people derive happiness from doing or experiencing something, rather than from the value they obtain in an exchange. Happiness sometimes come from the pleasure of working itself, for example, rather than from the paycheck that is the outcome of exchange. Welfare and satisfaction come from the relationships people create and develop with other people, more than from the results of exchanges. Exchange is only one small part of a relationship. As the political psychologist Robert Lane puts it:

> By definition, activities that are satisfying in themselves do not depend for their full worth upon exchange value (how much the activity is worth in the market), nor from their "use value" in the conventional sense of the usefulness of the activities. Rather they derive their *value in use by the actor*.[11]

Much of the activity people undertake and care about falls outside the realm of exchange, and a society conceived only as a network of exchanges fails to capture what are perhaps the most important sources of human happiness and well-being. A large body of psychological research suggests, moreover, that extrinsic rewards, such as payment, bonuses, praise, or other things not part of the activity itself, actually decrease people's intrinsic motivations to work and to learn. People try less or engage less in a task that they once found enjoyable if they are then paid for it.[12] Organizing those activities as market exchanges probably decreases human productive energy and so decreases net social welfare. Thus, a social system organized entirely

[11] Robert Lane, *The Market Experience* (Cambridge, England: Cambridge University Press, 1991), p. 364, emphases in original.

[12] See Alfie Kohn, *Punished by Rewards* (Boston: Houghton Mifflin, 1993); and Marc Lepper and David Greene, eds., *The Hidden Costs of Rewards: New Perspectives on the Psychology of Human Motivation* (Hillsdale, N.J.: Wiley / Erbaum, 1978).

as market exchange will not be able to provide all of the social welfare that is potentially available, as the efficiency criterion and market paradigm promise.[13]

Another line of challenge is to argue that the basic conditions of a perfectly competitive market never exist in actual societies, and thus a system of voluntary exchange can never work the way it is supposed to in theory.

In the polis, as we have seen, the line between voluntarism and coercion is very fuzzy, so the concept of purely voluntary exchanges is itself questionable. Because the polis is characterized by influence, groups, and loyalty, subjective preferences are never independently formed. They are shaped by peer pressure, family pressure, the pressure of historical tradition, the pressure of public opinion, the pressure of political alliances—all pressures from outside a market that undermine the independence and voluntariness of any individual choice inside a market.

The problem of manipulation of preferences from *inside* the market poses another serious challenge to the argument that voluntary exchange leads to efficiency. Advertising is only one way individual preferences are shaped from inside the market. Doctors, for example, rarely advertise but exert tremendous influence over what medical services a patient will "buy." They provide advice about what tests and procedures a patient needs, and then sell the diagnostic and therapeutic services they recommend. Any suppliers who sell a combination of services and advice—lawyers, engineers, psychotherapists, consultants, stockbrokers, insurance agents, architects, interior decorators, funeral home directors, building contractors—directly shape the preferences of their customers.

Arguably, all services are really a combination of actual service and advice about what the consumer needs. This means that as an economy evolves away from agriculture and manufacturing toward a larger service sector, the degree of voluntarism in market exchanges may decrease, because consumers are much more dependent on sellers than market theory acknowledges. And if consumer preferences are not really individual but shaped by sellers, we can no longer assume that each transaction does increase the welfare of both parties.[14]

[13] For a careful development of this critique, see Robert Lane, *The Market Experience*, op cit. (note 11), esp. chaps. 17–18 and 23–25.

[14] Adam Smith held an even more radical view of persuasion in the market: "The offering of a shilling . . . is in reality offering an argument to persuade one to do so-and-so

Yet another reason to question the possibility of purely voluntary exchanges is the vastly unequal distribution of income and wealth. The threat of starvation or homelessness is pervasive for poor people. The need to work for a livelihood is a coercive force in all labor markets. And, perhaps more important, need in the polis is relative as well as absolute. People can feel coerced not only by the need for sheer subsistence, but also by the need to meet the living standards of their peer or reference groups. Since 1946, a standard Gallup Poll question has asked people "What is the smallest amount of money a family of four needs to get along in this community?" Each year, people's answers hover just above the average weekly take-home pay of nonagricultural workers. This finding demonstrates "the squeeze for ordinary workers between what they earn and what is demanded of them in order to hold their heads up as 'good providers.' "[15]

Loyalty raises another dilemma for the assumption of voluntarism. In the polis, most exchanges are not merely one-time events but rather part of long-term relationships. Formal contracts are one type of long-term relationship, and indeed, in many markets, firms hold long-term contracts with suppliers and buyers.[16] Even without long-term contracts, many exchanges take place in the context of informal but still very strong long-term relationships; shopping at neighborhood stores, medical care, rental housing, and banking are examples.

Long-term relationships can add a coercive element to exchanges in two ways. One is that they generate expectations of continued exchanges, so that if one side terminates the relationship, the other side feels pressure. When long-term relationships are broken, as for example in worker layoffs, somebody is always left in the lurch. Although the theory of markets requires that people enter into trades voluntarily, it says nothing about voluntarism in the termination of exchanges. Clearly, freedom to enter exchanges requires freedom to

---

for it is in his interest." He thought the human propensity to "truck, barter, and exchange" derived from "the natural inclination every one has to persuade." *Lectures on Jurisprudence* (New York: Oxford University Press—Clarendon Press, 1978), chap. 2, cited in Robert Heilbroner, "The Murky Economists," *New York Review of Books*, April 24, 1986, p. 46.

[15] Lee Rainwater, *What Money Buys: Inequality and the Social Meanings of Income* (New York: Basic Books, 1974), pp. 41–63; quotation is on pp. 53–54. The concepts of absolute and relative need are discussed more fully in Chapter 4.

[16] In fact, long-term contracts are one of the principal devices used by firms to protect themselves against the uncertainties of the market. See John Kenneth Galbraith, *The New Industrial State*, 2nd rev. ed. (New York: New American Library, 1971), chap. 3.

terminate them. Yet termination is often felt as coercive, and people then enter into other exchanges out of a need created by a previous termination. In the context of long-term relationships, it may be impossible to talk about the voluntarism of individual exchanges.

Long-term relationships may also be coercive because they are often between parties with unequal power. Think of exchanges between landlords and tenants, insurance companies and policyholders, universities and students, doctors and patients, employers and employees. In every one, there is a buyer and a seller, yet "voluntarism" means something quite different for the two sides. Long-term relationships offer greater possibility for the more powerful side to take advantage of the weaker side. A new job applicant can bargain for higher wages by holding out the possibility of other job options. An employer deciding on a pay raise for a long-term employee can actually influence the employee's job prospects elsewhere, by blacklisting or by providing negative references, leaving the employee little leverage.

Another broad set of challenges from the polis questions the second assumption of the market model—namely, that individuals make exchanges on the basis of full information about the objective alternatives and their subjective preferences. The challenge here is that it is impossible to have the type of information necessary for voluntary exchanges to result in efficiency.

The market model requires accurate and complete information. But in the polis, information is always incomplete, interpretive, and deliberately controlled. People can never have full information about all the alternatives available for satisfying their goals. Even if the money costs of information were zero, there would still be enormous time costs to process all the free information. Moreover, we simply cannot know all the long-term consequences and side effects of every possible exchange. Yet for the most important decisions people have to make— how and where to educate oneself and one's children, where to live, what career to pursue, and what job to take—the long-term consequences are everything. Long-term consequences are at issue in many public policy decisions as well—whether to use nuclear power as a major source of energy, whether to stake national defense on space-based weapons, or whether to treat AFDC as a federal entitlement or a matter of state discretion. The argument here is not that somebody conceals information or that other people cannot understand it, but rather that critical information simply does not exist. No one knows, or can know, the long-range consequences of most decisions. In the polis, the impossibility of full information undermines the ability of voluntary exchanges to produce efficiency.

Even more important than the impossibility of what economists call *perfect information* is the strategic character of information in the polis, and indeed, in most real markets. Secrecy is central to competitive strategy. Sellers usually do not divulge plans for new products or for future price discounts; if they did, they would undercut their own sales in the present. Insurance companies and other firms that sell through contracts typically conceal restrictions and other negative features in fine print, technical jargon, or innocent-sounding phrases with arcane legal meanings. Buyers conceal information as well. The most notable examples are the purchase of consumer credit and insurance. Buyers may gain advantage by concealing information about their past history that would help creditors or insurers estimate their future risks—information such as outstanding debts for consumer loans or driving records for car insurance.

The parties to exchanges, therefore, necessarily make decisions on the basis of incomplete information about the past and the future, and about the services and the products in the exchange. While advocates of market mechanisms for policy making might argue that an exchange is efficient if it maximizes welfare at the present moment, inhabitants of the polis live over the long run and consider the time dimension a crucial part of most decisions.

Advocates of markets tend to believe that the problems of deliberate concealment are solvable through regulation. It is possible to require price disclosure, content labeling, and hazard warnings, for instance. In the polis, though, concealment is an essential part of strategy in economic and political life, and no amount of regulation can prevent people from behaving strategically. Concealment is so important to the economic livelihood of some industries that they will fight any attempt to limit it. That is why the funeral home industry mounted a huge lobbying effort to defeat price disclosure requirements proposed by the Federal Trade Commission.[17]

If incompleteness and deliberate concealment undermine the possibility of full information about the more objective side of exchanges, the interpretive character of information undermines the possibility on the subjective side. Remember that voluntary exchanges are said to result in efficiency because each exchange converts the universal market value of something into a higher value for the individual or firm. We have already considered how people's assessments of the value of exchanges to them are influenced by sellers, by public opinion, and by

[17]Martin and Susan Tolchin, Dismantling America (New York: Oxford University Press, 1983), pp. 164–79.

peer pressure. Assessments are also influenced by the presentation of information—the choice of words and images, the spokespeople, the timing, and the context. If the assessment of subjective value is so much influenced by others who have a stake in the same exchanges and by forms of presentation of information, then the independence of market value and individual value is called into question. And without independence, how can we ever know whether exchanges indeed result in shifting resources to their best possible use?

4　A third set of challenges focuses on market theory's equation of societal welfare with individual welfare. These challenges reject the idea that there is no meaningful concept of social welfare other than the aggregate of individual situations. People are not simply isolated beings whose welfare is affected by no one else. In a community, as in a family, individuals derive some satisfaction from others' well-being and feel some pain—and sometimes pleasure—from others' misfortunes.[18] Thus, even individual welfare depends on the welfare of others.

Individual welfare is influenced not only by the welfare of others, but also by all the complex activities and decisions of a community. The corollary is that all individual actions have side effects on others. However indirect or hard to determine some side effects might be, the economist's conceptual boundaries around exchanges are necessarily artificial, and they are often used to deny the significance of effects beyond those boundaries.[19] To ignore side effects, or to pretend that

[18] Some economists, recognizing the possibility that individual welfare might in part depend on other people's welfare, have subsumed this phenomenon as another type of market failure, calling it "interdependent utilities." In such situations, which they deem to be relatively few, government intervention into markets is justified.

[19] Duncan MacRae, Jr., and James A. Wilde, in *Policy Analysis for Public Decisions* (North Scituate, Mass.: Duxbury Press, 1979) distinguish between effects internal and external to a market, and hold that externalities properly involve only the latter. I find even this distinction hard to sustain in any meaningful way. They use the example of a market for bread, and include as *internal* all impacts on bread consumers and manufacturers, bread industry workers, wheat growers, plastic bag manufacturers, and even the potato industry (because potatoes are a substitute for bread). Why not also barley growers and barley product manufacturers, pasta producers and rice growers, the petroleum industry (petroleum goes into plastic), and the aluminum foil industry (aluminum foil is a substitute for plastic bags), *ad infinitum?* MacRae and Wilde might include these effects as internal to the bread market but their generic definition doesn't help me decide. Externalities are only those consequences that "involve people who did not participate in the market decision and thus are experiencing impacts external to the voluntary exchange mechanism" (p. 178). We are now off on a wild goose chase for the meaning of "participation."

externalities are a defect in a minuscule area of human affairs, is to undermine the ability of public policy to achieve efficiency in any important sense.

Finally, many goals of public policy cannot be broken down into situations of individuals: community survival, the security and pride that come from membership in a community, social trust, camaraderie, and the enrichment and dignity of participating in collective decisions are examples. None of these types of welfare would retain its essential qualities if it were divided up and parceled out among individual citizens, and so it is impossible to conceive of them as the aggregate of individual conditions.

Markets do not work, even on the terms of classical microeconomic theory. But there is an even more important reason to be skeptical of the claims that markets are the best way to organize society. The whole enterprise of proving that markets lead to efficiency is predicated on the idea that efficiency is objectively determinable. If, as the library conundrum showed, efficiency is a political claim, a portrait of a situation that makes some people and some things look more important than others, then we should doubt the very possibility of proving that some social system leads to "the greatest good given our collective resources."

Markets are a way of organizing social activity, just as other forms of governance are. They require a set of rules about who can sell, what can be sold, what constitutes a valid contract, and how valid contracts will be enforced. They also happen to be a mode of organizing social activity that gives more power to people who control money and property than to people who do not. If we start from the premise that efficiency itself is a contestable idea about what constitutes social welfare, then the best way to organize society to achieve efficiency is to provide a democratic governing structure that allows for these contests to be expressed and addressed in a fair way.

THE EQUALITY-EFFICIENCY TRADE-OFF

Equality and efficiency are often thought to be in a zero-sum relationship: the more we have of one, the less we have of the other.[20] Many

---

[20]The idea of a trade-off between these two policy goals was popularized by Arthur Okun's Godkin Lectures, published under the title *Equality and Efficiency: The Big Tradeoff* (Washington, D.C.: Brookings Institution, 1975).

policy debates therefore take the form of asking what is the best "mix" of equality and efficiency, or how much of what we currently have in one dimension we should give up in order to obtain more in the other dimension. Tax and welfare policy are two areas where the belief in a trade-off is strongest. Since there are good reasons to think the relationship between equality and efficiency is not zero-sum, it is worth summarizing the logic of the trade-off view.

There are three reasons why efficiency and equality are thought to be in a trade-off. The first and most common is the motivation argument. It holds that equality eliminates the differential rewards necessary to motivate people to be productive. Any move toward equalization of incomes—such as welfare grants, progressive taxation, or restructuring of wages—will reduce individual effort, personal savings, and eventually, the level of productive investment a society can generate. The motivation argument goes back at least as far as Reverend Malthus's eighteenth-century treatise on poverty, in which he postulated that the stimulus of providing for oneself and bettering one's condition in life is necessary to "overcome the natural indolence of mankind." Thus, greater equality through income redistribution to the poor would necessarily lead to less work and lower production.[21]

The second reason for the trade-off is that to maintain equality, government must continuously interfere with individual choices about how to use resources, and in doing so, it curbs useful experimentation and productive innovation. One element of this innovation argument is that the more we have a policy of equality, the larger the government bureaucracy has to be, and the larger the government bureaucracy, the more inflexible it is likely to be. In large organizations, innovators tend to be suppressed.[22]

The third reason is the waste argument. To maintain equality requires a large administrative machinery that uses up resources but is not itself productive. The administrative machinery of equality—tax bureaus, welfare agencies, labor departments, and the judicial apparatus for resolving conflicts generated by these entities—represents an actual loss of valued resources. The labor, buildings, computers, and paper they use could go to producing other things. Arthur Okun dramatized this argument with his metaphor of a leaky bucket: any redis-

[21] T. R. Malthus, *An Essay on the Principle of Population*, Anthony Flew, ed. (Harmondsworth: Penguin, 1970), p. 245.

[22] This is one of Okun's major arguments, and it seems to be the one that most convinces him of a zero-sum relationship. See Okun, op. cit. (note 18), pp. 56–60.

Challenges to Efficiency as a Criterion for Social Welfare

Market Imperfections

Imperfect competition:
: One or a few suppliers or buyers dominate the market and can control prices.

Imperfect information:
: Sellers may conceal information; information may be too technical or too costly for buyers to acquire.

Externalities:
: An exchange between two parties has bad side effects on third parties who have no say in the exchange.

Collective goods:
: People have no incentive to produce and pay for goods that are used collectively and that cannot be divided and charged to individuals.

Polis Realities

Nature of welfare:
: People derive welfare from doing, participating, and experiencing, apart from the output of exchanges; output is too narrow a measure of welfare.

: Personal welfare is not separable from collective welfare, nor is societal welfare simply the aggregate of individual welfare.

Nature of exchanges:
: Purely voluntary exchange is a fiction; line between coercion and voluntarism is blurry.

Nature of information:
: Information is incomplete, interpretive, and deliberately controlled.

TABLE 3.1
DISTRIBUTION OF EARNINGS IN 1977

| | Full-time, Full-year | |
Quintiles	White males (%)	All other workers (%)
1	7.7	1.8
2	13.9	7.2
3	18.2	15.8
4	23.5	27.0
5	36.7	48.2
Mean Earnings	$16,568	$5,843

Source: U.S. Bureau of the Census, *Current Population Reports, Consumer Income 1977*, Series P-60, no. 118 (March 1979), p. 228.

tributive policy is like carrying money from the rich to the poor in a leaky bucket. The policy question for him is how much waste society will tolerate before deciding it is not worth engaging in transfer at all.

The motivation argument is familiar from the great debate about equity. If you do not accept need as the primary motivator, if you believe people work also for the inherent satisfactions, for self-esteem, or for a sense of belonging, then you will probably not be terribly convinced by the argument here. But the most important critique of the motivation argument comes from another corner. Even if people are motivated by need and by the desire to increase differences of status and wealth between themselves and others, such enormous differences as we currently have are not necessary to sustain motivation. We could move in the direction of more equality without sacrificing efficiency. As Lester Thurow has pointed out (see Table 3.1), there is only a five-fold variation in earned income between the top and bottom quintiles for white males, but a 27-fold variation between the top and bottom quintiles for all other workers. If we are satisfied with the productivity of white males, then we can certainly reduce the income differentials in the rest of society to about fivefold without any loss of efficiency[23]— unless, that is, we are willing to argue that women and nonwhites are lazier than white men and need a greater economic stimulus to make them work.

The innovation argument falls under a similar line of reasoning. Some redistribution—and after all, no one in the policy mainstream is

[23] Lester Thurow, *The Zero-Sum Society.* (New York, Basic Books, 1980), pp. 201–2.

talking about redistribution to maintain completely equal incomes— ⟩*historical arg.*
obviously does not halt experimentation and innovation. If it did, tax
and welfare systems would long ago have killed the American economy, not to mention the West European and Japanese economies. Of
course, we can always wonder what marvelous innovations might have
happened had the last tax dollar not been extracted, but then again,
we can also wonder what marvelous innovations might have happened
had the next tax dollar gone to finance education or basic research.

Neither is it clear that administrative machinery is wasteful. Merely
calling something "administrative" as opposed to "productive" is a way
of prejudicing the argument. For example, to win political support for
a plan to reduce state aid to suburban school districts, New Jersey's
education commissioner devised a plan that would penalize districts
for excess administrative spending, and then categorized school libraries, nurses, and guidance counselors as "administrative."[24] Furthermore, much administrative work, such as record keeping, scheduling,
and monitoring the budget, does contribute to an organization's output. And, administrative machinery employs people, integrates them
in a social group, and gives them dignity, if it accomplishes nothing
else. In a society that stakes personal worth on paid employment but
cannot provide employment for everyone, that is no small contribution.

[24]Mark Walsh, "Wealthy N.J. Districts Assail Spending Categories," *Education Week*,
Feb. 22, 1995, pp. 10–11.

IS THERE AN EQUALITY-EFFICIENCY TRADE-OFF?

Yes	*No*
1. Maintaining equality eliminates people's motivation to work.	People are motivated to work by inherent satisfactions, self-esteem, and sense of belonging.
2. Maintaining equality requires government interference with individual choice, and free choice is necessary for exchanges to produce efficiency.	Redistribution does not stifle experimentation and innovation; some security is a stimulus to work and risk taking.
3. Maintaining equality requires a large bureaucracy and bureaucracy equals waste.	Administration is a productive activity in itself.
4. A trade-off between equity and efficiency is inevitable.	Society can have both equity and efficiency by managing political and policy choices.

Finally, the administrative machinery necessary for equity is arguably no less productive, no less useful to society, than some of the innovations spawned by the pursuit of profit and the unfettered use of resources—hula hoops and pet rocks, fruit loops and fruity pebbles, gold fingernails and green hair.

The most telling evidence against an immutable equality-efficiency trade-off comes from cross-national studies. Japan has steeply progressive taxes on personal income, fairly high inheritance taxes, and very low taxes on consumption (such as sales taxes), yet it has one of the highest rates of personal savings in the world, is a leader in technological innovation, and leads the industrial countries in productivity growth. West Germany has high corporate taxes, a generous pension system, a comprehensive universal health insurance system, and a far more equal income distribution than the United States, and yet it, too, has much higher rates of savings and productivity than does the United States.

As Robert Kuttner has shown, there are many different ways of reconciling equality with economic performance. There are many ways a society can go about providing economic security, collecting taxes, maintaining full employment, stimulating investment, promoting economic development, and distributing income. These are political choices. Where labor is well organized and shares significant political power, where in other words there is someone to "articulate the self-interest of the nonrich," economic policies tend to reconcile equality with efficiency. The idea that the two are incompatible is a politically useful myth for the rich and powerful.[25]

efficiency — most output for given input
but comparative idea
who gets benefits/costs².?
how do we measure them.
what mode of organizing human activity
will yield best results?

+ what objective, specifically¹²

mkt: rules are made outside mkt
assumptions — exchages val. (incl. numerous buyers/sellers
— perfect info. doesn't affect others indiv. use)

Social welfare ≠ Σ indiv welfare.
~~but~~ and perfect mkt
vastly unequal distrib.
↓
most power to those who control $ + power.

---

[25] Robert Kuttner, *The Economic Illusion: False Choices Between Prosperity and Justice* (Boston: Houghton Mifflin, 1984); the quotation is on p. 267.

4

Security

"Government is a contrivance of human wisdom to provide for human wants," wrote Edmund Burke in his *Reflections on the Revolution in France.*[1] In the original and primary sense of lacks or needs, wants tend to structure our vision of government's responsibilities. The quest for security—whether economic, physical, psychological, or military—brings a sense of urgency to politics and is one of the enduring sources of passion in policy controversies.

Need is probably the most fundamental political claim. Even toddlers know that need carries more weight than desire or deservingness. They learn early to counter a rejected request by pleading, "I need it." To claim need is to claim that one should be given resources or help because they are essential. Of course, this raises the question "essential for what?" In conflicts over security, the central issues are what kind of security government should attempt to provide; what kinds of needs it should attempt to meet; and how the burdens of making security a collective responsibility should be distributed.

[1] Edmund Burke, *Reflections on the Revolution in France*, J. A. Pocock, ed., (Indianapolis: Hackett Publishing Co., 1987), pp. 52–3. (Orig. pub. 1790.) Burke in fact would have disparaged the expansive definition of wants I am about to depict. With a touch of irony, he counted as first among the wants for which government should provide "the want . . . of a sufficient restraint on [men's] passions" (ibid.) Shortly after this passage, he went on to ask: "What is the use of discussing a man's abstract right to food or medicine? The question is upon the method of procuring and administering them. In that deliberation I shall always advise to call in the aid of the farmer or the physician rather than the professor of metaphysics" (p. 53).

Just as most people are all for equity and efficiency in the abstract, most people believe that society should help individuals and families when they are in dire need. But beneath this consensus is a turbulent and intense conflict over how to distinguish need from mere desire, and how to preserve a work- or merit-based system of economic distribution in the face of distribution according to need. Defining need for purposes of public programs becomes an exercise much like defining equity or efficiency. People try to portray their needs as being objective, and policymakers seek to portray their program criteria as objective, in order to put programs beyond political dispute. As with equity and efficiency, there are certain recurring strategies of argument that can be used to expand or contract a needs claim.

DIMENSIONS OF NEED

The simplest, most common, and in some ways intuitively most appealing definition of need is what is necessary for sheer physical survival. By this minimal standard, government should ensure that people have enough food and shelter to stay alive. The appeal of such a standard is obviously not its generosity, but its promise of objective, scientifically verifiable criteria of need. This line of thinking produces some rather dreary menus, on which, we are told, human beings could survive. For example, a diet of liver, soybeans, lard, and orange juice would provide medically excellent nutrition, and cost only a few dollars a year.[2]

When carried to its logical conclusion, the definition of security in terms of biological requirements reduces humans to metabolic machines. The exercise only prompts us to search for more satisfying definitions of security. Still, it is worth tracing this criterion to its logical extreme, because the minimal definition of security is commonly the starting point in policy debates.

In conservative arguments for the minimal state, a persistent refrain is "but, of course, no one should starve." Starvation becomes the floor of protection below which no one will be allowed to fall. In fact, it is hard to think of any social institutions that actually use near-starvation as their explicit standard of care, unless one includes concentration

[2]Victor E. Smith, *Electronic Computation of Human Diets*, M.S.U. Business Studies (East Lansing: Michigan State University Press, 1964), p. 20, cited in Lester C. Thurow, *The Zero-Sum Society* (New York: Basic Books, 1980), p. 197.

defining minimum standards [handwritten margin note]

camps and prisoner-of-war camps. But most social welfare programs do base their standard of aid on some concept of what is minimally necessary. In the United States, the poverty line, which serves as the official definition of poverty, is designated each year as a level of income necessary to purchase an adequate diet and other essentials. Eligibility for many public programs, even ones such as Medicaid and public housing that provide services instead of income, is often pegged to the poverty line. In the Federal Republic of Germany, public health insurance entitles people to medical care that is "appropriate and sufficient" for a cure but does not "exceed the limits of what is necessary."

In a curious way, this same minimalism is at the heart of defense policy, too. Defense budgeting is basically a tug-of-war between the military sector—the armed services and defense contractors—and the executive and legislative branches. Every year, the Joint Chiefs of Staff issue an estimate of the "minimum-risk capabilities" required to maintain U.S. security. This estimate is a list of various manpower, aircraft, submarines, missiles, and equipment without which our national security would be in jeopardy. Needless to say, as in any budget game, the military estimates of their minimum requirements are higher than everyone else's estimates. But defense policy and welfare policy are alike in their generally accepted fiction that what government provides is the minimum necessary for security.

The idea that security can be reduced to objective and countable needs, whether they are calories or cannonballs, is as conceptually enticing as the equal-slices solution to equity—and as politically problematic. We can see how problematic it is by examining the case of food. If there is anything for which it should be possible to specify precise minimum requirements, food would seem to be the leading candidate. And if such an exercise does not work for food, it is doubtful it could work for anything else.

The first and perhaps most important challenge to the idea of objectively definable needs is that material things have symbolic meanings which are often more important than their material value. As Michael Walzer says, "People don't just have needs, they have ideas about their needs."[3] Food is not just calories, but a sign of membership, social status, and spiritual worth.

ideas about needs [handwritten margin note]

Eating the same food as others is a basic mark of belonging. Partaking of meals is a sign of intimacy, and refusal to share food is a sign of difference, distrust, and being a stranger. Serving or being served liver

[3] Michael Walzer, *Spheres of Justice* (New York: Basic Books, 1983), p. 66.

and lard in a society where those are not traditional meals would be a form of exclusion. Eating turkey on Thanksgiving Day or hamburgers on the Fourth of July has little to do with nutrition, or even seasonal availability, and is instead a form of connection to a nation through historical tradition. Food connects people to specific places, as well. Pouring molasses on waffles makes you a Southerner, while using maple syrup identifies you as a New Englander. To guarantee people liver and lard might keep them alive, but it would not include them in these forms of participation. Food is also a sign of social status. Calf's brains and pig's feet, though equally unappealing to me, are clearly associated with different social classes. To guarantee people the security of lard in contemporary America is also to mark them as unworthy of a normal (and healthy) human diet.

cultural acts

Perhaps the most important aspect of food is its ritual significance. The saying "you are what you eat" means more than a description of humans as metabolic machines. Every culture has its beliefs about the proper foods for humans to eat, so that what people eat not only locates them within a particular social structure but also within a structure of spiritual worth. Beliefs about food as defining our humanity are by no means the province of "primitive" societies. Corn, a traditional part of the American diet, is something Europeans consider animal fodder. Most Americans, in turn, recoil at the thought of humans eating dog meat or horse meat. Cows are unthinkable to many Hindus and pigs to many Jews.

rituals...

Mary Douglas.

Ritual fasting sheds another light on the idea of objective needs. In Islamic culture, Ramadan is a month-long holy period when people fast during the daytime. They become tired, listless, and unable to work. Business and government come to a standstill because of the sheer lack of human energy. By objective standards, or even the standards of other cultures, these people might be seen as starving or at least malnourished. By their own standards and the standards of the Koran, their abstention from food elevates their spiritual worth. Would they or their government say they "need" more food? Absolutely not. The biological definition of minimum metabolic requirements fails us here.

The minimum survival concept of need turns people into living bodies, in much the same way that high school chemistry texts reduce people to $2.43 worth of chemicals. That sort of biochemical thinking renders us all equal. In fact, if there is any sense to the term natural equality, this may be it. The enterprise of defining minimum biological requirements does not differentiate among people, except perhaps

biological, reductionism

among men, women, and children. The symbolic concept of need, by contrast, recognizes and gives weight to human differences—different cultures, histories, social groups, classes, and even tastes. If we accept the symbolic dimension of need as important, then security means protecting people's identities as well as their existence. Issues of security then become fundamentally linked with issues of privilege, power, membership, and mobility. That is why definition of need is a political question rather than a biological one.

Lest it seem that food was too easy a case on which to stake an argument about symbolic meanings, let the reader try the same exercise with some other items over which there has been recent controversy. Try guns, in the context of physical security and gun control laws. Or water, in the context of pollution debates, hazardous waste disposal, and water rights disputes. Or air, in the context of smoking bans and clean air laws. Or land, in the context of farm policy, strip mining, and third-world land reforms. Or automobiles in the context of public transportation debates; television in communications policy; or books and prayers in educational policy. In every one of these policy debates, there is a fight about whether the item is needed: What kind of thing is needed? Who needs it? What does it provide? And what does it represent?

Because of its symbolic dimension, need is relative as well as absolute. Absolute concepts peg the definition of need to a fixed, usually numerical, point. An example is the poverty line, which defines need in terms of a fixed dollar amount of yearly income. Relative concepts peg the definition of need to one's place in a distribution. For example, poverty can be defined as having less than half the median income in a society, regardless of the dollar value of the median.

People's sense of deprivation or satisfaction comes in part from comparison with others. By any absolute standard, many poor rural families in the United States have more money and eat lavishly compared with the homeless in Calcutta. But the Indian standard of living is not their point of reference. They feel poor because they are poor in their own social context; they lack what is usual and necessary in American society.

The concept of relative need is usually meant to describe how people arrive at their standards of what is necessary. But John Maynard Keynes went so far as to assert two distinct types of needs—"those . . . which are absolute in the sense that we feel them whatever the situation of our fellow human beings may be, and those which are relative only in that their satisfaction lifts us above, makes us feel superior to, our fellows."[4] Economists talk of prestige goods or status goods, whose only (or major) function is to put people higher in the social hierarchy.

In light of the symbolic meanings of virtually everything people use and have, almost all needs have a relative dimension, in the sense that people define them in accordance with community standards, norms, and customs. Still, Keynes was probably overly cynical in saying that relative needs can be satisfied only by being in a position of superiority. Surveys indicate that people are most happy with their economic position when they are a little above average for their own reference group. They don't compare themselves to the richest people in society, or feel needy because they lack the resources of the richest. Rather, they compare themselves to a narrower circle of people similar to themselves.[5] They don't necessarily want to be at the top of society, superior to almost everyone, as long as they can feel superior to someone.

There is a thought experiment often invoked to show that the concept of relative need is nonsensical: If a whole community or society increases its standard of living and everyone in it retains the same relative position, would we say that no one is better off? If the inhabitants care only about their relative position, if their only "need" is to be superior, then none of their needs have been satisfied and they are no better or worse off than before. But from the point of view of an outside o)server, or even one of the inhabitants with a memory, clearly everyone is better off.

The trick in the experiment, as in an optical illusion, is its shift in perspective. Relative need is the perspective of people in society, in the present. Absolute need is the perspective of people outside society or people continually living in the past alongside the present. The choice of which criterion to use in policy making—absolute need or relative need—is a choice about which perspective to privilege.

In societies with much economic growth at all, most people are indeed materially better off than their parents. The intergenerational comparison as a point of reference could be an important source of satisfaction and might be one criterion for judging whether people are better off. But real people live in society and live mostly in the present. Studies consistently find that as national income or standard of living

---

[4]John Maynard Keynes, *Essays in Persuasion*, "Economic Possibilities for Our Grandchildren," pp. 365–66; cited in John Kenneth Galbraith, *The Affluent Society* (Boston: Houghton Mifflin, 1958), p. 122.

[5]Richard Esterlin, "Does Money Bring Happiness?" *Public Interest*, no. 30 (Winter 1973): 3–10; and Lee Rainwater, *What Money Buys* (New York: Basic Books, 1974), pp. 41–63.

Relative need

increases, the proportion of people who say their needs are met stays constant. Most people assess their needs by comparing themselves with neighbors or "mainstream standards" in the present.[6]

Relative need is not simply a phenomenon of individuals. The same dynamic is at work in organizations, industries, and firms as well. Occupations increasingly specialize and professionalize because if one attains the trappings of certification and licensure, members of related occupations feel they need the same trappings to maintain their own status and economic security. When an industry such as steel gets import quotas to protect it from competition with foreign companies, other industry leaders feel they deserve similar protection. Or when firms such as Chrysler and Lockheed get government assistance, others are encouraged to imagine it for themselves.

Relative need is important enough in politics to be enshrined in public policies. Many social welfare programs recognize relative need, rather than absolute, in their eligibility standards. Disability insurance, which provides income when people are unable to work due to physical or mental disabilities, offers some rich illustrations. The U.S. Social Security Disability Insurance program requires applicants to be unable to earn about $500 per month doing any job in the entire national economy. Here is an absolute standard analogous to the bare-survival standard for food. In contrast, the disability insurance program for federal employees will provide compensation if they are merely unable to perform their most recent government job, whether it was operating a jackhammer or a typewriter. This definition of disability protects people's occupational identity; no one has to become something else in order to earn a living. The major disability insurance program of the Netherlands uses a relative income standard: You are disabled if a physical or mental impairment prevents you from earning the prevailing average wage in your own community. Finally, the major German disability insurance program explicitly protects people's relative position in the social hierarchy: you are eligible if you are unable to do your previous job and if any other job you could do would entail a significant decline in social status.[7]

In defense policy, relative need is far more important than absolute. Our sense of national security (and hence our need for weapons) depends entirely on comparison with the countries we perceive as ene-

[6] Robert E. Lane, "Markets and the Satisfaction of Human Wants," *Journal of Economic Issues* 12, no. 4, (December 1978): 799–827, especially 803–4 and 811.

[7] Deborah A. Stone, *The Disabled State* (Philadelphia: Temple University Press, 1984).

mies. And here Keynes is probably right: The need for weapons can only be satisfied by feeling superior to "them." Thus, it doesn't matter how many people our warheads can kill or how many cities they can destroy. What matters is what retaliatory capacity we have left after an attack by the other side, or whether *our* capacity to sustain an offense is greater than *their* capacity to destroy it. The paradox of nuclear weapons is that the more security we gain in terms of absolute capability (i.e., kill potential), the more insecure we make ourselves with respect to the consequences of nuclear explosion. We gain superiority only by producing weapons we ourselves are terrified to use.

Absolute need as a criterion may hold some appeal for its analytic precision and its stability over time and across communities. But, as the examples from social welfare and defense policy show, relative need is usually the more salient criterion in public policy. Communities generally try to protect their internal social structure as well as their sheer existence, and relative need is the standard that allows them to do that. Similarly, relative strength and weakness as standards for national defense allow countries to protect or advance their positions in the international order.

A third dimension of need is direct versus instrumental. We need some things not for the direct satisfactions they provide but for what else they enable us to have and do. Education is typically justified in this way. Students are thought to need it because it will enable them to get good or satisfying jobs, to be more productive workers, or to be more informed citizens. In a climate of contraction of public welfare spending, child-care assistance for mothers on AFDC is often justified not on the basis of children's direct need for supervision, but rather as something that would enable mothers to go to work.

For John Rawls, social primary goods (rights and liberties, opportunities and powers, income and wealth) are important not for their own sake but because they enable people to fulfill their individual purposes and dreams (or what he calls "rational plans"). "With more of these goods men can generally be assured of greater success in carrying out their intentions and in advancing their ends, whatever these ends may be."[8] The instrumental view of need is crucial to egalitarian theories of justice, because it allows them to go beyond the requirements for sheer survival in their list of fundamental needs.

Like the symbolic and relative concepts of need, the instrumental

[8] John Rawls, *A Theory of Justice* (Cambridge, Mass.: Harvard University Press, 1970), p. 92.

concept is harder to define than an absolute concept, but it is more important in politics. For example, when industries such as steel or electronics press the government for import quotas, they assert both direct and instrumental need. Because some other countries can produce the same products at lower cost, they would drive American producers out of the market if they could export freely to the U.S. Thus, these industries claim, import restrictions are necessary for the immediate survival of American producers. This is direct need. But sensing the resistance of American consumers to the permanently higher prices that protection implies, industry executives add an instrumental argument: import restrictions will give them time to modernize their plants, make other cost-cutting changes, and will enable them to preserve jobs for Americans. Government protection is often sought and justified in the name of instrumental needs.

A fourth dimension of need has come to increasing prominence in this century—protection from possible future needs as opposed to compensation for present or past lacks. To take the example of food again, people need not simply calories but food that is free of poisons and infectious agents, that does not cause cancer, and that does not exacerbate heart disease or high blood pressure over the long run.

Safety, or the prevention of future needs, has become a major preoccupation in public policy. It is arguably the driving force in food and drug regulation, environmental policy, nuclear power politics, consumer product regulation, and occupational health. It plays a significant role in the regulation of automobiles (seatbelts, air bags, child restraints, drunk driving laws, mandatory inspections), of airplanes (pilot training requirements, ground maintenance, air traffic control), and of public buildings, dams, and bridges (fire safety requirements, structural requirements, earthquake tolerance). One mark of how recent this concern with future needs is, is that Harold Lasswell, in his 1936 classic book on politics, had only one thing to say about safety and its distribution in society: He examined the likelihood of death by violence, chiefly battles and assassinations, and noted that rulers and elites were more likely to be victims of violence than the general population.[9]

---

[9]Harold Lasswell, *Politics: Who Gets What, When, and How?* (New York: McGraw-Hill, 1936; 2nd ed. with postscript, Cleveland: World Publishing, 1958, p. 14 and chap. 3). In his 1958 postscript, Lasswell did suggest that an important question about government is whether it reduces "accidents, disease, physical violence and public nuisances" (p. 184). But posing the question, he had nothing more to say.

In many current policy debates, people are said to have needs based on a condition of being "at risk." We talk about health risks, risks to fetuses and unborn children, children at risk for child abuse, teenagers at high risk for drug addiction, and high-risk pregnancies. All of these risks and the protective behavior they engender concern harms that have not yet happened. Needs arising from potential harms exist only in the future. Of course, much of our awareness of safety and risk comes from previous accidents. But the focus of safety-related regulatory activity is always on potential future needs. Potential future needs often have a political potency far greater than actual needs, because fear of the unknown plays a bigger part. The human imagination is capable of creating infinite terrors, and terror explains why there is often an emotional fervor to arguments about this type of need, even when the risks are described in passionless statistics.

Finally, physical survival as a criterion of need is challenged by what we might call relational needs. Humans require community, solidarity, a sense of belonging; dignity, respect, self-esteem, and honor; friendship and love. We need not only to have and receive, but to give and to help. These are needs for relationships, not "things" that individuals can claim from a community, and in fact, we know very little about how communities can deliberately provide for them.[10] But social scientists have demonstrated how potent these needs are. In her study of an urban ghetto, Carol Stack found that people who receive a large sum of money from an inheritance or insurance policy typically give it away to meet other people's needs rather than spend it to increase their own material well-being.[11] William Foote White showed that urban street gangs fulfill a desperate need for social structure and stability and that they operate on a well-defined, if unspoken, code of mutual obligation.[12] Kai Erikson's study of the Buffalo Creek flood revealed that the victims missed their sense of connectedness to their past and their neighborhoods far more than their possessions.[13] Studs Terkel's interviews about work showed people more intensely concerned with dignity than with pay.[14]

These needs are no less real for being intangible and unmeasurable. In politics, these are the inchoate feelings that drive conflict and lend force to political demands, although politics often requires people to translate these needs into more tangible and measurable claims. For example, after the Buffalo Creek flood, when survivors sued the owner of the faulty dam, their lawyers and a consulting psychiatrist helped them translate their losses into a medical condition called "survivor's syndrome" so that they could claim greater damages than the very low economic value of their material possessions.[15] In a fight against a superhighway that would cut across their neighborhood, residents of the Crest Street community in Durham, North Carolina, documented their potential losses in a "community impact statement" patterned after environmental impact statements designed to forecast tangible physical, biological, and economic changes.[16]

[10]The best essay I know on this concept of need is Michael Ignatieff, *The Needs of Strangers* (New York: Viking Penguin, 1984).

[11]Carol B. Stack, *All Our Kin* (New York: Harper & Row, 1974).

[12]William Foote White, *Street Corner Society* (Chicago: University of Chicago Press, 1943).

[13]Kai T. Erikson, *Everything in Its Path* (New York: Simon and Schuster, 1976).

[14]Studs Turkel, *Working* (New York: Pantheon, 1974).

[15]Gerald Stern, *The Buffalo Creek Disaster: The Story of the Survivors' Unprecedented Lawsuit* (New York: Random House, 1976).

[16]Carol B. Stack, "A Critique of Method in the Assessment of Policy Impact," in S. M. Miller and M. Lewis, eds., *Research in Social Problems and Public Policy*, vol. 4, (Greenwich, Conn.: JAI Press, 1987), pp. 137–47. See also Elizabeth Friedman, "Crest Street: A Family-Community Impact Statement," working paper, Duke University, Institute of Policy Sciences and Public Affairs, 1978.

These five dimensions of need are not meant to be a hierarchy or sequential order, so that as one type is fulfilled, people move on to the next.[17] Rather, the dimensions are alternative ways of conceptualizing needs. These conceptions lead to competing political claims about security. In the polis, the boundary between needs and wants is unclear, unstable, and constantly contested.

The natural sciences tend to treat human need as if it were objective and determinable through the experimental method. Efforts to define the minimum requirements for biological survival fall into this tradition, but so do psychological studies seeking to define the requirements for development of a "healthy personality." What is significant, and appealing to some, about this approach is that it does not rely on individuals to tell us what they need. Instead, objective observers test people under different conditions and draw conclusions purportedly independent of the wishes of either the subjects or the scientists.

Need in the polis, however, does not operate by the standard physical laws. It is not a container with fixed dimensions, either full or not. Instead, need seems to expand as it is satisfied, and to draw its meaning from the surrounding situation. Part of the human condition is that people imagine the fulfillment of needs before they act, and are often disappointed by the actual experience of having or achieving the things they sought. Ability to imagine some kind of fulfillment is probably essential to progress—it spurs us on—but it is also fatal to contentment.[18]

Economists of all persuasions have offered explanations of this puzzling phenomenon of insatiable needs. Marxists attribute it to the class structure of capitalism. In order to maintain their predominant position, owners of capital must generate artificial needs among workers so that the demand for production (and the entire system of labor relations) can be sustained. Liberals hold that in a society where work is the only source of income for most people (rather than, say, inheritance, gifts, or mutual aid), unemployment is the greatest threat to

[17] In the best-known theory of hierarchical needs, Abraham Maslow postulated that people have five types of needs, which they try to fill in sequential order: physiological needs, such as hunger and thirst; safety and shelter needs; social needs; the need for self-esteem; and finally the need for self-actualization. Abraham Maslow, "A Theory of Human Motivation," *Psychological Review* 50 (July 1943): 370–96.

[18] For a fascinating exploration of the role of disappointment in economic and political life, see Albert O. Hirshman, *Shifting Involvements: Private Interest and Public Action* (Princeton, N.J.: Princeton University Press, 1982). Lane, op. cit. (note 6), also discusses this problem of insatiable needs.

CONCEPTS OF NEED

Simple Definition Minimum requirements for biological survival

Complications in the Polis

Dimension	Issue
1. Valuation of resources:	In assessing needs, should we count only material uses of resources or also symbolic meanings and satisfactions provided by resources?
2. Standard of comparison:	Should we measure needs according to a fixed (absolute) standard or a relative one (how people's resources compare to those of other members of the community)?
3. Purposes of resources:	Should we provide only resources that meet immediate, direct needs for survival, or also resources that enable people to fulfill broader goals?
4. Time:	Should society secure only people's current needs or also provide protection against future needs and risks of harm?
5. Unit of analysis:	Should society secure only the needs of people as separate individuals or also people's relational needs (such as dignity, a sense of belonging, trust, and community)?

economic security; therefore, production is essential to provide jobs. But the very production of goods and services creates new needs. Relative need means that "one man's consumption becomes his neighbor's wish."[19] Symbolic need means that goods become badges of prestige, which can work only by being new, different, and scarce. Advertising and promotion manipulate people's psychological needs. Conservatives are likely to argue that meeting people's needs—especially poor people's—encourages them to become or remain dependent. Need satisfaction alters people's character, so that even if their material needs don't grow, their ability to meet their needs through work declines while their need for social assistance actually grows.[20] Notably, all three views recognize need as infinitely expandable.

This analysis of the dimensions of need is helpful in explaining the dynamics of a policy conflict centered on the goal of security. It provides a framework to show how political actors can make plausible yet competing claims about security. It also shows how any minimal and allegedly objective definition of need, such as sheer survival of an individual, a firm, a group, an organization, or a nation, can be expanded using the five dimensions: material versus symbolic, absolute versus relative, direct versus instrumental, present versus future, and physical versus communal. The definition of security, like other policy goals, is an exercise in political claims-making.

NEEDS IN THE POLIS

Since the multiple ways of defining need for any problem result in different claims about what government ought to do, politics is centrally concerned with arbitrating the different claims. Through politics, a society decides whether needs are real or legitimate.

The policy-making process is full of devices for validating claims about need. In welfare policy, where needs are met primarily by distribution to individuals, eligibility requirements are essentially tests of applicants' need. Earnings and assets tests are used to measure whether people need income, food stamps, or medical insurance. Contributions to Social Security are used in disability insurance to screen out people who have never or hardly ever worked, on the theory that previous willingness to work indicates honest motives in applying for

[19] Galbraith, op. cit. (note 4), p. 125.

[20] The contemporary revival of this Malthusian view is best articulated in Charles Murray's *Losing Ground: American Social Policy 1950–1980* (New York: Basic Books, 1984).

benefits. Many state public assistance programs use home visits and inspections to determine whether recipients are truly needy. Doctors are asked to judge need for a variety of programs. To take only one example, many state laws restrict publicly funded abortions to women for whom they are "medically necessary."

Even in other policy areas, where needs are satisfied by making arrangements for whole groups rather than for individuals, political decision making takes the form of validating claims about need. When manufacturing industries seek protection from foreign competition, they must petition the U.S. International Trade Commission to restrict imports, demonstrating that their industry is on the verge of ruin because of a high foreign market share or unfair foreign trading practices. Farmers and dairy producers seeking price supports from Congress or state administrative agencies must document their need with measures of market saturation, low prices, and farm profitability.

Legislative hearings are often used to collect and test information about needs. They are usually sponsored by a representative who is already disposed to take action on some problem, and so the witnesses are all chosen because they will give an informed or passionate description of a need. Hearings on health insurance bills typically include a mixture of health policy experts reciting statistics and generalizations, and poor people telling their personal stories in vivid, ungrammatical prose.

Budgeting is another mechanism through which groups play out their claims. Agencies submit budget requests, which are their claims about how much money they need to carry out essential functions. Budget hearings and negotiations then force the different players to justify their needs and make choices among their own programs.[21] For better or for worse (probably worse), budgeting is the primary vehicle for determining what is needed for national security. There is comparatively little public discussion about defense policy outside of the decisions about investing in different weapons technology.

Much of politics is thus an effort to define needs collectively, and this is another sense in which there is a public interest in the polis. Even though many, if not most, of the needs government attempts to satisfy are not needs of society as a whole, the very process of determining needs through public agencies and institutions assumes a public interest in knowing and satisfying needs.

---

[21] For a delightful portrait of budgeting, see Aaron Wildavsky, *The New Politics of the Budgetary Process*, 4th ed. (New York: Harper-Collins, 1988).

Those needs that a community recognizes as legitimate and tries to satisfy as a community might be termed "public needs." The conception of public needs in real political communities is far broader, more varied, and more closely tied to specific cultures than the economic concept of public goods. (Remember that a public good is something that can be used jointly and is not used up as it is consumed.) In welfare economics, the inherent characteristics of goods determine whether they are "public." A lighthouse is a public good because it is in the nature of light signals to be visible to many users at one time and to persist even after being "used." By contrast, public needs are determined in a political process and have far more to do with people's ideas than with inherent characteristics of things. Public needs are always under dispute.

The pattern of public needs is the signature of a society. In its definition of public needs, a society says what it means to be human and to have dignity in that culture. In medieval Jewish communities, government's function included maintaining what was necessary to the practice of religion: synagogues and their officials; religious courts; education (for boys only, since the purpose of education was to enable men to participate in religious services and discussions); and rescuing captive Jews from persecution in other communities. In ancient Athens, a different set of public needs was recognized: a large army and navy; the supply of corn; roads; funerals for the war dead; and the famous drama festivals.[22] It is perhaps the signature of contemporary American society that we devote major resources to protecting the abstract potential victim of future harm through safety research and regulation, while letting bag ladies go homeless in the streets.

If societies are marked by their unique blend of public needs, there are also some common patterns. By and large, Western nations have tended to adopt social welfare programs in the same order, as though there were a universal hierarchy of needs: industrial accidents, old age, sickness, unemployment, and family allowances.[23] Within disability programs, blindness, deafness, and missing limbs are usually recognized before mental illness and chronic diseases.

Whatever the similarities and differences among societies in their concept of public needs, all communities strive to provide collectively for the recognized needs of their members and for their own survival

---

[22] Walzer, op. cit. (note 3), chap. 3.

[23] Phillips Cutright, "Political Structure, Economic Development, and National Social Security Programs," *American Journal of Sociology* 70 (1965): 532–50.

as communities. In fact, the urge to communal provision for security is so strong that it often gives structure to mob actions. Food riots in eighteenth-century England, for example, while seeming to be undisciplined and destructive crowd movements, in fact proceeded by a very orderly pattern that closely mimicked official regulations for emergencies.[24] Peasant revolts in Southeast Asia follow predictable patterns if they are viewed as rational efforts to protect the economic security of villagers.[25] That mob actions have a coherent structure when understood as collective efforts to assess needs and provide for them suggests that collective provision for security may be the vital force in community formation.

Communal provision for security may be the most important force holding communities together as well. When people in need receive aid, they are usually grateful to, and perhaps dependent on, the giver. Gratefulness and dependence create loyalty. As Carol Stack found in the black urban neighborhood she studied, "The value of an object given away is based upon its retaining power over the receiver; that is how much and over how long a time period the giver can expect returns on the gift."[26] Bismarck saw this point clearly when he established national health and accident insurance in Germany in the late nineteenth century. With these programs, he sought to lure workers from the emerging socialist movement by tying their futures to the national government. The political bosses of American cities built their machines on the same principle: help a person in need and you will gain his vote forever. And so it is a peculiar twist to American thinking about welfare policy that it is dominated by the opposite idea—that social aid somehow gives something away and diminishes the government, the public treasury, and the economy (since welfare supposedly destroys work incentives). Here is another aspect of the polis where the laws of matter do not apply. Charity creates loyalty and political cohesiveness, which can motivate people and harness their energies. Thus, charity may indirectly increase the supply of valuable resources as it gives things away.

The major theories of politics differ dramatically on how they understand the process of claims-making about needs. In the classic liberal

---

[24] E. P. Thompson, "The Moral Economy of the English Crowd in the Eighteenth Century," *Past and Present*, no. 50 (1971): 76–136.

[25] James C. Scott, *The Moral Economy of the Peasant: Rebellion and Subsistence in Southeast Asia* (New Haven: Yale University Press, 1976).

[26] Carol B. Stack, *All Our Kin*, op. cit. (note 11), p. 42.

tradition (now associated with economic conservativism), needs find expression in behavior. In one variant of this tradition, classical micro-economic theory, needs are expressed in consumption decisions, or "consumer demand"; in another variant, classical pluralist political science, needs are expressed in the formation of organized interest groups and then translated into political demands upon government. These theories hold that all important or strongly felt needs will be translated into action.[27]

In the reformist liberal tradition, called *neopluralism* in political science, not all needs are equally likely to find expression. Some people carry greater weight, either in the marketplace because they command more money, or in politics because they command more political resources, such as money, education, influence, or organization. Not all needs are transformed into political organization, and of those that are, some are consistently more successful in the political arena.[28]

The Marxist tradition rejects the liberal idea that needs automatically get translated into demands and even the reformist idea that only some needs are squeezed out. It holds that in capitalist society, where a minority controls the means of production, one class permanently dominates another. Crudely put, capitalists, property owners, or elites dominate workers, the poor, and the powerless. The needs of the subordinate class, who are also the majority, are suppressed to the point where people do not even recognize their true needs. This is one meaning of false consciousness—that some people (perhaps most) do not understand their true needs. Capitalism forces people to concentrate on their short-term material interests at the expense of their longer-term interest in a different political system.[29]

We cannot resolve these disputes here (or else I would be rich and famous), but it is worth stopping for a moment to humble ourselves by noting that the question of security—how we know what humans need—has occupied great minds for centuries. And although it is impossible to settle the question of how we can know and prove to ourselves what needs are real, it is possible to say a great deal about how the question of real needs is answered in practical politics.

[27] David Truman, *The Governmental Process* (New York: Knopf, 1951).

[28] Peter Bachrach and Morton Baratz, "The Two Faces of Power," *American Political Science Review* 56 (1962): 947–52; E. E. Schattschneider, *The Semi-Sovereign People* (New York: Holt, Rinehart and Winston, 1960).

[29] For a lucid explanation of this position, see Joshua Cohen and Joel Rogers, *On Democracy* (Harmondsworth, England: Penguin Books, 1983), chap. 3. For a summary of all three positions, see Steven Lukes, *Power* (London: Macmillan, 1974).

THE SECURITY-EFFICIENCY TRADE-OFF

Security and efficiency are often thought to be incompatible. The first reason is the motivation argument, quite familiar from the equality-efficiency trade-off. If people are secure, if they have their needs met without working, so the argument runs, then they will work less or not at all, and productivity will decline. Neither result is true. The New Jersey Negative Income Tax Experiment showed that labor supply (hours worked) did not go down with increased levels of welfare payments, and for black males—who have been the greatest victims of stereotypes about laziness—labor supply actually increased with greater income guarantees.[30]

Nor does productivity decline with increased economic security. In fact, the opposite seems to be true. Productivity, measured as output per labor hour, was much higher in the United States in the decades after the New Deal than before, as was the rate of growth in productivity. Productivity in Japan during the 1970s and '80s was nearly three times the U.S. level, even though Japanese workers typically had lifetime job security and their pay was based on seniority and company performance rather than their own performance.[31]

The idea that material security undermines work motivation and productivity holds a peculiar tenacity in American thinking. It may be that we have designed our welfare policy in a way that this idea becomes a self-fulfilling prophecy. With our reliance primarily on selective rather than universal welfare programs, eligibility tests require an applicant to assemble a dossier that demonstrates his or her helplessness publicly. It is not surprising, then, that people who have been forced by society to construct a helpless persona should come to believe in the role and play it faithfully. If they are caught stepping outside the role (earning a little money, for example), they are considered "frauds" and "abusers." In societies where social programs are universal and social aid is expected for everyone, including, incidentally, the United States during the Great Depression, the receipt of social aid probably has far less tendency to diminish motivation and productivity through this impact on people's self-image.

[30] Joseph Pechman and Michael Timpane, eds., *Work Incentives and Income Guarantees: The New Jersey Income Tax Experiment* (Washington, D.C.: Brookings Institution, 1975).

[31] Thurow, op. cit. (note 2), pp. 8, 84; Galbraith, op. cit. (note 4), pp. 94–96. See also Robert Kuttner, *The Economic Illusion: False Choices Between Prosperity and Justice* (Boston: Houghton Mifflin, 1984).

A second aspect of the security-versus-productivity argument concerns the way productivity is officially measured. To compare productivity across industries, some standardized unit of measurement is needed. The output-per-labor-hour definition for the agricultural and manufacturing sectors becomes something like "number of people processed" for the service sector, since handling people is what service industries do. Thus, hospital productivity is measured in "patient-days" and airline productivity in "passenger-miles." Extra personnel in these industries, such as nurses and ombudsmen in hospitals or flight attendants and security guards in airlines, no doubt add to people's comfort, peace of mind, and well-being; but they lower productivity statistics, because there are more workers spread over the same number of patients or passengers.

Think of this problem from a consumer's point of view. In choosing a school or a day care center, you would look for a high teacher-to-student ratio. In selecting a nursing home or mental hospital for a relative, you would look for a high staff-to-patient ratio. The very qualities that make human services more attractive to users make them less productive in our statistics. As services generate more security, meet more needs, they necessarily become less productive because of the way productivity is defined. It is no wonder that productivity is (officially) very low in the service sector as compared with manufacturing, finance, utilities, and mining. And, as services grow relative to the traditional economic sectors, measures of productivity cannot help but make the economy look less productive, even though it is probably producing more security.

A third and far more troubling reason for a security-efficiency trade-off is the progress argument. It holds that progress for society as a whole cannot happen without individual losses, because there can be little investment in new areas without disinvestment from the old. New businesses, products, services, and methods could not come into being if existing ones—and the people attached to them—were not allowed to wither or fail. New technologies can create better or cheaper goods, but only by rendering some workers' skills obsolete and putting them out of work. The rise of manufacturing in Southeast Asia and the growth of industry and services in the Sunbelt all produce improvements for some Americans—perhaps for the majority—but heavy losses are sustained by particular cities and industries in the Frostbelt and the Rustbelt. If government protects firms such as steel manufacturers and automakers that are no longer competitive on the world market, Americans will pay higher prices for these goods and will fail to transform the economy so that labor and capital go to their most productive uses. Security can be had only at the cost of inefficiency.

One solution to this dilemma is to have government protect people, not places; individuals, not firms and institutions.[32] It is possible to conceive of protecting individuals without incurring the rigidities of the status quo. Japan has large conglomerate firms that can move resources and people from declining areas to growing ones, still within the same firm. Sweden uses an extensive welfare system to create a safety net for individuals, along with job retraining and relocation programs to make disinvestment less costly to the individual. The key to such a strategy is a strong program of retraining and temporary support while individuals are moved from one type of job to another and one place to another.[33]

Although the protection of individuals offers some hope for the security-efficiency dilemma, it is not a complete resolution. For one thing, not everyone can be retrained, especially when new jobs involve shifting from unskilled to skilled labor or sedentary to heavy physical labor. A more important obstacle is that we protect organizations, occupations, firms, and localities because that is how political power is organized. There is no lobby of unemployed workers needing job training, but the industry trade associations and state governors are camping outside congressional doors. It is possible that the reorganization of protection would lead to the reorganization of power, but because (as we saw above) arrangements for security are the primary glue of communities, old groupings will die hard. Finally, the individual protection solution might work if people had no ties to place, to neighbors, and to friends. But people do value community and roots, especially as they reach middle age and have their own families. The Swedish and Japanese solutions work as well as they do because those countries are so tiny and homogeneous. Transfer within a Japanese conglomerate can never involve the geographic and cultural dislocations possible within the United States. Any system of security will always be a blend of direct aid to individuals and protection of the organizations and communities in which people work and live.

[32] This solution was advocated by the President's Commission for a National Agenda in its report, *Urban America in the Eighties: Perspectives and Prospects* (Washington D.C.: Government Printing Office, 1980). See also James Fallows, "America's Changing Economic Landscape," *Atlantic Monthly*, March 1985, pp. 47–68; and Thurow, op. cit. (note 2), pp. 81, 210.

[33] See Robert Reich, *The Next American Frontier* (Baltimore: Penguin Books, 1983), pp. 240–47, for a more detailed proposal of the retraining strategy.

Is There a Security-Efficiency Trade-Off?

Yes	No
1. People are not motivated to work when they are secure, so productivity declines with increased security.	Human productivity increases with increased security, especially in societies that provide a high level of security as a universal norm.
2. The more security society provides, the bigger its service sector. The service sector has the lowest rate of productivity in the economy.	Productivity is low in the service sector only because it is measured in a way that makes services unproductive by definition.
3. Economic efficiency requires technological changes and innovations that necessarily make some people worse off (and insecure).	Public policies can mitigate, though not eliminate, some of the insecurities and displacements that come with economic change.

Security / need   minimal   symbolic
                                  relative
                                  instrumental
                        ↖   future
                                  relational
—— defining needs is political ——

devices for validating claims about need
        eligibility
        hearings
        budgeting

politics as effort to define needs collectively

5

Liberty

In 1989, the Supreme Court ruled that since burning the American flag is a form of speech, no state can prohibit citizens from expressing themselves in this way. A member of one of the most proud veterans' associations, the American Legion, went on the *Today* show to explain why many patriotic people like himself thought the Supreme Court was wrong, and government should ban flag burning. The flag is a symbol of the nation, he said, and government should prevent people from defacing it. When Jane Pauley pushed him to explain what the flag symbolizes and why government should protect it, he replied: "It stands for the fact that this is a country where we have a right to do what we want."[1]

For many Americans, freedom is the essence of what America is about—it is the central reason why the colonists fought for independence and the most fundamental principle at the heart of American democracy. But freedom is no less ambiguous and complex than other goals and values that motivate politics. The legionnaire's paradox captures the dilemma of liberty very well: Do we always have a right to do what we want, and if so, don't we also have the right to burn the flag, the very symbol of liberty? The legionnaire seemed to intuit the crux of the liberty problem: Sometimes curtailing individual liberty may be necessary to preserve a community in which individuals can thrive and exercise free choice.

[1] Quoted in Mary Ann Glendon, *Rights Talk: The Impoverishment of Political Discourse* (New York: Free Press, 1991), p. 8.

The dilemma of liberty surfaces in public policy around the question of when government can legitimately interfere with the choices and activities of citizens. When, if ever, should community or social purpose be allowed to trump individual choice? Under what circumstances should public policy ever limit individual privacy and autonomy? The most famous and influential answer to these questions is John Stuart Mill's essay *On Liberty*, written in 1859. In it he attempted to find a single criterion for deciding when society ought to interfere with individual liberty:

> The sole end for which mankind are warranted, individually or collectively, in interfering with the liberty of action of any of their number is self-protection. . . . [T]he only purpose for which power can be rightfully exercised over any member of a civilized community, against his will, is to prevent harm to others.[2]

Mill believed that deliberation and the exercise of choice are the essence of what it means to be human and that therefore government should interfere with individual choice as little as possible. In reconciling the need for social control with individual freedom, he defined a sphere of action where the individual reigns supreme. The sphere includes all those purely "self-regarding" actions that do not have adverse consequences for others. A government is justified in restricting only behavior that concerns or affects other people.

Mill's resolution of the problem is the dominant way of thinking about liberty in American political thought, so it is worth highlighting the elements of this tradition. First, it holds that there is a single criterion by which we can judge whether interference with individual action is justified—namely, harm to others. Second, it is predicated on the possibility of a clear distinction between behavior that affects other people and behavior that does not. Third, it sees liberty as an attribute of individuals, not social roles or groups or organizations. And finally, it defines liberty in a negative way—that is, as the lack of interference with individual action. To provide liberty in this sense is to do nothing, to refrain from acting, rather than to do something. (There is a positive concept of liberty, to be explored later in this chapter, which holds that liberty requires active provision of opportunities and resources.) Each of these elements is a focal point for challenges.

[2]John Stuart Mill, *On Liberty*, first published in 1859. Quotations are from Penguin edition (Harmondsworth, England: 1974).

To define liberty as Mill does requires us to think about what counts as "harm to others." Policy issues are then cast as a choice between protecting the liberty of individuals and preventing harms to others. To ask in this framework when government should interfere with individual liberty is to ask what types of harms society should prevent. The question of liberty is then redefined as the nature of harms. As with equity, efficiency, and security, the intuitively appealing simple criterion is another battlefield upon which people fight for contradictory interpretations.

The most obvious type of harm is physical injury. Bodily assault and its extreme consequence of death would seem to be a self-evident type of harm that everyone would agree should be prevented. Actions that cause injury or death do not belong in the sphere of liberty. Yet, like the sheer-physical-survival definition of need, the injury-or-death definition of harm is not as simple as it first appears.

What about the action of exposing people to small but toxic doses of chemicals, either in the workplace or in air and water supplies? Should the long-term and cumulative effects of exposure count as a harm that justifies restriction of action? This, of course, is the rationale for most environmental, chemical, and drug regulation. What if the effects of exposure caused by one person (say, an employer) are magnified or compounded by activities of the person who is harmed (say, the worker)? Many potentially harmful substances, such as asbestos and birth-control pills, are known to have far greater likelihood of harm in smokers than in nonsmokers. Should asbestos manufacturers have to provide greater protection for smokers, or should they be allowed to fire smokers and hire only nonsmokers? Should smokers be prohibited from taking birth-control pills?

The image of simple physical assault hardly captures the array of indirect and poorly understood mechanisms by which individual actions harm other people. The harmful effects of chemicals are in part determined by the social organization of their use—how work is organized spatially, how long and consistently workers are exposed to chemicals, how wage systems reward or penalize the use of protective equipment, and whether there are incentives for safety in the transport of chemicals. Moreover, in the modern era much physical injury results from the failure of large and complex systems rather than from individual action. Dangerous activities such as chemical manufacturing plants, nuclear power plants, air traffic systems, and dams are controlled by a combination of mechanical devices (e.g., thermo-

stats and valves, electronic monitors) and human operators. Accidents and their consequences can rarely be traced to a single source.[3]

Thus, the connection between individual human action and harm to others is not as clear as Mill's theory of liberty would require. If we are seeking a clear criterion to evaluate public policy—to decide when preventing harms to others should override the basic value of individual liberty—even the relatively clear idea of physical harm is not so clear. When we move beyond physical harms to other kinds of harm, Mill's criterion for deciding questions of government interference in a private sphere is even less determinate.

Before examining some other kinds of harms, though, let us consider another serious problem of Mill's resolution. Even when an action is known to produce harm to others, there are many possible ways of preventing the harm, each of which interferes with different types of liberties for different sets of people. For example, some chemicals used in manufacturing are known to be teratogenic (that is, they cause injury to fetuses). Fetal injury might be prevented in several ways. Should the production and use of teratogenic chemicals be banned entirely? Should manufacturers be required to make expensive modifications to protect workers from exposure to the chemicals? Should employers exclude fertile women of childbearing age from jobs involving exposure to the chemicals, on the theory that every potential fetus deserves protection from harm? Identification of the harmful consequences of actions does not tell us which actions ought to be prevented or whose liberty to curtail. This point is equally true of the other types of harms discussed below.

Beyond bodily harm, we might consider *material* harms to others as a legitimate reason to interfere with individual liberty. An activity may cause someone else to suffer a loss of income. For example, slander

[3] For an excellent analysis of such system failures, see Charles Perrow, *Normal Accidents* (New York: Basic Books, 1984).

causes a loss of reputation for a businessperson and for that reason is an exception to the doctrine of freedom of speech. Or, actions may cause a loss of resources. For example, reckless driving damages others' cars and property. But how far do we want to go in protecting people from suffering material losses at the expense of other people's liberty? Is there a difference between behavior that physically destroys property (say, my driving a car into your living room) and behavior that destroys the market value of property (say, my operating a junk car lot next door to your house)? Even material losses have different degrees of urgency and reality that might be considered relevant for decisions about liberty.

Another type of harm involves *amenity effects*. Some activities cause aesthetic harms, such as placing advertising billboards on highways or satellite dishes on rooftops. Some types of environmental harms might be considered amenity harms rather than material—actions that change the character of a landscape or destroy wildlife habitats, for example. Similarly, tearing down historic buildings, destroying the architectural unity of an historic district, or changing the character of a neighborhood are all harms to some people that cannot be adequately described in material terms. Disturbances of quiet (blaring radios on buses) and invasions of privacy (paparazzi stalking celebrities) fall in this category, too. Zoning, environmental regulation, and historic preservation are all examples of policy areas where government limits certain activities in order to mitigate amenity harms, and where, in other words, claims about amenity harms are deemed legitimate.

As we move from more physical to more abstract types of harms, it becomes more evident that harms are political claims asserted by one set of interests against another. But the imprecision of these harms and our inability to measure them, either in market values or other quantifiable units, makes them no less important. If anything, the more abstract and symbolic types of harms are usually the most politically contentious.

Emotional and *psychological* harms are difficult to grasp yet important as types of harms. We all know this basis for the restriction of liberty in the classic parental argument: "If you do that, I will worry about you." No doubt everyone has wrestled with the question of whether a parent's emotional suffering due to fear of possible harms is a legitimate reason for curtailing a child's liberty.

The question has its counterparts in the public sphere, where government is often asked to restrict behavior of one set of people to prevent psychological damages to another group. Many educators and parents think schools should be required to use curriculum materials portraying women and minorities in responsible positions, in order to avoid the psychological harm of leading them to believe they can attain only menial and low-status jobs. Pornography is opposed (among other reasons) because it is demeaning to women and leads both women and men to regard women as sexual objects.

The dilemma posed by claims of psychological harm was crisply stated by Justice Rehnquist in a case concerning nuclear power. The dispute centered on whether the Three Mile Island plant should be allowed to resume operations after its accident in 1979. Some residents claimed that risks to their psychological health should be considered by the Nuclear Regulatory Commission and the plant should be kept shut. If the plant were to operate, they said, they would suffer stress and anxiety from worrying about another accident. The Supreme Court rejected their claims. It would be difficult, Justice Rehnquist pointed out, to differentiate among

> . . . someone who dislikes a government decision so much that he suffers anxiety and stress, someone who fears the effects of that decision so much that he suffers similar anxiety and stress, and someone who suffers anxiety and stress that "flow directly" . . . from the risks associated with that same decision. It would be difficult for agencies to differentiate between "genuine" claims of psychological health damage and claims that are grounded solely in disagreement with a democratically adopted policy.[4]

Psychological harm spills over into the area of *spiritual* and *moral harms*. Frequently in history, a group has sought to have government prohibit behavior forbidden by its own religious laws or compel behavior mandated by its religious tradition. John Stuart Mill was adamant that religious belief should never be a permissible ground for government regulation of behavior. Claims that a group is morally offended or revolted by some practice, such as eating pork or working on the sabbath, should never be recognized by government as the basis for policy. It is "the logic of persecutors," Mill argued, "to say that we may persecute others because we are right."[5]

Despite the strong tradition of separation of church and state in the

[4] *Metropolitan Edison Co. v. People Against Nuclear Energy*, 460 U.S. 766 (1983); quotation is on pp. 777–78.

[5] J. S. Mill, *On Liberty*, p. 156.

United States, claims about spiritual harms continue to be heard in American politics. The school prayer issue can be understood as a conflict between those who believe that their children are spiritually harmed if denied the opportunity to pray in school and those who believe that their children may be psychologically harmed if pressured to choose between participating in prayer and remaining conspicuously silent. The abortion issue has many facets, but one is surely that people who believe the fetus to be a person from the moment of conception feel spiritually harmed by actions they understand as murder. Because American political tradition has generally accepted Mill's strictures against granting legitimacy to claims of spiritual harm, opponents of abortion have sought to translate their claims into ones of physical injury by focusing on "viability" of the fetus.

The abortion issue illustrates another important point about the categories of harms. Harms to others are not objective phenomena, to be discovered or documented by science, but rather political claims, which are granted more or less legitimacy by government. Natural science is only a weapon in the struggle of groups to prove their claims of harm. It is probably fair to say that there is a rough hierarchy among the categories. Claims based on physical injury are easier to assert successfully (i.e., to attain a restriction on someone else's activity) than claims based on other material harms, and material harms are stronger than amenity harms, and so on down the line. Thus, a significant aspect of political strategy is to move claims from one category to another, to redefine harms as types that have a higher or more generally recognized legitimacy.

The harm-to-others criterion, which Mill thought was "one very simple principle,"[6] thus turns out to be exceedingly complex. There are many types of harms, and their recognition is a matter of political struggle—not rational discovery. Moreover, the restrictions on behavior necessary to prevent one type of harm often result in another type of harm. Protecting workers from physical injury by granting them "rights to know" about chemicals in the workplace runs up against employers' rights to protection of trade secrets. Protecting severely handicapped infants from death imposes emotional and financial burdens on parents and siblings. Questions of liberty as defined by the harm criterion are inevitably also questions of equity, for they entail decisions about who bears harms, whose activities should be curtailed, and who bears the costs of preventing harms.

[6] Ibid., p. 58.

LIBERTY IN THE POLIS

Even if the harm-to-others criterion were unambiguous, it would not provide a very good picture of how issues of liberty are handled in the polis. Because the polis is a community with some collective vision of a public interest, the liberty of individuals is also limited by obligations to the community. In the polis, there is a more active conception of legitimate compulsion that requires individuals to participate in collective efforts, if only the effort to maintain order and stability. Government is not merely a referee in a giant boxing match, restraining people when they get unruly; it acts also as an impresario, coordinating cooperative ventures.

Mill paid brief tribute to this political reality at the beginning of his essay: "There are also many positive acts for the benefit of others which [a person] may rightfully be compelled to perform."[7] He gave as examples the duty to testify in court, to contribute to the common defense or "any other joint work necessary to the interest of society," and to perform "acts of beneficence" such as saving someone's life. Mill, however, did no more than list these examples, and devoted the rest of *On Liberty* to the analysis of harms to individuals.

In the polis, the sphere of compulsion based on the interests of society (as distinct from harm to individuals) is actually quite large. In addition to the duties Mill mentioned, most societies require their members to honor contracts and promises, pay taxes in support of government, give up land for public projects (eminent domain), educate their children, and aid the needy. Above all, societies require their members to obey the law, regardless of whether violations cause harm to someone else. A driver will be punished for running a red light, even if no one else is harmed by the action. Such restrictions of individual liberty are not meant so much to protect particular individuals from harm, but rather to protect social order itself. These types of liberty issues—questions of when government can legitimately interfere with individual choice in order to promote social cohesion and maintain community—are even more conflictual than questions entailing harm to particular individuals.

If community is the starting point of analysis, then there are several kinds of harms that cannot be accounted for in Mill's framework of individually calculated harms. One is *structural harms*—effects on the

[7] Ibid., p. 70.

ability of a community to function as a community. When private schools are allowed to compete with public (or to put it in another way, when parents are given the liberty of sending their children to private schools), the ability of schools to integrate children of different social backgrounds suffers. Funding public education through a system of vouchers rather than through appropriations to public schools would no doubt diminish discussion of the quality of schools on the public agenda. Perhaps the most serious defect of the individualist conception of liberty is that in seeing only harms to individuals, it fails to protect communal life and community institutions.

A second kind of harm which escapes from the individualist concept is what the philosopher Joel Feinberg calls *accumulative harms*.[8] Some actions, like walking across the grass, dumping sewage in a river, withdrawing one's money from a savings bank, or dropping out of a group insurance plan, are not harmful when one person does them, but they can be devastating if a lot of people do them. In order to protect the things people use in common, such as natural resources and cooperative institutions, policy makers need to take into account accumulative harms in defining the sphere of liberty.

A third kind of nonindividual harm, one at the heart of the affirmative action conundrum, is *harm to a group that results from harm to individuals*. In the polis, people live and work in groups and the effects of injuries to individuals carry over into those groups. When an applicant for a job is rejected on the basis of race, for example, the harms go beyond the person's immediate loss of job and the denial of pay, status, respect, and work experience. His or her children are denied emotional and financial security, and perhaps also the resources and motivation to continue their education. Others in the minority community are deprived of a potential "friend in the business," a role model, a supervisor, a co-worker of the same race, or a mentor. Others, too, are discouraged from applying for similar jobs and even from aspiring to and training for them. Arguments that remedies for past discrimination should be available only to "actual victims" but not to other members of the minority group fail to recognize that discrimination against an individual on the basis of group membership inevitably imposes harms on the entire group.[9]

[8] Joel Feinberg, *Harms to Others* (New York: Oxford University Press, 1984).

[9] This example is from an insightful analysis by Paul J. Speigelman, "Court-Ordered Hiring Quotas After *Stotts:* A Narrative on the Role of the Moralities of the Web and the Ladder in Employment Discrimination Doctrine," *Harvard Civil Rights—Civil Liberties Law Review* 20, no. 2 (Summer 1985): 339–424.

If the individualistic conception of harm is a distortion of how liberty is defined in the polis, so is the conception of liberty as an attribute of individual action. People in the polis occupy roles and offices, and liberties are usually assigned to the roles instead of the individuals. Spanking is a form of physical assault, and while it is not allowed for most people, it has always been a prerogative of parents vis-à-vis their children, and until at least the mid-twentieth century, often also a prerogative of teachers vis-à-vis students, and husbands vis-à-vis their wives.

In many ways governments are far less restrictive of the behavior of public officials and business executives than that of ordinary citizens. In theory, officials and executives need more freedom to be able to do their jobs. Under a doctrine known as sovereign immunity, government agencies, officials, and employees cannot be held liable for certain kinds of damages they cause, as when police destroy property in the course of a high-speed chase or domestic search. At one time, immunity extended to virtually everything a government official did; increasingly, however, government's sphere of liberty has been curtailed.[10] Corporation owners and managers are protected from personal liability for financial losses and for unemployment caused by their decisions. Thus, for example, American law creates few obligations for corporate owners who want to close a plant, destroying a community in the process.

For the most part, the domain of liberty is enlarged for business and government officials, but in some ways their behavior is more restricted or their protection from harm more diminished than that of the average person. Corporate executives are not allowed to trade stocks in companies about which they have inside information. Public figures find it harder to win libel and slander suits than private citizens, because they are assumed to expose themselves to criticism as part of their role.

Whether the liberties of officials are greater or smaller than those of ordinary citizens, the key point is that liberty in the polis is to a significant extent an attribute of roles rather than of individuals. We grant liberties to certain types of people and allow them to cause certain types of harms because we define their duties and obligations according to their roles and believe that different roles require different kinds of freedoms.

[10] Jethro K. Lieberman, *The Litigious Society* (New York: Basic Books, 1983), chap. 6. For a more extensive treatment see Peter Schuck, *Suing Government: Citizen Remedies for Official Wrongs* (New Haven: Yale University Press, 1983).

To see liberty as an attribute of individuals—even individuals in social roles—and to judge it only as applying to individual action is to miss the far more significant political question of the freedoms accorded to corporate actors. Churches, trade unions, sports franchises, professional associations, business corporations, trade associations, trusts, political parties, and many voluntary associations are corporate actors.[11] Since individuals are affected, and restricted, as much by these types of actors as by other individuals, public policy must address conflicts between the liberties and interests of individuals and those of corporate actors.

Among the most important corporate actors are government agencies themselves. Agency actions can perpetrate both harms to the community and harms to individuals. New surveillance techniques and computerized data banks provide a good example. Increased monitoring and record sharing may create a sense of distrust in a community. People will be more afraid to file grievances against employers or join in petitions against a local housing authority if they fear their actions will become public information. The spirit of reform can be destroyed. Potential blood donors might decline to donate if records of AIDS screening tests were available to landlords and employers. The spirit of altruism can be destroyed. People might forgo mental health treatment if their records were to become available to insurance companies and potential employers. Individual health can be diminished.

Because corporate actors can have far greater impact on individuals and community than the actions of other individuals, a theory of liberty must consider corporate actors as well as individuals. Since their power is so great, the consequences of their actions so magnified, and their potential for causing harm so enormous, the criteria for granting them liberty of action should be exceptionally stringent. One of the ironies of American politics is that we pretend that private corporate actors are very weak, and so we impose relatively few limits on their activities. Trade unions and professional associations, for example, exercise tremendous control over their members' working conditions and abilities to get and hold jobs, yet they offer few democratic safeguards to their members.[12] In many European countries, by contrast, corporate actors

---

[11] For a fascinating description of the origins of corporate actors and their significance in the structure of society, see James S. Coleman, *Power and the Structure of Society* (New York: Norton, 1974).

[12] Grant McConnell analyzes this phenomenon brilliantly in *Private Power and American Government* (New York: Knopf, 1966), chap. 5.

are explicitly recognized as creatures of the state, with serious power over members; because their power is acknowledged, the state is also able to impose limits and hence they are more closely regulated than their American counterparts.

Every community permits some kinds of deliberate or foreseeable harms while it punishes others. As Oliver Wendell Holmes pointed out nearly a century ago, "a man has a right to set up a shop in a small village which can support but one of the kind, although he expects and intends to ruin a deserving widow who is established there already."[13] We allow all kinds of harms to occur in the name of the free market. A real estate developer has the right to demolish low-income housing and replace it with high-priced condominiums, even though he knows he will harm the current residents. Employers can fire employees or provide detrimental information in recommendations, despite the foreseeable harms.

Americans have a distinctive legal culture concerning the proper role of government in restricting individual liberties to promote social cohesion, security, and solidarity.[14] U.S. courts have been very reluctant to create a legal obligation for citizens or even government officials to help one another. First-year law students are immersed in the doctrine that no one has a legal duty to rescue another person, not even a champion swimmer who happens by a drowning baby in a wading pool. To be successful, law students must shed their ideas of ethical obligation, recognize that law and morality are separate spheres, and get over the popular but naive view that law ought to incorporate ideas about moral behavior.

Even government officials and employees in social service agencies, the Supreme Court has ruled, cannot be held accountable for failing to protect vulnerable citizens under their jurisdiction. Thus, when a little boy in Wisconsin was beaten to the point of permanent brain injury by his father, the Court said the mother and boy could not collect damages from the state social services department—even though the department was responsible for preventing child abuse, had taken on the little boy as a client, and had received overwhelming evidence over two years that the father was abusing the boy.[15] Ameri-

[13] Oliver Wendell Holmes, Jr., "Privilege, Malice, and Intent," *Harvard Law Review* 8, no. 1 (April 25, 1895): 1–14; quotation is on p. 3.

[14] This is the central argument of Mary Ann Glendon, *Rights Talk*, op. cit. (note 1).

[15] *DeShaney v. Winnebago County Department of Social Services*, 109 S. Ct. 998 (1989).

CONCEPTS OF LIBERTY

Simple Definition People should be free to do what they want unless their activity harms other people.

Complications in the Polis
- What harms to individuals should trigger government restraints on liberty?

  1. Material harms (e.g., bodily injury, loss of income, loss of property value, higher taxes)?
  2. Elevated risk of injury or loss (as opposed to actual, immediate injury)?
  3. Amenity harms (e.g., aesthetic, environmental, quality-of-life)?
  4. Emotional and psychological harms (e.g., distress, anxiety, loss of self-esteem)?
  5. Spiritual and moral harms (e.g., behavior that offends religious or moral beliefs)?

- What harms to communities, organizations, and groups should trigger restraints on liberty?

  6. Structural harms (actions or policies that reduce an organization or community's ability to function)?
  7. Accumulative harms (activities that are harmful only if a lot of people do them)?
  8. Harms to a group caused by harms to one of its members?
  9. Harms to society or community caused by individual failure to undertake helpful actions?

- Whose liberty should be curtailed?

  10. When the activities of several different people (groups, organizations) contribute to causing harms, whose activity should be restrained? Who should bear the burden of change?
  11. When corporate actors cause harms, should their activities be restrained? In what ways?

 can political culture, in comparison to that of European nations, is not terribly receptive to creating *affirmative* legal duties for the promotion of social goals. Even though we have a variety of social aid programs written into Progressive- and New Deal–era statutes, these programs were themselves objects of intense conflict and scaling-back at the time of their establishment. Moreover, the apparent ease with which the 1996 Congress could abolish entitlements to AFDC and other forms of relief with a stroke of the legislative pen shows just how fragile American commitments to compulsory social obligations really are.

Just as every community has its pattern of publicly recognized needs, so each also has its pattern of allowable harms. In the U.S., superstore chains are allowed to put small family enterprises out of business as part of "normal" market competition. In Germany, government prohibits supermarkets and department stores from opening on Sundays and evenings, precisely to protect mom-and-pop stores from ruin at the hands of unfettered competition. To postulate or seek a simple criterion of harm that tells us what activities are or should be forbidden is a complex enterprise, because the domain of liberty is constructed in political life. It is a matter of cultural history and political choice as to which kinds of harms are privileged in any society and which are punished.

THE LIBERTY-SECURITY TRADE-OFF: TWO DILEMMAS

Can a society provide its members both liberty and security? Can it protect them from harm without restricting their freedom of action? The liberty-security trade-off seems inescapable, and a consideration of these questions leads to two dilemmas.

First is the dilemma of *dependence.* On the one hand, "poverty forces the free man to act like a slave."[16] Without the security of having one's basic needs met, a person cannot make free choices. Where a choice involves taking some risk, it cannot be a true choice if the consequence of failure is starvation, injury, or death. On the other hand, security creates dependence. As the old city machine bosses understood so well, whenever people depend on government (or any other institution or person) for their essential needs, they feel constrained to obey and support their provider. Security seems to be necessary for liberty and yet undermines it.

The ancient Greek solution to this dilemma was to place security

[16] Hannah Arendt, *The Human Condition* (Chicago: University of Chicago Press, 1958), p. 64.

entirely in the realm of the private household. A man had to secure life's necessities by himself, by good management of the household economy, before he could enter the realm of politics where truly free decision making could occur.[17] Because he was master of his material needs, such a man could be independent and free. This solution worked, of course, because the small class of free men controlled (and depended on) a far larger number of women and slaves, whose lack of liberty was ignored in practice as well as in political theory.

Many contemporary thinkers offer a similar resolution to the dilemma of dependence: If public policy promoted self-sufficiency instead of dependence, then people would not become dependent and suffer the inevitable constraints on liberty that accompany dependence. The ideal of individual self-sufficiency is a false promise, however. Even in the early days of the Republic and the pioneering days of the Westward expansion, the mythical self-sufficient farmer or pioneer was in fact highly dependent on a web of relationships and community institutions. In the late twentieth century, with highly developed industrial economies, regional and global specialization in production, and electronic information and communication systems, the possibility of an economically self-sufficient individual is even more remote.

In a society where liberty is deemed appropriate for all citizens, the solution of "freedom for those who can provide for themselves" is not an acceptable answer. Yet that solution persisted until relatively recently, and in some respects is still with us. In the extensive welfare system of nineteenth-century England, paupers could receive aid from their towns, but in accepting it, they had to give up the right to travel, the right to live with their families (they were forced into poorhouses), and the right to vote. In New England through much of the nineteenth century, citizens who applied to their towns for economic support were auctioned off to the lowest bidder at town meeting, and in exchange for room and board with another family, were subject to employment and control by the head of that family. Many contemporary state AFDC programs restrict the liberties of recipients in similar ways, such as requiring young women to live with their parents or requiring recipients to accept certain jobs. In imposing these requirements, states curtail the liberties of welfare recipients more than those of other citizens.

[17] Arendt, *The Human Condition*, ibid., part 2.

In other ways, the history of the twentieth-century welfare sta
story of gradually expanding rights for people dependent upon the
state. These rights include not only rights to aid in more and more situations (e.g., mental illness as well as physical, occupational illness as
well as injury, learning problems, family problems, or drug addiction),
but also procedural rights aimed at protecting recipients from abuse by
providers. For example, informed consent requirements seek to protect
institutionalized populations, such as hospital patients and prisoners,
from being coerced into medical procedures or acting as research subjects; due process requirements are meant to protect public aid recipients from arbitrary terminations. (To be sure, these protections are not
fully effective. Informed consent is sometimes a sham, as in the famous
case of Willowbrook, where mentally retarded children were inocu-
lated with hepatitis virus with the "consent" of their parents.)

One might well question whether formal political rights can have
much significance in a dependent relationship. When one side is dependent on another for basic material needs, the weaker side will always
be preoccupied with securing basic needs.[18] But the failures should not
obscure the point that modern democracies attempt to reconcile security and liberty by creating formal political rights for the dependent.
Given the problem of dependence, formal rights are the best device we
have for protecting the liberty of those to whom we guarantee security.

The second dilemma is the problem of *paternalism:* When, if ever,
should government prevent people from acting voluntarily in ways that
harm themselves? Is it legitimate to coerce people to do something
against their will in order to promote their own good? In other words,
should government curtail liberty in order to promote security?

This question is at the heart of debates about health and safety regulation. Should automobile passengers be required to wear seat belts or
purchase air bags? Should motorcyclists have to wear helmets? Should
very sick and disabled people be allowed to refuse medical treatment?
Should anyone be allowed to hang glide? Should people be prohibited
from taking addictive drugs, smoking tobacco, or consuming alcohol?
Should all homeowners be required to install smoke detectors? When,
in short, should the goal of security be allowed to override the goal of
individual liberty?

John Stuart Mill's answer was characteristically simple—"Never!"

[18] See Joshua Cohen and Joel Rogers, *On Democracy* (Baltimore: Penguin Books, 1983),
pp. 50–59, for a lucid and perceptive critique of formal political rights in a capitalist
society.

[A person's] own good, either physical or moral, is not a sufficient warrant [for interference with his liberty of action]. He cannot rightfully be compelled to do or forbear because it will be better for him to do so, because it will make him happier, because, in the opinions of others, to do so would be wise or even right. These are good reasons for remonstrating with him, or reasoning with him, or persuading him, or entreating him, but not for compelling him or visiting him with any evil in case he do otherwise.[19]

But, just as characteristically, Mill felt compelled to make one exception to his rule. Society can legitimately prevent people from entering into contracts to enslave themselves, even though no one but the slave is harmed by slavery. Why would Mill allow this exception? Because by entering into slavery, a person gives up his liberty, and protecting individual liberty is the very purpose of prohibiting paternalism in the first place.

The slavery exception in Mill's argument exemplifies a larger issue in contemporary policy: Are there other situations in which a person's freedom to choose some course of action should be denied in order to enable him or her to have other choices in the future? Or, to put the question in the form of a paradox, can a person be forced to be free? Most governments have made policy based on this sort of logic. Its underlying premise is that some types of choices are equivalent or analogous to enslaving oneself. Terminating one's life, either by deliberate suicide or by forgoing medical care necessary to survival, is an action often prohibited under this logic. Prohibitions on alcohol and drugs are usually justified on the basis of their impairment of a person's future judgment. The problem with the slavery metaphor is that it is only a metaphor, and does not escape the trap of imposing on someone else a judgment about what sorts of experiences are "as bad as" slavery.

Another approach to the problem of paternalism is to allow it for certain categories of people. Children and the mentally incompetent are usually thought proper objects of paternalistic policy; that is, they are forced to do things "for their own good," and denied ordinary liberties. John Stuart Mill, by the way, allowed these exceptions, too, and added yet another: backward societies, or as he put it, "backward states of society in which the race itself may be considered as in its non-age."[20] The logic of this exception is that certain categories of people

[19] J. S. Mill, *On Liberty*, op. cit. (note 2), p. 68.
[20] Ibid., p. 69.

are incapable of deliberating and exercising meaningful choice, so that no liberty is violated by protective coercion. This same logic leads to a lesser civic status for members of groups deemed incapable of acting as free citizens.

The exclusion of whole categories of people from rights and liberties to which other citizens are entitled is the great loophole in liberal political thought. There is always a danger that powerful citizens can simply declare less popular and less powerful groups to be "of non-age," as Mill so delicately put it. The U.S. has a long tradition of declaring entire peoples as immoral, backward, incompetent, or otherwise incapable of exercising the responsibilities and freedoms of citizenship.[21] Our public policy and law developed a variety of lesser civic statuses for people the white male majority regarded as "nonage." Women and blacks were for a long time denied basic rights to vote, own property, serve on juries, or testify in court, all on grounds of alleged mental inferiority. Henry Cabot Lodge, a senator in 1896 with a Ph.D. in politics and history from Harvard, argued for a literacy test for immigrants because, he said forthrightly, it would exclude Italians, Russians, Poles, Hungarians, Greeks, and Asiatics, and so preserve "the quality of our race and citizenship."[22] Claims about the backwardness and moral inferiority of many races and nationalities were consistently used to exclude groups from immigration, from becoming naturalized citizens, and from various civic rights if they were naturalized.

Paternalism may indeed be warranted for some people. The criteria for deciding whether a group is incapable of exercising true liberty, however, are highly susceptible to interpretation and manipulation. Leaving aside the obvious and egregious cases of racism, sexism, and gross stereotyping as a substitute for genuine inquiry into people's competence, there is even room for dispute—and stereotyping—in assessment of people who are genuinely restricted by severe mental and physical disabilities. For example, the question of paternalism frequently arises when people with terminal illnesses or their family members request cessation of medical treatment. One study compared how courts assessed requests to stop medical care from family members of male and female patients who were no longer mentally competent to express their own wishes. In these so-called "right to die" cases,

---

[21] There is a large literature on this topic, but for an excellent overview and analysis of group exclusions in American political thought and practice, see Rogers Smith, "Beyond Tocqueville, Myrdal, and Hartz: The Multiple Traditions in America," *American Political Science Review* 87, no. 3 (Sept. 1993): 549–65.

[22] Quoted in Rogers Smith, "Beyond Tocqueville" (previous note), p. 560.

courts try to reconstruct the patient's wishes from statements he or she made while still competent. The study found that the judges tended to take the men's wishes more seriously than the women's. They often characterized the men's statements as reasoned and rational, and the women's statements as emotional or mere "immediate reactions." They often viewed the women patients as childlike.[23] In short, the categorical resolution of the paternalism dilemma—defining categories of people who are incapable of exercising liberty—is not straightforward, and not beyond politics.

One more approach to paternalism is the so-called "Ulysses contract." Ulysses, knowing he could not resist the temptations of the beautiful Sirens, had himself tied to the mast and ordered his mates not to obey him if he should later beg to be freed as the ship passed the Sirens. The philosopher Ronald Dworkin has suggested that paternalism is justified whenever a rational individual would consent in advance to restrain himself in some way. Thus, there are certain goods, like health and education, which any rational person would want to have in order to pursue his own welfare, however conceived. Government could legitimately force people to acquire these things. People would also want to be restrained from making decisions that produce irreversible changes (such as taking drugs), from making decisions under extreme psychological or social pressure (such as suicide or dueling), and from making decisions involving hazards they don't sufficiently understand (such as smoking).[24]

The dangers of Dworkin's solution are obvious. There is a big difference between respecting a person's actual request to be treated in some fashion in the future, and imputing wishes to him by surmising what a rational person would want. Furthermore, none of the criteria Dworkin sets forth is very well bounded. How much health or education is necessary for liberty? Isn't food necessary, too, and should we force people to consume a medically perfect diet? (Liver and lard, soybeans and orange juice for everyone. . . .) What counts as extreme social pressure? Decisions to marry and have children are often made under extreme social pressure, often with harmful results for those involved. Should we forbid these choices because they are made under duress? Clearly, any hypothetical rational person is invested with his or her creator's own values, not some universal values shared by all.

[23] Steven Miles and Allison August, "Courts, Gender and 'The Right to Die,' " *Law, Medicine and Health Care* 18, no. 1–2 (1990): 85–95.

[24] Ronald Dworkin, "Paternalism," in Richard Wasserstrom, ed., *Morality and the Law* (Belmont, Calif.: Wadsworth, 1971), pp. 107–26.

Is There a Liberty-Security Trade-off?

Yes	No
1. Security creates dependence on the provider of security.	Insecurity deprives a person of capacity to make truly free choices; security creates true liberty.
2. People need to be self-sufficient in order to be truly independent and free.	The ideal of complete self-sufficiency is illusory; being able to rely on a community creates a sphere of freedom for individuals, and public policies can protect recipients of aid from domination by providers (including the state itself).
3. If government acts paternalistically, protecting people from harming themselves, it must necessarily limit people's freedom.	Public policies can make honest, nondiscriminatory distinctions between people who are competent to make decisions affecting their well-being and those who are not.

The desire not to be coerced for our own good resonates in everyone. So does the desire for protection. And everywhere societies enact paternalistic rules and policies. No one has yet found a satisfactory single criterion to guide these decisions about when liberty ought to be overruled by security. No doubt the enduring appeal of Mill's essay, beyond its affirmation of the supreme rights of the individual, lies in its promise of a single criterion for reconciling individual and social interests. In this it fails (as have all subsequent efforts), but in the attempt, Mill and his audience are forced to grapple with a complex array of exceptions, and we come to understand why questions of liberty are never settled by formulas, but rather are continuously reformulated by politics.

THE LIBERTY-EQUALITY TRADE-OFF

In Chapter 2 ("Equity"), we already encountered the argument that liberty and equality are incompatible. Now, with some more differentiated concepts of liberty at our disposal, we are in a position to explore the argument more fully.

The liberty-equality trade-off argument runs like this: People have different talents, skills, and abilities to secure the valued resources and opportunities in society. To maintain equality, government would have to take away resources and positions from some people (the advantaged) and give them to others (the disadvantaged). This taking away of resources and positions interferes with the freedom of action of the advantaged.

Such a conclusion can only be drawn from a negative concept of liberty, one that defines it as the absence of restraint. There is another tradition that sees liberty as the availability of meaningful choice and the capacity to exercise it. In this positive view, liberty is expanded whenever a person's control over his or her own life is increased.[25] There are two aspects to control: first, the range of issues or problems over which one can exercise control; and second, the resources, both material and non-material, that enable one to envision alternatives and carry out one's will.

Liberty conceived as control leads to a very different set of questions than those about the nature of harms. Positive theorists ask what kinds of resources are necessary or helpful in exercising effective choice. They include political rights—active rights, such as voting and participation in decision making of schools, unions, or firms; more defensive rights, such as the protection of free speech and assembly and freedom from unreasonable searches; wealth (the more material resources one has, the more one can think about issues other than physical security); and knowledge (because knowledge enables people to imagine more solutions to their problems).[26]

Power, wealth, and knowledge are thus prerequisites to liberty in the

[25] The classic essay on positive and negative liberty is Isaiah Berlin's "Two Concepts of Liberty," in *Four Essays on Liberty* (New York: Oxford University Press, 1969), pp. 118–72.

[26] An excellent argument for the inseparability of liberty and equality, as well as a thorough presentation of the positive concept of liberty, can be found in Richard Norman, "Does Equality Destroy Liberty?" in Keith Graham, ed., *Contemporary Political Philosophy* (Cambridge, England: Cambridge University Press, 1982), pp. 83–109.

positive view, because they are sources of capacity to exercise choice. *power wealth knowledge* Liberty in this view is a matter of degree: those with more power, wealth, and knowledge have more freedom than those with less. In the negative view, by contrast, liberty is often treated as an all-or-nothing concept. It is imagined as a space or territory within which the individual resides and around which there is a fence to prevent intrusions. If the fence is broken at all, liberty is ruined. It is possible to think of degrees of liberty in the negative concept as well. The more types of actions one can do without interference, the greater the liberty. But believers in the liberty-equality trade-off typically take any interference with property acquisition as the destruction of liberty, without asking how important the restricted activity is or how many activities are curtailed.

If liberty is understood as the ability to make choices about matters of serious concern, then inequalities of power, wealth, and knowledge also create inequalities of liberty. A society that maximized liberty would be one that equalized the prerequisites to liberty—power, wealth, and knowledge. Such an ideal democracy does not (and probably cannot) exist. But for those who value liberty in the positive sense, it is worth striving for.

Finally, the positive concept of liberty links individual and social freedom. Liberty in the negative sense is the absence of coercion by other human beings. A person's own physical or mental limitations, not to mention the resources and opportunities of family and community, are taken as givens, much like the weather. That a snowstorm prevents me from carrying out my plans is not to be regarded as an infringement of my liberty.

Those who interpret liberty in the positive sense see the range of human control as more plastic and expansive. Certainly the distribution of power, wealth, and knowledge is the result of socially created arrangements; arguably, so are intelligence, skill, talent, and good health. As leaders of the disability rights movement point out, physical handicaps are as much the product of building design as of human anatomy and physiology. The social mechanisms of "interferences" with individual liberty are far more complex than the image of individually caused harm implicit in negative liberty. The central issue for the positive view is, then, not what kinds of harms should be prevented, but what constraints on individual freedom are within the realm of human agency. The individual's scope of freedom is broadened by the capacity and willingness of his or her society to bring problems under human control.

IS THERE A LIBERTY-EQUALITY TRADE-OFF?

Yes	*No*
1. To maintain equality, government has to take away from the better off, thereby restraining their liberty.	Power, wealth, and knowledge are prerequisites to genuine liberty. By equalizing these resources, government enhances "positive liberty," the control over one's own life.
2. Liberty is all-or-nothing; only the complete absence of interference with individual decisions counts as genuine liberty.	There are degrees of liberty. Relatively minor restrictions on some people might enable relatively major expansions of liberty for others. Liberty itself can be equalized.
3. Liberty is decreased whenever some people are coerced by public policies aimed at creating more equality for others.	Human freedom can be expanded by society's willingness to bring problems (even natural disasters) under control, sometimes by compelling cooperation in collective endeavors.

Liberty — Mill.
prevent harm to others
INDIVIDUALISTIC conception
1 criterion, clearcut!, −ve.
what is harm? bodily, material, accum., emotional,
                        spiritual... ?
what about corporate actors.
                                    2
also Qs of equity — who bears harms.
                whose activities are curtailed?
                who bears costs of preventing harms?

—vs collective vision
structural harms
accumulative "
group harms → indiv harms
                                    · paternalism p 123.

PART III

PROBLEMS

Part III is about how problems are defined and demonstrated in politics. In conventional policy analysis textbooks, as well as in the larger rationality project, a problem definition is a statement of a goal and the discrepancy between it and the status quo. In this conception, problem definition is a matter of observation and arithmetic—measuring the difference between two states of affairs.

What should be clear from Part II is that there are no fixed goals or fixed positions in the polis. Since there are competing conceptions of abstract goals, people fight about which conception should govern policy. They may implement a policy that satisfies one, only to realize they wish they had another. The ideal of equality can yield multiple distributions. Efficiency is a standard amenable to numerous conflicting interpretations. Security encompasses complex needs that change even as they are satisfied. Liberty conceived as activity without harms to others turns out to be a very small sphere in modern society; and conceived as control over one's life and well-being, it is a perennial quest. The goals of policy are thus vague, contradictory, and protean. The status quo is equally unstable. It looks very different depending on which standard one uses to interpret it.

In the polis, then, problem definition is never simply a matter of defining goals and measuring our distance from them. It is rather the strategic representation of situations. Problem definition is a matter of representation because every description of a situation is a portrayal from only one of many points of view. Problem definition is strategic because groups, individuals, and government agencies deliberately and consciously fashion portrayals so as to promote their favored course of action. Dissatisfactions are not registered as degrees of change on some universal thermometer, but as claims in a political process. Representations of a problem are therefore constructed to win the most people to one's side and the most leverage over one's opponents.

Each chapter in this section concerns a type of language for defining and portraying policy problems: symbols, numbers, causes, interests, and decisions. "Symbols" (Chapter 6) deals with words and more particularly with some literary devices usually associated with fiction rather than policy analysis. It introduces the concept of stories—good old-fashioned stories with heroes and villains and moments of tri-

congratulations
Campbell

. Like speaking prose, we all know the language of stories, but it so deeply embedded in our political discourse that we are usually unaware of its presence. Stories are so useful in politics because their drama is emotionally compelling, and sometimes blinding. One theme of Part III is that every language of problem definition, even the language of numbers, makes use of stories. "Numbers" (Chapter 7) is about the language of counting, but its argument is that symbolic devices are as important in numerical language as in the language of words. Counting is at bottom metaphor-making, because to count requires making judgments about how things are like one another in important ways. Counting is used in the construction of explicit stories, but counting and measuring create implicit stories as well.

Symbols and numbers, as the two most elemental languages, are essential to each of the other frameworks of problem definition. "Causes" (Chapter 8) is about the language of cause, effect, and responsibility. More generally, causal theories are origin stories, stories of how a problem came in to being. Every origin story implies a resolution—we learn how to get out of a mess by knowing how we got into it. Causal theories are also stories of control; they locate responsibility and blame, and assign the moral statuses of victims and perpetrators. In contemporary society, counts and statistics are the most important tools for authenticating causal stories.

Another language, perhaps the one most strongly associated with politics in popular discourse, is the language of "Interests" (Chapter 9). In this language, problems are portrayed as a contest between competing interests. Again we have a story of heroes and villains, this time cast as a contest between good, but weak, interests and bad, but strong, interests. Implicit in these stories are also measures of strength.

"Decisions" (Chapter 10) takes up the framework of rational decision making that has dominated the study of policy and policy analysis in the postwar period. In this framework, the hero is cast as a decision maker, lost in the forest of complexity and confusion. He or she explicitly uses numbers to get out of the woods, by counting up the costs and benefits of alternative pathways. To model a problem as a rational decision is to portray it as leading ineluctably to a single best choice.

The central theme of this section is that there is no universal, scientific, or objective method of problem definition. Problems are defined in politics, and political actors make use of several different methods, or languages, of problem definition. Each of these languages has room for moral conflict and is a vehicle for expressing moral values, but there is no universal technical language of problem definition that yields morally correct answers. To become fluent in these languages is to learn to see problems from multiple perspectives and to identify the assumptions about both facts and values that political definitions don't usually make explicit. The goal of mastering these languages is not to find some Esperanto, some formula that tells how to combine these perspectives to arrive at the best or most accurate problem definition. With multiple perspectives, however, one can achieve an understanding of problems that is more comprehensive and more self-conscious and explicit about the values and interests any definition promotes.

problem definition

as representation

symbols

numbers

causes

interests.

no universal, sci, obj. method

of problem def".

6

Symbols

We talk of policy problems in words. How words are used to represent things is a subject usually treated in the domains of rhetoric and literature, but symbolic representation is the essence of problem definition in politics.

A symbol is anything that stands for something else. Its meaning depends on how people interpret it, use it, or respond to it. It can be an object, a person, a place, a word, a song, an event, even a logo on a T-shirt. The meaning of a symbol is not intrinsic to it, but is invested in it by the people who use it. In that sense, symbols are collectively created. Any good symbolic device, one that works to capture the imagination, also shapes our perceptions and suspends skepticism, at least temporarily. Those effects are what make symbols political devices. They are means of influence and control, even though it is often hard to tell with symbols exactly who is influencing whom.

Four aspects of symbolic representation are especially important in the definition of policy problems. *Narrative stories* provide explanations of how the world works. These explanations are often unspoken, widely shared, and so much taken for granted that we are not even aware of them. They can hold a powerful grip on our imaginations and our psyches because they offer the promise of resolution for scary problems.[1] *Synecdoches* are figures of speech in which a part is used to represent the whole. They are important symbolic devices in political life because we often make policies based on examples believed to be

[1] See Bruno Bettelheim, *The Uses of Enchantment: The Meaning and Importance of Fairy Tales* (New York: Knopf, 1976).

representative of a larger universe. *Metaphors* are sometimes held to be the essential core of human thought and creativity.[2] Metaphoric reasoning—seeing a likeness between two things—is essential to classification and counting. To make a metaphor is also to make a political claim: "There is a likeness that is important." This chapter, along with "Numbers" (Chapter 9), explores how metaphorical claims work in politics. *Ambiguity*, the capacity to have multiple meanings, is a feature of symbols, and for better or worse, of the human condition. While this entire book is about struggles for the control of ambiguity, this chapter focuses on the role of ambiguity in enabling coalition and compromise.

STORIES

Definitions of policy problems usually have narrative structure; that is, they are stories with a beginning, a middle, and an end, involving some change or transformation. They have heroes and villains and innocent victims, and they pit the forces of evil against the forces of good. The story line in policy writing is often hidden, but one should not be thwarted by the surface details from searching for the underlying story. Often what appears as conflict over details is really disagreement about the fundamental story.

Two broad story lines are particularly prevalent in policy politics. One is a *story of decline,* not unlike the biblical story of the expulsion from paradise. It runs like this: "In the beginning, things were pretty good. But they got worse. In fact, right now, they are nearly intolerable. Something must be done." This story usually ends with a prediction of crisis—there will be some kind of breakdown, collapse, or doom—and a proposal for some steps to avoid the crisis. The proposal might even take the form of a warning: Unless such-and-such is done, disaster will follow.

The story of decline almost always begins with a recitation of facts or figures purporting to show that things have gotten worse. Poverty rates are rising, crime rates are higher, import penetration in U.S. markets is greater, environmental quality is worse—you have heard these all before. What gives this story dramatic tension is the assumption, sometimes stated and sometimes implicit, that things were once better than they are now, and that the change for the worse causes or will soon cause suffering.

[2] Jacob Bronowski, *Science and Human Values* (New York: Harper Torchbooks, 1972).

The story of decline does not necessarily have to be about human beings to be gripping. Consider the accompanying article about government data from the *New York Times*, by a former director of statistical policy for the Office of Management and Budget, portraying the decline of federal economic statistics. (Go ahead, turn the page, and read the article. I'll get a cup of coffee while you read, and we'll continue when you're ready. By the way, can I get you a piece of cake?)

Like most pleaders for budget increases, Mr. Duncan tells a story of decline and doom. He tells us that things were once better by referring to the "high-quality statistical procedures and data bases that we have developed over the last 40 years." In the second paragraph, he uses six words in only 12 lines to connote deterioration: "undermining," "decline," "dissolved," "cuts," "reduced," and "failure." There we have the beginning of the story; the author has established a bygone era of well-being and placed us, his audience, on the precipice of decline. We are ready to roll.

From here to the last paragraph, the author presents examples of government statistical records and procedures that have not kept pace with economic change. In each example, he shows that some lack in the data prevents policy makers from making effective policy. The middle of this story, then, is a compilation of small steps in the direction of decline. The end comes in the final paragraph, with its prediction of doom: "Unless this potential crisis is addressed, the effectiveness of policy decisions will be severely undercut." (Not the worst crisis most people can imagine, I grant, but for analyst types, having your effectiveness undercut is the equivalent of 8.3 on the Richter scale.) And just in case we have so far missed the emotional tenor of the story, the author cues us by introducing the denouement with the word "Regrettably."

The drama of heroes, villains, and innocent victims is part of every problem definition, even though one sometimes has to read between the lines to find it. I selected the article on statistics as an illustration precisely because it has very little in the way of obvious human actors, feelings, motives, and morals, and yet it still has all the elements of a good yarn.

The story of decline has several variations. The *stymied progress story* runs like this: "In the beginning things were terrible. Then things got better, thanks to a certain someone. But now somebody or something is interfering with our hero, so things are going to get terrible again." This is the story told by every group that wants to resist regulation. In the 1970s and 1980s, the American Medical Association, fighting government cost-containment efforts, reminded us about the days of

ARE GOVERNMENT NUMBERS ACCURATE

The Economy Has

By JOSEPH W. DUNCAN

IT is fashionable today to blame economists for the confusion and contradictions in economic forecasting. But we may be ignoring a more basic source of error: the quality of Federal economic statistics.

A combination of factors is undermining the high-quality statistical procedures and data bases that we have developed over the last 40 years. The decline can be traced to deregulation, which dissolved regulatory agencies that had collected data; to budget cuts, which have reduced the flow of information from Government departments to statistical agencies, and — most important — to a failure to update statistical systems.

For example, the Bureau of Economic Analysis, which provides data used to compile the gross national product, still uses statistics that are heavily weighted toward the manufacturing sector, even though an estimated 70 percent of total employment is in service industries.

Joseph W. Duncan, director of statistical policy for the Office of Management and Budget from 1974 to 1981, is corporate economist and chief statistician with the Dun & Bradstreet Corporation.

This lopsided emphasis also is reflected in the Standard Industrial Classification system, which is crucial for tracking activity in specific industries. The system has 140 classifications for manufacturing companies but only 66 for services.

The lack of detailed information on services has profound implications. The strong dollar has produced a tremendous influx of less expensive foreign goods that compete with domestic products. While this puts strong and well-documented pressure on domestic manufacturers, the benefit of increased imports to domestic service businesses, such as the warehousing, finance, distribution and retailing industries, is unmeasured.

How is Congress supposed to make informed policy decisions on economic and trade issues when it is, at least to some extent, groping in the dark? Without accurate information, decision-making becomes arbitrary.

Statistical policy has not kept pace with the restructuring of the economy. In 1982, the Office of Federal Statistical Policy recommended that Standard Industrial Classification group 7392 — management, consulting and public relations services — be divided into six new industries. The revision was never made. Now, it is difficult to confirm evidence that large corporations are using outside technical services rather than rebuilding their staffs.

Such information is crucial to Federal policy makers. Employment regulations are intended to encourage hiring of permanent workers, who usually gain tax-subsidized benefits

Source: Joseph W. Duncan. "The Economy Has Left the Data Behind," *New York Times*

Left the Data Behind

packages. Yet there is evidence that some companies may be hiring temporary workers solely to avoid Federal employment rules, such as unemployment compensation.

Dated industrial codes for the financial sector inhibit accurate appraisals of the impact of deregulation on banking services. Automated teller machines, for example, are rapidly replacing bank clerks. But without detailed data, the impact of such technological developments on inner-city employment, future demand for skills and other trends is difficult to determine.

The deterioration of Federal statistics has become particularly evident during current efforts to revise the nation's tax code. For example, one of the key features of the Reagan Administration's proposed revision concerns business taxes. Current government statistics show that, in 1984, corporate profits and non-farm proprietors' income totaled $402 billion, or 11.2 percent of total G.N.P., down from 12.2 percent in 1979 and 14.6 percent in 1969. The decrease is especially perplexing because of the recent reduction in corporate taxes.

Interpreting the decrease, however, is not an easy matter. The size of the Internal Revenue Service's corporate sample declined from 105,000 companies in 1969 to 93,000 in 1981. This, coupled with the fact that the I.R.S. estimated that the total universe of companies increased by 75 percent in the same period, means that the actual sample has been cut in half, from 6 percent to 3 percent of the total universe of firms.

WHILE improved sampling design and estimating methodologies may have reduced errors caused by smaller samples, there are no studies that have gauged the effect smaller samples may have on measuring long-term trends or trends by industry or size of company. Both of these factors are crucial for accurately evaluating the potential impact of the proposed new tax laws.

Measures of personal savings also have been clouded by a lack of data on participation in the four-year-old Section 401(k) programs, under which employees may defer income. Although there may be as many as 2 million workers participating in such programs, there are no statistics on either the extent of the coverage or its impact on reported income.

Personal savings, as measured by the B.E.A., is simply the difference between total reported income and calculated personal consumption expenditures. Currently, income deferred under the 401(k) program is not included as reported income. As a result, the nation's overall savings rate is probably understated by between 5 percent and 10 percent.

We are currently faced with a number of major policy challenges, such as evaluating the impact of imports, stimulating savings and investment and revising the tax code. Regrettably, the quality of the statistics on which we will base our decisions on these issues is deteriorating. Unless this potential crisis is addressed, the effectiveness of policy decisions will be severely undercut. ∎

plagues, tuberculosis, and high infant mortality, and warned that government restrictions on the profession would undo all the progress doctors had brought us. Biotechnology firms, through their trade association known as "BIO," told a very similar story to fight President Clinton's medical cost-containment plans in the 1990s: biotechnology had brought us miracle medicine, but Clinton's planned regulation and price controls threatened the very survival of the nascent industry.[3] Manufacturing concerns, such as automakers, steel companies, and textile firms, tell a story of how minimum wage legislation, mandatory health benefits, and occupational safety regulations threaten to destroy America's once-preeminent position in the world economy. The CIA tells us that restrictions on its operating methods prevent it from maintaining the security it once could provide, and the Pentagon tells how budget constraints have undermined our once-dominant military position.

Another variant of the decline story is the _change-is-only-an-illusion story_. It runs like this: "You always thought things were getting worse (or better). But you were wrong. Let me show you some evidence that things are in fact going in the opposite direction. Decline (or improvement) was an illusion." Examples of the revisionist story are everywhere. Medical researchers tell us that the improved survival rates for cancer patients are really an artifact of measurement; it is only because we can now diagnose cancer at earlier stages that patients appear to live longer.[4] Child abuse (or rape or wife-battering) is not really on the rise; it only appears to have increased because we have more public awareness, more legislation, and more reporting.

The other broad type of narrative in policy analysis is the _story of helplessness and control_. It usually runs like this: "The situation is bad. We have always believed that the situation was out of our control, something we had to accept but could not influence. Now, however, let me show you that in fact we can control things." Stories about control are always gripping because they speak to the fundamental problem of liberty—to what extent do we control our own life conditions and destinies? Stories that purport to tell us of less control are always threatening, and ones that promise more are always heartening.

Much of the analysis in the areas of social policy, health and safety,

[3] "BIO" stands for Biotechnology Industry Organization. See Peter H. Stone, "Lost Cause," _National Journal_ Sept. 17, 1994, p. 2133.

[4] Alvan R. Feinstein et al., "The Will Rogers Phenomenon: Stage Migration and New Diagnostic Techniques as a Source of Misleading Statistics for Survival in Cancer," _New England Journal of Medicine_ 312, no. 25 (June 20, 1985): 1604–8.

and environment is a story of control. What had formerly appeared to
be "accidental," "random," "a twist of fate," or "natural" is now
alleged to be amenable to change through human agency. For example, much modern economic policy—the use of government fiscal and
monetary tools to stabilize fluctuations in the economy—is based on a
grand story of control. In the 1930s, when national economies had
lurched into rampant inflation and disastrous depressions, they
seemed to behave more like the weather than like social institutions.
Lord Keynes wrote a highly influential treatise whose central premise
was that seemingly random fluctuations in economies are really manageable through government manipulation of spending and money
supply.[5] The story of control governs in a vastly different policy area—
public health—as well. Cancer, previously thought to strike victims
unpredictably, now turns out to be related to diet, smoking, and chemicals—all things humans can control. Increasingly, cancer is linked to
mutant genes, and though we cannot control our genes, the knowledge
of genetic contributions to cancer can help us target screening and
prevention programs, and may eventually help design genetically
based therapies. Stories that move us from the realm of fate to the
realm of control are always hopeful, and through their hope they
invoke our support.

A common twist on the control story is the *conspiracy*. Its plot moves
us from the realm of fate to the realm of control, but it claims to show
that all along control has been in the hands of a few who have used it
to their benefit and concealed it from the rest of us. Ralph Nader's
famous crusade against automobile manufacturers was a story that
converted car accidents into events controllable through the design of
cars, and even willingly accepted by automakers. Advocates of industrial policy tell a story in which unemployment, thought to be intracta-
ble, is actually caused by "capital strike" (businessmen refuse to invest
in new plants and ventures) and "capital flight" (businesses invest their
capital in other regions or other countries). Conspiracy stories always
reveal that harm has been deliberately caused or knowingly tolerated,
and so evoke horror and moral condemnation. Their ending always
takes the form of a call to wrest control from the few who benefit at the
expense of the many.

Another variant of the control story is the *blame-the-victim* story.[6] It,

[5] John Maynard Keynes, *The General Theory of Employment, Interest and Money*, (New
York: Harcourt & Brace, 1936).

[6] The phrase became a byword in social science after William Ryan's *Blaming the Victim*
(New York: Random House, 1971).

too, moves us from the realm of fate to the realm of control, but locates control in the very people who suffer the problem. In one recent analysis of homelessness, "it was the fact that unskilled women not only married less but continued to have children that pushed more of them into the streets."[7] Homelessness, in this view, is the result of women's knowing choice between two alternatives:

I bad choices

> Few unskilled women can earn enough to support a family on their own. For many, therefore, the choices were stark. They could work, refrain from having children and barely avoid poverty, or they could not work, have children, collect welfare and live in extreme poverty. Many became mothers even though this meant extreme poverty.[8]

There are many versions of the blame-the-victim story. The poor are poor because they seek instant pleasures instead of investing in their own futures, or because they choose to live off the dole rather than work. Third World countries are poor because they borrow too eagerly and allow their citizens to live too extravagantly. The sick are sick because they overeat, consume unhealthy foods, smoke, and don't exercise. Women are raped because they "ask for it." Workers succumb to occupational diseases and injuries because they refuse to wear protective gear or to act with caution. Just as the conspiracy story always ends with a call to the many to rise up against the few, the blame-the-victim story always ends with an exhortation to the few (the victims) to reform their own behavior in order to avoid the problem.

What all these stories of control have in common is their assertion that there is choice. The choice may belong to society as a whole, to certain elites, or to victims, but the drama in the story is always achieved by the conversion of a fact of nature into a deliberate human decision. Stories of control offer hope, just as stories of decline foster anxiety and despair. The two stories are often woven together, with the story of decline serving as the stage setting and the impetus for the story of control. The story of decline is meant to warn us of suffering and motivate us to seize control.

Policy stories use many literary and rhetorical devices to lead the audience ineluctably to a course of action. They have good guys and bad guys, even though nonhuman entities may be cast in these roles, and they have a moment of triumph. Look back at the article on fed-

---

[7] Christopher Jencks, *The Homeless* (Cambridge, Mass.: Harvard University Press, 1994), p. 58.

[8] Christopher Jencks, "The Homeless," *New York Review of Books*, April 21, 1994, p. 25.

eral statistics. The author starts right in telling us we have been pursuing the wrong villain ("economists") in our quest to find the perpetrator of the evil deed of "confusion and contradictions in economic forecasting." The real source of error is the poor quality of federal economic statistics. But these statistics are not the villain—they are the innocent victims of larger evil forces ("deregulation," "budget cuts," and "failures"). The heroes of this story are the struggling statistical agencies, such as the Bureau of Economic Analysis, the Internal Revenue Service, and the Office of Federal Statistical Policy, who have been unable to carry out their own recommendations and to implement changes they know to be "crucial." The good guys have had their weapons undermined: the IRS has to make do with a smaller sample, the Bureau of Economic Analysis doesn't have enough categories, and Congress is groping in the dark. The whole story is a plea for Congress to come to the aid of the innocent victims (statistics) by strengthening the heroes (agencies) who could perform the rescue.

Let's look more closely at three of the most common and powerful literary devices in policy stories.

SYNECDOCHE[9]

Synecdoche is a figure of speech in which a whole is represented by one of its parts: "Ten thousand feet moved down Pennsylvania Avenue toward the White House." This form of symbolism is very common in politics, where examples are offered up as "typical instances" or "prototypical cases" of a larger problem. These typical cases then define the entire problem and frame the policy response.

In the mid-1970s, Wisconsin passed a major reform of its divorce law. The reform was fashioned on the assumption that the problem with the old law was its treatment of the displaced homemaker, the woman who spent her marriage years as a housewife and mother and then received no economic assets in a divorce settlement. The reformers deliberately collected and publicized examples of the displaced homemaker to mobilize support. Because the displaced-homemaker image dominated policy thinking, the new law presumed there should be an equal division of property upon divorce. In doing so, it neglected other types of marital situations, such as women who were homemakers *and* income earners, and women who brought substantial eco-

[9] Pronounced *sin-ECK-da-key*.

nomic assets to the marriage, perhaps from a business or a prior marriage. The "equal division" standard made it difficult for these women to get more than half of the marital assets at divorce. According to one scholar, the reigning image of the displaced homemaker and the horror stories that supported it "came to substitute for a more generalized articulation of the problems of women in divorce. . . . 'Displaced homemakers' became the exclusive measure against which reforms would embody the ideals of fairness or justice."[10]

It is common in politics that one part of a problem particularly catches the popular imagination and confines the policy response to that part of the problem. In discussions of welfare reform, the "welfare queen" has become the dominant representation of the problem. She is a mother of many children who has been on the rolls for ten or twenty years, and has adopted welfare as a way of life. In fact, only about a fifth of current welfare recipients have been on the rolls for ten years or more. If we look at all "spells" of welfare, that is, entrances and exits from the rolls, instead of at current recipients, only 14 percent of these spells last ten years or more.[11] A reform that is targeted to the long-term welfare recipient, then, will affect only a small part of the welfare population, and a small part of the welfare problem.

One common genre, the horror story, is itself a form of synecdoche. Politicians or interest groups deliberately choose one egregious or outlandish incident to represent the universe of cases, and then use that example to build support for changing an entire rule or policy that is addressed to the larger universe. Horror stories are a staple in political fights against industry regulation, and against liability suits such as malpractice or product safety. Often these stories are not only atypical, but also highly distorted. In early 1995, as the 104th Congress rushed to dismantle much of the safety and environmental regulation of the seventies and eighties, antiregulation crusaders claimed the Occupational Safety and Health Administration (OSHA) had abolished the tooth fairy (by requiring dentists to discard any baby teeth they pulled), and had required all buckets to be built with holes in the bottom. Such absurdities could be counted on to generate hostility to regulation, but they grossly distorted the actions of the agency. OSHA never required

[10] The story of Wisconsin's divorce reform is from Martha L. Fineman, "Implementing Equality: Ideology, Contradiction and Social Change," *Wisconsin Law Review* 1983, no. 4 (1983): 789–887; quotation is on p. 866.

[11] Mary Jo Bane and David T. Ellwood, *Welfare Realities: From Rhetoric to Reform* (Cambridge, Mass.: Harvard University Press, 1994), p. 29.

"Once upon a time there was a wicked Welfare Queen who had the power to destroy entire economies with one AFDC check. . . ."

disposal of baby teeth, only that dentists protect themselves and their assistants from blood-borne pathogens when handling the teeth. As for the leaky buckets, it turns out that about 50 babies drown every year by falling into large plastic buckets—the kind left over from construction projects that people often save for use around the garden or house. OSHA suggested that the buckets be redesigned to tip over if a child fell in, but left it up to industry to make a voluntary effort.[12]

As with other forms of symbolic representation, the synecdoche can suspend our critical thinking with its powerful poetry. The strategy of focusing on a part of a problem, particularly one that can be dramatized as a horror story, thus is likely to lead to skewed policy. Yet it is often a politically useful strategy. It is a good organizing tool, because it can make a problem concrete, allow people to identify with someone else, and mobilize anger. Also it reduces the scope of the problem and thereby makes it more manageable. The extreme version of this strategy is reducing a large-scale problem to a single instance. This happens, for example, when the president makes a plea for a donated liver for a single child in need of transplantation. The plea, and the joy we all feel when it succeeds in turning up an organ, makes invisible the rest of the people who need organ transplants.

[12]John H. Cushman Jr., "Congressional Memo: Tales from the 104th: Watch Out, or the Regulators Will Get You!" *New York Times*, Feb. 28, 1995, p. A20.

METAPHORS

Take another a trip down memory lane to recall that a metaphor is an implied comparison. It works by using a word that denotes one kind of object or idea to describe another—for example, "Clinton blasted the press;" "Industry is being strangled;" "We live on spaceship earth."

Metaphors are important devices for strategic representation in policy analysis. On the surface, they simply draw a comparison between one thing and another, but in a more subtle way they usually imply a whole narrative story and a prescription for action. Take this example:

> One of the most pervasive stories about social services diagnoses the problem as "fragmentation" and prescribes "coordination" as the remedy. But services seen as fragmented might be seen, alternatively, as autonomous. Fragmented services become problematic when they are seen as the shattering of a prior integration. The services are seen as something like a vase that was once whole and now is broken. Under the spell of the metaphor, it appears obvious that fragmentation is bad and coordination good.[13]

Merely to describe something as fragmented is to call for integration as an improvement, without ever saying so. The jump from description to prescription in policy metaphor is what Martin Rein and Donald Schon have called the "normative leap."[14]

Buried in every policy metaphor is an assumption that if *a* is like *b*, then the way to solve *a* is to do what you would do with *b*. Because policy metaphors imply prescription, they are a form of advocacy. The claim that "*a* is like *b*" takes on political importance in another way as well. In a culture where the common understanding of fairness is "treating likes alike," to claim a likeness is also to posit an interpretation of equity and to demand equal treatment.

Metaphors are pervasive in policy language. Once you are sensitized, you will find them everywhere. One common metaphor is to see social institutions as *living organisms*. Communities or groups are said to have a "life of their own" and organizations have "goals." The

[13]Donald Schon, "Generative Metaphor: A Perspective on Problem Setting in Social Policy," in Andrew Ortony, ed., *Metaphor and Thought* (Cambridge, England: Cambridge University Press, 1980).

[14]Martin Rein and Donald Schon, "Problem Setting in Policy Research," in Carol Weiss, ed., *Using Social Research in Public Policy Making* (Lexington, Mass.: Heath, 1977).

image of "life cycle" is used to explain why political issues seem to experience periods of rapid growth and then decline, why regulatory agencies go through periods of fervent reform-mindedness and then passive acceptance of the status quo, or why elected officials seem to follow predictable patterns of popularity and behavior in their terms of office.[15]

The assertion that something is like an organism is implicitly a claim that it must be viewed as a whole whose importance is more than the sum of its parts. To see something as an organism is to assert that it is "natural," which in turn implies that however it is, that is "the way it is supposed to be." (In fact, the word "natural" is a good hint that there is an underlying metaphor of organism.) Deliberate human interference with it then becomes artificial and perhaps even futile. The normative leap in the organism metaphor is usually a prescription to leave things alone, and it is often used by those who want to resist change. They argue that tampering with any part of an organism (community, neighborhood, family) will upset a delicate balance, destroy the whole, or interfere with nature.

One common and potent variant of the organism metaphor is the idea of _natural laws_ of social behavior. Many famous social scientists have claimed to discover laws that govern the social world and that set limits, and even total barriers, to the changes humans can bring about through deliberate policy.[16] Two influential nineteenth-century sociologists, Gaetano Mosca and Vilfred Pareto, argued that all societies were naturally and inevitably divided into rulers and the ruled, elites and non-elites, so that democratic reforms such as expanded voting rights could not possibly bring about real change. Another sociologist of the late nineteenth century, Roberto Michels, formulated the "iron law of oligarchy," according to which all organizations, no matter how participatory and egalitarian they begin, inevitably evolve toward a concentration of political power among a few leaders. George Stigler, a contemporary economist, has postulated a "law of public income redistribution," according to which any attempt at redistribution

[15] See Anthony Downs, "Up and Down with Ecology: The Issue Attention Cycle," *The Public Interest*, no. 28 (Summer 1972): 38–50; Marver Bernstein, *Regulating Business by Independent Commission* (Princeton, N.J.: Princeton University Press, 1955); Paul Light, *The President's Agenda* (Baltimore: Johns Hopkins University Press, 1982), especially pp. 36–52.

[16] This paragraph draws on Albert O. Hirschman, *The Rhetoric of Reaction* (Cambridge, Mass.: Harvard University Press, 1991), esp. chap. 3, "The Futility Thesis." This is a brilliant book about deep stories in policy argument.

toward the poor inevitably takes money from them and redistributes it to the middle classes. Albert O. Hirschman groups these kinds of stories under the heading "futility thesis," because their common underlying story is that it is futile for people to attempt social change (of the democratic and redistributive sort). They are all stories about the impossibility of human control.

Undoubtedly, the most influential "law" of social behavior in contemporary public policy is Charles Murray's "law of unintended rewards": "Any social transfer increases the net value of being in the condition that prompted the transfer."[17] In plain English, this law says that helping people who have problems (such as poverty, illness, homelessness, or drug addiction), especially giving them money or services, actually *rewards* them for having the problem and *creates an incentive* for them to stay or become poor, sick, homeless, or addicted. Therefore, it is impossible to mount any kind of social welfare programs that don't simply perpetuate or even increase the problems they purport to ameliorate. Though no one in Washington or the state capitals is going around quoting Murray's law, the equation "helping hand equals incentive to be needy" is the driving force in today's social policy debates.

Machines and mechanical devices form the basis of many policy metaphors. Eighteenth-century political thought, from which our Constitution is derived, conceived of a political system as a machine with working parts that had to be kept "in order" and "in balance." Thus, "checks and balances" are central to our way of thinking about how political power should be allocated. The idea of balance also appears in international relations, where a "balance of power" is thought to ensure international peace. With the advent of nuclear weapons, strategists talk of a "balance of terror," where mutual fear prevents either side from taking action. The very term "balanced budget" implies that either revenue surpluses or deficit spending would be bad, when of course most people believe that saving for the future, or borrowing to invest in education or business, is a perfectly sensible (and even virtuous) strategy. The metaphor of balance implies a story about the decline from balance to imbalance and prescribes addition of something to one side or subtraction from the other.

Wedges and inclines (think of a rubber doorstop) abound in political language. Government regulation is often portrayed as a wedge: Once they get their foot in the door, the regulators will be pushing through

[17]Charles Murray, *Losing Ground* (New York: Basic Books, 1984, 2d. ed. 1994, pp. 213–16.

with more and more. (An animate version of this metaphor is "the nose of the camel in the tent.") The image of a wedge suggests that a seemingly small beginning can have enormous leverage. The image of an incline suggests that once something starts on a downward path, it will be irresistibly drawn further by gravity. Metaphors of wedges and inclines thus contain stories warning of future decline, and the implied prescription is that policy should avoid the "first move" in order to prevent the inevitable "slide" or "push" in an unwanted direction.

From the metaphor of the incline comes a very common and potent genre of policy argument, the "slippery slope." Much argument over behavior seen as immoral is based on the slippery slope: a drink, a cigarette, a lapse from a diet, a white lie, or a small bit of cheating are seen as a the first step down the slippery slope. The "twelve step" metaphor of Alcoholics Anonymous and other recovery programs promises to counteract the unbroken slippery slope by reconstructing it and dividing it into steps with firm footing.

Slippery slope arguments have a common form.[18] They begin by acknowledging that the phenomenon (a law, a proposal, a rule, a program, a drink) is not in itself wrong or bad or dangerous. But then they proceed to declare that permitting the phenomenon would inevitably lead to situations or cases that *are* wrong or bad or dangerous. For example, opponents of laws permitting physicians to assist terminally ill people with euthanasia usually concede that euthanasia is justified, and even desirable, under certain conditions. Then they shift ground, claiming we still should not permit euthanasia, even under conditions where it is justified, because it might be carried out in the wrong circumstances. Slippery slope arguments are usually used in this fashion, to resist changes even when the opponent can't find any good reasons against the change itself. Philosopher Dan Brock has called slippery slope arguments "the last refuge of conservative defendants of the *status quo.*"[19]

Herman Kahn's early and well-known theory of the arms race, *On Escalation*, uses the metaphor of a ladder, yet another form of incline. Kahn portrays possible "steps" in international crises as rungs on a ladder. He says that the purpose of the ladder metaphor is to show that "there are many relatively continuous paths between a low-level crisis and an all-out war, none of which is necessarily or inexorably to be

---

[18] See Fred Schauer, "Slippery Slopes," *Harvard Law Review* 99, no. 2, (1985): 361–83; and Wilbren van der Berg, "The Slippery Slope Argument," *Ethics* 102 (1991): 42–65.

[19] Dan Brock, "Voluntary Active Euthanasia," *Hastings Center Report*, March–April 1992, pp. 10–21, quote on p. 19. The euthanasia example is from Brock.

followed." Explicitly, he reassures his readers that "there is no necessity that one inexorably go up the ladder—rung by rung. One can go down as well as up, or even skip steps."[20] The metaphor, though, conveys another story: we all know the urge to climb a ladder, the sense of being drawn from one step to another, the increasing scariness as one ascends, and the overwhelming temptation to go up against one's better judgment. Kahn's metaphor is emotionally compelling because it tells a threatening story in between the lines of the more reassuring formal narrative. The ladder metaphor, too, evokes an uncertain narrative about control; it makes us ponder whether we really can or will do anything but climb.

 Another set of policy metaphors is based on _containers_ and the idea of a fixed space. The problem might be that a space is overfilled; thus, for example, Mexican workers "spill over" the borders into the United States. Or, a container is underfilled, as when journalists declare a "power vacuum" when a politician "vacates" an important position. If a container has holes there will be "leaks" (e.g., of information) or "seepages" (e.g., of power). Foreign policy in the 1950s was dominated by the image of "containing communism." If a container is not big enough, there might be "spillovers" which require "mopping-up operations." Or too much "pressure" might develop, leading to "outbursts" and "explosions," as people seek "outlets" for their frustrations. The "dense" cities were always "exploding" in the 1960s.

The solutions to such problems are varied, but appropriate to the metaphor. One can "drain off" some of the contents of the container ("draining off the opposition") for example, by transferring disgruntled employees to another location or appointing them to low-level management positions where their loyalties will be split. One can allow a gradual release of pressure through a "pressure valve," such as letting enraged community residents or agency clients "blow off steam" in public hearings or grievance procedures. Some scholars have argued that what often appear as acts of resistance by the relatively powerless in a society are really just "safety valves" consciously designed by elites to maintain their position of dominance.[21]

 Disease, especially the contagious variety, forms the basis for many policy metaphors. Cults, communism, crime—in fact any behavior or

---

[20] Herman Kahn, _On Escalation_ (Hudson Institute, 1965; rev. ed., Baltimore: Penguin Books, 1968). The quotations are from pp. 37 and 40, respectively.

[21] For an extraordinarily insightful (and skeptical) analysis of safety-valve theories of social control, see James Scott, _Domination and the Arts of Resistance: Hidden Transcripts._ (New Haven: Yale University Press, 1990), chap. 7.

set of ideas one wants to condemn—are said to "spread." Members and advocates "infect" others with their ideas. Teenage pregnancy, unwed motherhood, and high school dropping out are declared "epidemics." Universities and slums are "breeding grounds" for all kinds of troubles. We talk almost unthinkingly about "healthy" economies, businesses, and institutions, and from there it is a short step to diagnosing "urban blight" and "dying industries."

Disease metaphors imply a story about deterioration and decline, and about struggle for control between humans and nonhuman "germs." The disease label discredits opponents and implies the moral rightness of treating them as less than human. If a social process is conceived as contagion, then a "cure" of any single infected entity will not stop the phenomenon, and harsh measures may be needed to isolate the carriers and "stamp out" the disease. Some banks use a policy of "redlining," or marking off poor areas in cities where they refuse to write mortgages and homeowner insurance, almost as if they are quarantining a part of the city.

Perhaps the most pervasive disease metaphor in social policy is the image of the poor and disadvantaged as having some pathology. The dominant social-science interpretations of poverty, homelessness, teen pregnancy, drug addiction, and illegitimacy view all of these problems as outcomes of personal problems and deficiencies. In fact, the psychiatry profession has converted many a social problem into a mental disorder by creating a name and a set of associated symptoms in its official diagnostic manual. Thus, for example, the manual lists "antisocial personality disorder," whose symptoms are "significant unemployment," "repeated absences from work," and "abandonment of several jobs." Other symptoms are not obeying social norms, failing to plan ahead, traveling from place to place, and not having a fixed address for at least a month.[22]

As you might begin to suspect, this set of symptoms makes homelessness into a mental illness. Like all metaphors, this one creates political resources. For psychiatrists, the metaphor empowers them to diagnose and treat the problem of homelessness. (Other metaphors might empower construction businesses or labor economists to treat

---

[22] Antisocial personality disorder is listed in the American Psychiatric Association, *Diagnostic and Statistical Manual of Mental Disorders* (Washington, D.C.: American Psychiatric Association, 1987), p. 345. This example comes from David Wagner, *Checkerboard Square: Culture and Resistance in a Homeless Community.* (Boulder: Westview Press, 1993), pp. 92 and 95. Chapter 1 provides an excellent analysis and critique of the pathology metaphor in social science.

the problem.) For homeless people, the illness metaphor enables some of them to receive cash and health insurance from the Supplemental Security Income (SSI) disability program.[23]

The metaphor of *war* is ingrained in policy language. We wage "war on poverty," suffer the "invasion of privacy," declare "war on cancer," and go on "campaigns" against drunk driving or illiteracy. When something is portrayed as an invasion, the invader is foreign, and therefore not a citizen whose rights have to be respected or whose life is to be valued. When we are at war, survival is at stake and so we ignore the costs of waging war. (In medicine, for example, the military metaphor justifies an obliviousness to costs, and in the words of one commentator, a "technological arms race" among medical centers.[24]) If our government is at war, be it against poverty or fraud or crime, then we are traitors if we do not support the cause. The symbol of war is an obvious tactic used by leaders to create support for their policies.

Organisms, machines, containers, diseases, and wars are some of the most frequent and overarching metaphors in policy. But in all policy discourse, names and labels are used to create associations that lend legitimacy and attract support to a course of action. A liberal columnist chides conservatives that when government helps the private sector, the process is called a "partnership"; when it helps the middle class, through block grants to states or Social Security programs, it is called "spending." And when it helps the poor, the unemployed, and the disabled, it is called "a giveaway."[25] A conservative might well retort that to the liberal, aid to a private firm is a "bailout"; aid to a government agency imparts "fiscal stability"; aid to the middle class is a "stimulus to the economy"; and aid to the poor is a "moral duty." What is a "gasoline tax" to one side is a "user fee" to the other. What is a "Job Creation and Wage Enhancement Act" to the Republicans is a rollback of the New Deal regulatory state to the Democrats. Thus, the very labels in policy discourse evoke different stories and prescriptions. In the world of politics, language matters.

Problem definition in the polis is always strategic, designed to call in reinforcements for one's own side in a conflict. Since it is always the loser or weaker side who needs to call in help, strategic problem definition usually means portraying a problem so that one's favored course of action appears to be in the broad public interest. When

---

[23] David Wagner, op. cit. (note 22), p. 89.

[24] George Annas, "Reframing the Debate on Health Care Reform by Replacing Our Metaphors," *New England Journal of Medicine* 332, no. 11 (March 16, 1995): 744–47.

[25] Alan Lupo, "High Tech Cry Babies," *Boston Globe*, June 22, 1985, p. 19.

George Pataki proposed drastic budget cuts for New York's Medicaid program, the state hospital association took out a full-page ad in the *New York Times* with the message "Cutting Medicaid Cuts Your Health Care, Too." The ad detailed how all patients, not just the people on Medicaid, would be hurt by cuts in equipment and staff, and warned: "You [readers of the *New York Times* who are probably not on Medicaid] won't be able to escape the pain."[26]

When business asks for tax breaks, foreign import protections, or special favors from state or local government, it always casts consumers or workers as the beneficiaries, rather than its stockholders. Why, though, would business, arguably always the stronger side in any social conflict, want to expand the scope of conflict and appeal to a larger public? A contemporary Marxist interpretation of this phenomenon holds that since capitalists are far outnumbered by workers, they need to make the interests of business—such as higher investment and profits and lower wages—appear to be the interests of society as a whole.[27]

Strategic definition also means manipulating the scope of a conflict by making some people seem to be affected by it and others not. Certain symbols, such as individualism, freedom, privacy, private enterprise, localism, and states' rights, are calculated to restrict the scope of conflict, while others, such as equality, justice, and civil rights, are calculated to expand it.[28] For example, under the banner of "racial equality," black minorities have called in the help of federal courts in school integration; under the banner of "neighborhood schools" or "local control," white majorities have attempted to split blacks from their outside allies.

Problems, then, are not given, out there in the world waiting for smart analysts to come along and define them correctly. They are created in the minds of citizens by other citizens, leaders, organizations, and government agencies, as an essential part of political maneuvering. Symbols, stories, metaphors, and labels are all weapons in the armamentarium (to use a metaphor).

This strategic concept of problem definition does not mean there is a conspiracy or that every policy argument we read and hear is an attempt to dupe us. There is, after all, a long distance between strategic

[26] Advertisement by Greater New York Hospital Association, *New York Times*, March 9, 1994, p. B5.

[27] See Antonio Gramsci, *Selections from the Prison Notebooks*, ed. and trans. Quentin Hoare and Geoffrey Nowell-Smith (New York: International Publishers, 1971).

[28] E. E. Schattschneider, *The Semisovereign People* (Hinsdale, Ill.: Dryden Press, 1960), p. 7.

ıd venality. Symbolic representation is a fundamental part
urse, political or other, and by conveying images of good
ght and wrong, suffering and relief, these devices are instru-
e struggle over public policy.

ʒymᵇᵒⁿⁱᶜ devices are especially persuasive and emotionally compelling because their story line is hidden and their sheer poetry is often
stunning. "Spaceship earth" stops your mind for a minute and makes
you conjure up an image of cozy but fragile interdependence. When
Senator Phil Gramm promises to make the 40 million people who have
been "riding in the wagon get out and help the rest of us pull," we can
practically feel our burdens lighten.[29] Often a metaphor is so much a
part of our cultural way of saying things that it slips right by us, normative leap and all.

For these reasons, it is worth cultivating some skill in recognizing
symbols and questioning their assumptions. What is the underlying
narrative? Does it make sense? Does the metaphor tell a different story
from the one the author purports to tell? Does the metaphor seem to
obviate the need for evidence, or does it bias the kind of information
opponents might bring to bear on a conflict? Does a symbol offer a
"pig in a poke," and might we want to inquire into substance before
lending support to the symbol? These are the questions one is led to
ask in a symbolic analysis of problems.

AMBIGUITY

The most important feature of all symbols, both in art and politics, is
their ambiguity. A symbol can mean two (or more) things simultaneously: "equal opportunity in education" can mean giving everybody a
tuition voucher for the same dollar amount, as well as providing extra
resources for those with special needs. A symbol can mean different
things to different people: "religious freedom" means organized vocal
prayer in public schools to some people and absolutely no prayer in
public schools to others. And a symbol can mean different things in
different contexts: pictures of alligators conjure up very different
images on Izod knit jerseys than on T-shirts for the National Wildlife
Federation.

Ambiguity is a source of richness and depth in art. Symbols call forth

[29]This was Senator Gramm's famous and oft-repeated characterization of welfare
reform during the 1994 congressional election campaign. See Bob Herbert, "In America,
Scapegoat Time," *New York Times* Nov. 16, 1994, p. A16; and "Welfare Helps Kids,
Moms," *USA Today*, Nov. 16, 1994, p. 12A.

individual imagination, wish, and experience, and draw the observer into the work of art as an active participant. For these very reasons, ambiguity is anathema in science. Crucial to the scientific method is that experiments should be replicable over time and by different observers. The interpretation of events should remain constant and unambiguous, unaffected by the identity of the observer. Politics is more like art than science in that ambiguity is central. Some people think that is a good thing; others, a bad thing. But whatever one's assessment, a type of policy analysis that does not make room for the centrality of ambiguity in politics can be of little use in the real world.

Why is ambiguity essential in politics? What role does it play? Ambiguity enables the transformation of individual intentions and actions into collective results and purposes. Without it, cooperation and compromise would be far more difficult, if not impossible. As Charles Elder and Roger Cobb say, symbols provide the vehicle through which diverse motivations, expectations and values are synchronized to make collective action possible.[30]

Ambiguity allows leaders to aggregate support from different quarters for a single policy. For example, a president might succeed in unifying advocates and opponents of foreign military intervention by asking for a congressional mandate allowing him to send troops "only if American interests are threatened." Congressional representatives will agree to that phrase, even though they have very different ideas about what constitutes a threat to American interests. "Defending American interests" is an ambiguous idea around which everyone unites.

Similarly, ambiguity allows leaders of interest groups and political movements to bring together people with wishes for different policies. The postwar women's movement was initially portrayed in terms of equalizing the rights of women and men, a portrayal that seized on the common identity and interests of women. Later when specific policies were at issue, such as requiring employers to provide maternity leave benefits, old coalitions fell apart as subgroups coalesced around new symbols such as "mothers" and "small business owners." In their role as small business owners, many women did not see their bread buttered on the same side as women in their role as mothers or employees. As this example shows, the ambiguity so beneficial at early stages of a movement usually masks internal conflicts that will become evident as the movement seeks concrete policies.

Ambiguity can unite people who would benefit from the same policy

[30] Charles D. Elder and Roger W. Cobb, *The Political Uses of Symbols* (New York: Longman, 1983), p. 28.

but for different reasons. In California some people sought construction and development restrictions to preserve natural resources and wildlife habitats, while others supported the restrictions to preserve the low-density, high-priced, and exclusive character of their neighborhoods. On the national level, environmentalists from southern and western states found ready allies among northeastern members of Congress, because strong environmental controls on new industries hindered Sunbelt economic growth and helped the ailing Frostbelt industries to remain competitive.[31] These different groups would probably find themselves opponents on a variety of other political issues, but the symbol of "environmental preservation" united them around a common vehicle for preserving different things.

Ambiguity enables leaders to carve out a sphere of maneuvering hidden from public view, where they can take decisive action on a problem. Legislators can satisfy demands to "do something" about a problem by passing a vague statute with ambiguous meaning, then letting administrative agencies hash out the more conflictual details behind the scenes. For example, when the Interstate Commerce Commission (ICC) was formed in 1887 to deal with the problem of balancing the interests of railroads, manufacturers, and farmers in the setting of freight rates, it was given a congressional mandate to set "just and reasonable rates." Everyone could agree to "just and reasonable," although what the phrase meant to farmers, shippers, and railroad magnates certainly differed. Railroad owners were able to control the Commission and its rates, but the ICC stood for a long time as a symbol of scientific, impartial rate determination.[32] This particular use of ambiguity in American politics has been roundly criticized as a vehicle for moving political decisions into arenas where strong special interests dominate.[33] But it is also a feature of politics that allows highly conflictual issues to move from stalemate to action, for whatever that is worth.

Ambiguity allows policy makers to placate both sides in a conflict by "giving the rhetoric to one side and the decision to the other." The

[31] Bernard Frieden, *The Environmental Protection Hustle* (Cambridge: Mass.: M.I.T. Press, 1979); and Robert W. Crandall, "Environmental Ignorance," *Wall Street Journal*, April 22, 1985, p. 28.

[32] James A. Morone, "Representation Without Elections: The American Bureaucracy and Its Publics," in Daniel Callahan and Bruce Jennings, eds., *Legislative Ethics* (New York: Praeger, 1985).

[33] The best-known critic is Theodore Lowi in *The End of Liberalism* (New York: Norton, 1969).

Federal Communications Commission, for example, is charged with "protecting the public interest" by regulating the monopoly franchises it creates for radio broadcasters. "Nowhere does [it] wax so emphatic in emphasizing public service responsibility as in decisions permitting greater concentration of control in an area, condoning license transfers at inflated prices, refusing to impose sanctions for flagrantly sacrificing program quality to profits, and so on."[34] By portraying a decision one way in press releases, speeches, preambles, or surrounding language and yet executing it in another, leaders can perform the magic of making two different decisions at once.

Ambiguity facilitates negotiation and compromise because it allows opponents to claim victory from a single resolution. In negotiation, both sides must feel they are better off with an agreement than without, or a settlement will not occur. Since most aspects of a settlement— such as redrawing of boundaries or monetary payments—have symbolic value as well as material consequences, opponents can invest them with different meanings. For example, one party might accept a far smaller payment than it wants or thinks it deserves, but still claim victory by portraying the payment as an admission of guilt by the other side.

Negotiators can turn even seemingly unambiguous numbers into ambiguous affairs. That is what happened in the 1995 U.S.–Japan trade negotiations over automobiles, allowing both sides to claim victory. U.S. officials said they had gotten agreements that Japanese automakers would purchase more American-made parts and autos. The evidence? The U.S. trade representative, Mickey Kantor, wrote some hard numbers into the deal—for example, Japan would increase the number of its dealers selling American cars to 200 by the end of the year, and to 2,000 by the end of the decade. Japanese officials told their citizens that Japan had won, because the agreement didn't require Japanese businesses to do anything different from what they were already doing. The evidence? The agreement contained a stipulation by the Japanese government that "any purchase estimates were not formal commitments, did not carry government backing and were not enforceable."[35] Moreover, the Japanese trade minister, Ryutaro Hashimoto, and Mickey Kantor released a joint announcement saying, "Minister Hashimoto said that Ambassador Kantor's estimates are his

[34] Murray Edelman, *The Symbolic Uses of Politics* (Urbana: University of Illinois Press, 1964) p. 39.

[35] David E. Sanger, "U.S. Settles Trade Dispute, Averting Billions in Tariffs on Japanese Luxury Autos," *New York Times*, June 29, 1995, pp. A1, D6.

own and neither shared by minister himself nor the Government of Japan."[36] In these negotiations, the two negotiators were clearly cooperating in constructing an ambiguous agreement for the sake of being able to come to an agreement. Both sides wanted an accord rather than a trade war, an alliance rather than a split, and both sides were willing to fudge to get there.

Ambiguity helps individuals reconcile their own ambivalent and inconsistent attitudes so that they are capable of giving sustained support to leaders and policies. Most people do not have a coherent and logically consistent set of beliefs about policy issues and choices.[37] Opinion surveys are chock-full of seeming inconsistencies where people subscribe to a principle but not to an action that embodies the principle. So, for example, most Americans agree that citizens should be able to "influence public policy," but nearly half would not allow people to circulate a petition for the legalization of marijuana, and many would deny black militants the right to hold a demonstration.[38] Asked about "government spending on welfare," 48 percent think it should be cut, but asked about "spending on programs for poor children" (who comprise, incidentally, two-thirds of the beneficiaries of AFDC), 47 percent think it should be increased.[39] Sometimes, by emphasizing the symbol instead of the practice, politicians can get support for a policy when people hold contradictory views.

Sometimes entire policies gain their support from the ambiguity of their symbolism. Shelby Steele has argued that affirmative action is an "iconographic public policy—policy that ostensibly exists to solve a social problem but actually functions as an icon for the self-image people hope to gain by supporting the policy."[40] People can point to the mere existence of affirmative action programs as evidence of white social virtue and growing black power, even though in practice, according to Steele, affirmative action has benefited white women more than anyone else, and has done little to improve the situation of poor blacks. This kind of symbolic policy is particularly powerful

---

[36] Ibid.

[37] For the classic political science statement of this proposition, see Philip Converse, "The Nature of Belief Systems in Mass Publics," in David Apter, ed., *Ideology and Discontent* (New York: Free Press, 1964).

[38] Elder and Cobb, op. cit. (note 30), p. 119.

[39] Jason DeParle, "Despising Welfare, Pitying Its Young," *New York Times*, Dec. 18, 1994, p. E5.

[40] Shelby Steele, "Affirmative Action Must Go," *New York Times*, Mar. 1, 1995, A19.

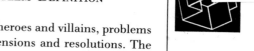

SYMBOLIC DEVICES IN PROBLEM DEFINITION

Stories   Narratives with heroes and villains, problems and solutions, tensions and resolutions. The most common are:

- Stories of decline, including the story of stymied progress and the story of progress-is-only-an-illusion.
- Stories of control, including the conspiracy story and the blame-the-victim story.

Synecdoche   A small part of a policy problem is used to represent the whole—for example, the horror story.

Metaphor   A likeness is asserted between one kind of policy problem and another. Common metaphors in politics include organisms, natural laws, machines, tools, containers, disease, and war.

Ambiguity   The ability of statements, events, and experiences to have more than one meaning. Ambiguity is the "glue" of politics. It allows people to agree on laws and policies because they can read different meanings into the words.

because "you cannot be against it without seeming to be against what it purports to represent."[41]

In summary, the ambiguity of symbols helps transform individual strivings into collective decisions. Symbols allow coalitions where pure material interests would divide people. They enable leaders to assemble broad bases of support for particular policies. They facilitate negotiation. They permit policy makers to retreat to smaller, less visible arenas to get things done. They quell resistance to policies by reassuring at the same time as the actual policies deprive. In all these ways, politics obeys the laws of poetry rather than the laws of matter: a pro-

[41] Ibid.

gram or policy or speech, unlike a physical object, can be two things at once. But if symbols are the invisible hand of politics, it is not because there is any overall force coordinating individual decisions, but because they enable us as individuals to "read ourselves into" social programs and collective actions.

Policy stories are tools of strategy. Policy makers as well as interest groups often create problems (in the artistic sense) as a context for the actions they want to take. This is not to say that they actually cause harm and destruction so they will have something to do, but that they represent the world in such a way as to make themselves, their skills, and their favorite course of action necessary.

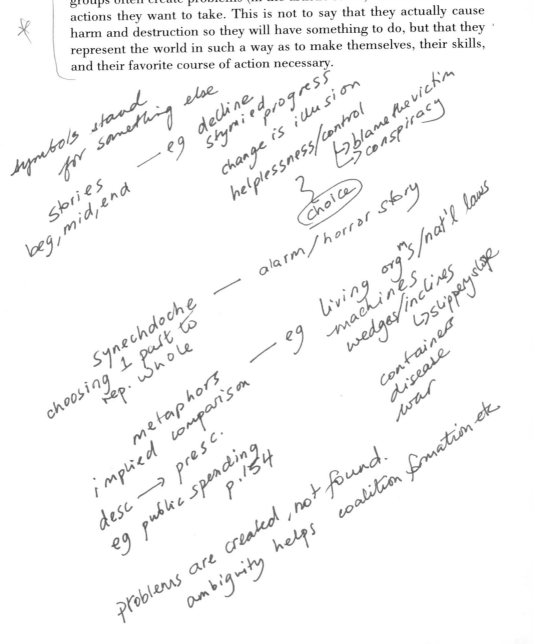

7

Numbers

One common way to define a policy problem is to measure it. Most policy discussions begin with a recitation of figures purporting to show that a problem is big or growing, or both. Although numbers have a preeminent status in our scientific culture, measuring is only one of many ways to describe. Literature describes with words, painting with pigments and brush strokes, and measurement with numbers. And just as there are infinite ways of describing a single object in words or paint, so there are infinite ways of describing with numbers. Numbers are another form of poetry. *measure what in particular?*

Suppose I hire you to measure an elephant. That may sound like a pretty straightforward job description, but think about it for a minute. Do you measure its weight? Height? Length? Volume? Intensity of its color gray? Number and depth of its wrinkles? Or perhaps the proportion of the day it sleeps? In order to measure this creature, you need to select one or a few features from many possibilities. That choice will be determined by your purpose for measuring, or rather mine, since I hired you. If I were manager of a railroad freight department, I would need to know the elephant's height, length, and weight. But if I were a taxidermist, I would be more interested in its volume and wrinkles. As a trainer, I might care more about the proportion of the day it sleeps. As a producer of synthetic animal skins, I would want to know its exact hue of gray. You, sensing a chance to stay on the payroll, would probably insist that I can't understand my elephant without knowing the seasonal variation in its body temperature.

There are many possible measures of any phenomenon and the

choice among them depends on the purpose for measuring. The fundamental issues of any policy conflict are always contained in the question of how to count the problem. The unemployment rate, for example, is designed as a measure of people wanting work, or the need for jobs. People are counted as unemployed if they are older than 16, have previously held a job, are available for work, and have looked for work within the previous four weeks. The official method of counting unemployment (which, make no mistake, is the official definition of the problem), leaves out a host of people who fit somebody's notion of unemployed but not the official definition: people unwilling to take available jobs because the jobs are too dangerous, unpleasant, or demeaning; people who can find only part-time jobs but would rather work full-time; people who quit a job to search for something better, but are still searching; people who are willing to work but can't find child care; or workers on strike. Should any of these count as unemployed?

The very question highlights the critical issue in numbers: Counting always involves deliberate decisions about *counting as.* To count peas, one needs to decide first which things in the world are peas and which aren't. Counting must begin with categorization, which in turn means deciding whether to include or exclude. We categorize by selecting important characteristics and asking whether the object to be classified is substantially like other objects in the category. Categorization thus involves the establishment of boundaries in the form of rules or criteria that tell whether something belongs or not. (If it's green and round and small, it's a pea.) Only after categorizing does mere tallying come into play. Tallying, by the way, is what arithmetic is about.

All that may seem a terribly abstract description of counting, but notice how political the language sounds. It is impossible to describe counting without talking about inclusion and exclusion (terms that in themselves suggest community, boundaries, allies, and enemies); selection (a term that implies privilege and discrimination); and important characteristics (a term that suggests value judgments and hierarchy). Remember, too, that it was impossible to talk about the goals of public policy without using the language of counting. Who should count as a recipient or what should count as a relevant item in equity issues? What use of resources gives the most for the least in efficiency issues? What should count as a harm or a need in liberty and security issues?

Counting resolves questions like these by assigning things to one group or another. When children learn to count, they learn that things are either peas or beans and must be assigned to a pile. In arithmetic, there are no borderline cases. In that sense, numbers are the opposite of symbols—they are not ambiguous. Something is either counted or it isn't. But ambiguity—the range of choices in what to measure or how to classify—always lies just beneath the surface of any counting scheme. Before a decision is made, things could go either way.

Numbers as Metaphors

The resolution numbers offer is nothing more than a human decision about how to "count as." Numbers, in fact, work exactly like metaphors. To categorize in counting or to analogize in metaphors is to select one feature of something, assert a likeness on the basis of that feature, and ignore all the other features. To count is to form a category by emphasizing some feature instead of others and excluding things that might be similar in important ways but do not share that feature. To count as unemployed only people who have looked for work in the past month is to see unemployment as active job hunting. That vision excludes from the unemployed people who desperately want to work but are unable or too discouraged to pound the pavement.

Because counting requires judgment about inclusion and exclusion, counting schemes are always subject to two possible challenges. The first asserts a real likeness where the measure finds a difference, and insists on inclusion of something the measure excludes. Claims that the unemployment rate should include "discouraged workers" and "underemployed workers" pose this kind of challenge. Counting the homeless population offers another example. Social scientists and government agencies usually count as homeless only people who sleep on the streets or in bus stops, doorways, train stations, and the like. Some count as homeless those people who sleep in shelters for the homeless. But advocates for the homeless believe the concept and the count should include people who are in jails, detox centers, and mental institutions who would have no home if and when they were released, as well as people who crowd into the living spaces of their family and friends but really have no private space of their own.[1]

Challenges of this sort are inevitable in policy politics because the need for clear rules drives policy makers to establish thresholds as

[1] My discussion draws from Christopher Jencks, *The Homeless* (Harvard University Press, 1994, chap. 1.

dividing lines. Agencies, legislatures, courts, and officials must decide who will receive benefits, loans, contracts, budget increases, jobs, fines, and penalties. For many policy purposes, we make fairly arbitrary classifications by setting a cutoff point or threshold on a numerical scale—law school admissions on the basis of LSAT scores, welfare eligibility on the basis of income level, or drinking and voting rights on the basis of age. But thresholds are always subject to the challenge that they differentiate among people or situations that should be considered the same. Is there any significant difference between the person earning $10,000 and the one earning $10,001, or the person aged 20 years and 364 days and the person aged 21? The commonsense understanding that numerical thresholds mask underlying similarities leads people to conceal, fudge, and bend the rules at the borderline.

The second kind of challenge asserts a real difference where a measure finds a likeness, and insists on exclusion of something the measure includes. This kind of challenge is possible, indeed inevitable, because no matter how small and precisely defined a category is, it still masks variety among the objects or people or events it includes.

The second type of challenge can be illustrated with the problem of counting beds. In the late 1960s, amidst belief that the country had too many health care facilities, there was a movement to plan health services by allowing new construction only where it was needed. "Need," in turn, was defined primarily by the ratio of hospital beds to population in a community. The bed ratio seemed a sensible measure of a community's capacity to provide health care, since beds are the places in hospitals where patients can be put, and they are manifestly easy to count. (If it has four legs and a mattress. . . .) But it soon became obvious that all hospital beds are not the same. A bed might be an iron cot or an electric multiposition unit. It might include a cardiac monitor and emergency equipment at its station or it might share equipment with a whole corridor of beds. It might be supported by a staff of four hundred specialists or fourteen general practitioners. It might be within five miles of its client population or within forty. Needless to say, health planners who denied applications for new facilities were besieged with protests about how they counted beds.

If it is hard to count beds because they can mean so many different things, imagine the difficulties in counting jobs for purposes of employment policy. Should unionized, secure, well-paying jobs be counted as equivalent to low-paying, high-turnover jobs? There are dead-end jobs and jobs with built-in career ladders, blue-collar and white-collar jobs, seasonal jobs, short-term jobs (elected officials), long-term jobs (midlevel managers), unpredictable-length jobs (political appointees), and virtually permanent jobs (civil servants and tenured professors). There are jobs with pension, health and life insurance benefits, and jobs without; there are make-work jobs and essential jobs. A job is simply not a job, and debates about employment, retraining, and welfare programs often hinge on the tremendous ambiguity lurking behind counts of jobs. For example, the *New York Times* reported good news for workers in the fall of 1994, saying that most of the new jobs created in the past couple of years were in categories with higher than average pay. In fact, most of the new jobs *were* in the category officially called "managers," but that category includes both corporate managers with six-figure salaries and assistant managers at McDonald's, with starting hourly wages in the low one-figure range. Most of the job growth was at the low end.[2]

Debating the size of a phenomenon is one of the most prominent forms of discourse in public policy. Although the debate usually appears to be about the tally—whether things were added up correctly—it is usually about categorization—how the different sides "count as." There are, to be sure, occasional conflicts over the actual tally, such as when candidates for public office ask for a recount of votes, or cities ask for a recount of the census. Almost always, however, the conflict in policy is over what legitimately counts as what, and numbers are invoked to give an air of finality to each side's opinions.

Every number is an assertion about similarities and differences. No number is innocent, for it is impossible to count without making judgments about categorization. Every number is a political claim about "where to draw the line." Projections, correlations, simulations, and every other fancy manipulation of numbers all rest on the decisions about "counting as" embodied in their numbers, so they, too, are claims about similarities and differences. And similarities and differences are the ultimate basis for decisions in public policy.

Numbers as Norms and Symbols

Like metaphors, numbers make normative leaps. Measures imply a need for action, because we do not measure things except when we

[2] Bob Kuttner "Inequality Sours Economic Recovery" *Boston Globe*, Oct. 24, 1994, p. 13.

[handwritten marginalia: "no diff between counting people (?)"]

want to change them or change our behavior in response to them. The reason we try to predict rain, after all, is to decide whether to carry an umbrella.

To call for a measurement or survey of something is to take the first step in promoting change. In the 1930s, amidst the Great Depression, Congress wanted the administration to begin a full-fledged unemployment census. Until then, the Bureau of Labor Statistics had collected data on employment, from which business and labor organizations as well as economists had tried to estimate unemployment. President Roosevelt did not want a formal unemployment census, because the mere presence of official unemployment figures would put even more pressure on him to lower them. Roosevelt eventually did create the Civilian Conservation Corps (CCC) and the Works Progress Administration (WPA) to provide jobs for the unemployed. The WPA began its own monthly survey of unemployment in 1939, first to dispute the administration's lower figures, and later to convince Congress of the continuing need for the WPA after World War II had begun to stimulate new jobs.[3] Everyone—first Congress, then Roosevelt, and then the head of the WPA—saw that unemployment figures could be a force in politics.

Not only does measuring a problem create subtle pressure to do something about it, but some level of the measure usually becomes a norm. In 1946, Congress passed the Employment Act, mandating that the administration should collect data on unemployment levels and also provide "full employment." The old WPA monthly survey was taken over by the Census Bureau. Since the survey revealed rather persistent rates of unemployment, those rates came to be seen as normal and inevitable. During the 1950s and 1960s, when unemployment averaged about 4.6 percent, economists defined full employment as an unemployment rate between 3 and 4 percent. (If that sounds like a contradiction, that's because it is. This is the political language of numbers.) In the early 1970s, unemployment climbed to more than 6 percent, and Nixon administration economists began claiming that employment should really be considered full at around 4.5 to 5 percent unemployment. With average unemployment rates of more than 7 percent in the 1980s and more than 9 percent in 1982 and 1983, Reagan administration economists began to define full employment as about 6 percent unemployment. The economics profession obliged politicians with textbook theories of a "natural rate of unemployment," below

[3] Judith Innes De Neufville, *Social Indicators and Public Policy* (Amsterdam: Elsevier, 1975), pp. 75–76.

which inflation would inevitably accelerate. Paul Samuelson's best-selling textbook declared in its 1970 edition that full-employment was about 3.5 percent unemployment; by time of its 1985 edition, the natural rate of unemployment had grown to around 6 percent.[4]

As norms, numbers are part of a story of helplessness and control. The administration is held responsible for the state of the economy, and much of the president's support is contingent on his seeming to be in control. So presidents weave a tortuous path between invoking numbers to prove they have reduced a problem through intelligent policy and invoking numbers to prove that some part of the problem is beyond human control. The unemployment rate, the prime interest rate, the inflation rate, the size of the budget, the GNP and the deficit are all characters in the drama of presidential control and failure.

The norms established by measures are sometimes ambiguous. In 1985, the U.S. Navy reported that it had saved $2.5 billion in shipbuilding costs over the previous three years. At first glance, savings would seem to be a good thing, and the navy ought to be proud. But navy officials were not sure whether to brag about the savings or conceal them. The secretary of the navy wanted to brag, thinking that the $2.5 billion saving showed thrift, successful use of competitive bidding, and good management. The vice admiral in charge of buying ships, on the other hand, thought the savings might be interpreted by Congress as proof of "fat" in the navy's budget, and he wanted to play them down.[5] Savings turned out to be a double-edged sword.

In politics, many measures are double-edged swords; that is, it is good to be high on the measure but also good to be low. This is another aspect of ambiguity in numbers, and it occurs when the things we measure are symbols, not just objects. Saving, for example, symbolizes both present thrift and past waste. Thus, far more important than the actual number of a measure is how the measure is interpreted. When measures have a double meaning, the people being measured are put in a double bind. The political fight then shifts from the correctness of the

[4]David Gordon, "Six Percent Unemployment Ain't Natural: Demystifying the Idea of a Rising 'Natural Rate of Unemployment,' " *Social Research* 54, no. 2 (Summer 1987): 223–46. For an argument that letting unemployment fall below the supposed natural rate does not bring about galloping inflation and might even be good policy, see Robert Eisner, "Our NAIRU Limit: The Governing Myth of Economic Policy," *The American Prospect*, no. 21 (Spring 1995): 58–63.

[5]Richard Halloran, "Savings by Navy Posing a Problem," *New York Times*, March 24, 1985, p. 32.

tally or the categorization to a struggle over the interpretation of the symbol.

Another double-edged sword is cost. We usually think of high costs as bad. All things being equal, it is better to pay less for something than more. That is the ideology of efficiency. But for many types of goods and services, high cost is itself a symbol of high quality (think of doctors' and lawyers' services) or prestige (think of designer clothes). To some extent, we all use cost as a proxy measure for quality ("It's so cheap it can't be any good"). In policy debates, measures of cost are often double-edged. Is a costly national defense system waste-ridden or extra secure? Does a high price tag on defense convey a certain toughness and strength to our enemies, independent of the system's actual military capability? Reformers tend to emphasize the waste side of cost, while people in the system trumpet the quality side and the symbolic benefits of high cost.

Cost is a double-edged sword in another way as well. A cost to buyers is income to sellers. Thus, the high cost of medical care for patients and insurers is simultaneously new job opportunities and higher incomes to health care providers and medical supply firms. The high cost of fighter planes to the Air Force represents more jobs and higher wages to contractors. Costs are always income to somebody else, so there is always a constituency for high costs to battle the one for low costs.

Efficiency (getting the most output for a given input) and productivity (output per hour of labor) can be double-edged swords. The terms themselves are value-laden, and we generally think that the more efficiency and productivity, the better. But when physicians open clinics to process Medicaid patients quickly and efficiently, critics complain about "Medicaid mills." High output can symbolize both perfunctory work and a job well done. In services where the output of jobs is personal attention or custom design, efficiency is not always a virtue.

Middles and averages often become norms in politics, and because they are symbols as well as mathematical concepts, they can take on conflicting meanings and put policymakers in a double bind. Promoting a policy as "helping the middle class" is a standard strategy for gaining broad support, because surveys show that most people think of themselves as middle-class, even when they fall substantially above or below the median income.[6] Yet the social science truism that most

[6]John Aldrich, Paul Abramson, and David Rohde, *Change and Continuity in the 1984 Elections* (Washington, D.C.: Congressional Quarterly Press, 1985).

people consider themselves middle-class collapses when survey takers change a few words. If people are given a choice among "lower-class," "middle-class," and "upper-class," about 90 percent will say they are middle-class, but if a category for "working-class" is added as an option, about 45 percent say they are working-class, and only about 45 percent identify as middle-class. People who identify themselves as working-class tend to want a more activist government and more redistributive social policy. Thus, if almost half the citizenry thinks of themselves as working-class, promoting a middle-class tax cut may alienate those voters rather than attract them: a broad tax cut not only depletes revenues available for tangible benefits for the working class, but working-class families don't have enough income to benefit very much from tax cuts.[7]

Politicians exploit the ambiguity and positive connotation of the idea of "middle." Republicans and Democrats both try to present their tax proposals as middle-class tax cuts, but Clinton's plan would cut taxes for families earning up to $75,000, while Newt Gingrich's plan would cut taxes for families earning all the way up to $200,000. As the

[7] S. M. Miller and Karen Marie Ferroggiaro, "Class Dismissed?" *The American Prospect*, no. 21 (Spring 1995): 100–104.

Reagan administration found out when it promoted a tax cut for middle-class families, defined as earning between $20,000 and $30,000, the *political* middle class is not the same as the economic middle class. The typical people who lobby, write letters, staff campaigns, and make contributions, define themselves as "middle-income," even though they earn $50,000 to $60,000 and are in no statistical sense average.[8] The political middle and the economic middle turn out to be different groups, and it is hard to write a tax plan that pleases both.

THE HIDDEN STORIES IN NUMBERS

In policy debates, numbers are commonly used to tell a story. Most obviously, they are the premier language for stories of decline and decay. Figures are invoked to show that a problem is getting bigger and worse, or to project present trends into the future to demonstrate that decline is just around the bend. Numbers are also important in stories of helplessness and control. As we will see in Chapter 8 ("Causes"), statistics have become the predominant form of identifying causal relationships and thus of identifying agents and factors of control. In both uses, numbers are invoked to authenticate the story. The author or speaker tells the audience, in effect, "The numbers show that my story is true."

Even more important than the explicit stories numbers tell are the implicit ones. The acts of counting and publicizing a count convey hidden messages, independent of the actual numbers or the explicit stories.

First, to count something at all is to assert that the phenomenon is at least frequent enough to bother counting. The initial demands to count something formally, such as the demands for the unemployment census, grow from recognition that the thing is common enough to worry about. Counting says a phenomenon is common, regular, and expected, even when the explicit story of a count is to show how rare the phenomenon is. Counts of "parts per billion" in pollution or chemical exposure, for example, tell a story of extreme rarity at the same time as standards of permissible levels expressed in this measure tell a story of common occurrence. Counting moves an event from the singular to the plural.

[8] Alan Murray, "Reagan's Tax-Overhaul Plan Faces Criticism from Upscale, Politically Active Middle Class," *Wall Street Journal*, July 12, 1985, p. 50.

Demands for record keeping often intensify after an apparent accident, and the impetus for counting is a suspicion that numbers will "prove" a connection between some controllable human action and the problem that was once thought to be pure natural accident. Thus, for example, when a few people in the same neighborhood or manufacturing plant develop cancer, a grassroots group will often demand that a public health agency or an employer begin to keep records on cancer occurrence. Their hope is to pin the blame for cancer on something government or firms control, such as chemical disposal or electric wires.

To count something is, second, to assert that it is an identifiable entity with clear boundaries. No one could believe in a count of something that cannot be identified, so to offer a count is to ask your audience to believe the thing is countable. That is no trivial request. In designing the first U.S. population census of 1790, James Madison argued for counting people's occupations. He wanted to have three categories—manufacturing, agriculture, and commerce—because he believed these categories represented the only important political interests to which congressmen should attend. (He thought the learned professions should not be counted in the census because Congress would not make policy concerning them anyway.) Samuel Livermore, a fellow congressman, opposed counting occupations, because he thought it impossible to distinguish the categories Madison set forth. A tobacco grower worked in both agriculture and commerce; or a man might be a farmer in the summer and a shoemaker in winter. Livermore said, in effect, you can't count something you cannot distinguish, and he denied that the political interests Madison wanted to represent were in fact distinguishable. Madison lost.[9]

Many contemporary policy debates involve the question of countability. In education policy, people argue over whether it is possible to measure aptitude for learning, and if so, whether current tests really measure it. Insurance programs worry about whether they can measure disability, and managers about whether they can measure productivity. Civil rights lawyers ponder how to measure "hate crimes." Early in every policy issue, there is usually a serious discussion of whether a phenomenon is measurable at all. Once a measure has been proposed, the debate centers on challenges to the measure as too inclusive or exclusive. But one should not forget that even in debates about the

[9]This story is from Patricia Cline Cohen, *A Calculating People* (Chicago: University of Chicago Press, 1982), p. 163.

validity of a particular measure, both sides have already accepted the underlying premise that a phenomenon is distinguishable and countable.

③ To count something is, third, to create a community. Any number is implicitly an assertion that the things counted in it share a common feature and should be treated as a group. Sometimes numbers represent members of what we might call natural communities or primary groups—people who actually interact regardless of whether they are counted. The population of a village, size of a family, or size of a school are examples. Other numbers represent artificial or statistical communities; they lump together people who have no relationship other than the shared characteristic that determined the count. Age groups, income classes, and mothers of young children in the labor force might be examples.

demographics

The distinction between natural and artificial communities is itself somewhat fuzzy, however, and most communities in the polis are somewhere between the natural and the artificial. The number of citizens in the United States expresses a statistical community in one sense (I have had more interaction with some French citizens than with most Americans) but a natural community in another (I grew up with the same history and culture as most Americans).

epidemiology

In the polis, counting is often part of a deliberate effort to stimulate creation of a natural community by identifying a statistical community in order to demonstrate common interests. Early in the issue of asbestos as a health hazard, for example, trade unions and physicians devoted most of their efforts merely to counting people who developed certain types of cancer and had been exposed to asbestos. That kind of counting created a community of "victims of industry" out of a mass of cancer patients. As cancer patients, people are tied together only by a common diagnosis but no human relationships; as "victims," they are tied together through common relationships to particular employers.

Counting, because it creates groups, is an essential instrument of political mobilization. To identify shared characteristics or problems among individuals is to draw people into a group, however artificial the group may be at first. When leaders of the women's movement talk of the "women's vote" and the "gender gap," they are counting up all women of voting age and asserting a similarity of interest among them. The task for women's leaders, as for leaders of any non-primary group, is to convert statistical members (ones who share important characteristics but have no real relationship with the group) into natural members (ones who actually participate).

A fourth hidden story is that numbers offer the promise of conflict resolution through arithmetic. It is common wisdom among negotiators that irreconcilable demands can often be handled by breaking them up into smaller components and trading the parts off against each other. Numbers are a vehicle for dividing, weighing, and balancing, because putting a number on something makes it susceptible to arithmetical manipulation.

One of the most striking examples of this strategy is Justice Blackmun's majority opinion in the 1973 Supreme Court decision *Roe v. Wade*, the case that established a legal right to abortion.[10] To supporters of a woman's right to have an abortion, motherhood changes women's lives in a quantum fashion, so that their future life course is qualitatively different, not just a little bit more or less of this and that. To opponents of abortion, a fetus is a living person for whom abortion means death, not just a little bit less of life. It is hard to find a compromise between such absolutist views. After all, pregnancy and abortion are all-or-nothing states; a woman can't be a little bit pregnant, nor can a fetus be a little bit aborted.

In his opinion, Justice Blackmun acknowledged the fundamental importance of childbearing to women's identity and acknowledged that the Supreme Court couldn't settle the debate about when life begins. Then he made two brilliant arithmetical moves. First, he imagined these concerns as bundles of "interests"—a pregnant woman's interests in her own life, on the one side, and a state government's interests in prenatal life, on the other. Once he had made this metaphorical leap of conceptualizing the two concerns as divisible bundles, he could assert that it was possible to "weigh" and "balance" them against each other. Next, he divided pregnancy into three trimesters (as medicine had been doing for a long time), and asserted that as a pregnancy progresses, the state's interest grows larger in comparison to the mother's. "These interests are separate and distinct," he wrote. "Each grows in substantiality as the woman approaches term, and at a point during pregnancy, each becomes 'compelling.' " Continuing with his metaphor of a balance, with bits of "interest" being added and subtracted from the two sides of the scale, he said that during the first trimester, the risk of dying from abortion was less than the risk of dying from childbirth if the woman carried her pregnancy to term, so the mother's interest was heavier, or "compelling" in legal language; thus, a state couldn't interfere with her and her doctor's decision to

---

[10] *Roe v. Wade*, 410 U.S. 113, 93 S.Ct. 705.

WHY COUNTING IS POLITICAL

1. Counting requires decisions about categorizing, about what (or whom) to include and exclude.

2. Measuring any phenomenon implicitly creates norms about how much is too little, too much, or just right.

3. Numbers can be ambiguous, and so leave room for political struggles to control their interpretation.

4. Numbers are used to tell stories, such as stories of decline ("we are approaching a crisis").

5. Numbers can create the illusion that a very complex and ambiguous phenomenon is simple, countable, and precisely defined.

6. Numbers can create political communities out of people who share some trait that has been counted.

7. Counting can aid negotiation and compromise, by making intangible qualities seem divisible.

8. Numbers, by seeming to be so precise, help bolster the authority of those who count.

---

abort. By the beginning of the third trimester, the fetus had presumably reached the point of viability outside the womb, and so the state's interest had now gotten heavier and tipped the scale, or reached the "compelling point" in Blackmun's language. At this point, a state could prohibit abortion if it wished.

Like pregnancy, once a phenomenon has been converted into quantifiable units, it can be added, multiplied, divided, or subtracted, even though these operations have little meaning in reality. Numbers provide the comforting illusion that incommensurables can be weighed against each other, because arithmetic always "works": arithmetic yields answers. Numbers force a common denominator where there is none. They make it possible to reduce conflicts to a single dimension of size—big versus little, more versus less.

Finally, in our profoundly numerical contemporary culture, numbers are symbols of precision, accuracy, and objectivity. They suggest mechanical selection, dictated by the nature of the objects, even though all counting involves judgment and discretion. By the time we are adults, the categorization part of counting is so much second nature that we tend to forget we do it. One has only to watch a child learning to count to see how self-conscious, learned, and precarious are the categorizations adults take for granted. Numerals hide all the difficult choices that go into a count. And certain kinds of numbers—big ones, ones with decimal points, ones that are not multiples of 10—not only conceal the underlying choices but seemingly advertise the prowess of the measurer, as if to say he or she could discriminate down to the gnat's knees. To offer one of these numbers is by itself a gesture of authority.

MAKING NUMBERS IN THE POLIS

Counting of any sort is a complex mental process, but measurement in the polis is a complex social process as well, nothing like counting up piles of peas and beans. Numbers in politics are measures of human activities, made by human beings, and intended to influence human behavior. They are subject to conscious and unconscious manipulation by the people being measured, the people making the measurements, and the people who interpret and use measures made by others. George Washington knew he had this kind of trouble on his hands in 1790, when the numbers from the first census began rolling in:

> Returns of the Census have already been made from several of the States and a tolerably just estimate has been formed now in others, by which it appears that we shall hardly reach four millions; but one thing is certain: our real numbers will exceed, greatly, the official returns of them; because the religious scruples of some would not allow them to give in their lists; the fears of others that it was intended as the foundation of a tax induced them to conceal or diminished theirs; and thro' the indolence of the people, and the negligence of many of the Officers, numbers are omitted.[11]

Measuring social phenomena differs from measuring physical objects because people, unlike rocks, respond to being measured. Try measuring people's heights and watch how they stretch their spines upward. Measurement is something like a mirror. When people know

[11] From J. C. Fitzpatrick, ed., *The Writings of George Washington* (Washington, D.C.: Government Printing Office, 1939) 31:329, cited in E. J. Kahn, Jr., *The American People* (Baltimore: Penguin Books, 1975), p. 45.

they are being measured, they try to imagine the results beforehand. They do a kind of stocktaking, whether of themselves or their program, organization, or firm. Because measures always carry implicit norms, people wonder whether "their" measurements will meet the norms.

Measurement, like a mirror, triggers the natural desire to look good. People want to conform to their own ideals as well as to general social values. Measurement provokes people to "play the role" and to present themselves as they want to be seen. Such changes of behavior in response to being observed and measured are often called *reactive effects*, and reactivity is as pervasive among organizations as it is among individuals. Reactivity derives from two of the central features of the polis: influence and the interpretive nature of information. Since information is an instrument for shaping alliances and influencing others' behavior, it is no wonder that people try to control the impressions of themselves and their activities created by measures. And since people's choices are partly determined by other people's expectations and choices, it is no surprise that people try to give impressions of themselves as doing what they think other people want.

When something is measured, people tend to notice it more. Counting and measuring require looking and thinking, so the very process focuses people's attention on the things being measured. When the Head Start program was given a mandate to enroll handicapped children and required to submit enrollment figures, local directors started perceiving children as handicapped. One director noted, "We didn't know we had so many handicapped children until we started counting."[12] When the census added a category of ethnicity for Cajuns, the number of self-identified Cajuns shot up dramatically; as one commentator notes, "merely placing such an option on the census invites people to consider choosing it."[13]

The establishment of reporting and record-keeping mechanisms always brings out cases, as if the records exerted some kind of magnetic force on the things they record. Sometimes this happens because a formal count normalizes a problem thought to be rare, and so can legitimize something people were previously afraid or ashamed to discuss. This phenomenon is thought to be a major reason why reports of rape have escalated. Moreover, by creating groups, counting enables the victim of a stigmatized condition to come forward as a group mem-

[12] Robert Bogdan and Margaret Ksander, "Policy Data as a Social Process: A Qualitative Approach to Quantitative Data," *Human Organization* 39, no. 4 (1980): 304.

[13] Lawrence Wright, "One Drop of Blood," *New Yorker*, July 25, 1994, pp. 46–55; quote on p. 47.

ber rather than as an individual. Record keeping also provides a channel for reporting. Once an agency publicizes that it is keeping a count,
people turn to that agency to report instances.

Record keeping is especially apt to stimulate reporting in the early
phases of a policy issue. When a problem first gathers public attention,
reformers begin to collect statistics and compare the present with the
past. Every reform group needs to show that the problem it fights is
not only big but somehow new and not something that has been tolerated for centuries. Reformers actively seek out cases, and because
there is usually a relative lack of statistics for the previous period, the
proportions of the problem loom large.

Many public problems are in fact things that have been tolerated for
decades, if not centuries—alcoholism, child abuse, wife beating, elder
abuse, environmental degradation, unequal access to health care, poor
public schools, and congested cities, to name a few. Apparently dramatic growth rates in these problems reflect a decline in social tolerance of the phenomenon more than an increase in the phenomenon
itself. As people's tolerance for any annoyance diminishes, their perception of the problem grows, just as annoying noises seem to get
louder once we feel annoyed. Child abuse, some have argued, shows
such a rapid rate of increase because the historically high level of violence toward children is no longer acceptable. People define child
abuse more broadly, see it where they used to see parental prerogative
and discipline, and report it because they can no longer tolerate it.[14]

If dissatisfaction induces counting, counting can also induce dissatisfaction and the desire for change. Stepping on the scale leads people
to diets; surveying the wardrobe leads them to department stores; and
balancing the checkbook leads them to the boss's office. When communities or organizations do a survey of their resources, the survey
increases general awareness of problems and feeds demands for
change. Conventional wisdom has it that the British National Health
Insurance program got its critical stimulus from the army's induction
exams for the Boer War at the turn of the century. The army found a
high proportion of men unfit to serve, and the revelation prompted
political leaders to invest in health care as a way of strengthening
national manpower. Or, to take an American example, surveys of illiteracy and tests of students' knowledge almost always lead to curriculum reforms.

In public policy, measures are explicitly evaluative and are used to

[14]Bogdan and Ksander, op. cit. (note 12), p. 304.

determine how people and organizations will be treated. Therefore, when people are measured in the polis, something more than their self-image and their desire to please is on the line: their fate is at stake. Some measures evaluate performance—of organizations, officials, employees, firms, or government agencies. They are used to determine rewards and punishments. Other measures evaluate needs—of individuals for social welfare benefits, of firms for small business loans or special tax treatment, of agencies for budget resources, for example. These measures are used to legitimize or dispute claims for resources and privileges.

People thus have a strong incentive to manipulate measures in the polis. When teachers' salaries are determined by how well their students perform on standardized tests, teachers start "teaching to the tests," focusing their entire efforts on boosting students' scores. When hospitals are judged by the cost per patient they incur, hospital administrators dump the difficult-to-treat and uninsured patients onto other hospitals. When job training programs are evaluated by the proportion of trainees they place in jobs, they tend to select the most employable people as trainees rather than the people who most need training, and they eagerly place trainees in easy-to-find, dead-end jobs. In all these examples, no one actually falsifies the numbers. Rather, people change their behavior in response to being measured, and the changed behavior leads to results that are actually different from what they would have been without the measure.

Understanding reactivity is so important in policy analysis because, unlike deliberate falsification of numbers, it is an inextricable feature of social measurement.[15] Moreover, reactivity violates the canons of good scientific practice, on which all statistical reasoning is based. Scientific method assumes a strict separation between the observer and the observed. The subject of measurement should never measure himself or herself. To do so would be the essence of subjectivity, and scientific measurement pursues the ideal of objectivity, where neither the subject nor the observer has incentive or opportunity to manipulate the way a measure appears. In experimental research involving human

[15] One very influential, if not predominant, school of thought in social science aspires to eliminate reactivity in social measurement and thus to make the social sciences meet the presumed standards of the physical sciences. (In fact, measurement in the physical sciences is not devoid of some of these problems.) The classic work in this tradition is Eugene J. Webb et. al, *Unobtrusive Measures: Nonreactive Research in the Social Sciences* (Chicago: Rand McNally, 1966). I argue the folly of such a dream in this chapter.

Good title for paper

subjects, scientists use the term "blindness" to mean lack of knowledge about whether the subject is in the control group or the experimental group. In a single-blind experiment, the subject does not know which group he or she is in, but the observer does. In a double-blind experiment, a third party codes the subjects so that neither the subject nor the observer (measurer) knows. Double-blindness is thought to make for the most accurate, unbiased, nonreactive measurement. Measurement in the polis is more appropriately characterized by heightened vision on the part of subjects and measurers rather than by any kind of blindness.

Separation between the people being measured and the people doing the measuring is rarely, if ever, possible in politics. The vast majority of measures in policy debates are official statistics, gathered, analyzed, and reported by the agencies whose performance and needs they assess. Crime statistics are produced by crime-fighting agencies and housing statistics by housing development agencies. Thus, the measures often reflect as much on the behavior of the measurers as the measured, and measurers, too, have an incentive to manipulate.

The clearance rate, for example, is supposed to measure police effectiveness in solving crime. It is loosely defined as the percentage of crimes known to the police that police believe they have solved. The clearance rate can be raised either by solving more crimes (increasing the numerator) or reducing the total number of crimes known to the police (decreasing the denominator). Police, it turns out, have a fair amount of discretion in classifying complaints as "unfounded" or "suspicious," and these complaints are not entered as "crimes known to police." A man reports a burglary, for example, but police can't find physical evidence of a break-in and suspect the man really wants to claim a loss to his insurance company. Since police performance looks better the lower the total crimes and the higher the clearance rate, there are subtle pressures for them to regard reports as unfounded or suspicious. Thus, because the clearance rate is used as an evaluative measure, it influences the way police count.[16]

Even when the measurer is organizationally separate from the measured, such as when an accounting firm audits a business firm or one government agency monitors another, the separation is only nominal. The very fact that one organization is measuring another links them in a relationship of cooperation and influence. The accounting firm

[16] Jerome Skolnick, *Justice Without Trial: Law Enforcement in Democratic Society* (New York: Wiley, 1975), chap. 8.

needs the business of the firms it audits, and so must be responsive to its client firms' desires; and it is still dependent on the data provided by client firms. The government monitoring agency needs the cooperation of the agencies it monitors, both because it needs data and because the people in the monitoring agency would rather have pleasant working relationships than hostile ones. Measurers need the people they measure.

Measurers also have power over the fate of the measured, since measuring is done to help decide on policy actions. The census taker not only counts heads, but also determines the apportionment of seats in the House of Representatives and the allocation of federal revenue-sharing funds. The health inspector makes bacteria counts, but with them closes down restaurants and destroys reputations. The Antitrust Division of the Justice Department measures market concentration to decide whether to allow mergers and acquisitions. Because policy measurement is always linked to benefits and penalties, the measured try to influence the measurers, occasionally with outright bribes, but more often with pleading, cajoling, and selective disclosure.

Evaluative measurement sometimes makes strange bedfellows. A suspect who confesses to many crimes is more valuable to police than a suspect who confesses to only one, because the multiple offender helps "clear" several crimes at once. Police are more willing to bargain with a suspect who can potentially raise the clearance rate, by offering reduced charges and counts, arranging for only one of the offenses to go on the record, and promising immunity from prosecution for the other crimes. The use of the clearance rate as an evaluative measure thus actually reverses the hierarchy of punishments in the criminal justice system in that the multiple offender is treated with relatively more leniency than the single offender.[17]

A similar logic seems to have supported the Justice Department's decision not to prosecute E. F. Hutton executives when the brokerage firm was caught in an elaborate check overdraft scheme. According to the *New York Times*, the Justice Department "contended that Hutton's guilty pleas to 2,000 counts of mail and wire fraud were far more valuable to the interests of justice, including deterring any such practices by other companies, than would have [been] the prosecution of individuals in a trial that might have gone on for many months."[18]

[17] Ibid.

[18] Nathaniel C. Nash, "Rep. Hughes Criticizes Hutton," *New York Times*, July 12, 1985, p. D5.

The check-writing scam illustrates how, in a measuring relationship, the thing being counted can become a commodity that is strategically traded between the measurer and the measured. It is bad to commit a crime, and committing a large number is worse than committing a small number; but since guilty pleas are counted in the justice system as a measure of crime-fighting success, crimes become bargaining chips, and it is better for the criminal to have a lot of crimes to confess than a few. At different points in the investigation of E. F. Hutton's behavior, its executives had strong motivations first to conceal the number of check overdrafts and later to reveal as many as possible. On the other side, the incentives for the Justice Department were to collect a lot of guilty pleas for trivial crimes rather than to prosecute and seek to change a large, systematic pattern of crime.

This dynamic in which the thing measured becomes a strategically traded commodity occurs whenever the measurer is rewarded or punished for finding instances of the thing measured. All regulatory agencies are in this position. They monitor the behavior of regulated firms by counting violations. They may be encouraged and rewarded by Congress (with higher budget appropriations) for finding violations, or punished by Congress in a period of antiregulatory sentiment. Regulators may be rewarded by regulated firms with lucrative jobs for not finding too many violations, or for devising sophisticated ways of "counting as" that minimize violations.

A more conscious aspect of number manipulation in the polis occurs in the selection of measures from the vast range of possibilities. (Remember my elephant). If, as the saying goes, where one stands depends on where one sits, so does how one counts. In election campaigns, incumbents and challengers choose different measures of inflation or poverty or unemployment. One side wants measures to make these perennial problems look low and declining, while the other wants to make them look high and growing.

Congress and the defense agencies play cat-and-mouse games with measures of cost. The cost of the F-14 fighter plane (the Tomcat) has been figured at anywhere from $26 million to $35 million per plane. One measure is program cost, or the total cost for developing and building the planes divided by the number of planes actually built. That gives a very high cost per plane. Another measure is marginal cost, or the cost of building the next plane, assuming production is already running. That gives a lower cost per plane. Yet another measure is the hypothetical cost for a large package deal of, say, 1,000 or 1,500 planes, which turns out to give the lowest cost of the three

555 - Students needing help vs autonomy

measures.[19] I leave it to readers to guess which measure might have been touted by the Air Force as it sought original funding from Congress, which one was bandied about as Congress reconsidered the budget midway through the building program, and which one was thrown back at the Air Force by an angry Congress years later.

People in their role as fund-raisers, either as philanthropic leaders or as heads of agencies, always use measures that make "their" problems seem as big as possible. But once an agency has been in operation, allegedly working to solve the problem, its leaders also need to show that the problem has diminished, so that the agency will look effective. Thus, agencies might choose absolute number of cases as a measure of a problem early in the life of a policy issue, but proportion of known cases treated in later stages of an issue. And, agencies are very likely to present different measures of the problem to different audiences. For example, an environmental regulatory agency might count total sources of pollution to justify its budget, but count number of sources closed or number of disciplinary actions to show its own effectiveness.

Business firms, too, select measures to show their performance in a certain light. They want to look highly profitable to investors, but not so profitable to the Internal Revenue Service. Firms can manipulate the value of their assets by allocating depreciation. They can change their cost and productivity figures by how they allocate overhead and other fixed costs to individual products. If they have lost big environmental or consumer product liability suits, they can tally up estimated future payments, guessing how many suits they might lose, in order to wipe out their assets altogether. With the help of its accountants, Johns-Manville, a large asbestos manufacturer, used this trick to show bankruptcy, despite its ranking as number 181 in the Fortune 500 and its assets of over $2 billion.[20]

Measures tend to imply certain solutions to a problem, so people who have particular solutions to peddle will promote the measures that point to their solutions. Social workers benefit from such definitions of poverty as the number of broken families (another metaphor) or the number of families with children at risk of abuse. The medical industry is wont to measure poverty as the number of people who cannot

---

[19] The example comes from James Fallows, *National Defense* (New York: Vintage Books, 1981), p. 37.

[20] Paul Brodeur, "The Asbestos Industry on Trial," *New Yorker*, June 10, 1985, p. 49.

afford its services, the so-called medically indigent. Building contractors benefit more from a definition of poverty based on housing, such as the number of families who live in substandard dwellings. Educators tout measures of illiteracy as indicators of poverty. Farmers with surplus agricultural products might like a definition based on malnutrition. Economists, to their credit, are among the few who measure poverty as the number of people lacking in income. Measures, in short, obey the law of the hammer: Give a small boy a hammer and he'll find plenty of things that need pounding.[21]

Measures in the polis are not only strategically selected but strategically presented as well. Numbers never stand by themselves in policy debates; they are clothed in words and symbols and carried in narrative stories. Articles and speeches rarely say simply that a rate changed from this to that number. They give stage directions, telling the audience that rates "rose rapidly," "dropped substantially," "moved sluggishly," or otherwise behaved dramatically. Without these cues, we would not how to react to the naked numbers.

News stories about employment data provide great examples of number costuming, because unemployment is a double-edged sword. (It's good for unemployment to be low so fewer people need assistance, but bad for unemployment to be *too* low—any lower than 5 percent economists deem inflationary.) Because unemployment figures had been hovering just above 5 percent for the first half of 1996, policymakers awaited the August reports with trepidation. Would the unemployment rate trigger the Federal Reserve to raise interest rates again? When the news came, unemployment had risen from 5.3 percent in June to 5.4 percent in July, only a tenth of a percent. The economy had added 193,000 new jobs in July, "much more tame than June's huge gain of 220,000," said the *Wall Street Journal* with an audible sigh of relief. (Neither June's "huge" gain nor the average monthly gain of 237,000 jobs in the first half year probably offered much solace to the 7 million people out of work.) The story's lead played the numbers as a melodrama: "Somewhat subdued job growth and declining hourly wages in July offered the clearest signs yet that the economy is throttling down from the second quarter's torrid pace." Torrid pace? This was the same week Congress passed welfare reform, and directly above the story about the "benign" new unemployment

---

[21] This law probably has folk origins, but I learned it from Abraham Kaplan, *The Conduct of Inquiry* (New York: Harper & Row, 1968).

data was one about state governors "in a cold sweat" over "the unenviable task of finding full-time jobs for two million of the least skilled, least employable Americans."[22]

Numbers in policy debates cannot be understood without probing how they are produced by people: What makes people decide to count something and then find instances of it? How are the measurers and the measured linked together? What incentives do people have to make the numbers appear high or low? And what opportunities do they have to behave strategically? People change the activities that are being measured. They try to influence the measurers. The exercise of counting makes them notice things more. Measurers change the way they count because their measures affect how they, not only the measured, are treated. The things being counted become bargaining chips in a strategic relationship between the measurers and the measured, so that at different points in the relationship, there are very different pressures to reveal or conceal. The choice of measures is part of strategic problem definition, and the results of measures take on their political character only with the costume of interpretive language.

If numbers are thus artifacts of political life, and if they are themselves metaphors, symbols, and stories, are they "real" in any sense? Numbers are always descriptions of the world, and as descriptions, they are no more real than the visions of poems or paintings. Their vision of experience may correspond more or less with popular visions, just as realist, impressionist, and abstract expressionist paintings correspond more or less with common visions. Numbers are real as artifacts, just as poems and paintings are artifacts that people collect, recite, display, and respond to. But the dominance of numbers as a mode of describing society in public policy discussions is only a recent, and perhaps temporary, phenomenon in cultural history—not the result of some underlying reality of numbers.

[22] "Economy Shows Signs of Slower Pace; Benign Employment Data Lift Markets," and "Welfare Law's Work Rules Worry States," both in *Wall Street Journal*, August 5, 1996, p. A2.

NUMERICAL STRATEGIES IN PROBLEM DEFINITION

1. People react to being counted or measured, and try to "look good" on the measure.

2. The process of counting something makes people notice it more, and record keeping stimulates reporting.

3. Counting can be used to stimulate public demands for change.

4. When measurement is explicitly used to evaluate performance, the people being evaluated try to manipulate their "scores."

5. The power to measure is the power to control. Measurers have a lot of discretion in their choice of what and how to measure.

6. Measuring creates alliances between the measurers and the measured.

7. Numbers don't speak for themselves, and people try to control how others will interpret numbers.

numbers as one way to define problem.
measure what? how? interpretation?
need to categorize / draw boundaries —
imply need for action
create group (useful for mobilization)
numbers tell story eg of decline
of helplessness

numbers are authoritative
hide what goes into count
counting brings out cases.

8

Causes

> Men do not think they know a thing till they have grasped the "why" of it (which is to grasp its primary cause).
>
> *Aristotle's Physica*, Book II

Aristotle's treatise on causes speaks to a fundamental human instinct to search for the cause of any problem. We often think we have defined a problem when we have described its causes. Policy debate is dominated by the notion that to solve a problem, one must find its root cause or causes; treating the symptoms is not enough. Analysis of causes is so much taken for granted that it is scarcely mentioned in policy analysis textbooks. What most scholars have to say about causal analysis is that it is difficult, that policy problems are complex, and that we often lack a good understanding of underlying causal processes. But they are unanimous in their belief that one cannot solve a problem without first finding its underlying cause or causes.

The effort to define a problem by identifying the causes of bad conditions rests on a certain conception of cause. In this conception, any problem has deep or primary causes that can be found if one only looks hard enough and does enough careful research. Causes are objective and can, in principle, be proved by scientific research. We speak of suspected causes and true causes as though once a true cause is found, suspected causes are off the hook and the true cause, like the convicted criminal, bears some known relationship to the problem. Once "the" cause is identified, policy should seek to eliminate it, modify it, reduce it, suppress it, or neutralize it, thereby eliminating or reducing the problem.

Causal reasoning in the polis is something quite different from this mechanistic model. In politics, we look for causes not only to understand how the world works but to assign responsibility for problems. Once we think we know the cause of a problem, we use the knowledge to prevent people from causing the problem, to make them compensate other people for bearing the problem, and to punish them for having caused suffering. To identify a cause in the polis is to place burdens on one set of people instead of another. It is also to tell a story in which one set of people are oppressors and another are victims.

In the polis, causal stories are strategically crafted with symbols and numbers and then asserted by political actors who try to make their versions the basis of policy choices. Causal stories are essential political instruments for shaping alliances and for settling the distribution of benefits and costs.

CAUSAL STORIES AS PROBLEM DEFINITION

We have two primary frameworks for interpreting the world: the natural and the social. In the natural world, we understand occurrences to be "undirected, unoriented, unanimated, unguided, 'purely physical.' "[1] There may be natural determinants—the clash of a cold front and a warm front causes a storm—but there is no willful intention behind the occurrences (at least not without invoking a purposeful God). The natural world is the realm of fate and accident, and we believe we have an adequate understanding of causation when we can describe the sequence of events by which one thing leads to another.

In the social world we understand events to be the result of will, usually human but perhaps animal. The social world is the realm of control and intent. We usually think we have an adequate understanding of causation when we can identify the purposes or motives of a person or group and link those purposes to their actions. Because we understand causation in the social sphere as related to purpose, we believe that influence works. Coaxing, flattering, bribing, and threatening make sense as efforts to change the course of events, and it is possible to conceive of preventing things from happening in the first place. In the natural world, influence has no place. We laugh at those who would bring rain with their dances or sweet-talk their computer

[1] Erving Goffman, *Frame Analysis* (New York: Harper & Row, 1974), p. 22.

TABLE 8.1
TYPES OF CAUSAL THEORIES WITH EXAMPLES

Actions	Consequences	
	Intended	Unintended
Unguided	MECHANICAL CAUSE	ACCIDENTAL CAUSE
	intervening agent(s)	nature
	brainwashed people	weather
	machines that perform	earthquakes
	as designed, but	machines that run
	cause harm	amok
Purposeful	INTENTIONAL CAUSE	INADVERTENT CAUSE
	oppression	intervening conditions
	conspiracies that work	unforeseen side effects
	programs that work as	avoidable ignorance
	intended, but cause	carelessness
	harm	omission

into compliance. In the natural world, the best we can do is to mitigate effects.

In everyday discourse, as Erving Goffman points out, we use the term causality to refer to both "the blind effect of nature and intended effect of man, the first seen as an infinitely extended chain of caused and causing effects and the second something that somehow begins with a mental decision."[2] Yet in policy and politics, the distinction between actions that have purpose, will, or motivation and those that do not is crucial. So, too, is the distinction between effects that are intended and those that are not, since we know all too well that our purposeful actions may have unintended consequences.

These two distinctions—between action and consequences and between purpose and lack of purpose—can be used to create a framework for describing the causal stories used in politics. Each section of Table 8.1 contains a type of causal story commonly asserted in policy argument. The types are rough categories with fuzzy boundaries, not clear dichotomies. Once you recognize the different types, though, you can analyze how political actors strategically represent issues by framing them as different types of causal stories, or metaphorically, by pushing them around from one box to another.

In the upper right box are *accidental causes*. These include natural

[2]Ibid., p. 23.

disasters such as floods, earthquakes, droughts, and hurricanes. Here, too, goes anything our culture understands as belonging to the realm of fate—perhaps personal looks, some aspects of health, a person's good fortune to have bet the right lottery number or purchased a company's stock just before a takeover bid. Here we might also put machines that run amok—the car that careens out of control or the CAT scanner that crushes its captive patient. These phenomena are devoid of purpose, either in their actions or consequences. In fact, one cannot properly speak of actions here, but only of occurrences. This is the realm of accident and fate. Politically, this is a good place to retreat if one is being charged with responsibility, because no one is responsible in the realm of fate.

At the opposite pole politically are *intentional causes* (in the lower left section). Asserting a story of intentional cause is the most powerful offensive position to take, because it lays the blame directly at someone's feet, and because it casts someone as willfully or knowingly causing harm. In this kind of story, problems or harms are understood as direct consequences of willful human action. Either someone acted in order to bring about the consequences, or someone acted with full knowledge of what the consequences would be. When the consequences are perceived as good, this is the domain we know as rational action. But when the consequences of purposeful human action are perceived as bad, we have stories of oppressors and victims. One interpretation of immigration policy, for example, holds that the plight— and to some extent the sheer presence—of illegal immigrants is directly traceable to deliberate decisions on the part of American legislators and bureaucrats. Many politicians support permissive immigration rules for agricultural workers and other very low wage industries, and the Immigration and Naturalization Service accommodates the needs of employers by being lax in enforcing the law. Yet many of these same politicians, such as California's governor Pete Wilson, accuse illegal immigrants of flouting the law and of taking social aid they don't deserve, when in fact (the interpretation goes), American recruitment and underpayment of illegal workers is the cause of whatever problems illegal immigrants generate.[3]

In this box also belong conspiracy stories. Here, the argument is that problems are the result of deliberate but concealed human action. For example, congressional hearings in 1994 developed the line of argument that smoking-related disease and death was due not so much to

[3] Peter Shuck, "The Message of 187," *The American Prospect*, no. 21 (Winter 1995): 85–92.

personal choices about smoking as to tobacco companies' deliberate efforts to conceal scientific evidence about the dangers of smoking. Cigarette manufacturers advertised and promoted smoking, knowing full well that nicotine is addictive and that smoking is a health hazard.[4]

In the lower right section are *inadvertent causes,* or the unintended consequences of willed human action. (Actions often have good side effects, but I will ignore these, since politics is usually concerned with problems.) One type of story here is the tale of harmful side effects of well-intentioned policy. Here, the consequences are predictable but still unforeseen. Proponents of free markets and deregulation often tell such stories, whose gist is that knowledgeable economists could have predicted why government interference with markets would fail. Rent control, for example, is intended to make housing affordable but drives landlords out of the market by restricting their income, reduces rental housing stock, and raises the price of remaining housing.[5] Minimum wage laws are passed by softhearted politicians who want to protect the standard of living of low-wage workers, but any first-year student of economics knows that if the cost of hiring workers goes up, employers will hire fewer of them, and so higher unemployment will result.[6] The larger, more general, argument that governments inevitably make things worse when they interfere with private markets is an example of what Albert Hirschman calls "the perversity thesis," and as he notes, this is a common pattern of conservative argument against social change, whether the change is increasing voting participation, redistributing income, or expanding the welfare state.[7]

The story of inadvertent cause is a common interpretation of poverty, malnutrition, and disease. Accordingly, the poor don't realize how important it is to get an education or save money; the elderly don't understand how important it is to eat a balanced diet even if they are not hungry; and the sick don't understand that overeating leads to diabetes and heart disease. Inadvertence here is ignorance. Ordinary peo-

[4] Philip J. Hilts, "Scientists Say Cigarette Company Suppressed Findings on Nicotine," *New York Times,* Apr. 29, 1994, A1; and Alix M. Freedman and Laurie P. Cohen, "How Cigarette Makers Keep Health Question 'Open' Year After Year," *Wall Street Journal* Feb. 11, 1993, p. A1, A6.

[5] William Tucker, *Zoning, Rent Control, and Affordable Housing* (Washington, D.C., Cato Institute, 1991).

[6] For the story and a critique, see David Card and Alan Kruger, *Myth and Measurement* (Princeton: Princeton University Press, 1995).

[7] Albert O. Hirschman, *The Rhetoric of Reaction* (Cambridge: Harvard University Press, 1991), chap. 2.

ple do not understand the harmful consequences of their willful actions, even though the consequences are predictable by experts. These stories are soft (liberal) versions of "blaming the victim:" if the person with the problem only became more informed and changed his or her behavior, the problem would not exist. (A conservative version of blaming the victim is intentional causation: the victim actually chooses to have the problem. Many people, so the story goes, calculate the economic returns of working versus the returns from welfare, and choose to go on AFDC, and thus to remain poor.)

Another type of inadvertence is carelessness or recklessness. Problems in occupational safety and health are often explained in this rubric, although carelessness is alternately attributed to labor or management. In management's version, workers understand the dangers of machines or chemicals but decline to use protective gear and safety devices because their tasks are easier, more comfortable, or faster without the precautions. In labor's version, management understands the hazards, but does not monitor equipment conscientiously or provide safety gear, hoping it can keep productivity up without any undue mishaps. And in a more radical labor version, management knowingly stints on safety in the interests of profits, a conscious trade-off that pushes the problem into the sphere of intent.

In the upper left section are *mechanical causes,* which include things that have no will of their own but are designed, programmed, or trained by humans to produce certain consequences. The idea of mechanical cause is that somebody acts purposefully, but their will is carried out through other people, through machines, or through "automatic" social procedures and routines. Their purposeful actions are guided only indirectly, through an intervening agent. When, for example, a policy or program is implemented by subordinates who rigidly follow orders and fail to exercise their own discretion, problems might be understood as the result of humans acting like automatons.

In mechanical cause, the exact nature of human guidance or control is then at issue. Often, a fight about the cause of a problem is a debate about whether certain people are acting out of their own will or mechanically carrying out the will of others. To return to the example of malnutrition, a liberal causal story rests on unintended consequences of purposeful action: malnourished people do not know how to eat a proper diet. A conservative story rests on intended consequences of purposeful action: malnourished people knowingly choose to spend their food money on beer and junk food. And a radical causal story rests on indirect control: food processors and advertisers, in their quest for profits, manipulate people into eating junk food and unbalanced diets.

If the nature of human control over other humans is problematic, so is human control over machines. After a chemical leak at its plant in West Virginia, Union Carbide officials immediately blamed a computer for their delay in notifying local authorities. The computer had erroneously predicted that a toxic gas cloud would not leave the plant site. This was a story of accidental breakdown. Then the president of the company that produced the computer safety system said the computer had never been programmed to detect the toxin in the cloud, aldicarb oxime. "The computer worked exactly the way it was supposed to," he affirmed, changing the story to pure mechanism. He revealed that his company could have provided a more expensive safety system that would have detected the leak, predicted the flow of the cloud, and automatically notified local authorities, but Union Carbide had ordered only the "basic model."[8] With this information, it began to look like Union Carbide had intentionally stinted on safety, deliberately choosing not to buy a more comprehensive safety system while knowing that some hazards would not be prevented.

By the end of the week, the Union Carbide story had grown hopelessly complex. The injuries from the leak could be traced to a tank that wasn't designed to hold aldicarb oxime, faulty meters on another tank, defective safety valves, weak gaskets, pipes too small for the job, mistaken transmission of steam to the tank, failure of control room operators to notice pressure and temperature gauges, failure of the computer to detect the spreading gas cloud, failure of executives to purchase a program that could detect the chemical, and failure of government to regulate the chemical industry.[9]

The Union Carbide incident suggests a type of causal story far more complex than can be contained in the table. The ideas of accidental, mechanical, intentional, and inadvertent causes all conjure up images of a single actor, a single action, and a direct result. This underlying image remains even when the ideas are applied to corporations, agencies, and large groups, or to sequences of identifiable actions and

[8] David E. Sanger, "Carbide Computer Could Not Track Gas That Escaped," *New York Times*, Aug. 14, 1985, pp. 1, 18.

[9] See, in addition to the Sanger article in the previous note, Stuart Diamond, "Carbide Blames a Faulty Design for Toxic Leak," *New York Times*, Aug. 13, 1985, pp. A1, B8, and "Chemical Pipe Size Called Key Safety Factor," *New York Times*, Aug. 14, 1985, p. A19; and Robert E. Taylor, "Carbide Tank Wasn't Designed to Hold Chemicals that Leaked," *Wall Street Journal*, Aug. 16, 1985, p. 2.

results. Many policy problems—the toxic hazard problem notable among them—require a more complex model of cause to offer any satisfying explanation. There is a wide variety of such models, but let me paint three broad types.

One type might be called complex systems.[10] This model holds that the social systems necessary to solve modern problems are inherently complex. Today's technological systems, such as chemical production, involve parts that serve multiple functions, juxtaposition of different environments (say, high and low temperatures), complicated feedback loops, multiple human decision-makers, and interactions between different parts of a system. In such complex interactive systems, it is impossible to anticipate all possible events and effects, so failure or accident is inevitable. Failures also involve so many components and people that it is impossible to attribute blame in any fashion consistent with our cultural norm that responsibility presupposes control.

A second type of complex cause might be called institutional. This model envisions a social problem as caused by a web of large, long-standing organizations with ingrained patterns of behavior. The problem of cost overruns and "gold plating" in weapons acquisition—symbolized by $91 screws and $630 toilet seats—has been explained in these terms. The armed services operate with a basic drive to "have the edge in operational performance" over the other side. They believe that it pays to develop the best-quality weapons during peacetime because Congress will certainly authorize high-quantity production during wars. The different service branches gain by colluding for overall increases in the defense budget rather than competing with each other for a fixed pie. The services also gain by colluding with industry contractors to push programs through Congress on the basis of low initial cost estimates and coming back later for increased appropriations once there have been sunk costs. As one analyst says, "the causes of gold plating in its broadest sense are rooted in the institutional interests and professional outlooks of the military."[11]

A third type of complex cause might be called historical. Quite simi- 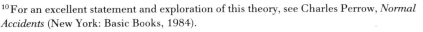 lar to institutional explanations, this model holds that social patterns

---

[10] For an excellent statement and exploration of this theory, see Charles Perrow, *Normal Accidents* (New York: Basic Books, 1984).

[11] Robert J. Art, "Restructuring the Military-Industrial Complex: Arms Control in Institutional Perspective," *Public Policy* 22, no. 4 (Fall 1974): 423–59. A more theoretical version of institutional causation can be found in Douglas C. North, *Institutions, Institutional Change, and Economic Performance* (Cambridge, England: Cambridge University Press, 1990).

tend to reproduce themselves. People with power and resources to stop a problem benefit from the social organization and resource distribution that keeps them in power, and so maintain these patterns through control over selection of elites and socialization of both elites and non-elites. People who are victimized by a problem do not seek political change because they do not see the problem as changeable, do not believe they could bring about change, and need the material resources for survival provided by the status quo.[12]

In politics, ironically, models of complex cause often function like accidental or natural cause. They postulate a kind of innocence, because no identifiable actor can exert control over the whole system or web of interactions. Without overarching control, there can be no purpose—and no responsibility. Complex causal explanations are not very useful in politics, precisely because they do not offer a single locus of control, a plausible candidate to take responsibility for a problem, or a point of leverage to fix a problem. Hence one of the biggest tensions between social science and real-world politics: social scientists tend to see complex causes of social problems, while in politics, people search for immediate and simple causes.

[12] An excellent example of this type of argument is Joshua Cohen and Joel Rogers' explanation of how capitalist democracy reproduces itself, in their *On Democracy* (Harmondsworth, England: Penguin, 1983), chap. 3; see also Arthur Stinchcombe, *Constructing Social Theories* (New York: Harcourt Brace, and World, 1968), pp. 101–30.

In politics, causal theories are neither right nor wrong, nor are they mutually exclusive. They are ideas about causation, and policy politics involves strategically portraying issues so that they fit one causal idea or another. The different sides in an issue act as if they are trying to find the "true" cause, but they are always struggling to influence which idea is selected to guide policy. Political conflicts over causal stories are therefore more than empirical claims about sequences of events. They are fights about the possibility of control and the assignment of responsibility.

MAKING CAUSES IN THE POLIS

In 1995, Massachusetts governor William Weld went to President Clinton seeking federal disaster assistance for the state's fishing industry, because the fish stocks in the state's water were at historic lows. The low fish supply put many fishermen out of work, but since most of them were self-employed, they were not eligible for state unemployment compensation. If the fishing industry were declared a natural disaster, fishermen would be eligible for unemployment compensation from the federal program.

In order to qualify for federal relief, a state has to show that its problem is the result of uncontrollable forces of nature. Weld therefore told a story of accidents of nature: fluctuations in water temperature and rising predator populations had killed off the cod, haddock, and flounder, he claimed. But many scientists, and especially government experts outside the state, countered with a story of human control. Overfishing was the most important reason for declining fish populations. Massachusetts fishermen were therefore responsible, at best because they didn't know better (inadvertence through ignorance), and at worst because they scrambled for individual profit though they knew collective resources were limited (intention, albeit only in the sense of deliberately ignoring information about harms). Moreover, said the federal experts, the Massachusetts state government was also responsible; it knew about the problem and should have done something to curb overfishing. The state's leaders, too, could be accused of deliberately ignoring information, hoping to help local constituents in the short run and to get bailed out by the federal treasury in the long run.[13]

[13] "Massachusetts Seeks Aid for Fishing Industry," *New York Times*, Mar. 22, 1995, p. A14.

Table 8.1 can be used as a "map" to show how political actors push an issue from one territory to another in the struggle for political power. Two positions are relatively strong: accident, with its story of no possibility of human responsibility, and intent, with its story of direct control and knowing action leading to full responsibility. Two positions are relatively weak: mechanical cause, with its story of human control mediated by other people, by machines, or by systems; and inadvertent cause, with its story of action without full knowledge. In the contest over problem definition, the sides will seek to stake out the strong positions but often will move into one of the weaker positions as a next-best option.

As one side in a political battle seeks to push a problem into the realm of human purpose, the other side seeks to push it away from intent back toward the realm of nature, or to show that the problem was intentionally caused by someone else. The side accused of causing the problem is best off if it can show the problem was accidentally caused. Second best is to show that the problem was caused by someone else. This strategy is only second best because anyone else accused of causing the problem will fight back and resist the interpretation, as Union Carbide's computer manufacturer did, while the accidental causal story does not generate a live opponent. A third strategy for the side accused of causing the problem is to show inadvertence, especially of the unforeseen-consequences variety. Carelessness and neglect do not look very good, but they are probably better defenses than planned or designed failures.

Books and studies that catalyze public issues have a common structure to their argument. They claim that a condition formerly interpreted as accident is actually the result of human will, either indirectly (mechanical or inadvertent cause) or directly (intentional cause); or alternatively, they show that a condition formerly interpreted as indirectly caused is actually pure intent. Crystal Eastman's *Work Accidents and the Law*, usually deemed the trigger event for state Workers' Compensation laws in the early decades of the twentieth century, showed that workplace injuries were not primarily caused by worker carelessness (inadvertence) but by employer refusal to provide safe machines and working conditions (intent). Eastman's framing of the problem is illustrative of the political logic in all these arguments:

If adequate investigation reveals that most work-accidents happen because workmen are fools, like Frank Koroshic, who reached into danger in spite of every precaution taken to protect him, then there is no warrant for direct interference by society in the hope of preventing them. If, on the other hand, investigation reveals that a considerable proportion of accidents are due to insufficient concern for the safety of workmen on the part of their employers, . . . then social interference in some form is justified.[14]

Rachel Carson's *Silent Spring* argued that deterioration of animal and plant life is not a natural phenomenon (accident) but the result of human pollution (inadvertence), and with this book, she catalyzed the environmental movement.[15] Ralph Nader's *Unsafe at Any Speed* claimed that automobile crashes were not primarily due to unpredictable mechanical failures (accidents) or even to reckless drivers (inadvertence) but to manufacturers' decisions to stint on safety in car design (intention).[16] As the leader of a widespread consumer movement, Nader popularized the notion that manufacturers design light bulbs, appliances, and tools to wear out so that consumers will have to buy new ones frequently. This theory of "planned obsolescence" is an assertion that a problem once thought to be unintended machine failure (accident) is really a case of intended machine failure (intention).

[margin note: tech designed for overconsumption]

A common strategy in causal politics is to argue that the effects of an action were secretly the intended purpose of the actor. The conspiracy story is one version of this strategy. Rational choice theory is another variant. Rational choice theory holds that whatever people do, their behavior is largely the result of conscious (or even unconscious) deliberate choice among alternatives. If people sleep in the streets or work in dangerous jobs, they must have chosen to do so because they get more satisfaction from those activities than anything else.

To assume that the effects of an action are its purposes is to commit what philosophers call the teleological fallacy. Purpose must always be demonstrated with evidence of the actor's wishes or motives, apart from the effects of his or her actions. Still, teleological reasoning is a good political ploy, because the person who turns out to have willed harm while concealing malevolent intent is a doubly despicable character; the symbolism of the disguised malefactor is a potent rallying cry.

[14] Crystal Eastman, *Work Accidents and the Law* (New York: Russell Sage, 1910); quotation is on p. 5.

[15] Rachael Carson, *Silent Spring* (New York: Fawcett, 1978).

[16] Ralph Nader, *Unsafe at Any Speed* (New York: Pocket Books, 1966).

The concept of risk has become a key strategic weapon for pushing a problem out of the realm of accident into the realm of purpose. Risk serves this function in two ways. First, when the (harms) at issue are bodily injury or death (as in food and drug regulation, occupational safety, consumer product safety, environmental pollution, or nuclear power), the probabilistic association of harmful outcomes with human actions is widely accepted as a demonstration of a cause-and-effect relationship.[17] If the harms associated with an action or policy are predictable, then business and regulatory decisions to pursue a course of action in the face of that knowledge can be made to appear as a "calculated risk." Similarly, business and regulatory decisions justified by risk-benefit analysis can be portrayed as the intentional causation of harms to others, or at least toleration of them, in the pursuit of benefits to oneself.

Increasingly, courts are willing to hold companies liable for calculated risks. This is the heart of the revolution in product liability law over the past twenty-five years. In 1981, in a suit against Ford Motor Company for its alleged disregard of safety in the design of its Pinto models, a federal appeals court first articulated the idea that a company could be held responsible for knowingly tolerating risks of injuries. The court construed Ford's business decision to trade off safety for cost as "conscious disregard of the probability that [its] conduct will result in injury to others," and therefore as "malicious intent."[18] The idea of calculated risk is central to some of the major product liability suits. For example, in both the silicone breast implant litigation and tobacco litigation, consumers (and some government regulators) assert that manufacturers ignored studies showing their products to be harmful. In these political conflicts, consumer advocates portray manufacturers as having *intended* to cause harm, because they *knowingly disregarded* studies showing some probability of harm to users of the products.[19] In

---

[17] On the predominance of the probabilistic interpretation of causation in twentieth-century scientific culture, see Jacob Bronowski, *The Common Sense of Science* (London: William Heinemann, 1951).

[18] *Grimshaw v. Ford Motor Co.*, 119 Cal. App. 3d 757, 174 Cal. Rptr. 348 (1981), citing language from *Dawes v. Superior Court*, 111 Cal. App. 3d. 82 (1980); emphasis added.

[19] On the silicone breast implant controversy, see Philip J. Hilts, "Maker of Implants Balked at Testing, Its Records Show," *New York Times*, Jan. 13, 1992, p. A1. A jury found Dow Corning Corporation guilty of "malice and fraud" after seeing internal company memos that showed scientists and executives knew of the risks but marketed the implants anyway. See Jean Seligman et al., "Another Blow to Implants," *Newsweek*, Jan.

short, then, predictable probabilistic outcomes have been transformed by reformers into conscious intent, and the idea of calculated risk is a way of pushing a problem from inadvertence to intent.

A second way the idea of risk serves to push harms into the realm of purpose is in the area of civil rights. In the early 1970s, statistical evidence became the primary tool to prove discrimination in employment, jury selection, schools, voting districts, housing, and other government service programs. Before 1971, the only way to win a discrimination suit was to show evidence of intent to discriminate on the part of an employer, a prosecutor, or whomever. In cases where a policy or rule did not explicitly mention race or gender as a criterion, this requirement usually meant adducing evidence of a person's motives and intentions, showing that a seemingly neutral rule was really a just pretext for discrimination, or showing that a rule was administered in an obviously discriminatory fashion.

In 1971, the Supreme Court for the first time allowed statistical evidence of a rule's "disproportionate impact" on a minority group to stand as proof of discrimination, without a showing of intent to discriminate.[20] Since then, plaintiffs could sometimes succeed in discrimination suits if they could show that the results of a selection process (e.g., for jobs, juries, school assignment, or public housing) were highly unlikely to occur by chance. If the risk of not being selected is higher for a minority group than for another group, or higher than it would be with random selection from a pool of both groups, then a court might find discrimination. Beginning in the late eighties, though, there was push in the other direction, when first the Reagan and then the Bush Justice Departments advocated returning to a standard of actual discrimination against a specific plaintiff. Some judges became less willing to accept statistical evidence of discrimination.[21]

6, 1992, p. 45. On the use of the calculated risk argument in tobacco litigation, see Dan Zegart, "Breathing Fire on Tobacco," *The Nation*, Aug. 28/Sept 4, 1995, pp. 193–196; and Dan Zegart, "Buried Evidence," *The Nation*, Mar. 4, 1995, pp. 11–15.

[20] *Griggs v. Duke Power Co.*, 401 U.S. 424 (1971). Duke Power Company required either a high-school diploma or a minimum score on an intelligence test as a condition for internal promotion. The Court found that neither requirement was related to ability to learn or perform jobs. Far fewer blacks than whites (proportionately) could satisfy either of these requirements, and so blacks fared poorly in job advancement.

[21] For good overviews of the legal issues and politics of the 1991 Civil Rights Act, see Andrew Rosenthal, "Reaffirming Commitment, Bush Signs Rights Bill," *New York Times*, Nov. 22, 1991, p. A1; and Linda Greenhouse, "Morality Play's Twist," *New York Times*, Nov. 3, 1991, p. 26.

The significance of statistical evidence in civil rights cases is that it broadens the concept of discrimination to encompass systematic or patterned effects, without a direct link to individual human intent and motivation. Civil rights advocates have long argued that economic and occupational differences between blacks and whites or women and men are partly caused by the lingering effects of *past* discriminatory treatment, even though there may be no discernible current intentional discrimination. In legal language, the concept of discrimination came to include not only explicit "discriminatory treatment" of minorities and women, but also behavior and rules that had a "disparate impact" on them. In effect, advocates successfully created the problem of "institutional discrimination" by pushing a causal story from the realm of intent to the realm of inadvertence. The acceptance of statistical evidence by courts as proof of discrimination converts "discriminatory impact" into the moral and political equivalent of calculated risk.

Complex cause is sometimes used as a strategy to avoid blame and the burdens of reform. When a group or organization comes under the fire and appears to be losing in the struggle to prove itself innocent, it may argue that the problem is really due to a complex structural cause and can only be solved by larger institutions. The widespread adoption of Workmen's Compensation in the early twentieth century can be seen as a successful move by employers, who were increasingly losing liability suits, to define the problem of industrial accidents as the "natural" result of modern technology and to socialize the costs through insurance.[22]

In the polis, causal stories need to be fought for, defended, and sustained. There is always someone to tell a competing story, and getting a causal story believed is not an easy task. Research on public opinion suggests that to some extent, people have stable, overall outlooks on responsibility for social problems. Roughly speaking, conservatives tend to hold individuals responsible for problems such as poverty, illness, and family breakdown, while liberals tend to hold society or its organizations responsible. But public acceptance of causal stories is also strongly influenced by the way television news frames stories. In general, when news coverage casts a problem like poverty as a series of individual cases and personal stories, the audience is likely to hold individuals responsible. Conversely, when the coverage is more thematic, discussing trends, making generalizations, and featuring com-

---

[22] Lawrence Friedman and Jack Ladinsky, "Social Change and the Law of Industrial Accidents," *Columbia Law Review* 67 (1967): 50–82; and James Weinstein, *The Corporate Ideal and the Liberal State: 1900–1918* (Boston: Beacon Press, 1968), chap. 2.

CAUSAL STRATEGIES IN PROBLEM DEFINITION

1. Show that the problem is caused by an accident of nature.

2. Show that a problem formerly interpreted as accident is really the result of human agency.

3. Show that the effects of an action were secretly intended by the actor.

4. Show that the low-probability effects of an action were accepted as a calculated risk by the actor.

5. Show that the cause of the problem is so complex that only large-scale policy changes at the social level can alter the cause.

mentary by experts, the audience is more likely to attribute responsibility to society at large.[23]

Being accepted by the general public is one test of success for a causal story, but the ultimate test of political success is whether it becomes the dominant belief and guiding assumption for policy makers. A causal story is more likely to be successful if its proponents have visibility, access to media, and prominent positions; if it accords with widespread and deeply held cultural values; if it somehow captures or responds to a "national mood";[24] and if its implicit prescription entails no radical redistribution of power or wealth. One major causal story—that the capitalist economic and political system is the cause of innumerable social ills—is consistently shut out.[25]

The political success of causal theories is also constrained by two powerful social institutions for determining cause and legitimating claims about harms: law and science. Law is a whole branch of government devoted to hearing claims, examining evidence, pronouncing verdicts, and enforcing them. Science is an intellectual enterprise with

[23] Shanto Iyengar, *Is Anyone Responsible? How Television Frames Political Issues* (Chicago: University of Chicago Press, 1991).

[24] John Kingdon, *Agendas, Alternatives, and Public Policies* (Boston: Little, Brown, 1984), pp. 153–57.

[25] For both the story and an analysis of the reasons why it is shut out, see Cohen and Rogers, op. cit. (note 12).

its own vast social and economic organization devoted to determining cause-and-effect relationships. And if law carries greater formal authority by virtue of its status as part of government, science commands enormous cultural authority as the arbiter of empirical questions. Not all battles over causal stories will be resolved in the court of law or science, but most significant ones will find their way into one or both of these forums.

Using Causes in the Polis

Causal theories, if they are politically successful, do more than convincingly demonstrate the possibility of human control over bad conditions. First, they can either challenge or protect an existing social order. Second, by identifying causal agents, they can assign responsibility to particular political actors so that someone will have to stop an activity, do it differently, compensate the victims, or possibly face punishment. Third, causal theories can legitimize and empower particular actors as "fixers" of the problem. And fourth, they can create new political alliances among people who are shown to stand in the same victim relationship to the causal agent. Let's look more closely at these different functions.

Bringing a condition under human control often poses a challenge to old hierarchies of wealth, privilege, or status. In the nineteenth and early twentieth centuries, many poor rural whites in the South were afflicted with a chronic sickness later discovered to be caused by the hookworm parasite. People with the disease were listless and eventually became slow-witted. Popular belief held that the condition reflected the laziness and lax moral character of the victims. When Charles Stiles demonstrated in 1902 that hookworm was the cause and that the disease could easily be cured with a cheap medicine, he was widely ridiculed in the press for claiming to have discovered the "germ" of laziness." The discovery was resisted because it meant that Southern elites had to stop blaming poor whites for their laziness and stupidity, and stop congratulating themselves for their superior ability to work hard and think fast—a supposed superiority that served to justify political hierarchy.[26]

---

[26] Deborah A. Stone, *The Disabled State* (Philadelphia: Temple University Press, 1984), pp. 93–94. The history of medicine is full of stories of resistance to discoveries that would make disease controllable. See, for example, Charles Rosenberg, *The Cholera Years* (Chicago: University of Chicago Press, 1962).

The abortion issue is a more recent example of political resistance to the extension of human control into an area formerly deemed natural. Much of the rhetoric against abortion is couched in terms of "interference with nature" and the "sanctity of life." Religious beliefs aside, the control over childbearing made possible for women by abortion threatens the social order in which a woman's status and social protection is determined by her role in the family; at the same time, it enables a social order in which her status is determined by her role in the work force. And in fact, women who actively oppose permissive abortion policies tend to be those who do not work outside the home and whose social identity is tied to motherhood, while pro-choice activists tend to be career women whose identity depends on work outside the home.[27]

One more example will show how a causal theory can buttress an old social order. The theory of maternal deprivation—that children whose mothers work suffer developmental deficits and delays—arose just as middle-class women entered the work force in large numbers. Consciously or unconsciously, the theory served as a brake on disintegration of the standard middle-class pattern in which the man is breadwinner and the woman is child rearer. Struggles over causal definitions of problems, then, are contests over basic structures of social organization.[28]

Such struggles are also about the assignment of responsibility and the burdens of reform. Any bad situation offers multiple candidates for the role of "cause." In the old nursery rhyme, the fall of a kingdom can be traced back through a lost battle, a fallen soldier, an injured horse, and a loose horseshoe, all the way to a missing nail and a careless blacksmith. In the real world, problems rarely come with such a neat lineage, but, like the leak at Union Carbide, always are replete with possible causes.

In the world of policy, there is always choice about which causal factors in the lineage to address, and different choices locate the responsibility and burden of reform differently. In the issue of deaths and injuries resulting from drunk driving, both our laws and cultural beliefs place responsibility with the drunk driver. There are certainly alternative ways of viewing the problem: we could blame vehicle design (for materials and structure more likely to injure or kill in a crash); highway design (for curves likely to cause accidents); lack of

---

[27] Kristin Luker, *Abortion and the Politics of Motherhood* (Berkeley: University of California Press, 1984), esp. chap. 10.

[28] This illustration is from Mary Douglas, *Risk Acceptability According to the Social Sciences* (New York: Russell Sage, 1985), pp. 53–60.

fast ambulance service or nearby hospitals; lax enforcement of drunk-driving penalties by police; or even easy availability of alcoholic beverages.[29] Grassroots organizations of victims, such as Mothers Against Drunk Driving, have successfully moved the issue beyond moral exhortation by looking for targets of responsibility other than the driver—restaurants, taverns, private hosts, and even governments. They have pressured legislatures to pass laws making hosts and servers liable for damages caused by drunk drivers, and lobbied to ban "happy hours" in bars.[30]

Even when there is a strong statistical and logical link between a substance and a problem—such as between alcohol and car accidents, handguns and homicides, tobacco and cancer deaths, or illicit drugs and overdose deaths—there is still a range of places to locate control and impose sanctions. Each of these problems has a virtually identical chain of causation: substance–user–seller–manufacturer–raw materials suppliers. In the case of alcohol, we have traditionally seen drinkers as the cause and limited sanctions to them, although sellers have more recently been made to bear the costs. In lung cancer deaths we have blamed the smoker primarily, but to the extent that people have sought to place the blame elsewhere, they have gone after cigarette manufacturers, not sellers or tobacco growers. With handgun homicides, we have limited blame to the users of guns, rather than imposing sanctions on either the sellers or manufacturers. And with drugs we cast the widest net, with attacks against users, sellers (importers, street peddlers, pharmacies, physicians), and growers.

Finding the true or ultimate cause of harms in these policy areas is not what is at issue. Rather, the fight is about locating moral responsibility and real economic costs on a chain of possible causes. The location is dictated more by the political strength of different groups (e.g., tobacco growers, the gun lobby) than by any statistical proof or causal logic.

Just as different causal stories place the burden of reform on some people rather than others, they also empower people who have the tools, skills, or resources to solve the problem in the particular causal framework. People choose causal stories not only to shift the blame but to enable them to appear to be able to remedy the problem.

[29]This observation is the starting point for Joseph Gusfield's insightful study of problem definition in public policy, *The Culture of Public Problems: Drunk Driving and the Symbolic Order* (Chicago: University of Chicago Press, 1981).

[30]Jilian Mincer, "Victims of Drunken Driving Press Suits on Drivers' Hosts," *New York Times*, Aug. 9, 1985, pp. A1, B5.

Political scientist Lloyd Etheredge tells a wonderful story about the problem of unreturned cafeteria trays when he was president of his high school student council. The student council, not wanting to get involved in policing other students but still needing to oblige the principal's request for help, chose to adopt the theory that offending students were ignorant of the consequences of their actions (inadvertent cause). That way, the student council could offer to run an "awareness campaign" without accepting any form of coercion. The principal, believing in the school as a training ground for life and having at his disposal a host of teacher-employees and disciplinary powers, adopted instead an intentional-cause theory. He asserted that students left trays on tables because "it wasn't worth it" for them to walk the trays back to the kitchen. Not surprisingly, he instituted a system of teacher monitors, moralistic lectures, and "the familiar repertoire of high school discipline."[31]

Like the famous six characters in search of an author, people with pet solutions often march around looking for problems that need their solutions. Causal stories then become mechanisms for linking a desired program to a problem that happens to be high on the policy agenda. Health Maintenance Organizations (HMOs) were promoted as reforms to increase health care for the poor during the liberal 1960s, on the theory that limited access of poor people to health care was caused by the inefficient solo-practice system of delivery. The same advocates of HMOs then pushed them to the Nixon administration as answers to the cost-containment problem, on the theory that high health care costs were caused by fee-for-service payment.[32] Similarly, urban mass transit was billed as the answer to traffic congestion during the urban-growth-conscious 1950s and early 1960s; to pollution during the environment-conscious late 1960s and early 1970s; and to energy conservation during the energy-conscious late 1970s.[33] Causal theories serve as devices for building alliances between groups who have problems and groups who have solutions.

Shifting the location of responsibility on a causal chain can restructure alliances. Under the old view of drunk driving, where the driver bore sole responsibility for accidents, the drunk driver was pitted against everybody else. In the new view, the driver becomes a victim

[31] Lloyd S. Etheredge, *The Case of the Unreturned Cafeteria Trays* (Washington, D.C.: American Political Science Association, 1976).

[32] Paul Starr, "The Undelivered Health System," *Public Interest*, no. 42 (Winter 1976): 66–85.

[33] This example comes from Kingdon, op. cit. (note 24), p. 181.

(of the server's negligence) along with the people he or she injured, and the server is cast outside this alliance. The relationship between taverns and their customers is altered, because all customers—indeed, especially the best customers—now represent a potential liability. Tavern owners may seek new alliances with other antiregulation groups. One can also imagine alcoholic beverage manufacturers facing a difficult political choice whether to ally themselves with the taverns (their most important customers) or with the injured victim and the driver (in the hopes that victims won't go after the manufacturers next).

Causal theories predicated on statistical association can create alliances by mobilizing people who share a "risk factor" but otherwise have no natural communication or association. An example is the DES issue involving women who took this drug over 30 years ago to prevent miscarriages, and their now-grown daughters who have developed or are at greater risk of developing certain cancers because of the drug. Organizations of these women sprung up out of nowhere as soon as the initial publicity about the DES-cancer link occurred. The trigger for Vietnam veterans' mobilization around the Agent Orange issue was a benefits counselor in the Chicago Veterans Administration office who thought she saw a pattern of illnesses and exposure to Agent Orange. She collected her own statistics, publicized them on television in 1978, and soon Agent Orange–based disability claims began pouring into the VA.[34] Dr. Irving Selikoff's early studies of cancer in asbestos workers stimulated unions to sponsor more studies, organize their members for research and litigation, and ally with other unions on issues of occupational safety. Causal theories thus can be both a stimulus to political organization and a resource for political leaders seeking to create alliances.

In summary, causal theories, like other modes of problem definition, are efforts to control interpretations and images of difficulties. Political actors create causal stories to describe harms and difficulties, to attribute them to actions of other individuals and organizations, and thereby to invoke government power to stop the harm. Like other forms of symbolic representation, causal stories can be emotionally compelling; they are stories of innocence and guilt, victims and oppressors, suffering and evil. Good political analysis must attend to all the strategic functions of causal interpretation.

---

[34] Peter H. Schuck, *Agent Orange on Trial* (Cambridge, Mass.: Harvard University Press, 1986), p. 23.

THE USES OF CAUSAL ARGUMENT IN THE POLIS

1. Challenge or protect an existing set of rules, institutions, and interests

2. Assign blame and responsibility for fixing a problem and compensating victims

3. Legitimize certain actors as "fixers" of the problem, giving them new authority, power, and resources

4. Create new political alliances among people who perceive themselves to be harmed by the problem

finding cause → ability to solve problem.
mechanistic and scientistic model

causes are contested.
/ assign responsibility to some actors
+ not others
this struggle is struggle over social structure

| mechanical / accidental |
| intentional / inadvertent |

} struggles try
to shift
bet. those
categories.

complex causes —— complex systems
—— institutional
—— historical

9

Interests

The quintessential political point of view defines problems not by their causes but by their effects. Who is affected? In what way? Do they know it? What do they do about it? Ask a politician to define a problem and he will probably draw a battlefield and tell you who stands on which side. The analytical language of politics includes "for and against," "supporters and enemies," "our side and their side."

The sides in politics are said to be "interests." They are groups that have a stake in an issue or are affected by it. Effects, in the language of policy analysis, are simply there to be discovered; they are underlying, enduring consequences of actions that exist whether we know about them or not. Interests, in the language of politics, are the active side of effects, the result of people experiencing or imagining effects and attempting to influence them.[1] Effects do not become important in politics until they are translated into demands. Thus, one of the central questions in political analysis of public policy is how, when, and why effects are converted to political interests.

CONCEPTS OF "INTEREST"

There is much political wisdom in the old proverb, "The squeaky wheel gets the grease." The proverb is usually invoked to show that it pays to complain, but there is another, equally important meaning: just

---

[1] I have used here what is traditionally a subjective concept of interests. An extensive discussion of subjective and objective concepts comes later in this chapter.

because a wheel doesn't squeak doesn't mean it has enough grease. The proverb captures a fundamental commonsense idea that there is a difference between real interests—what problems and needs people have—and political demands—what people ask for from government. Political theorists have put a great deal of effort into elucidating that idea.

affected ↓ action. why not?

One of the big debates that fueled political science during the 1950s and 1960s was whether people who are affected by something automatically translate their passive situation ("being affected by") into an active stance ("trying to affect"). The debate seems rather naive in retrospect, but suffice it to say that an influential school of thought known as pluralism held that if people were adversely affected by some social condition or change, they would organize to rectify the situation.[2] By now, most political scientists thankfully take for granted that the transition from passive victim to active agent is neither automatic nor easy.

The most important challenge to the idea of automatic transition is that people can be mistaken about their interests. To account for mis- > takes, political scientists sometimes distinguish between objective and subjective interests.[3] Objective interests are those effects that actually impinge on people, regardless of people's awareness of them; subjective interests, are of course, those things that people believe affect them. The difference is captured in our everyday language: we speak of "having an interest" in something to refer to the objective sense that people are affected by it, and of "taking an interest" in something to refer to the subjective sense that people actively pay attention to it.

When objective interests are "correctly" perceived and converted to subjective interests, liberals speak of political awareness and Marxists of development of consciousness. People might be affected by something but not realize it—a mistake called either lack of awareness or lack of consciousness, depending on your political persuasion. Or, they might not be affected by something but still believe they are—a situation called mistaken belief or false consciousness. In fact, the two kinds of mistakes usually go together: when people search for causes of their problems and mistakenly blame one factor, they usually ignore some other causal factor. So, for example, car accident victims may blame their own fatigue or slow response time (false consciousness) when in fact mechanical defects in cars are to blame (lack of consciousness).

[2] David Truman, *The Governmental Process* (New York: Knopf, 1951).

[3] Isaac Balbus, "The Concept of Interest in Pluralist and Marxian Analysis," *Politics and Society* 1 (1971): 151–77.

Objective and subjective interests are thought to be connected. As one political scientist says, "An individual's subjective interests are not merely given, or randomly generated," but rather are systematically determined by the way in which his life-chances are objectively affected by objective conditions.[4] Before we even consider how objective interests determine subjective interests, it is worth pausing to consider the meaning of objective interests themselves.

The concept has enormous intuitive appeal, yet people have had a terrible time agreeing on its meaning. One approach holds that we can identify objective effects of policies and situations—that is, what happens to people as a consequence of certain actions or policies—and that objective interests are the actions or policies that would serve people best, given these effects. But even this fairly narrow idea of objective effects is problematic, because one person at one moment is affected by innumerable objective conditions, each of which has multiple effects. The effect of food, for example, is neither unitary nor unambiguous: it satisfies (or does not satisfy) taste, marks some kind of social status, connects a person to a culture or tradition, provides (or perhaps does not provide) nutrition, and protects against (or perhaps leads to) disease, all at the same time. What can it mean to speak of a food's objective effect(s)? And food is just a simple case. War increases inflation but also employment opportunities; it increases death rates but also birthrates; it destroys a nation's productive capacity but stimulates it at the same time.

Another approach to defining objective interests is to identify essential human needs and assume that it is always in a person's interest to have those needs met and against his or her interests to have them denied. We saw in Chapter 4 ("Security") how difficult it is to define even minimum human needs. Food, water, and medical care come to mind as candidates for the position of objective interests, but they are quickly surrounded by troubling questions. What about severely disabled or terminally ill people who ask to be deprived of these things because they find life unbearable?[5] What about politically motivated

[4] Ibid., p. 153, emphasis added.

[5] For example, Elizabeth Bouvia, a young social worker afflicted with severe cerebral palsy, wanted to die and asked a hospital to help her commit suicide by giving her pain medication while she starved herself to death. Her doctors refused and force-fed her instead. See George J. Annas, "When Suicide Prevention Becomes Brutality: The Case of Elizabeth Bouvia," *Hastings Center Report* 14, no. 2 (April 1984): 20–21, 46.

hunger strikes?[6] Food, and more importantly staying alive, might be objectively in these people's interest, but certainly not everyone would agree. Individual motivations and attitudes toward something as "objectively necessary" as food make a difference in our assessment of whether having it is in someone's interest. If even at the level of life-and-death questions we cannot define some objective interest without imposing our will on others, if we cannot have biological survival as an enduring, all-inclusive, objective interest, it is hard to imagine how we can make the case for anything else.

An approach that seeks to avoid the problem of imputing interests to others defines objective interests as what a person would want or prefer if he or she had experienced all the alternatives and were free to choose.[7] This definition might be called rationality under freedom. It says that it is always in a person's interest to be free to choose, and we can know what objective interest is by doing the mental experiment of imagining what the free person would choose given all the alternatives and all the information.

The rationality-under-freedom approach raises all sorts of problems, not the least of which is that for many situations, people do not have all the relevant experience, so we (the theorists) or they have to guess at what those experiences would be like and what people would choose. Moreover, this definition leaves us with complicated questions about when a person is really free. In political society, where influence is pervasive, it is impossible to know and futile to think about what a person would choose without parents to disappoint or make proud, a boss to please or annoy, a network of friends to preserve, and a set of images of what is "normal." And finally, if we acknowledge that different people in the same circumstances and with the same information might choose different alternatives, we are back to something pretty subjective. To preserve the concept of objective interests, we have to

---

[6] See George J. Annas, "Prison Hunger Strikes: Why Motives Matter," *Hastings Center Report* 12, no. 6 (December 1982): 21–22.

[7] I have paraphrased here William E. Connolly, "On 'Interests' in Politics," *Politics and Society* 2, (1972): 459–77. His definition, more formally stated, is: Policy x is more in A's interest than policy y if A, were he to experience the results of both x and y, would choose x as the result he would rather have for himself" (p. 472). The article provides an excellent discussion of other concepts of interest, as well as some problems with Connolly's own definition. See also Steven Lukes, *Power: A Radical View* (London: MacMillan, 1974), pp. 34–35.

postulate that all people would choose the same. For anyone with a little bit of life experience, that is an implausible assumption.[8]

Up to this point, we have tried to define objective interests by considering the interests of individuals. The Marxist tradition in social science holds that people have interests as classes rather than as individuals, and that certain common situations—such as occupation, race, or religion—have an overwhelming impact on people's well-being and life opportunities. People have several facets, of course, but politics and history often render one of them far more crucial than others to a person's well-being. Thus, in Ireland, whether you are Catholic or Protestant is an overwhelming determinant of your life chances; in Mississippi or South Africa, whether you are black or white; and in Detroit whether you are a factory owner or an autoworker, as well as whether you are black or white.

The notion of group or class interests is as intuitively appealing as the idea of objective individual interests, but it, too, is fraught with conceptual difficulties. First, it is far easier to see common problems of a group than to see a common solution. Black Americans certainly have a common interest in ending segregation and discrimination; we might call this a "negative interest" or an interest in being rid of a certain condition. But it is not clear that they share the same interest in a single new situation. Some will benefit more than others from almost any new set of legal rules and selection practices designed to prevent and remedy discrimination. It is hard, if not impossible, to specify a positive group interest. (That is why all revolutionary tracts are far more satisfying in their critique of the present than in their vision of the good society.)

Second, it is hard to know what a group or class interest is unless there is someone to articulate it. No "general will" of a community has ever manifested itself without a human being (or group of humans) who claims to express it; and no voice of the proletariat or of capitalists has ever sounded apart from some real individuals who claim to be the "vanguard" or the "enlightened spokespeople." Someone has to articulate what class interests are and speak for them—in short, to represent them.

Even in the most conflictual of times and places, neither individual nor class interests are strictly determined by socioeconomic characteristics. A person may have needs and problems as a woman (gender), a

---

[8] Connolly (preceding note) might say that objective interest is different for each person—that is the central tenet of liberal individualism. But then the notion loses its meaning, for "objective" in its everyday usage means knowable by everyone.

black (race), a small business owner (class), and a parent (family status). Numerous political organizations clamor to represent her and her kind and to make her identify her interests in common with them. NOW (the National Organization for Women) wants her to see gender as the fundamental determinant of her life chances. The NAACP (National Association for the Advancement of Colored People) wants her to see race as primary. The Chamber of Commerce wants her to see her position as a small business owner as key. Mothers Against Drunk Driving and perhaps a day care advocacy group try to convince her that her role as a parent is central to her well-being. Moreover, her multiple roles might make her interests in any particular issue absolutely contradictory. A law requiring all employers to provide unpaid parental leaves hurt her as a small employer but help her as a parent, especially if she were married to someone with a good job so either of them could actually take the unpaid leave and they could live on the salary of the other. Each of these many interests is only abstract and hypothetical until it is defined and activated.

Representation is the process by which interests are defined and activated in politics. Political organizations, electoral candidates, officials, and representatives seek to describe an issue such as mandatory parental leave in ways that make it appear advantageous or disadvantageous to different sets of people. Individuals and groups, in turn, decide which organization or candidates to support depending on which portrayal they find more convincing. Representation thus has a dual quality: representatives give expression to an interest by portraying an issue, showing how it affects people and persuading them that the portrait is accurate; and representatives speak for people in the sense of standing for them and articulating their wishes in policy debates. The paradox is that what representatives say when they speak for their constituents is not the constituents' own words (figuratively speaking), but words the representatives composed and used to persuade their constituents in the first place.[9]

Interests must be understood as deriving from these two senses of representation, the artistic and the political. Groups, sometimes led by

---

[9] Hannah Pitkin formulated a different paradox of representation. On the one hand, true political representation requires that a representative must do what his or her constituents want, but on the other hand, it requires that the representative do what he or she thinks best. See Hannah F. Pitkin, "The Paradox of Representation," in J. Roland Pennock and John W. Chapman, eds., *Representation, Nomos* vol. 10, Yearbook of the American Society for Political and Legal Philosophy (New York: Atherton, 1968). See also her book *The Concept of Representation* (Berkeley: University of California Press, 1967).

CONCEPTS OF INTERESTS

Subjective 1. Those phenomena, social arrangements, and policies that people perceive as affecting them

2. Actions or policies that affect people *and* that the affected people understand as affecting them

Objective 1. Things that affect people, even if the affected people aren't aware of the effects

2. The actions or policies that would serve people best, given the objective effects and consequences of those policies

3. The things or policies that meet people's essential human needs

4. The things or policies a person would want if he or she had knowledge about all the alternatives and were free to choose

5. The things or policies that would increase the well-being of an entire social class (class interest)

---

outstanding individuals, deliberately portray issues so as to win the allegiance of large numbers of people who agree (tacitly) to let the portrait speak for them. In this way, the definition of interests is inextricably linked with the definition of issues. Whether one accepts the classical liberal vision of interests as fundamentally individual, or the Marxist vision of interests as fundamentally class based, representation in this dual sense is necessary to give life to interests.

In the end, although it seems there ought to be something that fits the idea of objective interests, when we try to find it, it disappears into the elusive process of representation. What matters in the polis is how the complex ball of wax that is "objective effects and conditions" is perceived, interpreted, and acted upon. Just as there is choice in politics about which elements in a causal chain to focus upon, so there is

Coherently

No on 200
didn't have a
face

choice about which effects of any situation to focus upon—and we cannot focus on them all. The problem in explaining how effects are translated into interests is to explain *why* some effects are selected and emphasized and *how* they are represented, both artistically and politically.

Making Interests in the Polis

In political science, the process by which effects and experiences are converted into organized efforts to bring about change is called *mobilization*. One of the enduring questions of politics is whether certain types of interests are more likely to mobilize than others, more likely to draw a large number of active adherents, and therefore more likely to win in the sense of finding expression in public policy. In everyday language, we want to know what kinds of wheels squeak.

Virtually all brands of political science and homespun political philosophies hold that some interests are stronger than others, but the brands differ by how they explain what makes an interest strong and mobilizable. Conservatives tend to believe that most important problems lead people to action, and if some do not, it is because they are not important enough to command scarce attention. In other words, all potential problems have an equal chance of stimulating political organization, but people ration their energy by paying attention to the things they care about most.[10] Liberals tend to hold that objective needs and problems will naturally lead to political mobilization unless the process is somehow blocked. Liberal theories look for temporary and artificial obstacles such as ignorance, masking of some problems by other, temporarily more important ones, and outright suppression of information. Marxist theories hold that the structure of capitalism privileges some kinds of interests over others. The fact that most people do not own and control any means of production other than their own labor systematically but subtly focuses people's attention on short-term material conditions, such as having a job or maintaining a standard of living, rather than on long-range nonmaterial effects, such as reduction of personal autonomy or destruction of community.

One theory of mobilization has captured the imagination of the entire political spectrum. It sees the *free-rider problem* as a major obstacle to interest mobilization. Most significant political interests

[10] The pluralist school of thought in the 1950s came closest to this view.

involve collective goods—goods, services, or programs whose benefits go to many people if they are provided at all. Individuals have little or no incentive to join groups and work for a collective good, since they will receive the benefit if others work for it and succeed in obtaining it (hence the term "free ride"). If the free-rider problem holds, then groups will be able to mobilize only if they can offer selective benefits to people who join—benefits that are individual and exclusive, such as subscriptions to newsletters, access to special information, or low-cost life and health insurance. Therefore, the types of interests most likely to get activated are those that satisfy individual and private wants.[11]

The free-rider problem is thought to be less of a force in small groups, where peer pressure and a sense of camaraderie in collective work are apt to overcome purely self-interested motives. Otherwise, this problem is thought to result from an inexorable logic of human behavior and indeed, the theory is often called the logic of collective action.[12] In contrast to the optimistic bias of classic pluralism, which predicts that all important interests will automatically organize, the logic of collective action theory predicts that none but the smallest or most individually oriented groups will organize. The essential point is that the theory purports to predict behavior on the basis of a universal logic of human motivation.

The logic's prediction is betrayed by reality. How can we explain the emergence and staying power of numerous large organizations that offer few, if any, selective benefits: environmental groups, antinuclear groups, pro-choice and pro-life groups, antiwar groups, coalitions for the homeless and the hungry, or even trade associations? Readers will surely recognize that the logic of collective action is a logic of markets, where individual traders exist outside the reach of influence, cooperation, loyalty, or the pursuit of common interests. If we start instead with a model of the polis, we will see several forces that lead to mobilization for collective interests and make the free-rider problem less formidable than market logic would suggest.

First, people exist in the polis not as autonomous, isolated atoms, but as subjects of influence by parents, friends, lovers, spouses, children, teachers, bosses, and general cultural ideas. Those relations of influence create structures of moral and social leadership, if not formal political leadership. Political society, with influence, cooperation, and

---

[11] Mancur Olson, *The Logic of Collective Action* (Cambridge, Mass.: Harvard University Press, 1965).

[12] The theory takes its name from the title of Olson's book (see preceding note). The exception for small groups is discussed by Olson, pp. 33–35.

loyalty as essential features of its structure, creates norms of altruism and ready channels for collective effort. People might participate in collective efforts because their parents do, because their friends ask them to join, because they are intimidated or shamed into joining by superiors, because their education and socialization make them believe in the value of sacrifice for the common good, or because collective action groups are a ready source of social contact. All of these are likely forces of mobilization in the polis.[13]

Second, participation in collective efforts tends to follow the laws of passion rather than the laws of matter. Even though the nominal purpose of collective effort is to achieve some result, the rewards of participation come as much or more from participation itself than from the achievement of purpose. Collective action in politics is more like a sports competition than a bargain hunt. One plays to win, and winning gives the game its direction and structure; but one plays even more just to play, and the greater satisfactions come from being in the game. Seen in this light, the costs of collective action (such as time and effort) are its benefits. Or, to see it another way, collective goods, because they provide the satisfactions of collective action, in effect provide selective incentives in the form of participation.[14]

Sometimes interest groups seem to form in waves, almost as if political mobilization were contagious. The 1960s was a period of blossoming interest groups and social movements, as were the Progressive era (roughly 1890s to the beginning of World War I) and the 1930s. These periods of vigorous interest group formation suggest that mobilization obeys the laws of passion in another way: that is, the energy for collective action feeds on itself. Groups set examples for other groups; they inspire each other with their heroism; they help each other; and the success of one group motivates others.[15]

---

[13] A narrow version of this argument says that dynamic and charismatic individual leaders can overcome the normally self-interested calculations of potential free-riders. Thus, Ralph Nader inspired a corps of law students and young lawyers to defend previously unrepresented interests, all for very low salaries. In this view, leadership can sometimes provide large groups with the social cohesion of a small group. See Norman Frohlich, Joe A. Oppenheimer, and Oran R. Young, *Political Leadership and Collective Goods* (Princeton, N.J.: Princeton University Press, 1971).

[14] For an especially illuminating discussion of this point, see Albert O. Hirschman, *Shifting Involvements: Private Interest and Public Action* (Princeton, N.J.: Princeton University Press, 1982), pp. 82–91.

[15] For an alternative explanation of this phenomenon of waves of public action, see Albert Hirschman (preceding note). His explanation rests on disappointment with private material consumption as the impetus to seek satisfactions in collective action.

According to a recent theory, relations of influence and loyalty, norms of altruism and participation, and a past tradition of organized cooperative efforts constitute a form of capital. Communities are best able to overcome the barriers to collective action when they have a large stockpile of these attitudes, norms, and existing groups. A widespread sense of trust comes from shared experience with other members of the community and encourages people to participate in collective efforts. Norms of reciprocity, of give-and-take and responsibility for the well-being of others, encourage civic engagement as well. And lastly, if a community has a dense network of voluntary associations, these serve as channels of participation for the collective good, so that a history of civic engagement builds on itself. All of these factors create "social capital," which, like physical assets or material wealth, can be used to harness individual energies for the common good.[16]

The third reason the logic of collective action does not always obtain in the polis has to do with the importance of symbols and ambiguity. The logic of collective action theory is expressed as a collective goods problem. But every political goal can be portrayed both as a good to be obtained and a bad to be avoided. Striving for a clean environment is also fighting against pollution; working for disarmament is also working against nuclear destruction. These labels may be flip sides of the same coin, but as symbols, they conjure up radically different images. People respond differently to bads and goods. They are far more likely to organize around a threatened or actual loss than around a potential gain. They are more ready to sacrifice and take risks in order to avoid a loss. Taking away something a person already has will stimulate strong emotions: anger, resentment, and a sense of injustice. The promise of something new is likely to stimulate fantasies, hopes, and desires, but when people are already used to living with the status quo, when they have adapted to it, hopes and desires are weak emotions. Hope becomes strong only when accompanied by a sense of deprivation, when the promise of something better is linked to perception of a deteriorating and intolerable present.[17]

[16] Robert Putnam, *Making Democracy Work: Civic Traditions in Modern Italy* (Princeton: Princeton University Press, 1993), esp. chap. 6.

[17] There are some interesting explorations of the relative strength of losses and gains as motivations for political change. Peter Marris, *Loss and Change* (New York: Pantheon, 1971) examines the topic from a psychological and sociological perspective; Russell Hardin examines it from a rational-actor perspective in *Collective Action* (Baltimore: Johns Hopkins University Press, 1982; and Amos Tversky and Daniel Kahneman examine the question of losses in utility theory using experimental evidence in "The Framing of Decisions and the Psychology of Choice," *Science* 211 (Jan. 30, 1981): 453–58.

The asymmetry of potential losses and gains in psychology and politics contrasts sharply with one of the fundamental assumptions of economic theory—that opportunity costs are equivalent to any other kind of costs. Opportunity costs are the imputed costs of not doing something, of missing an opportunity to use resources in some way other than the one chosen. Thus they represent potential gain rather than actual costs. The differences between actual costs and opportunity costs, between collective goods and bads, and between losses and gains are enormously significant in politics. These notions may be mathematically symmetrical, differing only by a plus or minus sign, but psychologically they exert different degrees of power as motivating forces. If a group can portray an issue in a way that emphasizes bads, losses, and costs, it can more effectively harness individual energies for collective purposes.

Another very influential theory of mobilization rests on the idea that the substance of an issue determines whether and how organizations get involved in promoting and expanding it. James Q. Wilson devised a widely used scheme that relates political mobilization to the types of effects that policies produce.[18] He begins with the simple idea that there are two kinds of effects—good and bad—and says that the way good and bad effects are distributed among people will determine whether organizations are likely to form and be active on an issue.

Wilson assumes (quite plausibly) that people are more likely to organize and fight hard about something that affects them intensely than about something that affects them only weakly. He uses the terms "benefits" and "costs" to describe good and bad effects, and the terms "concentrated" and "diffused" to capture the intensity or strength of policy effects. Effects are concentrated if they are spread over a small number of people, such as a tax on a particular type of business, and diffused if they are spread over a large number, such as a general sales tax. The degree of concentration also depends on how much of a person's life is affected. If a policy touches a major portion of people's time or resources (especially their livelihood), its effects are more con-

[18] James Q. Wilson has published at least three versions of his theory, each with some minor differences and modifications. They are: *Political Organizations* (New York: Basic Books, 1973), chap. 16; "The Politics of Regulation," in James McKie, ed., *Social Responsibility and the Business Predicament* (Washington, D.C.: Brookings Institution, 1974), pp. 135–68; and "The Politics of Regulation," in James Q. Wilson, ed., *The Politics of Regulation* (New York: Basic Books, 1980), pp. 357–94.

The general idea that different types of policies generate characteristic styles of politics was first put forward by Theodore Lowi in "American Business, Public Policy, Case Studies, and Political Theory," *World Politics* 16 (July 1964): 677–715. Lowi identified three types of policy–distributive, regulatory, and redistributive. *remediating civil rights abuses*

centrated than if it touches only a peripheral area of their life (say, a hobby or a minor tax deduction).

Wilson's answer to the question of what types of policy effects are likely to lead to political mobilization is quite straightforward: Diffusion of effects, whether costs or benefits, inhibits organization, whereas concentration fosters it. For Wilson (and many others who find his typology useful) what is interesting is how different types of effects create very different political contests. From the two dimensions of policy effects—costs versus benefits and concentration versus diffusion—Wilson derives four possible types of contests, which are shown in Table 9.1.

Two of these contests are equal matches—those between two sets of concentrated interests and between two sets of diffused interests. Issues of the concentrated-versus-concentrated type (quadrant 4) are likely to result in either stalemates or alternating victories for the two sides, since neither side is strong enough to dominate the other. Programs of the diffused-versus-diffused type (quadrant 1) are likely to expand gradually, since elected legislators have every incentive to hand out widely distributed benefits. (Why don't legislators have equally powerful incentives to minimize widely distributed costs? Because, first, they need to be seen as doing something for their constituencies. Simply not creating any new costs does not give them an active stance. And second, they can manipulate the image of these programs by publicizing the benefits and disguising and downplaying the costs.)

The other two configurations yield unequal contests. Concentrated interests almost always win when pitted against diffused. In the case of concentrated benefits versus diffused costs (quadrant 2), the group that stands to gain will mount a strong organized effort, while the larger group whose members stand to lose smaller amounts will likely remain passive and unorganized. For example, state legislatures often make laws to require that all health insurance sold in the state must include coverage of a particular service—say, treatment by psychologists or infertility clinics. The providers of these services stand to gain a vastly enlarged market of customers who can pay; their livelihood is at stake. The costs of these mandatory benefits are widely dispersed among all the people who pay premiums for health insurance. Assuredly the state association of psychologists or infertility clinics will mount a concerted campaign for such a law, while the millions of affected premium payers remain unorganized.

Similarly, with concentrated costs versus diffused benefits (quadrant 3), an organized opposition to proposed new costs will easily defeat

TABLE 9.1
TYPES OF POLITICAL CONTESTS WITH EXAMPLES

Costs	Benefits	
	Diffused	Concentrated
Diffused	1. Social Security Homeowner mortgage deductions	2. State mandated health insurance benefits Taxicab medallions Veterans' benefits
Concentrated	3. Food and drug regulation Environmental regulation Auto safety regulation	4. Union-management bargaining Hospitals versus health insurance companies Cable companies versus telecommunication companies

the hard-to-organize potential gainers. For example, food makers will resist a new regulation prohibiting their use of a preservative if the regulation substantially increases their production costs. Food consumers, on the other side, might benefit from a healthier (if shorter-lasting) food product, but probably would not find it worth their while to organize over such a small aspect of their lives.

The essential idea of this analytical scheme is that the distribution of costs and benefits of any program—whether they fall in a concentrated or diffused way—determines the type of political contest it engenders. Thus, it is very tempting to think that the distribution of costs and benefits is inherent in a policy, and that knowing a little bit about a program or proposal, one ought to be able to map it onto the table and predict which kind of politics it will generate. More often than not, however, a political issue seems to fit into more than one quadrant.

Social Security is usually considered as a classic example of a policy with diffuse costs (payroll taxes spread out over millions of employers and employees) and diffuse benefits (pensions, survivor benefits and disability awards to millions of people). During the 1995 debates on the balanced budget amendment, however, Social Security was anything but a quiet program creeping up gradually. Democratic opponents of the amendment claimed it would require deep cuts in Social Security and portrayed themselves as protectors of the program and its beneficiaries. In contrast to the nebulous beneficiaries of balanced budgets—all American citizens taking their cod liver oil—Social Security beneficiaries were portrayed as a concentrated interest, a group of identifiable people who depended on the program for the bulk of their livelihoods, and who were easily organizable by the American Association of Retired Persons. Whether an interest is concentrated or diffuse, therefore, is only relative. Politically, what matters is whether the losers or gainers on an issue are *more* concentrated than other losers or gainers on the same issue.

Now consider the example of tariffs and import quotas on shoes. If U.S. shoe manufacturers, a small producer group, are able to get tariffs on foreign-made shoes, they receive a significant benefit and the costs are passed on in pennies or dollars to the buyers of shoes. It is unlikely shoe consumers will mobilize, shoes being a small part of their budget, but shoe manufacturers have every reason to camp in congressional offices. This is a situation of concentrated benefits versus diffused costs (quadrant 2). But we could just as easily interpret this contest as concentrated costs versus diffused benefits (quadrant 3): without tariffs, American manufacturers bear the relatively high and significant costs of losing market share to foreign imports, while consumers receive the relatively small but widespread benefit of having cheaper shoes. The two types of unequal contests are really only one. The labels change depending on whether one looks at the issue from the vantage point of the status quo or the proposed change. But in either case, the contest is unequal.

Our ability to move Social Security and shoe import restrictions from one box to another suggests a fundamentally different way of looking at the relationship between problems and politics. *Policy issues don't determine the kind of political contests that occur, but instead, politics shapes the way problems and policy issues are perceived in the first place.* Problems do not have inherent, fixed effects that fall in a certain pattern, willy-nilly. Rather, a large part of politics consists in trying to influence how other people perceive effects of policies and proposals. This interpretation explains why issues seem to move around on the table as they are played out over time.[19]

[19] Indeed, Wilson is clear that it is the perceived distribution of costs and benefits that determines politics. "Not everyone will agree on the distribution of costs and benefits, opinions about any particular distribution often change over time, and occasionally beliefs can be made to change by skillful political advocacy" (Wilson in McKie, in note 18 above, p. 139). But his work focuses on what kind of politics follow once a perceived distribution of costs and benefits is given, and does not deal with how the perception of distributions is created and manipulated as part of politics.

Take the case of national health insurance.[20] When first presented
in the early part of the century, and then again in the late 1940s,
national health insurance was supported by liberal reformers who portrayed the issue as diffused benefits for the entire population paid for
by diffused costs in the form of broad-based, but small taxes (quadrant
1). The American Medical Association (AMA) mounted a campaign to
persuade physicians that their freedom was threatened: national
health insurance would make them government employees as under
the British system, control their fees, and restrict their therapeutic
choices. The AMA presented the issue as one of concentrated costs for
the medical profession versus diffused benefits for the general population (quadrant 3). With this portrait, the AMA mobilized physicians
and many of their patients against national health insurance. In the
early 1960s, supporters of national health insurance, including this
time organized labor, regrouped and came back with a proposal for
health insurance restricted to the elderly (Medicare) and the poor
(Medicaid). Now the issue looked more like concentrated benefits for
labor unions and their allies, the elderly and poor, versus concentrated
costs for physicians (quadrant 4).

Medicare and Medicaid were enacted in 1965, and as the programs
grew, hospitals and physicians appeared to benefit as much as if not
more than the poor and the elderly, because they could now be reimbursed for care they used to provide as charity and because the pool of
paying patients expanded dramatically. Hospitals and physicians, as
concentrated beneficiaries, had every incentive to keep on expanding
health services, perhaps even to provide unnecessary services, as long
as they could spread the costs over the large, unorganized population
of taxpayers. They allied to preserve the system in the face of cost con-
tainment reforms. The politics of health insurance had become a contest between sides with concentrated benefits (health care providers)
and diffused costs (taxpayers) (quadrant 2).

By the 1990s, the politics of health insurance had shifted yet again.
Many employers had cut back on offering health insurance benefits,
and many insurers were refusing to insure people with pre-existing
medical conditions. Meanwhile, expenditures on medical care were

---

[20] My interpretation of the political battles over health insurance draws from several
historical accounts: Richard O. Harris, *A Sacred Trust* (New York: New American
Library, 1966); Theodore Marmor, *The Politics of Medicare* (Chicago: Aldine, 1972);
Paul Starr, *The Transformation of American Medicine* (New York: Basic Books, 1983);
and Gary Belkin and James Morone, eds., *The Politics of Health Care Reform* (Durham:
Duke University Press, 1994).

growing and growing, while fewer and fewer people were covered. Expanding access to medical care with some kind of universal health insurance could be seen as diffuse benefits for the millions of uninsured people. But how would the costs of such an expansion fall? In a sense, President Clinton's universal health insurance plan was defeated because various opponents used the strategy of portraying concentrated costs to rally support from a variety of interests who might otherwise have benefited from the plan. Opponents of Clinton's proposal described the costs as falling primarily on employers (who would be required to pay toward employees' health insurance), even though the plan would have reduced costs to employers in many ways (for example, by pooling small businesses to get volume discounts). The insurance industry, whose medium and small companies stood to lose business to the Clinton insurance-purchasing alliances, portrayed the costs as falling on them, indeed, as threatening the survival of companies and the livelihood of insurance agents and other employees. These opponents of universal health insurance rallied hospitals and doctors to their side by casting the plan as one that would have Big Government intruding into the affairs of hospitals and doctors with bureaucratic rules, in effect telling medical providers they would be concentrated losers, when in fact, universal insurance could only increase money available to purchase hospital and doctor services.

As the health insurance example makes clear, issues are portrayed in terms of who and how many people benefit precisely in order to mobilize support for and against proposals. Programs do not themselves have inherent distributions of costs and benefits.[21] Rather, political actors strategically represent programs as contests between different types of costs and benefits. We can now look more closely at how conflicts between different interests serve to define policy issues and, simultaneously, how the definition of policy issues helps structure political conflicts.

---

[21] Roger Cobb and Charles Elder, in one of the classic works on issue definition, identify five characteristics of issues (concreteness, social significance, temporal relevance, complexity, and categorical precedence) and argue that as issues can be shown to be higher or lower on each dimension, they are more or less likely to mobilize an expanded public. They seem to assume that issue characteristics are fixed or given, while I would argue that their issue characteristics are really perceptions shaped by politics. See *Participation in American Politics: The Dynamics of Agenda-Building* (Boston: Allyn and Bacon, 1972), especially chap. 7.

How Issues and Interests Define Each Other

The theories of mobilization we have just examined are part of the larger quest in political science for an understanding of recurring patterns in the contests among interests. Are some types of interests universally stronger than others? We have seen two answers. According to the logic of collective action theory, interests that can be fulfilled with individualistic, divisible, material means will triumph over those that must be fulfilled with collective, shared, and nonmaterial means. According to Wilson's distribution-of-effects theory, the interests of small minorities intensely affected by something will dominate the interests of large majorities only incidentally affected by something.

Let us put these theories in a still larger context. The central problem in democratic theory is that interests that are regarded as morally equal might be politically unequal. The good, legitimate, and virtuous interests are not necessarily the strong ones; in fact, they tend to be the weak ones. Therefore, the good interests do not emerge naturally. They need protection. The role of government is precisely to protect weak but legitimate interests against stronger but less virtuous ones. Democratic theories differ, of course, in what they identify as the weak and strong interests and in the means they assign to government for protecting the weak. But they share these two central assumptions: that at least some important, good interests are too weak to flourish on their own, and that at least one important function of government is to foster these types of interests.

Notice, too, that this is a key difference between the market and the polis as models of society. Market theories share the assumption that some interests are stronger than others—ones that satisfy the most important needs of the most consumers. But they differ from democratic theories in their abiding faith that the good interests are usually the stronger interests, and that therefore the good interests emerge naturally in market transactions, without the "artificial" protections of government.

There are many schemes for classifying the good/weak and bad/strong interests. The contest is often billed as one between strong "special interests" and a weakly defended "public interest." President Carter decried "a Congress twisted and pulled in every direction by hundreds of well financed and powerful special interests," and in his farewell address, warned that "the national interest is not always the

TABLE 9.2
RHETORICAL CHARACTERIZATIONS OF POLITICAL CONTESTS

Good weak interests		Strong bad interests
collective		individualistic
diffused		concentrated
broad		narrow
long-term	vs.	short-term
spiritual		material
social		economic
public		special
workers		capitalists

sum of all our single or special interests."[22] In American political discourse, to label something as a special interest is merely a way of denigrating it by subtly opposing it to an unspecified, hypothetical general interest. Table 9.2 lists some other characterizations of this grand political contest.

The underlying story in all these portrayals is that a small, selfish concern is able to dominate a larger, more virtuous concern. The interests on the right-hand side of the table are not necessarily bad because they are inherently evil, or even illegitimate interests. They might be bad simply because they are strong enough to squeeze out other more legitimate interests. The important point is that each pair is a vision of an unequal political contest.

In any political contest, both sides try to amass the most power, but it is always the weaker side, the underdog, who seeks to bring in outside help. In American political culture, where government is viewed as properly a referee rather than a strong power itself, the most important source of outside help is government. Ironically, then, portraying one's own side as weaker becomes strategically useful in order to attract both broad support from bystander groups and support of the government to one's side.

Defining an issue thus becomes a strategically complicated problem. For purposes of gaining active support of powerful groups, it is useful to portray the issue as involving highly concentrated costs or benefits to those groups, just as opponents of the Clinton health reform did. To take a sweeter example, a coalition seeking to expand the period of daylight saving time made sure that October 31—Halloween—was

[22] Speeches reported in *Boston Globe*, July 16, 1979, and Jan. 15, 1981, and cited in Graham Wooten, *Interest Groups: Policy and Politics in America* (Englewood Cliffs, N.J.: Prentice-Hall, 1985), p. 4.

included in the proposed new period, and then contacted candy man facturers to join the coalition.[23] Here is a case where the definition the issue—the boundary between standard and daylight saving time—was literally chosen to draw a particular group to one side.

For purposes of attracting the support of bystander groups, however, it pays to look like the weaker, public-spirited side rather than the stronger side defending intense but narrowly distributed interests. Making a particular interest appear to be in the interest of the general public is a classic political strategy, captured in the famous assertion of Charles Wilson that "what's good for General Motors is good for the country." Thus, when Bill and Hillary Clinton launched their health insurance reform campaign with an attack on the profiteering pharmaceutical industry, the industry responded with a huge public advertising campaign portraying drug companies as humanitarian sponsors of medical research and discoverers of cures; selling drugs seemed to be only a minor sideline.[24]

Rx R&D as public good

There are several strategies by which groups define issues so as to make a sectional (concentrated) interest appear general. One is to disaggregate the alleged special interest—to show that a single political actor accused of being self-interested is really composed of a large number of ordinary and average citizens. Proponents of environmental regulation often portray utility companies as obtaining large benefits (for example cheap, high-sulfur coal and corresponding higher profits) at the expense of the general public (people harmed by deterioration of lakes and plant life). Utility companies resist this portrayal, depicting themselves instead as shareholder companies owned by grandmothers, widows, and hardworking Americans who would bear the costs of regulation in reduced value of their investment. Meanwhile, the benefits of lower emissions would go to a small, elite group of outdoor enthusiasts and people with second homes who have the time and money to fish and climb mountains.

Another strategy is just the opposite—to transform what appear to be narrow, concentrated interests by aggregating potential winners or losers into a much broader class of "everyman." When Congress moved to dismantle the federal school lunch program in 1995, calling it wasteful and bureaucratic, children's advocates were naturally the first to squawk. But the program's defenders didn't stop at naming

[23] Arlen J. Large, "Congress Again Tinkers with Daylight Time; Candy Lobby Has a Big Hand in This Clock War," *Wall Street Journal*, July 22, 1985, p. 40.

[24] Rick Warzman, "Drug Firms' Lobbying to Defuse Criticism by Clinton's Pays Off," *Wall Street Journal*, Aug. 16, 1994, p. 1.

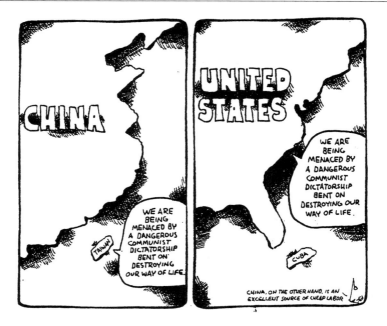

children as the only losers. They fought back by identifying the 200,000 program employees who would be laid off, the thousands of small businesses such as bakers and dairies who would suffer and probably lay off more employees, and the millions of ordinary taxpayers who would have to make up for the losses in payroll taxes from those now-unemployed workers.[25]

Similarly, economic interests can be transformed into social: Protection from foreign competition saves jobs, thereby saving communities. Agricultural price supports and farm loans save a "way of life," not an industry. Sole-source defense contracts, while appearing to provide monopoly guarantees to defense companies, actually build a stable national capacity to make specialized equipment.

In a similar vein, immediate short-term interests can be portrayed as long-run interests. Aid to industry is almost always portrayed as an emergency stabilization measure necessary for more thoroughgoing long-term restructuring. Public assistance, to be politically viable, must be shown as "a hand up, not a handout," President Clinton's metaphor for changing poor people's earning capacity instead of solving their immediate economic crisis.

Problems are defined in politics to accomplish political goals—to mobilize support for one side in a conflict. To define an issue is to

[25] Peter Viebling, letter to the editor, *New York Times*, March 2, 1995, p. A22.

make an assertion about what is at stake and who is affected, and therefore, to define interests and the constitution of alliances. There is no such thing as an apolitical problem definition. In confronting any definition of a policy problem, the astute analyst needs to ask how that definition also defines interested parties and stakes, how it allocates the roles of bully and underdog, and how a different definition would change power relations.

what is at stake?
who is affected? — diffused or conc.
costs/benefits?
interests try to appear as weak
public interest

why/how mobilization does/does not
occur

10

Decisions

It's not so easy to be president of the United States: "I listen to one side and they seem right, and then I talk to the other side, and they seem just as right, and there I am where I started . . . God, what a job!" Waffling, it seems, was a problem long before the 1990s, for this description of the anguish of decision making comes from Warren Harding, president from 1920 to 1924.[1] Like any president, we experience policy problems, if we are sentient creatures, as the need to act and the pressure to decide: "What should I do?" or "How can I help?"

In the realm of human experience, there are many ways to make decisions: by habit, social custom, impulse, intuition, or procrastination; by consensus, delegation, bargaining, mediation, trial, voting, or flipping a coin. The hallmark of contemporary policy analysis is its focus on rational methods of decision making. Problems are cast as a choice between alternative means for achieving a goal, and rationality means simply choosing the best means to attain a given goal.

In this approach, all policy problems become subspecies of a single metaproblem: how to make a decision that will attain given goals. These models of decision are prescriptive, rather than descriptive or predictive; they define policy problems as decisions, and they purport to show the best decision to solve a problem.[2] The main variants of this

[1] Quoted in Emmet John Hughes, *The Living Presidency* (New York: Coward, McGann & Geohegan, Inc., 1973), p. 135.

[2] A closely related type of model, often called "choice" or "public choice" or "economic," is used to explain behavior rather than to represent problems and prescribe solutions. Choice models are used, for example, to explain the behavior of organizations, nations,

approach are cost-benefit analysis, risk-benefit analysis, and decision analysis.

THE CONCEPT OF RATIONAL DECISION

A rational decision model portrays a policy problem as a choice facing a political actor. The actor is someone—an individual, a firm, an organization, or any entity capable of making a decision—who must choose a course of action in order to attain a desired end. The actor then goes through a sequence of mental operations to arrive at a decision. These steps are: (1) defining goals, (2) imagining alternative means for attaining them, (3) evaluating the consequences of taking each course of action, and (4) choosing the alternative most likely to attain the goal.

Stated simply, the model of rational decision sounds like speaking prose. We all do it every day without thinking, when we are not deciding by habit, intuition, voting, or other ways. But carried to its logical extreme, the ideal of perfect rationality would require a person to consider all possible alternatives (an infinite number), and evaluate all the possible consequences of each. He or she would soon become afflicted with "analysis paralysis" and would probably never make a decision at all. Rationality theorists, therefore, tend to assume that people operate with bounded or limited rationality. People consider only some alternatives, have limited information, and stop searching for a solution when they have found a satisfactory one, instead of holding out for the absolute best course of action.[3] The perfectly rational decision maker is to politics what the saint is to religion—an ideal everyone publicly espouses, most people would not want to live by, and precious few attain.

Decision models generally do not deal explicitly with steps 1 and 2. They assume the actor already has goals, knows what they are, and

---

or many individuals interacting within a group, and they are used either to explain past behavior or to predict future behavior. This chapter is not concerned with these descriptive and predictive choice models, simply because they are not themselves about the framing of policy issues. The classic political science introduction to this field is by James Buchanan and Gordon Tullock, *The Calculus of Consent* (Ann Arbor: University of Michigan Press, 1962). An excellent critical review of the literature is Donald Green and Ian Shapiro's *Pathologies of Rational Choice* (New Haven: Yale University Press, 1994).

[3] The concept of bounded rationality was developed by Herbert Simon in *Administrative Behavior* (New York: Free Press, 1947). For a recent collection of his essays, see his *Models of Bounded Rationality* (Cambridge, Mass.: MIT Press, 1982).

can articulate them. (Theories of political interests, by contrast, focus on exactly this question of where people get their goals.) Decision models concern themselves neither with where the alternatives come from nor which ones will be considered as possible candidates for the actor's choice. Instead, these models zoom in on step 3, assessing consequences. The essence of the model is to tally up the consequences of different alternatives and choose the one that yields the best results.

In all decision models, the decision in step 4 is made on the basis of a single criterion—*maximum total welfare.* Sometimes the criterion is called "satisfaction" or "well-being" or "utility," but the idea is the same: The decision maker should choose the alternative that maximizes overall welfare. If the decision maker is an individual, he or she should decide according to his or her own welfare. If the decision maker is an agent for an organization, a leader, or a policy maker, then the criterion should be the overall welfare of the entity in question. (Decision models, like the market model, define the welfare of an entity as simply the aggregate of individuals' welfare, an assumption we examined earlier.) Even though a decision might be very complicated and involve many factors, all considerations must ultimately be translated into a single scale or common denominator in order to yield a single measure of total welfare.

Decision models also assume that all the relevant considerations in a decision can be captured as *consequences* of the various alternatives. If we think that there are important considerations besides the consequences of actions, then to that extent the model will be unsatisfactory. One such consideration is moral principles and duties. Many philosophers of both the academic and armchair variety believe that certain actions whose costs outweigh their benefits are morally right and therefore should be taken nevertheless.[4]

Another consideration besides a decision's consequences is the very process of making a decision: sometimes we value the way a decision is made more than its outcome. People value town meetings not because they render correct decisions but because they offer individuals a chance to participate in making policy decisions. The process of deciding even affects the way we evaluate a decision's outcome. A decision whether to parole a prisoner seems qualitatively better and fairer if the process allows knowledgeable people to speak to his or her character than if it does not, regardless of the outcome of the decision. We might feel differently about an all-female jury convicting a male

[4]See Steven Kelman, "Cost-Benefit Analysis: An Ethical Critique," *Regulation,* January / February 1981: 33–40.

of rape if the prosecutor had systematically rejected all prospective male jurors than if the jury were composed by a random draw from the jury list.[5]

With this general picture of decision models, we can briefly describe the main variations. *Cost-benefit analysis* is probably the most widely used in both public policy and private lives. It consists in tallying up the negative and positive consequences of an action to see whether, on balance, the action will lead to a gain or a loss. The decision is then made according to a single criterion or rule: Take the action if its benefits outweigh its costs; or, in the mathematical language common to the genre, "Take the action if and only if net benefits are greater than zero." If the decision concerns not merely whether to take one course of action but which of several possible actions to take, the process is the same and the decision rule is: Take the action that yields the greatest net benefit.

You have probably used this method in your own decisions, if not in a formal quantitative way, at least by listing the "pluses" and "minuses" of an action you were considering. The only difference between your list of pluses and minuses and the formal cost-benefit analysis done by policy analysts is that the analysts have added numbers to theirs. For every plus and minus listed, they think of a way to measure it. And while you might be satisfied with an intuitive feel from your list as to whether the action is "worth it," formal analysts force themselves to measure all the consequences in the same terms so that the measures can be added up. The analyst is a stickler for arithmetic.

In cost-benefit analysis, the measures are usually dollars, since the impetus for the analysis is the puzzle of how best to spend money. Cost-benefit analysis is used to answer questions such as, "Is it worth investing in a major national campaign to reduce high blood pressure?" or "Is it worth requiring automobile manufacturers to equip cars with air bags?" An analysis would tally up the dollar costs and dollar benefits of the program or regulation, and give an answer.

When the consequences of an action are intangibles such as death, damaged political reputation, decline of a city, or destruction of a wilderness area, they must still be measured and valued in order to be used in cost-benefit analysis. Often such intangible factors are just left out, for lack of a convincing way to measure them, and the pressure to omit them is a major criticism of the method. At the other extreme, intangible elements of problems are often forced into the procrustean

[5] An excellent exposition of this criticism is made by Laurence H. Tribe in "Policy Science: Analysis or Ideology?" *Philosophy and Public Affairs* 2 (1972): 66–110.

bed of the analysis. One of the most controversial areas of cost-benefit analysis is health and safety regulation, where the consequences of policy choices are injuries, diseases, and deaths on one side, and health, longevity, and quality of life on the other. Analysts have come up with techniques for measuring the dollar value of a human life or the dollar cost of a permanent physical injury. This sort of thinking leads to pronouncements that (for example) the life of a construction worker is worth $650,000 and a safety standard should not be adopted if it will cost more than that for each life it saves.[6]

With many policy problems, the consequences we care most about are not the immediate ones but possible future effects that we are not even sure will materialize. For example, a new drug might have bad side effects years after its use, or a new weapon might turn out to be unreliable on the battlefield. Environmental, safety, and health regulation are all beset by problems involving uncertainty; that is, we have a suspicion, or a fear, or even some suggestive evidence that bad things will happen, but we do not know for sure. For these kinds of problems, *risk-benefit analysis* (or simply *risk analysis*) can be used to formulate the decision whether to undertake an action. It works exactly like cost-benefit analysis—you tally up the pluses and minuses—except that here the minuses incorporate measures of the *likelihood* of negative effects as well as of their magnitude. So, for example, if a new drug has a 10 percent chance of killing 100 people, its *expected cost* would be estimated at 10 lives (10 percent of 100 people).

The calculation of cost estimates in risk analysis is both simple and profound. The procedure is based on elementary arithmetic. Multiply a measure of the magnitude of an outcome, such as dollars or lives lost, by a decimal fraction that expresses its probability of happening. Since risk problems always involve probabilities of less than 100 percent (if the chance of happening were 100 percent, the event would be certain and it wouldn't be a risk problem), this *multiplication always reduces the original measure of magnitude.*

Here comes the profound part: *The technique builds in an assump-*

---

[6] Sometimes although the results we care about are not easily measurable in dollars, we want to compare several programs that have the same type of effects—for example, different safety programs designed to save lives, or management innovations that seek to raise worker productivity. For such problems, *cost-effectiveness* analysis defines the benefits in nondollar measures, such as number of lives saved or output per labor hour, and then compares the cost per unit of effectiveness of several programs. The decision rule here is: Choose the program with the lowest cost per unit of effectiveness.

assumption.

tion that a bad result is less bad if it is not certain to occur. Even if a result is 99 percent likely to happen, it counts for less in a risk-benefit analysis than a result we know will occur. And if a result is absolutely catastrophic but highly unlikely, it will count for almost nothing in the analysis. Thus, for example, a nuclear accident that would kill 10,000 people but is assumed to have only a 1/100,000 (or .00001) chance of happening would figure as an expected cost of only 1/10 of a life (.00001 × 10,000 lives).

The idea of *weighting* or reducing the value of a result by its likelihood of occurrence can be applied to positive as well as negative consequences of actions, to benefits as well as costs. For example, a management innovation that could lead to an extra million dollars in revenues but has only a 75 percent chance of working would count as an expected benefit of $750,000.

A measure of magnitude weighted by a probability factor is called *expected value or expected cost* and it is central to risk analysis. Here comes more profundity. In real life, the uncertain results of an action will eventually turn out one way or the other. Either there will be no accident and no one will be killed, or there will be an accident and 10,000 people will be killed. There is no middle ground. (Sure, it might be only 9,037 people, but they were all living people.) The felt consequences of an accident might be mitigated by the Red Cross, but they will not be any less painful for having been unlikely to occur. In risk analysis, by contrast, expected values are consequences mitigated by fractions from heaven.

Risk analysis assumes we can treat an expected value exactly like a certain value in doing arithmetic later on. To continue an oversimplified example, if all we care about in deciding on a safety standard is the cost of implementing it and the possible number of lives it would save, a risk analysis might look like this:

Cost of implementing safety standard =	$1 million
Expected value of standard =	0.1 lives
Cost per life saved =	$1 million ÷ 0.1 = $10 million

Notice that I divided a figure based on current market prices for labor and materials (the cost of the standard) by a figure based on a combination of a probability estimate and a number of real lives. Risk analysis allows us to treat an expected value the same as any certain value for purposes of arithmetic, even though the two types of values have

DECISION ANALYSIS

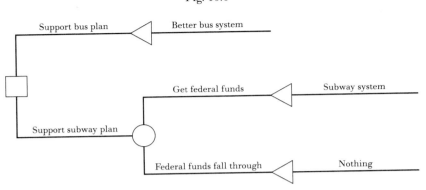

Fig. 10.1

very different meanings in human experience—one is experienced and has an empirical referent, while the other exists only as an arithmetic idea.

The concept of expected value is equally central to *decision analysis,* a framework for structuring problems when there is a great deal of uncertainty about the consequences of actions or when there are trade-offs between different consequences of the same action. Decision analysis explicitly adopts the point of view of a single person and uses his or her subjective estimates of values and probabilities as well as information from other sources. It makes use of probability not only to weigh uncertain outcomes, but also to establish value estimates of intangible outcomes. And it provides a visual map of decisions.

Suppose, for example, a mayor is considering which of two transit programs to support.[7] One will improve the current bus system at a moderate but known cost that could be covered by raising the property tax rate. The other, more ambitious, program will result in a new subway system if federal funding can be obtained, but the plan might get stalled permanently in federal budget politics. The subway system would be far superior to an improved bus system, but without federal funding, the city could not build it. Should the mayor gamble on the more ambitious program or go for the more certain one with less exciting results? In decision analysis, we would map the mayor's decision with a decision tree, as shown in Figure 10.1.

In the conventions of decision analysis, the tree is read from left to right. The square at the beginning denotes a person's decision. The

[7]I have borrowed and modified this example from Robert Behn and James Vaupel, *Quick Analysis for Busy Decision Makers* (New York: Basic Books, 1982), chap. 3.

Fig. 10.2

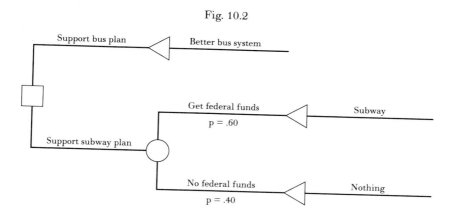

branching lines represent alternative courses of action. The triangles represent <u>final consequences to be evaluated</u>. The lower branch, choosing to support the subway plan, leads to <u>a circle, which denotes an uncertain event</u>; in this case, federal funding might come through or it might not. Each event then has a triangle at its end, representing the final consequences to be evaluated—in this case, getting a subway system or winding up with nothing at all.

To resolve the decision, the mayor needs to know the likelihood of getting federal funding as well as the value of each possible consequence of the decision. She might get information about federal funding by asking the state's congressional delegation, hiring an expert consultant, or simply making an informed guess (which is all the others would do). The mayor would then insert the proper numbers in the decision tree. For our example, we'll assume an estimate of the probability of getting funding at 60 percent, and of not getting funding at 40 percent. These probabilities are entered in Figure 10.2 and will be used, as in risk analysis, to weight the value of the outcomes.

To evaluate the outcomes, decision analysis always uses a scale from 0 to 1, where 0 is assigned to the worst outcome (here, getting nothing at all) and 1 to the best outcome (here, getting the subway). Evaluating any intermediate outcomes is slightly harder. To find out how much an improved bus system is "worth," the mayor would play a mental lottery game. She would imagine a series of gambles between the best and worst outcomes—subway or nothing—and figure out when she felt "indifferent" between taking a gamble on the subway plan and acquiring the improved but unexciting bus system. She might feel, for example, that if the chances of getting the federal funds were only 50

Fig. 10.3

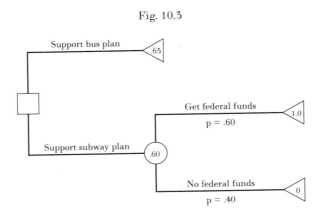

percent, she would rather take the bus system, but if the chances were as good as 80 percent, she would rather gamble on the subway system. However, if the chances were 65 percent, she wouldn't be able to decide and would be indifferent. Decision analysis would then conclude that, on a scale of 0 to 1, the bus system is worth ".65" to the mayor.[8]

With all of these numbers in place, the decision is easy. We multiply the value of each uncertain outcome by its probability of occurrence to get its expected value: $.60 \times 1 = .60$ for the subway system and $.40 \times 0 = 0$ for coming back to the citizens empty-handed. We add these two values together to get the total value for the lower branch—still .60. The bus option has a value of .65. It yields a greater overall benefit, given the uncertainties, and the mayor should choose the bus improvement plan (see Figure 10.3).

This is not the place to delve deeper into the arcane details of any of these decision techniques.[9] Suffice it to say that policy analysts have developed the most exquisite refinements. All the finery, however, does

---

[8] You are probably thinking, "That's a hell of a way to decide on the value of things." But I am only explaining how decision analysis works. When other quantitative measures are inappropriate or impossible, decision analysis evaluates outcomes by comparing them with a standard "reference gamble," and proponents regard this type of valuation as precise and unambiguous. See Behn and Vaupel, ibid., pp. 60–63 and 227–28. They call the values derived from this procedure preference-probabilities to indicate that values or preferences are expressed in terms of probabilities. Howard Raiffa, in his classic text, *Decision Analysis* (Reading, Mass.: Addison-Wesley, 1968), calls them Basic Reference Lottery Tickets or BRLT values.

[9] A good, readable introduction is Edith Stokey and Richard Zeckhauser, *A Primer for Policy Analysis* (New York: Norton, 1978).

not change the basic models. What is important is to understand the fundamental assumptions on which these models rest.

Some assumptions of cost-benefit, risk-benefit, and decision analysis have already been discussed, and need only brief recapitulation. First, actions are to be evaluated by their consequences, not, for example, by their causes, by principles of right and wrong, by the processes that produced them, or by their emotional appeal. Second, decisions should be made by specifying goals and means, and then by evaluating different courses of action and choosing the best one. Third, the best action can be found by a single criterion of "biggest." As long as all the possible consequences, negative and positive, are measured with a single measure or ratio (as in cost per life saved), it is trivial to find the action that yields the most benefits. And last, uncertain consequences can be measured by multiplying their likelihood times their magnitude, and the results can then be treated like certain values.

Behind these rather more explicit conventions of rational decision models are some less visible but no less important features. The rational decision model is avowedly individualist in its presentation of policy problems as the calculus of a single mind. Good decisions are portrayed as the result of cogitation, not bargaining, voting, or logrolling. The model depicts a problem from the point of view of someone— the "political actor" or "decision maker"—who has the psychological capacity and legal authority to make a coherent, single decision. At the same time, the construct of the abstract decision maker allows the model to be applied to organizations, agencies, governments, and nations, so long as the analyst assumes a single decision-making entity. Thus, the authors of a decision analysis textbook claim that decision analysis "can be used when a decision concerns election to public office or the outcome of a football game, bypass surgery on an individual or health policy for a nation. . . ."[10] They exclude, however, problems where "the power to make the decision is dispersed over a number of individual actors and / or organizational units" because "we assume in this book that the decision maker has the responsibility and authority to make the decision. . . ."[11]

In the polis, authority on issues of any significance is usually dispersed, shared, negotiated, and constantly contested. Most policy issues involve questions of who has the power to decide. The rational decision model assumes this problem has been resolved or does not

[10] Behn and Vaupel, op. cit. (note 7), p. 228.

[11] Ibid., p. 377.

exist. The adherents of rational decision models are hardly troubled by the omission, however. Quite the contrary, they tout as one of the virtues of these methods that "true" interests are revealed without the distortions of politics. Hence, Robert McNamara is credited by two of his disciples with having converted the Pentagon to "decision making based on explicit criteria related to the national interest, as opposed to decision making by compromise among various institutions and parochial interests."[12] (Notice the rhetorical construction of a contest between the good national interest and bad parochial interests.) And through cost-benefit analysis, we are assured by another pair of textbook authors, "the interests of individuals who are poorly organized or less closely involved are counted. . . . Benefit-cost analysis . . . has the effect of limiting the vagaries of the political process."[13] The advocates of rational decision models come close to promising that politics will become unnecessary.

MAKING DECISIONS IN THE POLIS

The rational decision model is itself a form of dramatic story. This point is key to understanding how it works in the polis. It asks us to identify with a protagonist—the decision maker—who is poised on the brink of a dilemma. Confusion and a sense of urgency, epitomized in President Harding's lament, are the emotional impetus for the story. The hero is a policy analyst, armed with rational decision models. The decision model offers a compelling resolution. It cuts through confusion, reducing heaps of information to a manageable amount. It provides a simple decision rule, a single criterion of "maximizing something good."

Most of all, the rational decision model offers determinateness, the promise that if you go through the process of analysis, you will get a definite answer. Even if what you find is an equivalence—say, that two programs have exactly the same cost-benefit ratio—you know definitely that it doesn't matter which one you choose. This promise of decision models and their response to the individual experience of difficult decisions is, I believe, the source of their appeal as a way to

---

[12] Alain Enthoven and K. Wayne Smith, *How Much Is Enough? Shaping the Defense Program 1961–1969* (New York: Harper & Row, 1971), p. 160; quoted in James Fallows, *National Defense* (New York: Random House, 1981), p. 21.

[13] Stokey and Zeckhauser, op. cit. (note 9), p. 151.

define problems—not their rather counterintuitive, politically unrealistic, and occasionally morally offensive use of numbers.

In the polis, rational choice models of problems are—no less than other types of problem definition—persuasive appeals mounted by people with stakes in the outcome. Portraying a problem as a decision is a way of controlling its boundaries: what counts as problematic and what does not, how the phenomenon will be seen by others, and how others will respond to it. Each step in the rational model can be seen as part of a strategy to control a decision rather than merely to get through the agony of deciding. We can understand better how the decision model functions in the polis by contrasting the strategic function of each step with its function in the "pure" analytic model.

In the rational model, stated objectives are the standard by which possible actions are evaluated. To serve that purpose, goals must be known to the decision maker, explicitly formulated, and fixed. If the decision maker could not articulate a goal, could not formulate it precisely enough to know whether it had been achieved, or changed his or her mind about goals frequently, there could be no stable standard of reference by which to judge the effectiveness of proposed alternatives. Explicitness and precision about goals are therefore not only virtues but necessities in the analytic model.

In the polis, statements of goals are not only wishes and intentions; they are means of gathering political support. They are portrayals of a future meant to enlist the aid of others in bringing it about. For this purpose, ambiguity is often far better suited than explicitness and precision. Recall some of the functions of ambiguity in politics: By labeling goals vaguely and ambiguously, leaders can draw support from different subgroups who otherwise might disagree on specifics, and can unite people who might benefit from the same policy but for different reasons. Vague goals in statutes allow legislators to vote for a law and pass the conflicts on to an administrative agency for interpretation and implementation.

Being ambiguous about one's intentions leaves a policy maker wiggle room in the future. Alan Greenspan, chairman of the Federal Reserve, is famous for using calculated ambiguity as a strategy to keep the Fed's actions secret until the last minute. With everyone guessing about whether the Fed would finally lower short-term interests in summer 1995, after seven consecutive increases in the prior year, Greenspan gave a speech that managed to intimate that the Fed might go either way with the interest rate. "I worry incessantly that I might be too clear," he quipped after the speech. Earlier in the day, while testifying before the Senate Banking Committee, he warned, "If I say

something which you understand fully in this regard, I probably made a mistake." There was a serious reason for him to be unclear. Greenspan was facing a meeting of his monetary policy committee in a few weeks, and if he announced his policy intention in advance, he would put the committee members in a bind: either they could go along with him and feel like rubber stamps, or they could recommend a different policy but be seen as undermining their chairman. Being ambiguous helped Greenspan deal with the internal politics of his organization.[14]

In short, it is rarely in anyone's interest—least of all a policy maker's—to articulate unambiguous goals. But we can go even one step further, and say that aside from deliberate uses of ambiguity in the polis, eliminating ambiguity is conceptually impossible. As Murray Edelman says, a political goal is a name, and every name is a metaphor.[15] To name something, just as to count it, is to place it in a class of objects or ideas and to assert a likeness between it and the rest of the class. Politicians can use this inherent metaphorical property of names to foster political alliances. The "Wage Enhancement and Job Creation Act" of the Republican Contract with America says nothing about either wages or jobs. It is a regulatory reform bill designed to hamper environmental, health, and safety regulation. Calling it a wage

[14] Keith Bradsher, "Fed Sees Signs of Weakness in Robust Economy," *New York Times*, June 22, 1995, pp. D1, D17.

[15] Murray Edelman, *The Symbolic Uses of Politics* (Urbana: University of Illinois Press, 1964), pp. 157–58.

and jobs bill, though, sends a different (if deceptive) message to labor and labor supporters, groups that might immediately oppose the weakening of occupational safety and health protection that is really the heart of the legislation.

The inescapable ambiguity of political goals means that they are more like moving targets than fixed standards. If goals are forever changing as different people read meanings into them, they cannot serve as a stable reference point for evaluating alternative actions. We cannot measure against them (as the rational model would have us do), but through their symbolic meanings we can inspire support or instill hostility. The relationship between goals and actions is interactive. As we take actions to achieve a goal, the meaning of the goal changes, the people who support and oppose it change, and the new meaning and alliances in turn change our ideas about what actions are appropriate.

The second step of the decision model, selecting alternative actions for consideration, is no less complicated in the polis. In the analytic model, alternatives spring miraculously from the head of the decision maker or, better yet, from the richly endowed brain of his policy analyst-advisor. Only two things limit the number and kinds of alternatives considered: poverty of imagination and considerations of practicality. To remedy the first condition, policy educators recommend mind-stretching exercises, such as "brainstorming," "lateral thinking," or "conceptual block-busting."[16] The second obstacle is simply the price we pay for living in a world with scarce resources, limited time, and multiple needs, and the good decision maker will accept such constraints without complaint.

In the polis, controlling the number and kinds of alternatives considered is the essence of the political game. Keeping things off the agenda is a form of power as important as getting them on.[17] If an alternative does not float to the surface and appear on the list of possibilities, it cannot be selected; to keep it off is effectively to defeat it. In fact, keeping an alternative from explicit consideration is even better than defeating it. Just as a losing political candidate in an election can become the rallying point for new political efforts, an alternative that

[16] Charles H. Clark, *Brainstorming: The Dynamic New Way to Create Ideas* (Garden City, N.Y.: Doubleday, 1958); Edward De Bono, *Lateral Thinking for Management: A Handbook of Creativity* (New York: American Management Association, 1971); and James L. Adams, *Conceptual Blockbusting* (San Francisco: W. H. Freeman, 1974).

[17] The classic political science essay on this point is Peter Bachrach and Morton Baratz, "Two Faces of Power," *American Political Science Review* 56 (1962): 947–52.

achieves a place on the decision maker's "short list" of possibilities acquires a reality in people's minds simply by having been considered. An alternative that remains unarticulated, unnamed, and unexamined does not lurk around as the focus of discontent, resentment, and renewed hope.

Another part of strategy in the polis is to make one's preferred outcome appear as the only possible alternative. For this purpose, construction of the list is crucial. An alternative is judged by the company it keeps. By surrounding the preferred alternative with other, less attractive ones, the politician can make it seem like the only possible recourse.

This strategy is so pervasive in social life that it has a name in rhetoric: Hobson's choice.[18] The author, speaker, or politician offers the audience an apparent choice, wearing all the verbal clothing of a real choice, when in fact the very list of options determines how people will choose by making one option seem like the only reasonable possibility. Thus, for example, Milton Friedman tells us in *Capitalism and Freedom*, his paean to free markets:

> Fundamentally, there are only two ways of coordinating the economic activities of millions. One is central direction involving the use of coercion—the technique of the army and of the modern totalitarian state. The other is voluntary co-operation of individuals—the technique of the market place.[19]

Once the audience accepts the structure of a Hobson's choice—that the alternatives presented are the only ones (cooperation and coercion), and that they have the qualities the author imparts to them ("free" versus "totalitarian")—then it is stuck with the offerer's preferred alternative.

Hobson's choice can become a fairly elaborate strategy of argument. It is the underlying structure of James Madison's classic essay *Federalist Paper No. 10*, in which he purports to demonstrate that federal government in a large republic is the best method for controlling factions:

> There are two methods of curing the mischiefs of faction: the one, by removing its causes; the other, by controlling its effects. There are again

[18] This name comes from Thomas Hobson, a seventeenth-century liveryman in Cambridge, England, who rented out horses but required each customer to take the one nearest the door, instead of giving them a choice.

[19] Milton Friedman, *Capitalism and Freedom* (Chicago: University of Chicago Press, 1962), p. 13.

two methods of removing the causes of faction: the one by destroying the liberty which is essential to its existence; the other, by giving to every citizen the same opinions, same passions, and the same interests.[20]

The essay goes on in this vein, leading us like sheep through a series of carefully controlled two-part choices, some of which are "obviously" unacceptable. (Here, both ways of removing causes are bad, so we must choose to curb the effects.)

The strategy of Hobson's choice is used not only to gain support for an alternative beforehand, but to gain legitimacy for actions already taken. (Here is a typical example of how a judge, when issuing a highly controversial opinion, presented his decision:

> The response of the courts can be either to adhere rigidly to prior doctrine, denying recovery to those injured by such products, or to fashion remedies to meet these changing needs.[21]

As with Friedman's or Madison's passages, this little sentence is all one needs to read to know how the judge decided.

The very image of a list of alternatives in the rational decision model is misleading because it implies that the items on the list are of equal standing. A list of alternatives in political decision making is a carefully constructed Hobson's choice, where one alternative is embedded among others, all portrayed as negatively as possible. By the time a problem has become formulated as a decision in politics, a lot has already been ruled out.

The construction of alternatives for a decision depends a great deal on conceptions of causation. Remember that political beings are always maneuvering to locate the blame somewhere else and to find solutions that either put the costs on other people or require their own services (well-compensated, of course), or both. Since causal chains are virtually infinite, there is potentially a wide range of choice about where to locate the blame, and correspondingly, about what type of corrective steps to take. The "drunk driving problem" (to repeat an example from Chapter 8) can be seen as caused by irresponsible drivers, uncrashworthy cars, poorly designed roads, insufficient ambulance and medical facilities, irresponsible tavern owners, or

[20] James Madison, "The Federalist No. 10," in Alexander Hamilton, and James Madison, and John Jay, *The Federalist* (New York: Tudor Publishing Co., 1937), pp. 62–70. Orig. pub. 1787.

[21] *Sindell v. Abbott Laboratories*, 163 Cal. Rptr. 132 (1980). This case held manufacturers of the drug DES liable for harms to daughters of women who had taken it.

overzealous promotional activities of the beverage industry. A set of cultural assumptions, perhaps bolstered by promotional activities of the auto and beverage industries, prevents consideration of anything but the driver as the source of the problem. The usual list of solutions—high school education programs, stiff penalties, better enforcement—therefore excludes all the alternatives directed at other conceptions of cause.

This process of focusing attention on a particular slice of an extended causal chain is called *issue framing.* A frame is a boundary that cuts off parts of something from our vision, and a list of alternatives is one of the most important ways of framing a policy problem and constructing a Hobson's choice.

Another very important technique in issue framing is the labeling of alternatives. It is no accident that Milton Friedman chose the names "voluntary cooperation" and "coercion" for his two alternatives, instead of, say, "cut-throat competition" and "public regulation," or that he further controlled our responses by appending the labels "totalitarian," "army," and "free market." We may have to put up with this kind of loaded writing in political treatises, but the rational model promises to eliminate verbal trickery from analysis and decision making. In rational analysis, the verbal labels attached to different alternatives should not affect their evaluation. Alternatives are actions that have objective consequences, and it is the measure of those consequences that counts in the final tally, not the decision maker's emotional responses to names.

In the polis, of course, language does matter. Try this mental experiment.[22] Suppose a serious flu epidemic is expected to kill 600 people. The government is considering two possible vaccination programs. Program A would use a conventional vaccine that can be counted on to save 200 people. Program B would use an experimental vaccine that has a 1/3 chance of saving 600 people but a 2/3 chance of being totally ineffective and saving none. You are the surgeon general of the United States. Which would you choose?

Now suppose you are considering a choice between two other programs. Program C would use a conventional vaccine that we know from past experience will result in the death of 400 people. Program D, using an experimental vaccine, would offer a 1/3 chance that no one will die and a 2/3 chance that all 600 would die. Which of these would you choose?

If you are like most people, you chose Program A in the first problem

[22]The experiment comes from Daniel Kahneman and Amos Tversky, "The Psychology of Preferences," *Scientific American* 286 (January 1982): 160–73.

and Program D in the second. In terms of decision theory, the choices are structurally identical. They offer the same probabilities of the same outcomes. The first options (A and C) will have as their result 400 people dying from the flu. The second options (B and D) are gambles whose expected values are 400 deaths. Both dilemmas, therefore, offer a choice between a certain outcome of 400 deaths and a gamble with an expected value of 400 deaths. Most people choose the certain outcome when the alternatives are labeled as "lives saved" but the gamble when the alternatives are labeled as "deaths." In the jargon of the trade, changing the labels determines whether we are *risk averse* or *risk seeking*. In the rational model of decision making, the switch most people make from the certain option to the gamble when the labels are changed is thoroughly irrational.

If you have always counted yourself among the rational, you will no doubt want to think about why you switched your preference (if you did). Psychologists believe the labels create different points of reference against which people evaluate alternatives. In the case of the flu vaccination program, the labeling of outcomes as "people saved" creates as a reference point a situation in which 600 lives are taken as already doomed; to choose the gamble seems like standing around doing nothing when you could be rescuing 200 people. The label "people die" suggests a starting point where the same 600 people are very much alive, and to shun the gamble seems tantamount to sentencing 400 of them to death.

The example illustrates that the way we think about problems is extremely sensitive to the language used to describe them. This observation will come as no surprise to most readers, but most proponents of rational decision models either ignore it or deny it. Theorists of rationality tend to believe that such framing effects of language are a distortion of rational thinking, and that a purely rational decision is based on objective consequences of actions, somehow purified of the poetic impact of words. Two leading scholars of the psychology of decision making hold that people's "susceptibility to the vagaries of framing" are "impediments to the achievement of rational decision." They are not sure whether the effects of framing "should be treated as errors or biases or whether they should be accepted as valid elements of human experience."[23]

In the polis, the way language affects people is undeniably a valid part of human experience. We think with and through language. To exclude the way words influence people's evaluation of the world as

[23] Ibid., p. 173.

Fig. 10.4
Thornburgh's decision: A simple tree

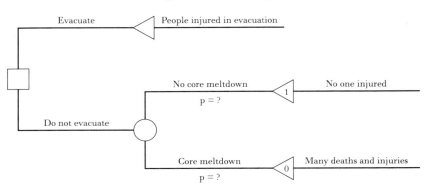

mere error or a distortion of some more objective reality is a strange conceit of rational analytic models. The conceit is more than silly. It is also antidemocratic. It denigrates the responses and opinions of ordinary people and elevates as "correct" or "objective" the evaluations performed by expert analysts. Moreover, to exclude this aspect of decision making is to miss (or perhaps even disguise) a major aspect of politics—the way metaphors and analogies are used to control people's evaluations of policy alternatives.

The significance of language in politics points up another very important difference between the rational decision model and decisions in the polis. In the rational model, the analyst is supposed to construct a list of alternatives that are mutually exclusive. Each alternative is distinct, and the point of the analysis is to choose one course of action when a decision maker cannot possibly do two things at once. (If he or she could, there would be no need to decide.) In the polis, symbols can combine and reconcile seemingly contradictory alternatives and thereby make possible a new range of options.

Consider Governor Thornburgh's decision whether to evacuate the area around the Three Mile Island nuclear plant after a leak in the cooling system was discovered in 1979.[24] No one knew whether the leak might ultimately lead to a core meltdown and consequent high radiation exposure in the surrounding area. A good decision analysis of this problem makes a clear distinction between the alternative courses of action: evacuate or do not evacuate (see Figure 10.4). With

[24]This example and Figure 10.4 are taken from Robert Behn and James Vaupel, *Fighting the Next War: Or Preparing to Analyze the Next Crisis*, Duke University Institute of Policy Sciences Working Paper No. 12791 (1979).

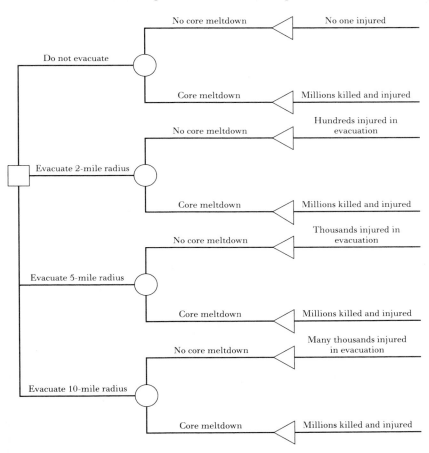

Fig. 10.5
Thornburgh's decision: A more complex tree

any evacuation plan, there are certain to be some injuries and deaths from car accidents, mass panic, and other side effects of declaring an emergency. If the governor did not evacuate the area and there were no core meltdown, virtually no one would be injured, but if there were a core meltdown, millions of people would be seriously injured by radiation. One could make the analysis even more sophisticated by adding more alternatives of various well-specified partial evacuations—for example, evacuate within a 2-mile radius, a 5-mile radius, a 10-mile radius, or do not evacuate (see Figure 10.5). The important point is that the analytic model requires the actions to be precisely defined.

In the event, Thornburgh did not order an evacuation or even a partial evacuation, but neither did he decide not to evacuate. Instead, he *recommended* that pregnant women and children under age 5 leave the area. Although his official message was that the area was safe, the unofficial message was that it was indeed unsafe. The symbol of "pregnant women and children" as vulnerable evokes fears of danger in all of us: If it's not safe for a child, is it safe for me? Mothers and children also symbolize the future and the importance of protecting the human species. With the governor recommending that pregnant women and children leave, lots of other people would leave as well. He thus could *cause* a partial evacuation without ordering one. The word "recommend," incidentally, symbolically puts responsibility for the decision whether to evacuate on residents themselves. With words and symbols, the governor could thus choose both alternatives at once—a feat of political magic rational analysis cannot duplicate.

Such deliberately ambiguous actions are a staple of the political world, because ambiguity permits a leader to escape difficult trade-offs. Especially when protecting public safety and health seem to con-flict with economic health of large corporations or organizations, polit-ical leaders can avoid seeming to favor one side or the other by taking ambiguous actions. Thus, when caught in a vise between Corning Cor-poration, maker of silicone breast implants, and consumer and medi-cal groups claiming the implants caused serious disease and death, the head of the Food and Drug Administration issued a "voluntary moratorium" on the implants and called for more studies. Two months later, the FDA's scientific advisory panel, unable to find conclusive evidence that implants are unsafe, used the same strategy Thornburgh had used to convey a double message. It recommended that only women with clear medical need (such as women with mastectomies following cancer) should have implants.[25] In a similar predicament a few years later, when several large public water supplies were contami-nated with a deadly parasite, the Environmental Protection Agency and Centers for Disease Control avoided warning that drinking water was unsafe by announcing that people with lowered immunity ought to boil their drinking water.[26] In the world of politics, the staff aid who presented the heads of the FDA or the EPA with analyses spelling out the exact consequences of banning or not banning would not be nearly

[25] See Philip J. Hilts, "F.D.A. Seeks Halt in Breast Implants Made of Silicone," *New York Times* Jan. 7, 1992, p. A1; and "Jean Seligman, "A Vote of No Confidence," *News-week*, Mar. 2, 1992, p. 75.

[26] John H. Cushman, Jr., "Federal Officials See Hazard for Some People in Tap Water," *New York Times* June 16, 1995, p. A20.

as welcome as the one who thought up clever ways to finesse the choice.

Moving to the third step in the decision model, evaluating the consequences of actions, we encounter another disjunction between the model and the polis. Much criticism of the analytic model focuses on how costs and benefits are counted. Is the correct dollar value assigned to an outcome? If the outcomes are intangible or not traded in markets, how should we establish prices for them? If the consequences occur far in the future, how should their values be "discounted" to account for the general belief that money available only in the future is worth less than money available immediately?

The way costs are counted is certainly important in controlling how a decision appears, but in the polis, there is a far more critical aspect of strategy: deciding which consequences to include in the analysis in the first place. Finding the consequences of an action is like finding the causes in reverse. Every action has infinite consequences, so there is no natural or correct place to draw the line around which ones to evaluate. Selection of what to include is both arbitrary and strategic. By simply including enough negative consequences to outweigh the positive ones, one can throw the decision one way, or reverse it by drawing the boundaries of consequences differently.

A child vaccination program, for example, can be made to appear highly cost-effective if one counts as a benefit the number of lives saved, and values each life as a person's expected lifetime earnings. But now, count as part of the program's costs all the future medical expenses of the people "saved," and the program appears to save less money. Add in their children's schooling and medical care costs—children they would not have had if they had died without the vaccine—and these beneficiaries of our policy become burdens on the public treasury. Now, count as benefits of the vaccination program the taxes paid by the people we rescued and the program begins to look better; add their children's taxes and it looks better still. Why not go to the next generation, including in the analysis the costs and benefits to society they generate? And why not include psychic consequences, such as the security of knowing you and your loved ones are protected? Or tilt the other way, and include the insecurity of worrying that you or a loved one might be the rarity who actually catches the fatal disease from the vaccine? For the creative mind, the possibilities are endless. By including some consequences and not others, the shrewd politician or analyst can construct a Hobson's choice.

What the rational model conceives of as abstract costs and benefits are in politics losses and gains to real people. They do not play an important role in politics unless someone mobilizes around them. Whether something is even noticed—much less counted—as a cost or benefit of a program depends on whether there are available cultural frameworks for identifying it and organized political interests for expressing it. Pollution was not even imagined as a cost of industrial processes until recently; violence against women was not considered a cost of pornography until feminist groups researched and publicized the issue. Any rational analysis is necessarily shaped by the structure of interests surrounding the issue. The harms and benefits to diffuse, unorganized interests are unlikely to be counted, while the losses and gains to concentrated interests will be weighed heavily.

The distribution of consequences plays a critical role in step 4 of the model, the choice among alternatives. Rational analysis uses the single criterion of maximum total welfare to make the ultimate decision among alternatives. The analyst purports to be neutral and omniscient, including in the calculations the losses and gains to everyone. The politician, too, pretends to be responsive to everyone, but is more responsive to organized constituencies. A program appears "rational" both to policy makers and to interest groups if it has net benefits for specific constituencies rather than society as a whole. For better or for worse, much policy choice is made by logrolling among powerful groups who trade support for policies that benefit the few at the expense of the many.

A decision is thus very sensitive to the way its costs and benefits are portrayed with words and images. Try another thought experiment. You lost your job as surgeon general but managed to be quietly confirmed as head of the Health Care Finance Administration (HCFA), the agency that runs Medicare and Medicaid. You have to decide whether Medicare and Medicaid should cover the cost of bone marrow transplants for people with terminal cancer. The procedure, at least in its current state of development, is very, very expensive (care can cost a few hundred thousand dollars per patient) and very ineffective (a very few patients go into remission, but most only have their lives prolonged a bit, and they spend most of the extra time being very, very sick in a hospital.) If you think of the costs as being met by taking small amounts of money from many, many people (everyone who pays taxes), the costs appear small and the action (saving some people from almost immediate death) might appear worthwhile.

Now imagine that the payment system works differently. Under congressional budget rules, any increase in one program must be financed

DECISION-ANALYSIS STRATEGIES OF PROBLEM
DEFINITION

Rational-Analytic Model	*Polis Model*
1. State goals/objectives explicitly and precisely.	State goals ambiguously, and possibly keep some goals secret or hidden.
2. Adhere to the same goal throughout the analysis and decision-making process.	Be prepared to shift goals and redefine goals as the political situation dictates.
3. Try to imagine and consider as many alternatives as possible.	Keep undesirable alternatives off the agenda by not mentioning them. Make your preferred alternative appear to be the only feasible or possible one. Focus on one part of the causal chain and ignore others that would require politically difficult or costly policy actions.
4. Define each alternative clearly as a distinct course of action.	Use rhetorical devices to blend alternatives; don't appear to make a clear decision that could trigger strong opposition.
5. Evaluate the costs and benefits of each course of action as accurately and completely as possible.	Select from the infinite range of consequences only those whose costs and benefits will make your preferred course of action look "best."
6. Choose the course of action that will maximize total welfare as defined by your objective.	Choose the course of action that hurts powerful constituents the least, but portray your decision as creating maximum social good for a broad public.

by a corresponding decrease in some other program. You have to raise the money for each bone marrow transplant by taking a few hundred thousand dollars from some other public health program—say, free vaccinations for poor children, or poison control centers. Each time you authorize a bone marrow transplant, a vaccination program or poison control center in one community must be closed. The decision undoubtedly looks different. The cost of the medical procedure is the same in the two cases, but how we pay for transplants, or even think of paying for them, influences how we evaluate their worth.

Political actors are dedicated to showing that a favored course of action benefits society as a whole and imposes costs on no one in particular. From this point of view, the maximum total welfare criterion of the rational model can be seen as a highly desirable costume with which people try to dress their own proposals. The construction of alternatives and selection of consequences contribute to the making of the final costume, the decision criterion. In the guise of numbers and the seeming logic of "maximizing welfare" (who could be against that?), the criterion appears as an irrefutable, unassailable, and even innocent way of deciding. In fact, the decision was made long before the criterion was invoked.

As a matter of your own strategy as audience or analyst, always be on the lookout for Hobson's choices. Whenever you are presented with an either / or choice, you should be tipped off to a trap. You can disengage it by imagining different alternatives other than those presented (there are always more), by giving new attributes to the ones presented (always keep a bag of adjectives handy to try on for size), and by expanding the range of consequences you bring into the analysis.

To return to the example from Milton Friedman, there are of course many "ways of coordinating the economic activities of millions" besides raw coercion and free markets. This dichotomy arises only in the market model of society, which can envision only two kinds of human relationships—brute force and self-interested exchange. In the polis, there are many other ways of relating, all of them more satisfying, and all of them resting on more ambiguous forms of influence. Part IV of this book is devoted to exploring some of them—incentives, deterrence, rules, persuasion, rights, and powers.

PART IV

SOLUTIONS

---

decision analysis.   ass^n = (1 person.)

(1 criterion)

[BUT] who has authority to make decisions?

dm method is — persuasive ≡ controlling boundaries

           — what counts as problem

           — what doesn't

           — how others see it

           — how others respond

           — how problem is. caused.

↓

Controlling #s & types of alternatives.

Keeping things off/on the agenda.

HOBSON'S CHOICE

The means of tackling policy problems are often called policy instruments or policy solutions. These terms give the misleading impression that public policies create permanent mechanical fixes. Policy actions, though, are really *ongoing strategies* for structuring relationships and coordinating behavior to achieve collective purposes. Effective maintenance of a community or pursuit of common goals cannot possibly be accomplished by governing every action or decision of individuals and organizations. Societies rely instead on broad structures and rules that will have a "multiplier effect," shaping people's behavior without continuous and specific directions. And because individuals, groups, and organizations within society have their own goals, they in turn use these structures and rules to help accomplish their own purposes.

Policy is more like an endless game of Monopoly than a bicycle repair. Hence the common complaint that policies never seem to solve anything. The process of choosing and implementing the means of policy is political and continuous. The actions we commonly call "new policies" are really somebody's next move, and in politics, as in a good game, nobody's move completely determines anybody else's future move. A sophisticated policy analysis will try to anticipate how other players will move in response to a new policy.

The strategies we call policy instruments are all ways of exerting power, of getting people to do what they otherwise might not do. Parts II and III, to be sure, are also concerned with power, but with the more subtle aspects of how goals and problems are strategically defined. Here in Part IV, the concern is with the forms of authority government explicitly uses to change behavior and policy. Chapters 11 through 15 are about generic strategies—generic in the sense that each is based on a general mechanism for changing or coordinating behavior and is not specific to a particular policy area such as agriculture or health or crime.

"Inducements" (Chapter 11) discusses changing people's behavior with rewards and punishments or incentives and sanctions. Although many social scientists treat rewards and punishments as two different forms of power, they are based on the same model of human motivation and behavior, and for that reason, they can profitably be analyzed as one type of policy instrument.

"Rules" (Chapter 12) are commands to act or not act in certain ways, and more broadly, they are classifications of people and situations that determine permissions and entitlements. Rules are usually backed up by sanctions, and inducements are predicated on rules for handing out rewards or punishments. Thus the two instruments, inducements and rules, are intertwined. Nevertheless, I think it is useful to separate them analytically: first, because policymakers and analysts often conceive of and promote these instruments as though they were separate, and second, because the effort to construct a pure model of each lays bare its inner assumptions.

"Facts" (Chapter 13) is my shorthand for strategies that rely principally on persuasion. They change people's behavior by operating on their minds and their perceptions of the world, rather than through rewards and punishments or through clearly delineated permissions and prohibitions. I use the imagery of facts as a vehicle for discussing the most fundamental assumption of persuasion strategies in liberal democracies—namely, that persuasion as a policy instrument rests on giving people information and letting them make up their own minds.

"Rights" (Chapter 14) are strategies that allow individuals or groups or organizations to invoke government power on their behalf. Rights describe those relationships between people or between people and organizations that government will uphold. A right is the policy instrument people have in mind when they say, "There should be a right to _____" (fill in the blank). Although rights must rest on authoritative rules from the state, they are a distinctive policy instrument in their heavy reliance on citizens for enforcement and their use of a special adjudication process.

"Powers" (Chapter 15) describes strategies that seek to alter the content of decisions by shifting the power of decision making to different people. These strategies include changing the membership or size of decision-making bodies, and shifting decision-making authority from one part of government to another. These strategies are usually promoted as efficient mechanisms for producing "better" decisions, but they are fundamentally ways of restructuring political power—hence the name "powers."

Market competition is frequently offered up as a policy instrument in current policy debates. I do not consider it a generic policy strategy because competition and free exchanges by themselves are avowedly not conscious and deliberate efforts to control behavior, and policy, it seems to me, is at least that. As we saw in Chapter 3 (Efficiency), economic markets are created and controlled by deliberate policy, but they are created and controlled with ordinary policy instruments, such as rules of ownership, rights of contractual relationships, and tax incentives for certain kinds of transactions.

Neither do I discuss force as a separate policy strategy, because when it is used legitimately in democratic polities, it is used as a sanction in the enforcement of previously articulated rights and rules. Even acts of war are governed by international conventions and treaties. Naked physical coercion is beyond the pale in the value system of democracies. The policy strategies in this section are ones that appear to me to be central in democracies and especially prominent in contemporary American policy debates.

The strategies as I describe them are ideal types. They represent underlying theories about how to change people's behavior and how to coordinate individual and organizational behavior in the service of collective goals. But no policy strategy is ever purely one type. In each of the following chapters, I will show how the pure model, in practice if not in theory, involves elements of the other strategies.

In the polis, a policy or program can be promoted simultaneously as two different types of strategies. Education vouchers, for example, have been promoted as an inducement scheme, because they give parents an incentive to choose the best school, and schools the incentive to offer educational programs parents desire. At the same time, they are promoted as a power strategy, because they give more power to parents vis-a-vis education professionals. Managed care health insurance can be described as an incentive scheme that promotes autonomy of health care providers: doctors and hospitals are paid a fixed price for each patient or type of disease they treat, and they can pocket the difference if they are able to provide care less expensively than the set price. But managed care can also be described as a power shift. Insurance companies sell managed care plans to employers by emphasizing that the insurer, no longer the doctor and hospital, will have decision-making authority about employees' medical care and through that new authority, insurers will be able to lower employers' premium costs. One of the most important aspects of policy choice in the polis is that people with pet solutions often know how to promote their program so it appears to be one kind of strategy to one constituency and another kind to another constituency.

Much discussion of these strategies in policy analysis is theoretical. People tend to advocate one strategy over another, in the abstract, asserting that one type is logically superior to another. For example, in the United States there has been a long debate about whether incentives are better than rules and standards. In these debate, the advocates of incentives typically compare an ideal incentive system with a real (necessarily imperfect) rule-making agency. None of these strategies exists in the abstract. Any policy strategy is a human creation, something designed, administered, responded to, and adjusted in a political world. Evaluation of the potential of any policy to ameliorate a problem has not really begun until it analyzes how the policy is likely to be crafted and conducted once it leaves the safe haven of the analyst's mind.

Each of the following chapters first describes the theory behind each strategy, particularly as held by its proponents. Next, each chapter shows how the various strategies work in the flesh—what happens when they are conducted by real people, subject to all the factors in our simple model of the polis.

11

Inducements   *either/both*   rewards/penalties

Our most commonsense notion of how to bring about change rests on the proverbial carrot and stick. The idea behind inducements is that knowledge of a threatened penalty or a promised reward motivates people to act differently than they might otherwise choose. Incentives and deterrence are flip sides of this same coin. With incentives, we make it easier or more rewarding for people to do something we want them to do; with deterrence, we make it harder or more costly for them to do something we don't want them to do. One uses the promise of rewards, the other the threat of penalties, but they both rely on getting other people to choose actions we would desire.

Some areas of public policy have traditionally relied on deterrence—most notably, the criminal justice system and defense policy, but also the income tax system with its penalties for tax avoidance, and occupational safety and health policy, with its (albeit weak) penalties for unsafe practices. Other areas have relied primarily on incentives—notably tax credits for activities we want to encourage, foreign aid in exchange for political cooperation, or federal funds to induce states and localities to undertake special programs.

In many, perhaps most areas, we rely on a combination of rewards and penalties—rewards so long as you cooperate and penalties as soon as you don't. Although there is a debate in both psychology and politics about whether rewards or penalties are the more effective instrument, in an important sense the distinction is false. Every reward contains an implicit or potential penalty of withdrawal, and every penalty short of death contains an implicit reward of cessation. The United States, for example, rewards its allies with "most favored nation" status in trade arrangements, but withdrawal of the privilege always looms as a possibility if our allies fail to cooperate; and once we impose an embargo on another country, as we have on Cuba since 1960, the possibility of lifting it inevitably dangles.

Because incentives and deterrence share a similar logic, I treat them as one type of policy strategy, although I will point out some important differences. In common parlance, the term incentives usually refers to positive inducements or rewards (as in "incentive pay systems"). The term sanctions usually refers to negative inducements or penalties, (as in "economic sanctions"). I will follow this usage and use the term inducements to refer to both incentives and sanctions.

THE THEORY OF INDUCEMENTS

Inducements are one possible response to commons problems. Recall that a commons problem exists when there is a divergence between private interest and public interest, or when individuals benefit (or lose) from doing something that harms (or helps) the community. The purpose of inducements is to bring individual motives into line with community goals. Inducements alter the consequences of individual actions so that what is good for the community is also good for the individual.

It is useful to think of inducements as a system with three parts: the inducement giver, the inducement receiver or target, and the inducement itself. In analyzing how inducements might work, we can then look at these elements separately and consider what is necessary for each part in order that the three parts function together to bring about the desired change.

Inducements work not through direct force, but by getting people to change their minds. The theory rests on a utilitarian model of human behavior. People are assumed to be rational. They have goals and each decision to act is predicated on conscious goal-seeking. Every action is first a mental decision based on an economic calculus: Which of the possible actions I could take will get me to my goal in the easiest or cheapest way? The theory of inducements says we can alter people's self-propelled progress toward their goals by changing the obstacles and opportunities they face.

Obviously, such a model makes many assumptions. One is that the targets of inducements have control over their own behavior, so that when confronted with new knowledge of a penalty or a reward, they can change their calculus and their behavior. Individuals, in other words, are *adaptable.* One issue in assessing a policy based on inducements, then, is the extent to which this assumption of adaptability holds true. We can simply note here that the phenomenon of loyalty in the polis is a force that works in the opposite direction of adaptability. People often hang on to old habits, choices, and actions out of loyalty, long after a rational calculus suggests they ought to change their ways.

The theory of inducements assumes, second, that givers and receivers are <u>*unitary actors*</u>. This means not that the actor is necessarily an individual, but that it is an entity capable of rational behavior. A giver must be able to implement a consistent policy of rewarding or penalizing behavior, and a target must be capable of making a unified calculus and taking a single course of action.

The mechanism of inducements is enormously complicated in the polis by the fact that the givers and receivers are likely to be, or to operate in, a collective entity. We can easily imagine a donkey responding to a carrot, but a trainer who proposed to motivate a hundred donkeys with a bunch of carrots would leave us pondering many questions: Should he put the carrots all in one place? Throw them into the middle of the herd? Should he have one carrot for each donkey? Do all donkeys like carrots? Will two or three aggressive donkeys get all the carrots, regardless of how the others behave? Will the latecomers and slow learners get no carrots anyway, and figure it's not worth changing their ways? Might the donkeys stampede the trainer and devour the carrots? And what if carrot distribution policy is decided by a committee of independent-minded, strong-willed trainers? The carrots might be given out according to several different standards, or the committee might be paralyzed and the carrots never given out.

The carrot-and-stick metaphor, played out a bit more fully than usual, suggests numerous ways an inducement strategy can go awry. Even though each person within a group may be a rational actor, likely to respond to inducements in predictable ways, membership in an organization or a community alters the way individuals respond. In designing and assessing inducements, therefore, one of the most critical tasks is to analyze how collective processes influence the way individuals will apply and respond to them.

In most policy situations, the target of inducements or the giver, or both, will be a collective entity with some inner conflict and some ability to act as a unified group. The giver is apt to be a small committee (such as a parole board or a zoning board), a large agency (such as the

Internal Revenue Service or the Environmental Protection Agency), or even a country (such as when the United States imposes a trade embargo). Commonly the giver is nominally a single person but is really acting on behalf of and with the authority of a larger organization or political entity. The school principal who disciplines students with penalties may well have to negotiate with teachers who have different educational philosophies before she can impose a penalty. Once having decided on a penalty—say, expelling a student—she may have to negotiate with parent groups as well. Even the top banana in an organization can rarely assign and implement penalties alone.

Similarly, the target of an inducement might be a single person heading a group, or a firm, an organization, a government entity (e.g., a town, a state, a nation), so that the target's response to an inducement cannot be the product of a single mind. Incentive reimbursement plans for hospitals offer a good example. Under such plans, an insurer such as Blue Cross or the federal Medicare program seeks to induce hospitals to operate efficiently by offering them a share of any savings below some target cost. These plans assume that hospital spending decisions are controlled by a unified organizational structure under a single administrator, when in fact, authority is widely dispersed: many key decisions that affect cost are made by individual physicians. On the other side, each hospital faces an array of different insurers who pay its patients' bills, somewhat like my imaginary committee of donkey trainers. Hospitals are able to play one insurer off against another and shift their costs to the ones with the least restrictive requirements.[1]

A third assumption of the theory of inducements is that the receiver has some *orientation toward the future*. Inducements can work only to the extent that the target cares about the costs or rewards to be faced in the future and is willing to modify current behavior in order to shape future results. There must be some correspondence between the time frame of the receiver and the time frame of the inducement itself.

Inducements that occur far in the future probably have less impact than ones that occur immediately.[2] If the "discovery time" between when an action takes place and when it becomes visible is very long, the effect of inducements is weakened. For example, we penalize hazardous waste dumping, but since dumps can be concealed until a slow-

[1] Judith Feder and Bruce Spitz, "The Politics of Hospital Payment," *Journal of Health Politics, Policy and Law* 4, no. 3 (Fall 1979): 435–463.

[2] In the vocabulary of economics, I am suggesting that there is a discount rate on future penalties and rewards. That is, gain or loss in the future is worth less than the equivalent amount in the present.

developing health problem affects a community, dumpers may not be particularly responsive to penalties. Moreover, the longer the discovery time for an activity, the more difficult it is to impose a penalty. Long-past activities are harder to document than recent ones because records and evidence disappear. The responsible people may no longer be in office or easily available to give evidence. Also, it is part of our general notion of fairness that people should not have to face the prospect of discovery and punishment forever. This notion leads us to have "statutes of limitation" for many crimes and negligent activities (such as occupational injury), and creates a climate of greater leniency toward long-past deeds than toward recent ones.

When the target of a sanction is a collective entity—a firm, an agency, or a country—its time frame as an actor is apt to be quite scrambled. The life span of individuals in an organization differs from that of the organization itself. To the extent that leaders and managers shift in and out of positions in shorter intervals than the cycle of activity, discovery, and sanction or reward, their motives will be less directly affected by inducements. Also, organizations often insulate their leaders from responsibility in ways that mitigate the effects of future sanctions; a corporate officer usually does not have to pay fines, tax penalties, or business losses directly out of pocket, nor does he or she personally reap all the rewards of successful business decisions. This does not mean that individuals within an organization are unaffected by inducements applied to an organization, but it does suggest that the design of inducements must take into account their attenuation as they are transferred from organizations to their members.

Even if inducements are targeted to individuals, individuals change over time so that a long time frame can play havoc with the effectiveness of inducements. The National Health Service Corps, a program to induce young physicians to practice in underserved cities and rural areas, works by offering a reward to prospective medical students just finishing college. Students can receive a medical school tuition fellowship from the program if they agree to practice in an underserved area when they finish medical training. Many who accept this inducement later change their minds. By the time they finish medical training some five or more years after they have been tempted by the fellowship, they are more likely to be married or seriously involved. They are no longer free to decide on a job location without considering the career needs of their partner, and so they are less willing to accept a no-choice assignment from the program. They are more likely to have been socialized by the lure and prestige of high-tech, specialized medicine, and therefore less willing to practice routine, primary-care medicine in places without prestigious medical centers. Moreover, a physician with five or more years of training may soon be in a position to pay back the fellowship with income from earnings, and no longer need to pay it back with labor.[3] The moral of the story? The longer the time span between the reward or penalty on the one side and the behavior change on the other, the more likely the situation of the target will change and along with it, the value of the inducement.

time span

Because the theory of inducements relies on a conception of the individual as a rational actor, it is also tied to a fourth assumption, that of *purposeful notions of cause* (the bottom row in Table 8.1). Inducements might be applied when the cause of a problem is understood as intentional—the effect of intended consequences of purposeful action. In that case, the incentives or penalties are designed to alter the consequences to the target of taking the action in question. Criminal penalties on burglary are an example. Or, inducements might be applied when the cause is understood to be inadvertent—the result of unintended consequences of purposeful action, such as unforeseen side effects or careless mistakes. In this case, inducements are designed to make formerly invisible consequences visible to the target, thereby making him or her consider possible negative side effects or missed opportunities of a planned action. Taxes on industrial pollution or consumer rebates for plastic bottles are examples.

Using inducements as a policy instrument does not require us to understand the causes of a problem or the reasons why people do what they do.[4] To increase high school completion among poor teenagers, we can offer prizes for staying in school or penalties for dropping out, and we might succeed in increasing school attendance as long as the inducements keep flowing. (New York City tried offering salutes, dictionaries and T-shirts to freshmen; Wisconsin uses penalties instead, cutting the welfare checks of mothers of whose kids are truant.[5]) But an inducement system doesn't require anyone to ask *why* kids drop out of school. Is it because they find the curriculum irrelevant? Because

[3] Frank E. James, "Despite Federal Aid, Doctors Are Still in Short Supply in Rural Areas," *Wall Street Journal*, June 23, 1987, p. 33.

[4] This point is made by Alfie Kohn, in *Punished by Rewards* (Boston: Houghton Mifflin, 1993), esp. pp. 59–62.

[5] Fred M. Hechinger, "New York Adds New Weapons in the War Against Dropping Out," *New York Times*, July 9, 1985, p. C8; Thomas Corbett, et. al., "Learnfare: The Wisconsin Experience," *Focus* (University of Wisconsin-Madison, Institute for Research on Poverty), vol. 12, no. 2 (1989): 1–10.

they are made to feel like failures? Because teachers don't teach in a way they can understand? Because they want to help their welfare-dependent mothers and siblings by earning money instead of going to school? Because their peers make fun of them for succeeding in school? Because they intuitively know that the economic rewards to a high-school degree are practically nil? Really "fixing" the dropout problem would require grappling with underlying causes such as these, but obviously, T-shirts and welfare cuts are politically much easier to accomplish.

The theory of inducements is not based on any complex notion of causation. When a social problem is rooted in a complex organizational system, a web of institutional patterns and practices, or a long-standing historical pattern of social and political relationships, inducements applied by one narrow set of actors to another are unlikely to have a significant impact. Inducements, because they rest on a notion of actors as unitary, autonomous, and single-minded, are in a sense the narrowest of policy strategies. At best, they can influence only simple causes but not complex ones.

Having considered some of the political complexities of inducement givers and targets, it remains to say something about the third part of the system—inducements themselves. Positive and negative inducements differ in some important ways, not the least of which is how the target experiences them. What determines whether an inducement is a reward or penalty is not the giver's intentions but the target's expectations.[6] A $1000 raise sounds like a reward, but if you had every reason to expect $2000, you will experience it as a penalty. Likewise, a notice that you will have to pay a $100 fine will feel like a reward if you expected to owe $200. Inducements are thus negative or positive only in relation to the target's expectations, and understanding the target's point of view is critical in designing them.

Positive and negative inducements are often treated as conceptually equivalent.[7] The more carrots offered, the more desired behavior we get, and the more sticks wielded, the less undesirable behavior we get.

---

[6]This point is from David Baldwin, "The Power of Positive Sanctions," *World Politics* 24 (1971): 19–38. More formally stated, positive sanctions are "actual or promised improvements in [the target's] value position relative to his baseline of expectations," and negative sanctions are "actual or threatened deprivations relative to the same baseline" (pp. 23–24). (He uses the term "sanctions" generally as I use "inducements.")

[7]Baldwin, ibid., is a notable exception. See also his "Thinking About Threats," *Journal of Conflict Resolution* 15 (1971): 71–78. The next five paragraphs build on his very useful analytical distinctions and suggestive hypotheses.

"Today I was awarded the 'Salesman Of The Year' trophy . . . and then I sold it to Larry for $150!"

The proportional relationship between inducement and behavior is the significant characteristic of both positive and negative inducements. Moreover, in the theory of rational decision making, the actual loss of seven carrots is treated as equivalent to the opportunity cost of not gaining seven carrots. As we saw in Chapter 9 (Interests), losses and gains have qualitatively different political and psychological effects, and therefore, carrots and sticks actually work differently. Politically, it is not a matter of indifference whether we chose to motivate with rewards or punishments.

Rewards and punishments, or promises and threats, can foster different kinds of political relationships. Positive inducements, such as wage productivity bonuses, foreign aid, or trade subsidies, may create an alliance and a spirit of good will. They can encourage the two parties to cooperate on other issues. If the giver's promise succeeds in getting the target to change its behavior, a bond is created between them. In fulfilling the giver's wish, the target creates an obligation for the giver to fulfill the promise, and the implicit bargain creates a sense of loyalty and mutual aid.

Negative inducements, such as fines, tariffs, and embargoes, create a climate of conflict and divide the two parties, even if the threats are not carried out. If, under threat of penalty, the target refrains from some action it would like to take, it is not likely to feel especially warmly toward the giver. If the target does not refrain and the penalty is imposed, the adversary relationship is made explicit. Thus, threats and penalties, even when they succeed from the point of view of the giver, build resentment and solidify an oppressor-victim relationship, making it likely that the giver will have to use more threats and penalties in the future.

When promised rewards are used to motivate a target, the giver does not have to do anything if the attempt fails. But if it succeeds, if the target does change its behavior in the desired way, then the giver must dispense the reward. The target gives up something by doing something it otherwise would not have done, and the giver sacrifices something by granting the reward. Rewards thus have a structure of reciprocity and compromise that further builds a sense of alliance.

Sanctions work in the opposite way. The sanction giver sacrifices something only if the threat fails; if the target does not comply, then the giver must carry out the sanction and incur the costs of its implementation. The target, of course, also loses. However, if the threat succeeds and the target refrains from doing what it otherwise wanted to do, the target bears costs but the sanction giver does not have to do anything. Successful threats are free—the powerful get something for nothing.

For all these important differences between rewards and punishments, there is one overwhelming political similarity: rewards, just as much as punishments, are efforts by one party to control the behavior of another.[8] Inducement systems of either stripe entail unequal power relationships. In reward systems, no less than punishment schemes, one party sets the terms, makes the rules, monitors the other's behavior, and decides when and whether to dispense the consequences.

Incentive schemes are often presented in political rhetoric as policy instruments that are non-coercive and respectful of individual autonomy. People are free to choose, so the argument goes. In practice, incentive schemes, especially monetary and material rewards, are most effective when the targets are somewhat needy or feel somewhat deprived, so that the potential reward really matters to them. Thus, the effectiveness of any reward system in getting people to change their behavior is increased the more the targets are dependent on the giver and unable to attain the "goodies" in other ways. (It is no accident that reward schemes are frequently used to manipulate the behavior of dependent populations—children, students, prisoners, people in mental institutions, and workers in large organizations.) Incentive systems

---

[8] This point is brilliantly explored in Alfie Kohn, *Punished by Rewards,* op. cit (note 4), and is one of the central elements of Kohn's critique of incentive plans in the workplace, in schools, and in the family.

work by capitalizing on the weakness of the targets, not by empowering them.

Making Inducements in the Polis

In the simple model of inducements, if society penalizes an activity, people will do it less, and if it rewards an activity, people will do it more. In the polis, things aren't so simple. Inducements are usually designed by one set of people (such as policy analysts, legislators, and regulation writers), applied by another (executive branch bureaucrats), and received by yet a third (individuals, firms, organizations, lower levels of government). The passage from one set to the next is treacherous.

There is never a direct correspondence between the inducement as proposed by the designer and as applied by the giver. The biggest problem is a lack of willingness to impose sanctions or hand out rewards on the part of officials charged with meting them out. Several elements of the polis make giving out inducements difficult.

Negative sanctions are divisive and disruptive to relationships, as we saw above, and therefore to the sense of community. People generally do not like causing suffering to those they work with. Physicians, for example, are extremely reluctant to report their colleagues for violations of ethics or extreme incompetence, and the professional disciplinary boards are correspondingly reluctant to revoke licenses or even give warnings. Physicians would far rather talk to an offending colleague with mild hints of the errors, or even better, simply isolate the colleague by not referring patients.[9] Even in more distant relationships such as that between a factory safety inspector and managers, or a restaurant health inspector and owners, inspectors know they need the ongoing cooperation of the establishments they visit. They often would rather cajole their targets into compliance than risk the strains on work relationships that would come with being known as "the tough guy." Thus, fear of poisoning one's social relationships and work environment restrains sanction givers.

Even positive incentive systems are sometimes resisted because people fear the divisive and competitive atmosphere they would generate. Incentive pay schemes, such as performance-based salary increases or wage bonuses, have often run afoul of employees. Teachers, physicians, and office workers have generally opposed the introduction of

[9] See Eliot Freidson, *Profession of Medicine* (New York: Dodd, Mead, 1970), pp. 149–151.

incentive pay, because the majority of employees would rather have the security of a fixed income and because employees do not want to be pitted against their co-workers in a competitive environment.[10]

Imposing a penalty on someone else often creates costs for the giver. At a university where I once taught, there was a writing requirement that students had to satisfy to graduate. They could take an essay examination or enroll in a writing course, but the easiest way to pass was to have a professor certify a short paper as meeting the (fairly nebulous) standards of the requirement. If the professor denied certification, he or she had to write a justification and assessment of the student's writing to the Committee on the Writing Requirement, and probably also have a somewhat painful conversation with the disappointed student. Signing off on the paper was by far the easiest thing for the professor to do.

Imposing penalties can have very concrete, material costs as well. Mandatory sentencing and so-called "three strikes and you're out" laws are efforts to deter criminal behavior by making prison terms more certain and more severe. A rather less visible side effect of these laws is their effect on taxes, since governments must construct new prisons to accommodate all the additional people who are now sentenced to serve time, and to pay for their room and board. (In 1990, the Federal Bureau of Prisons spent almost $18,000 per prisoner per year on housing and feeding inmates.[11]) After a twenty year trend of adopting tougher sentencing laws, and in a new political climate of both budget and tax reduction, people are beginning to question whether the costs of building and maintaining prisons are worth the sacrifices in education, health and welfare budgets. North Carolina recently moved to make the costs of crime control proposals explicit before policies are adopted: Every bill that affects prison space must be accompanied by a cost estimate. With the costs made more visible, proponents of long and tough sentences are more willing to soften their demands.[12]

---

[10] See for example, "Merit Pay for Teachers Runs into Union's Resistance," *Wall Street Journal*, November 11, 1986, p. 1. "Sharing the Wealth: Democrats Latch Onto Bonus Pay Systems," *Wall Street Journal*, April 28, 1985, p. 1. See also Kohn, *Punished by Rewards*, op. cit (note 4), chapter 7, which reviews a great deal of evidence that performance-based pay schemes don't work and anger employees.

[11] Matthew Brelis, "Mandatory Sentences Take Hit," *Boston Globe*, February 18, 1992, pp. 1, 7.

[12] Neil R. Peirce, "Seeing Prisons Through New Prisms," *National Journal* December 17, 1994, p. 2988.

Even handing out rewards can create costs for the giver. In my former university, there was some departmental money to award small prizes to the best theses in various categories. Faculty were asked to nominate the best theses they had supervised. Typically, very few nominations were made. Why? I suspect each professor knew that nominating a thesis meant writing a short summary and a statement of its virtues for the prize committee. That would be work, and moreover, would open the professor's judgment to the scrutiny of colleagues. These examples from university life are hardly atypical. Rewards and penalties never happen automatically. They must be decided upon and brought into being by people with toothaches, leaky basements, and buses to catch. Bureaucratic rules, especially requirements to document certain types of decisions, often make it costly for officials to apply an inducement, and so skew their incentives to take one kind of action rather than another.

Sometimes the designers of sanctions make them so drastic that the sanction givers are extremely loath to impose them. If the sanction givers regard their only sanctions as vastly out of proportion to the badness of a target's actions, they will go by their own sense of justice and either refuse to impose any sanction or fashion one they deem more appropriate. Shortly after California passed its "three strikes and you're out law" requiring a twenty-five-year prison sentence for someone convicted of three serious felonies, a certain Jeffrey Missamore got caught smoking marijuana in a low-security prison farm, where he was serving time for petty theft (not a serious felony). He had been convicted of a burglary in 1988 (strike one), and his jail joints counted as strikes two and three (he was charged with two counts of carrying drugs into a prison, classified as a serious felony). Missamore's lawyer, a public defender, said smoking marijuana was a stupid mistake, but Mr. Missamore was "not your typical thug." The judge refused to impose the twenty-five-year prison term, sentencing him to probation and drug treatment instead.[13] Judges often resist what they see as overly harsh required sentences by simply changing some felony charges to misdemeanors.

Sometimes inducements are designed so that by imposing a penalty, one hurts the very thing one is trying to protect. This is a very common problem in the United States, where the federal government often tries to induce the states to implement programs by means of federal tax credits, grants, or subsidies. Medicaid, federal highway subsidies, and

---

[13] "California Judge Refuses to Apply a Tough New Sentencing Law," *New York Times*, July 20, 1994.

public housing all work this way. The point of federal inducements is to get states to provide services to their citizens that are otherwise unavailable. But the only leverage the federal government has over state performance is to withdraw the funds, depriving the very people it is trying to help. The incentive (federal funds) contains an implicit penalty (withdrawal), but the penalty is virtually unusable. Unusable penalties convert an incentive into a guarantee.

The same problem occurs in regulatory systems meant to assure quality of social services. Most states have systems for monitoring the standards of care provided by nursing homes, group homes for the retarded, and even public schools. However, the ultimate stick for non-compliance with quality standards is either the loss of state funds or closure of the institution. Either one would hurt the clients of the institution, the very people whom the quality standards are meant to protect. Again, the sanction becomes virtually unusable.

If there is a gap between the design and the application of inducements, there is a virtual canyon between the designer and the target. A great deal of slippage occurs because of the possibilities for symbolic meaning of inducements. Whatever the actual reward or penalty in a material sense, the target might give it different meaning than the giver. A familiar problem in school discipline is that the most unruly students are usually also ones who take punishment as an emblem of prestige. To broaden the example, in any kind of revolutionary situation or political rebellion, rebels are apt to welcome punishment as proof of their victimization or as a test of their commitment. Sanctions may even harden resistance to change. For example, economic sanctions against political regimes we are trying to influence often stimulate broader support for the regime and stiffen its will to continue its policies. In these situations, what appears as a cost or a punishment to the giver may appear to the target as a resource for creating a martyr identity and for gathering more support for the target's cause.[14]

Just as penalties are sometimes perceived as resources by the targets, the costs of imposing sanctions may become resources for the givers. When, for example, one country imposes a trade embargo on another in order to induce some political change (say, abolition of apartheid in South Africa), the sanction giver incurs some loss of its export market as well as a loss of imports. But its willingness to make these sacrifices increases the credibility of its commitment to the policy change and

[14]See David A. Baldwin, *Economic Statecraft* (Princeton, N.J.: Princeton University Press, 1985), p. 142. This book is an excellent treatment of the use of economic sanctions in foreign policy.

signals its willingness to stand behind its commitment.[15] Here is yet another example of how costs are double-edged swords.

Symbolism is important in still another way. If the activity we are trying to change is something that defines the target's identity—what it stands for, what kind of organization it is, or what its principal mission is—then it is unlikely that the target will perceive the activity as something divisible, something of which it can do a little less and still survive as itself. In foreign policy we have often applied economic sanctions, such as trade embargoes or blockades, in attempts to induce other countries to make these kinds of changes: getting Italy to abandon its invasion of Ethiopia after it had already begun (1935); getting Fidel Castro to step down after the Cuban revolution (1962); getting the Soviet Union to abandon its invasion of Afghanistan after the fact (1979); and getting Saddam Hussein to withdraw from Kuwait after Iraqui forces had already invaded (1990).[16] These examples suggest the futility of designing sanctions that attack a target's fundamental identity or mission.

For the target, rewards and penalties do not come in isolation. They are merely additional consequences of taking certain actions, so that any new inducements simply join a broad array of consequences the target already faces. The designer tends to focus on only the inducements he or she designs, and the giver only on the ones he or she controls. But for the target, new inducements always fit into a web of reinforcing and crosscutting inducements.

This kind of narrow vision is illustrated in a recent analysis of welfare by some professors who became high-level officials in charge of welfare reform in the Clinton administration. According to them, "the primary mechanism for encouraging work [until 1981] was a system of incentives that allowed recipients to keep a portion of their earnings, without having them deducted from their grants."[17] In the daily economic world of the welfare recipient, though, other economic realities and possibilities loom far larger as work incentives. Surely, the low level of income attainable through public assistance and the virtual impossibility of supporting a family on a welfare grant have always been much greater incentives to work than a bureaucratic rule that merely lessens the penalties for working while on welfare. Indeed, research with welfare mothers has found that virtually all of them do

[15] Baldwin, ibid., pp. 106–107.

[16] Most of these examples are from Baldwin, ibid., p. 133.

[17] Thomas Kane, author of chapter 1 in Mary Jo Bane and David Ellwood, *Welfare Realities*, (Cambridge: Harvard University Press, 1994), p. 20.

off-the-books work without reporting their income to the welfare department, precisely because working on the side is the only way to make a go of things.[18] Poverty and budget shortfalls are the big stimuli to work for women on welfare. It is only from the program designer's point of view, not the welfare recipient's, that the latest wrinkle in program rules looks like an important incentive.

Perhaps the most important reason for slippage between the design of inducements and the target's response is that people—far more than rats and donkeys—are strategic as well as adaptive. They will try to reap a reward or avoid a penalty without changing their behavior. They can conceal information about themselves and their activities. They can manipulate the information, even, as we saw in Chapter 7 (Numbers), when the criterion for a reward or penalty is numerical.

Strategic creatures can always find ways to get around requirements. For example, when New Jersey began requiring owners of industrial facilities to develop and finance a clean-up plan before they could sell a plant, plant owners began immediately to talk of evasion strategies: they could close a plant without selling it, run it with a skeleton crew, declare bankruptcy, or, as one industrialist threatened, "find somebody's idiot nephew to act as a caretaker."[19] If all else fails, targets may be able to shift a penalty to someone else. A firm can pass on pollution taxes to its customers in the form of higher prices, which in the theory of inducements is supposed to make the firm less competitive. It can also pass on the taxes to its workers in the form of lower wage increases or reduced benefit packages, or to taxpayers in the form of lower profits and lower corporate income taxes.

Since the Family Support Act of 1988, mothers who apply for public assistance are required to give information about their children's fathers so the welfare department can pursue the men for child support payments. The child support collection system is basically a penalty scheme, since if the state succeeds in collecting any money from the father, the mother gets only fifty dollars a month and the state keeps the rest to reimburse itself for the cost of providing assistance to the mother. Someone who wrote the legislation might have thought the threat of no welfare would be enough to get women to cooperate, and the promise of an extra fifty dollars would be a significant inducement. But welfare mothers apparently don't see things that way. Most of

[18] Kathryn Edin, *There's a Lot of Month Left at the End of the Money: How Welfare Recipients Make Ends Meet in Chicago*, (New York: Garland Press, 1993).

[19] Barry Meier, "Pressure Builds for Cleanup of Closed Plants," *Wall Street Journal*, August 7, 1985, p. 6.

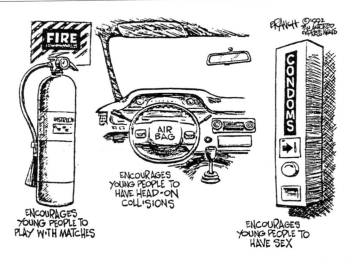

them get some assistance from their children's fathers, in the form of gifts and babysitting as well as money, without the coercive hand of the state, and they don't want to jeopardize their children's relations with their fathers by "putting the law on" the men. They are far better off pretending to comply with the welfare department by giving a false social security number or "not knowing" the father's whereabouts. By not turning the fathers in to the welfare department, they can use the threat of formal enforcement to get fathers to continue or increase their contributions.[20]

Evasion strategies are only the tip of the iceberg. In the polis, the targets of inducements rarely accept the structure of rewards and penalties as given. Targets are political creatures and they try to remake the world. Faced with an inducement system that seems to penalize them for doing what they want to do, they will first try to change the rules. They will cajole, bargain, or even bribe the givers.

Even more effective than trying to change the rules after the fact, however, is gaining control of the political institution that controls the inducement system. If there is a pollution control board meting out taxes on industrial discharges, for example, industry executives will demand some seats and try to influence the selection of members favorable to themselves. They might press for a division of seats that explicitly represents industry (along with perhaps labor, technical experts, and "the public"). They may succeed in having a former

[20] Kathryn Edin, "Single Mothers and Child Support: The Possibilities and Limits of Child Support Policy," *Children and Youth Services Review*, vol. 17, nos. 1 / 2, 1995, pp. 203–30.

industry employee appointed as the technical expert, or they might make it clear to the public representative that a high-paying job in industry follows a "cooperative" term on the board. Targets will do everything they can to make givers dependent on them—for future jobs, for information, for money—so that the givers will be restrained in meting out penalties or generous with rewards.[21]

The deliberate, officially created inducements of public policy—things such as taxes and tax credits, subsidies, low-interest special-purpose loans, mandatory sentences for certain crimes, and T-shirts—must always be placed in the perspective of the broader structure of inducements in society. Enormous disparities in power and economic resources shape the impact of the more temporary inducements of day-to-day programs. For the vast majority of people who do not control any wealth or productive assets, the overwhelming incentive is to acquire economic security by getting and keeping a job. In such a situation, a person may be more concerned with how an action will affect his or her future possibilities of work (e.g., relationships with and attractiveness to an employer, the stability of the employer's firm) than with its immediate consequences. Alternatively, a person on the brink of starvation is likely to focus on immediate consequences and ignore long-run effects. There is no general rule for predicting how inducements will affect someone's behavior, but the astute analyst should remember that every new inducement must fight for attention with an existing array of penalties and rewards, and will be filtered through the perceptions of the people to whom it applies.

Above all, it is important to remember that no system of inducements is self-executing, automatic, or apolitical. Inducement strategies are organized social systems involving two sets of people who are trying to influence each other. Not only do inducement-givers exert power over their targets, but targets are adaptive and strategic human beings who can influence the application of rewards and penalties. Even the inducements, whatever form they take, are not inert objects, passed from one set of people to the other. Their impact on people's behavior depends on how they are interpreted by both the givers and receivers, and their meaning is subject to on-going negotiation and change.

[21] For evidence that indeed industry is well represented on regulatory bodies in both the United States and abroad, see Giandocomo Majone, "Choice Among Policy Instruments for Pollution Control," *Policy Analysis* 2, no. 4 (Fall 1976): 589–614, especially pp. 603–613.

INDUCEMENTS IN THE POLIS

	Rationality Model	Polis Model
Giver	unified entity capable of consistent and rational decision	may be a collective entity with internal conflict and inconsistent decision-making
Target	unified entity capable of consistent and rational decision making	may be collective entity with internal conflict and inconsistent decision making
	oriented toward future; will change current behavior to obtain future rewards	may scramble time frame; actors within the entity may have different time frames, and their motivations may change over time
Inducements	meaning and value to targets is clear and unambiguous	may have different meaning/value to target than giver intends; may have symbolic meanings in conflict with surface meanings

INDUCEMENTS IN THE POLIS (*Continued*)

	Rationality Model	*Polis Model*
Rewards	the more rewards offered, the more likely the desired behavior change	may create alliances (and collusion) between givers and targets
		may create costs for the givers
Sanctions	the more sanctions threatened, the more likely the desired behavior change	may create conflict between targets and givers
		may harden target's resistance
		may be sabotaged by givers
		may hurt the people one is trying to protect instead of altering the behavior of the targets

gion keeps the poor from killing the rich.

12

Rules

Rules of behavior are the essential form of social coordination. General rules are necessary because, in the words of H. L. A. Hart, "No society could support the number of officials necessary to secure that every member of society was officially and separately informed of every act he was required to do."[1] Still less could society apply inducements for every action it wanted to influence. Policymaking relies heavily on official rules—rules consciously designed to accomplish social goals. Official rules in this sense are generally referred to as laws, although they might be rules made by legislative bodies (statutory laws), administrative bodies (regulations), courts (common law), or laws contained in constitutions (state or national).

Some kinds of official rules mandate behavior. They command people, organizations, and governments to act in certain ways. Other rules confer powers, either on private citizens and organizations, or on public officials and bodies. Such rules specify how people must act if they want to invoke the powers of the state to support their relationships with other people, in contracts, wills, and lawsuits, for example. And they specify how state agencies must act if their own decrees and actions are to be considered valid. We will discuss such "power-conferring" rules in Chapter 15 ("Powers") and restrict ourselves in this chapter to rules that impose obligations and duties.[2] The kind of rule

[1] H. L. A. Hart, *The Concept of Law* (Oxford: Clarendon Press, 1961), p. 21.

[2] This distinction is Hart's, ibid., Chap. 3 and pp. 78–79. He refers to primary rules (or coercive orders) and secondary rules (or power-conferring rules). My definition of rules in this chapter is quite close to his concept of primary rules: an order backed by a threat

at issue here is what is imagined when we say, "There is a rule against that."

Societies have many other types of rules to coordinate behavior in addition to formal laws and regulations—social customs and traditions, informal norms of small groups and families, moral rules and principles, and the rules and bylaws of private associations. These unofficial rules often have the force of laws, at least in their powerful impact on people's lives, and they can significantly reinforce or undermine official rules. More important, unofficial rules shape the categories and classifications used in official rules, as well as the interpretation and enforcement of rules in practice. Policy analysis is deficient if it does not account for the way formal and informal rules interact.

How a Rule Works

Rules are indirect commands that work over time. They are indirect in that they are stated once to the general class of people to whom they apply, rather than being told directly to each person in every situation that the rules cover. They apply to a broad class of actions as "standing orders," and although the threat of a sanction is always present, rules are intended to induce compliance without the necessity of invoking coercive sanctions for every action they govern.

Rules derive their enormous power from legitimacy, the quality of being perceived as good and right by those whose behavior they are meant to control. Legitimacy binds rule-follower to rule-maker. Like the "willing suspension of disbelief" that makes readers follow an author through all sorts of improbable situations, legitimacy makes citizens follow the commands of leaders, even at great costs to themselves. Legitimacy is in some sense the political scientist's equivalent of the economist's invisible hand: we know it exists as a force that holds societies together, but we cannot give very satisfactory explanations of how to create it or why it is sometimes very strong and sometimes seems to disappear. Nevertheless, we can say that rules work best when they are perceived as legitimate.

Rules generally have two parts. They prescribe *actions* to be taken in

that (a) applies to a general type of conduct and a general class of persons; (b) is generally obeyed; (c) is kept alive by a general belief that the threats are likely to be carried out in the event of disobedience; (d) is issued by a person or body who is "internally supreme" (within the nation) and externally independent.

Legit, is broken when rights are indiv.

certain *situations or contexts*. They can be formulated as "if . . . then" statements: if situation A holds, then do X. The context might involve personal identity. For example, if you are a male over eighteen, you must register for the armed services. If you hold a medical degree and a license, you may slit open people's bellies. The context might involve location. In this place you may smoke, but in that place you may not. The context might involve time. You may hunt deer only between the first Friday in October and the last Sunday of November. Or the context might involve a complex relationship defined by identity, space, and time: you may slit open someone's belly only if you are a licensed doctor, working in a medical setting under sterile conditions, after having received informed consent from the patient.

Rules depend on context because the way we regard actions—their value, their moral qualities, their acceptability—depends on context. Slitting open someone's belly is medical therapy when done by a doctor, assault when done by a hoodlum. Kissing a child is an expression of love when done by its parents, molestation when done by a stranger. Sexual harassment poses a difficult policy problem because it is so hard to define what contexts make sexual advances legitimate romantic courtship and what contexts make them exploitative uses of power. Sometimes the context part of a rule is only implied. A "No Swimming" sign on a deserted beach would seem to prohibit only an action, but the implicit message is "No swimming *here*." Who, after all, has not been driven by a hot summer day to consider the implied boundaries of "here," or for that matter, how wet one has to be before one is "swimming?"

Ask a lawyer whether something is legal, and the answer is always, "It depends." Lawyers cannot say whether actions are legal or illegal, because all rules include some context within which behavior is allowed or forbidden, and because all actions take their meaning in part from the surrounding context. Much of lawyers' work involves portraying clients' behavior in contexts that make the behavior legal (or illegal in the case of prosecutors). Lawyers thus *represent* their clients not only in the sense of speaking for them, but in the artistic sense of casting their behavior in a particular light.

Rules work by classifying situations and actions as like or unlike for purposes of action. In applying a rule, one asks whether the situation or action is "like" that defined in the rule; if so, the rule applies. For example, eligibility for workers' compensation requires a determination of whether a worker's injuries are substantially similar to those listed in a schedule of compensable injuries. Because rules classify,

Rules — sanctions as foundation

they necessarily create differences, or more accurately, consequences of differences.

Herein lies the essential political nature of rules: they include and exclude, unite and divide. Rules include and exclude by defining different treatment or permissible activity for different people. They unite and divide by placing people in different categories; those treated favorably by a rule have a common interest in preserving it, while those treated unfavorably share an interest in overturning it. Rules thus create natural alliances. Moreover, the classifications inherent in rules are far from automatic. They are made by human beings, first in the writing of rules, and later in their application and enforcement. Because the classifications determine other people's fates, rule making and rule enforcement are always acts of power.

Like the tempting "No Swimming" sign, every rule is ambiguous at the boundaries and so creates incentives for people to portray their behavior as falling within or outside its purview. These incentives to manipulate the boundaries of a rule operate on the rule enforcers as much as on the people whose behavior the rule is meant to control. The first person to be prosecuted under the 1994 federal "three-strikes-and-you're-out" law was caught in a botched convenience store hold-up in Iowa. Before the law, the man would have been charged with armed robbery, a state crime. However, a federal prosecutor saw the opportunity to use the new law, and perhaps also to make a name for himself as the first one to "put away" a hardened criminal for life. He asked a grand jury to charge the man with interfering with interstate commerce, a federal offense, and persuaded them to go along by arguing that the convenience store was part of a multi-state chain.[3]

Sometimes rules create rather surprising incentives to assume particular identities. Until fairly recently, "handicapped" had been a stigmatized identity, but a provision of the Rehabilitation Act of 1973 forbidding employment discrimination on the basis of handicap brought people into courts seeking to have obesity, short stature, left-handedness, and transvestitism classified as handicaps.[4] The Americans with Disabilities Act of 1990 expanded job protections for people with disabilities. By linking the handicapped identity to protection in the workplace, public policy attaches a benefit to it and induces people to expand its definition.

---

[3] Fox Butterfield, "A Criminal Resume Tailor-Made to Fit the New Three-Strikes Law," *New York Times*, Sept. 11, 1995, A1 and B11.

[4] See Mark Rothstein, *Medical Screening and the Employee Health Cost Crisis* (Washington, D.C., Bureau of National Affairs, 1989), esp. pp. 144–59.

The same dynamic is at work in every rule. Because rules sort people and activities into privileged and nonprivileged statuses, there will always be demands for reclassification as people seek to enter the realm of privilege or push others into the realm of disadvantage. Any classification scheme, as we saw in Chapter 7 ("Numbers"), is a matter of judgment and therefore vulnerable to two kinds of challenges: claims that truly like cases have been treated differently, and claims that truly different cases have been treated similarly. Rules gain legitimacy to the extent their classifications and those made by rule enforcers are perceived as making significant distinctions along the most important dimensions.

IN SEARCH OF GOOD RULES

The most important problem in the design of rules is the tension between precision and flexibility. The essence of precision is that both actions and contexts are (and can be) described without ambiguity. In several ways, the ideal of precision goes hand-in-hand with the ideal of the rule of law.

The argument for precise formal rules rests on three pillars. First, precise rules are said to ensure that *like cases will be treated alike,* and this type of consistency is part of what we mean by fairness and the rule of law. The formula itself conveys a deceptive precision, though. What counts as "alike?" Likeness—as we have seen in the earlier discussions of equity, symbols, and numbers—is not a quality inherent in objects, people, and situations; it is a perception on the part of observers. To judge things as like or different requires selecting some features and ignoring others. To claim that things *are* alike is really to say they *ought to be treated alike* for the purposes of achieving some end, or because prior moral principles require treating them alike.[5] Declaring a likeness is always an assertion, an act of both poetry and politics.

Second, precise rules are said to insulate people from the whims, prejudices, moods, or predilections of officials. This feature is related to the first: one reason not to give officials power to decide citizens' fates is that individual discretion will inevitably lead to like cases being treated differently. But more than the concern for consistency is at stake here. In theory, precise rules prevent officials from exercising improper power or giving their own prejudices the stamp of public

[5] See Peter Westen, "The Empty Idea of Equality," *Harvard Law Review* 95 (January 1982): 537–596.

authority. This is another interpretation of rule of law, captured by the phrase "a government of laws, not of men:" officials must look outside their own will, to known rules, for their criteria of decision.[6]

Third, precise rules are thought to provide predictability. They inform people in advance what is allowable and what will be the consequences of forbidden behavior. Being able to choose one's actions with knowledge of the consequences is part of what we mean by freedom. Also, precision ensures that no one will be punished or disadvantaged because of the way a rule is interpreted after his action. This is a third meaning of rule of law: "Government in all its actions is bound by rules fixed and announced beforehand."[7]

Protection from *ex post facto* laws is guaranteed by the Constitution (in Article I, section 9). Although the phrase usually refers to punishment under a law *promulgated* after an action, the distinction between promulgation and interpretation may be meaningless if laws are very vague and can only be implemented through *ad hoc* interpretation. As Justice William Douglas wrote in an obscenity case, "[To] send men to jail for violating standards they cannot understand, construe, and apply is a monstrous thing to do in a Nation dedicated to fair trials and due process."[8] Precision in laws thus helps prevent the injustice of after-the-fact lawmaking.

Precision has its disadvantages, however. Precise rules cannot be sensitive to some kinds of individual and contextual differences, so that inevitably, different cases will be treated alike. Rules cannot be perfectly tailored to individual circumstances. It is not necessarily only small or subtle differences that are ignored. Any rule is based on a classification scheme and will disregard features that belong to 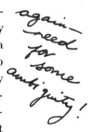 another scheme. To take a simple example, rules about town eligibility for federal economic development grants might be based on population size and per capita income, two scales that allow very fine distinctions. Yet two towns of the same size and per capita income might differ dramatically in other features relevant to economic development, such as unemployment rate, education level of the working-age population, or proximity to a metropolitan area. However refined the categories of a rule in one classification scheme, they will always be

---

[6]This formulation is Robert Cover's, in the *New York Times Book Review*, January 14, 1978, p. 27; cited by Leif Carter, *Reason in Law*, 2nd rev. ed. (Boston: Little, Brown, 1984), p. 310.

[7]Friedrich Hayek, *The Road to Serfdom* (Chicago: University of Chicago Press, 1944), p. 72.

[8]Justice Douglas, dissenting, in *Miller v. California*, 413 U.S. 15, 93, (1973).

too crude on dimensions of other schemes. The dilemma of classification is that we must always select some feature(s) as the basis for line-
drawing, and so we must always ignore others.

Precise rules stifle creative response to new situations. We can never
fully anticipate future circumstances, so it is impossible to write rules
that account for new facts, technologies, and contexts. Moreover, when
new circumstances do materialize, people typically revise or even radically change their goals. Precise rules are good for only short periods
of time and usually lag behind changes in circumstances and goals.

The failings of precision are claimed as the virtues of vagueness.
Vague rules, with very broad categories and lots of room for discretion,
can be flexible and allow sensitivity to differences. They enable creative responses to new situations. They can offer the opportunity for
efficiency by specifying general goals but letting individuals with
knowledge of particular facts and local conditions decide on the means
for achieving the goals. (The argument for block grants and state control of welfare policy is a variant of this more general argument for
vague rules.)

The case for vague rules and a high degree of discretion rests on still
other virtues. Vague rules allow for the incorporation of what Michael
Polanyi calls tacit knowledge, the things people know but cannot put
into words, much less formulate as rules.[9] Intuition is one kind of tacit
knowledge; criminal lawyers and judges often report a "sixth sense"
about whether people are guilty or innocent. Expert judgment is
another form of tacit knowledge. Some physicians are thought to have
exceptional powers of diagnosis that cannot be captured even by elaborate computer algorithms. Good politicians have a sense of how to
gather support on an issue but cannot put their skills into words.

Democracies typically have a certain distrust of tacit knowledge in
law and public policy—for all the reasons that vagueness and discretion
are criticized. A system of criminal law that relied on judges' unarticulated intuitions, for example, would seem to be the height of arbitrari-
ness. For this reason, we have developed a constitutional protection
against vague statutes. Yet we sometimes want to legislate in areas
where our knowledge is only tacit or partially tacit. Sexual harassment
might be one such area. The legitimacy of tacit knowledge was immor-
talized in Justice Potter Stewart's famous remark in a Supreme Court
obscenity case: "I can't define it but I know it when I see it."[10]

[9] Michael Polanyi, *Personal Knowledge* (Chicago: University of Chicago Press, 1962).

[10] Justice Potter Stewart, concurring, in *Jacobellis v. Ohio*, 378 U.S. 184, 197 (1964).

Vague rules, finally, also serve important symbolic functions. Ju precise rules symbolize fairness and predictability, vague rules allow for the expression of community ideals. Aspirations are better captured in general words, abstract concepts, and high-sounding slogans, such as the "public interest," the "best available technology," "pure air and water," or a right to trial by "a jury of one's peers." Vaguely stated rules can convey tough determination and commitment to eradicating a problem and, at the same time, allow lenient enforcement where strictness would be impossible or would disrupt entrenched relationships and ways of doing business. (Whether this is a good or bad feature of vagueness depends on whether you are one of the entrenched.)

The debate about precision versus vagueness in the design of rules is part of a larger debate about the proper balance of formal rules and discretion in the design of governments. How much should government officials be bound by formal rules, and how much should they apply their wisdom to individual situations? Do formal rules enhance fairness or promote rigidity? Does discretion produce refined and compassionate policy, or does it lead to favoritism and privilege?

CONCEPTS OF GOOD RULES

Precise Rules	*Flexible Rules*
Ensure fairness by treating likes alike	Ensure fairness by allowing sensitivity to contextual and individual differences
Eliminate arbitrariness and discrimination in officials' behavior	Allow officials to respond creatively to new situations
Create predictability for citizens	Create efficiency by letting officials use their knowledge of particular situations
Symbolize the rule of law	Symbolize ideals and aspirations of community, which are necessarily vague

Many of our current public policy debates are variations on these age-old questions: Is it better to regulate automobile safety through mandatory standards or through voluntary guidelines and individual discretion? Should social welfare programs be centralized, with uniform standards applying to all the states, or would decentralization allow local officials to apply their knowledge of local circumstances in ways that would make for better policy? Ultimately, even the debate about government regulation versus market arrangements is a variant of the rules-versus-discretion dilemma.

Philosophers have the luxury of conjuring up societies governed entirely by rules or by discretion. Policymakers confront the dilemma in a much narrower way: when to make a rule instead of leaving things to discretion, and how to make a good rule that helps accomplish their purposes. These questions are decided in politics rather than in theory, but it is worth dispensing with some unattainable ideals often bandied about in the scholarly world.

First is the rational ideal of *the optimum social balance* between discretionary power and control by formal rules. This ideal rests on a belief that rules and discretion each have virtues and proper uses, and that it is possible to distinguish between the necessary and unnecessary uses of either one. Kenneth Culp Davis, in his pioneering treatise *Discretionary Justice*, argues that American society has allowed far too much discretionary power to administrative agencies, and the solution is to require them to make formal rules whenever possible. Still, he is insistent that some discretionary power is necessary for an industrial society, and "the proper goal is to *eliminate unnecessary discretionary power*, not to eliminate all discretionary power."[11]

The problem with this ideal is how to identify the "unnecessary" component. Necessity is not an objective standard but rather a matter of power and resources at stake for people affected by a rule. The discretion police officers deem necessary to do their job is surely not the same as what arrested suspects and their defense lawyers think is necessary. Defense lawyers and civil libertarians say that citizens are not guaranteed their Fourth Amendment right to be free of unreasonable searches and seizures if the police are able to conduct searches without a warrant. Police claim they cannot effectively fight crime if they always have to obtain a warrant before searching in order to use the evidence against a defendant at trial. They prefer a regime that allows them to conduct searches at their discretion. The choice of how much

[11] Kenneth Culp Davis, *Discretionary Justice*, 3rd printing (Urbana: University of Illinois Press, 1971), p. 217 (emphasis added).

discretion to allow them is not between "necessary" and "unnecessary" discretion, but between the value of liberty of potential defendants and the value of security of potential victims of criminal activity.

The choice between rules and discretion is also a choice about *who* makes decisions. Mandatory sentencing laws that specify the required sentences for individual crimes take sentencing authority away from judges and give it to legislatures (since it is legislative bodies that write the guidelines and put them into law). Three-strikes-and-you're-out laws are not just a new set of rules, but a way for citizens to exert more control over judges, by demanding tougher penalties and getting their representatives to write tougher sentences into law. Thus, apparent fights about the proper degree of discretion are also power struggles between one set of actors and another. The power struggle between legislatures and courts represented in mandatory sentencing laws is evidenced by the relatively high degree of non-compliance and resistance by judges.[12] There is no possible way to determine what is the proper balance between a statutory rule and judicial discretion, or what amount of discretion is "necessary." The real issue is one of values: to what extent should society's response to crime be greater investment in prisons versus greater investment in education, good jobs, and equal opportunity? The idea of a neutral, technically optimum balance between precise and discretionary rules is an illusion that absolves us from resolving the value disputes.

A second unattainable ideal is *the perfectly precise rule*. It would spell out all the circumstances to which it applies, and would describe situations and actions with no ambiguity. The legal philosopher, Ronald Dworkin, holds that "[a] rule might have exceptions, but if it does then it is inaccurate and incomplete to state the rule so simply, without enumerating the exceptions. In theory, at least, the exceptions could all be listed, and the more of them that are, the more complete is the statement of the rule."[13] The perfectly precise rule would specify all classifications in advance and eliminate the possibilities for deliberate manipulation.

Problems worth making policy for are almost always complicated—full of fuzzy boundaries and subtle distinctions. Specifying all possible

[12] Recall the story in Chapter 11 of the judge who refused to give a 25-year prison sentence to the marijuana smoker; and see H. Laurence Ross and James P. Foley, "Judicial Disobedience of the Mandate to Imprison Drunk Drivers," *Law and Society Review* 21, no. 2 (1987): 315–323.

[13] Ronald Dworkin, *Taking Rights Seriously* (Cambridge, Mass.: Harvard University Press, 1977, 1978), p. 25.

applications and exceptions is impossible. The variety of human situations is always greater than the variety of categories in even the most precise rule, and people will insist on the importance of distinctions that the rules do not recognize. We can never fully anticipate all future circumstances in which a rule might have some bearing; more important, our goals change as circumstances change. Perfect rules would require, in Plato's words, "a legislator [to] sit at everyman's side all through his life, prescribing for him the exact particulars of his duty."[14] The perfectly detailed rule is one continuously in the process of making—it is the judgment of a wise person and not a rule at all.

Third is the ideal of *the perfectly flexible rule*. It would set forth goals but not specify any particular mechanism for achieving them. It would be elastic, capable of being stretched to fit the most peculiar circumstances and the newest, most unimaginable situations.[15] Such a rule would hardly be a rule, either. Just as the perfectly detailed rule would require constant formation, the perfectly flexible rule would be so vague as to be absolutely unconstraining.

The perfectly precise and perfectly flexible rules are static ideals, rules that work for all time and circumstances. In politics, rules can never be stable. Since the classifications in rules have important consequences, such as allocating government benefits or applying restrictive regulations, people who are disadvantaged by the rules will challenge them. And since classifications are interpretations of what is significant, they are always vulnerable to alternative interpretations.

A fourth ideal is *the neutral rule*. Neutral rules, in theory, affect everybody similarly and create no advantages or disadvantages for different people. According to philosopher Friedrich Hayek:

> They refer to typical situations into which anyone may get and in which the existence of such rules will be useful for a great variety of purposes. . . . They do not involve a choice between particular ends or particular people, because we just cannot know beforehand by whom and in what way they will be used.[16]

[14] Quoted by Jerome Frank in *Courts on Trial*, (Princeton, N.J.: Princeton University Press, 1949), p. 406.

[15] For a position advocating the perfectly flexible rule, see Robert Goodin, *Political Theory and Public Policy* (Chicago: University of Chicago Press, 1982); Chap. 4 "Institutional Framework: Loose Laws".

[16] Friedrich Hayek, *The Road to Serfdom*, op. cit. (note 7), pp. 74–75. He calls such rules "formal rules" rather than neutral rules, but his meaning is clear. See also Herbert Wechsler, "Toward Neutral Principles of Constitutional Law," *Harvard Law Review* vol. 73 (1959): 1–35.

Hayek's example is traffic rules, such as stop signs, speed limits, and right-side driving, which he contrasts with rules that command people "where to go" or "which road to take." One wonders where "one-way" signs fit in this schema, but even apart from this anomaly, the kinds of traffic rules Hayek imagines as neutral benefit some people and interests more than others. Stop signs and speed limits make for safer residential neighborhoods, but the extra safety comes at the cost of inconvenience and lost time for drivers.

All rules benefit some people and harm others, however trivial the effects may be. Once a set of rules exists for a period of time, such as tax laws or real estate laws or college admission rules, they benefit the people who have or can develop the skills and resources to manipulate them and succeed under them. Perhaps even more important, rules are never made by neutral legislators with no stakes in them, but rather negotiated by interested parties who stand to lose or gain. The ideal of the neutral rule rests on the ostrich fallacy: just because we cannot see or predict the effects of a rule on different people, we cannot assume that differential effects do not occur.

Finally, there is the perennial quest for *the perfectly enforced rule,* one that "operates with the deadly inevitability of a guillotine."[17] In

---

[17] J. Dickenson, "Legal Rules," *University of Pennsylvania Law Review* 79 (1931): 833; cited in Frank, op. cit. (note 14), p. 52.

part, this ideal is related to the perfectly precise rule: precision is said to guarantee unswerving and automatic application of rules. An influential if not dominant tradition in legal philosophy known as legal positivism holds that judges are mostly bound by formal, agreed-upon rules and most of their decisions are thus automatic. Even Benjamin Cardozo, a noted critic of this tradition, asserted that "nine-tenths, perhaps more, of the cases that come before a court are predetermined—predetermined in the sense that they are predestined."[18] The perfectly enforced rule holds out the promise of impartiality, even as it threatens cold, mechanical justice. But since rules are made and enforced in the polis, not in the mind, the perfectly enforced rule is a fantasy (or nightmare) that need not distract us.

MAKING RULES IN THE POLIS

Rules in the polis are not only objects of political conflict but also weapons. People fight with rules about rules, trying to shape them to accomplish public and private purposes. Rules are in constant tension between precision and vagueness, between centralization and discretion.

As rules are initially written, certain pressures create a tendency toward vagueness. New statutes and regulations generally get their impetus from some kind of crisis—natural disasters, major accidents and catastrophes, riots and rebellions, or scandals. The Social Security Act was triggered by the Great Depression. The Food and Drug Administration was formed after Upton Sinclair's exposé about the meat packing industry, and it received greater authority to regulate drugs after the thalidomide disaster. Marches, demonstrations, and urban riots catalyzed civil rights legislation. The Constitution, which shapes all our other political rules, was born of colonial rebellion and the need for order (or protection of private property, depending on your reading of history) in a society just cut loose from its governing framework. The Declaration of Independence is a document of crisis, cataloguing the intolerable "injuries and usurpations" of the king, portraying the separation as a desperate last resort, and setting the stage for a new set of political rules.

Crises—from suddenly intolerable tyranny to chemical plant accidents—create a mentality of absolute prevention. People want to ensure that "that kind of tragedy" never happens again. The crisis or

[18] Benjamin Cardozo, *The Growth of the Law* (New Haven: Yale University Press, 1927), p. 60.

disaster becomes the enemy, and, like a foreign invader, it unites a community and makes people temporarily forget other conflicts. Such an atmosphere produces slogans and war cries, not precisely worded rules. Citizens demand wholesale solutions ("eliminate the problem") and politicians often oblige them with vague but grandiose promises— "safe and effective drugs"; "equal opportunity"; "decent and afford- able housing"; "a safe workplace." At the same time as the crisis men- tality generates verbal hyperbole, the spirit of closing ranks on the enemy restrains policymakers from questioning feasibility or seeming to be soft on the problem.[19]

In the theory of democracy, formal rules are negotiated in elected legislative bodies by representatives of affected interests. As institu- tions, legislative bodies have certain characteristics that drive them toward the side of vaguer legislation. Legislators must worry about get- ting re-elected as well as about substantive issues. Each legislator faces not only conflict with representatives of other constituencies, but con- flicting interests within his or her own constituency. One way to escape conflict and avoid alienating potential supporters is to shun statutes that clearly harm some people. Legislators can do this by filling up their time with constituency service (helping citizens fight red tape and find information), by logrolling (obtaining programs with jobs and money for one's own district by supporting similar programs for other districts), and by purely symbolic legislation (creating National Home- makers' Week, authorizing commemorative postage stamps, renaming streets after local heroes).[20] But when they are forced to make substan- tive rules, ambiguity is a wonderful refuge. Nothing lubricates difficult bargaining and hides real conflicts so well. Who can blame a legislator for supporting "reasonable rates of return" for public utilities or for opposing "unfair methods of competition" in business?

The drive toward ambiguity in programmatic statutes described here is thought to be exacerbated by the U.S. electoral system, in which legislators face voters in single-member districts and stand and fall on their individual records. In European parliamentary systems, with their much stronger parties and proportional representation, a legisla- tor's electoral fortune depends far more on that of his or her political party and less on pleasing voters with tangible and symbolic rewards. Also, in parliamentary systems legislation is usually initiated, if not

[19] See Irving Janis, *Victims of Groupthink* (Boston: Houghton Mifflin, 1972), for a general treatment of how crises tend to restrain critical thinking and dissent in committees and other small policy-making groups.

[20] For an excellent analysis along these lines, see Morris P. Fiorina, *Congress: Keystone of the Washington Establishment* (New Haven: Yale University Press, 1977).

drafted, in the bureaucracy where the concern for workable guidelines and details is immediate.

Since rules are meant to make people do things they might otherwise not choose to do (or refrain from doing things they might choose to do), there is always some pressure on rules from potential evasion or disobedience. After all, if no one wanted to disobey a rule, there would be no need for the rule in the first place. Rules are made in the interplay between those they govern and those who enforce them. From this tension comes one of the most fascinating phenomena of politics, *perverse incentives.* Perverse incentives are incentives unwittingly built into a rule to comply with it in a way that creates new problems or exacerbates the very problems the rule is meant to cure.

Perverse incentives arise when there are trade-offs between objectives, but a rule rewards or penalizes only one of them. According to Western legend, Soviet economic planning in the 1930s epitomized perverse incentives. Textile factories were given production targets in terms of meters of cloth, so factory managers narrowed the width of looms and produced ribbons. Railroads were subjected to mandatory freight-hauling goals expressed in terms of weight. Since there were not enough goods to be shipped to meet the quotas, workers hauled goods in one direction, then filled up the cars with water for the return trip. Such stories were often told in the 1950s as proof of Soviet ineptness or the futility of economic planning, but they illustrate a profound and universal dilemma of rules: the dimensions of human activity we care about are always far more numerous and complex than what can be captured in formal rules, so rules always contain escape hatches.

You don't have to go to Siberia to find perverse incentives. Exhibit A: In an effort to contain hospital costs, Congress established Medicare payment rules that reimburse hospitals on the basis of the average durations and treatments for categories of diseases. (In the old days, hospitals were reimbursed on the basis of their costs as reported to the government.) Many hospitals, finding that the new system would reduce their income, responded by reporting some patients as having more severe (and costly) types of diseases, or worse, by discharging patients as soon as they had "used up" the amount of reimbursement allowed for their diseases.[21] Exhibit B: Many state utility commissions,

---

[21] Robert S. Stern and Arnold M. Epstein, "Institutional Responses to Prospective Payment Based on Diagnosis-Related Groups," *New England Journal of Medicine* 312, no. 10 (March 7, 1985): 621–627; and Jennifer Bingham Hull, "Medicare Payment Plan Is Blamed for Hasty Release of Aged Patients," *Wall Street Journal*, June 25, 1985, p. 33.

seeking to protect consumers from the high costs of delays and break-
downs in nuclear power plants, established rate formulas that penalize
utilities for shutdowns and let them earn more if their plants operate
steadily. Such formulas create perverse incentives to avoid or delay
shutdowns for repairs and general maintenance. The single-minded
pursuit of reliability (steady operation) undermines safety.[22]

Whenever we have multiple goals or care about several dimensions
of behavior, rules governing only one dimension may distort behavior
by pushing people to exaggerate or cut corners in another dimension.
An important aspect of this dilemma, especially in a federal system, is
the displacement of forbidden or restricted activity into other jurisdictions. If one state restricts drinking to those over twenty-one, younger
people will drive to more lenient states to purchase alcohol. If a state
tries to impose minimum wage laws or tough pollution laws, it may
drive businesses to other states where they can exploit labor and natural resources more freely.

The phenomenon of perverse incentives leads to a dynamic of ever
more elaborate rules. Rules are formulated to handle a pressing problem. The targets of rules avoid them by doing something that creates,
or brings to light, new problems. The original rules are then amended
and made more precise (so that literal compliance cannot be achieved
without meeting the spirit of the rule), more inclusive (additional
aspects of the targets' behavior are regulated), or more comprehensive
(so the would-be evader cannot escape to another jurisdiction).

Rules can create perverse incentives for the rule enforcers as well.
Formalization of rules leads officials to devote their time to enforcing
things that are part of the rules rather than things that are not. Factory
safety inspectors, for example, will diligently hunt for tangible violations specified in program regulations, no matter how trivial, but
ignore more significant or complicated problems. They know they
won't be penalized for not finding problems unlisted in the rules, and
if they do try to report unlisted problems, they cannot point to something "in black and white" when the factory owner protests.[23]

It is doubtful that perverse incentives could ever be eliminated,
although that is one of the hopes for the perfectly precise rule. We tend
to think that perverse incentives are caused by poorly designed rules,
and to some extent they are. But perverse incentives are to some extent

[22] See Matthew L. Wald, "Cutting Corners on Nuclear Safety," *New York Times*, December 8, 1985, p. F6.

[23] Eugene Bardach and Robert Kagan, *Going by the Book* (Philadelphia: Temple University Press, 1982), pp. 102–104.

inevitable. As long as rules seek to curb activities people want to carry out, and as long as people remain willful and creative creatures, rules will necessarily produce perverse incentives. Still, the designer of rules should stand in the target's shoes and ask: "How does this rule harm me, and how can I possibly get around it?" At the very least, a rule designed with these questions in mind might obviate one round in a cat-and-mouse game.

Writing rules is just the beginning. No rule or set of rules, even the Constitution, is written once and for all. Rules acquire their meanings and their effects as they are applied, enforced, challenged, and revised. Official rules are always backed up by sanctions, such as fines, revocation of privileges, or imprisonment, but they rely primarily on the magic of legitimacy to induce compliance. Most rules are usually followed out of goodwill and voluntary obedience. We don't know the real proportions for any rule, though some economists have tried to demonstrate exactly how much deterrent effect is created by each degree of severity and probability of a sanction.[24] To the extent that sanctions are part of the persuasive force of any rule, rules are subject to all the pitfalls of sanctions described in the previous chapter.

In the polis, formal rules are enforced and observed according to informal *rules of thumb.* Officials charged with enforcing rules rarely follow through on all the violations they observe or mete out penalties exactly in accordance with the formal rules. Rather, they develop informal, perhaps only intuitive, guidelines about the seriousness and blameworthiness of violations, and seek to fit the punishment to the crime in a way that matches their own sense of justice. Their own sense derives from informal rules—social customs, peer norms, moral beliefs, and existing practices.

District attorneys, for instance, have notions of normal or typical crimes based on the socioeconomic characteristics of the offender and the victim, the setting, and the manner of the crime. They may make deals (plea bargains) with suspects they deem to have committed normal offenses, offering a charge to a lesser offense in exchange for a guilty plea, but these deals are always conditioned by the prosecutor's sense that the suspect will "get his due."[25] Housing code inspectors,

[24] For a review of this literature see Phillip J. Cook, "Research in Criminal Deterrence: Laying the Groundwork for the Second Decade," in Norval Morris and Michael Tonny, (Eds.), *Crime and Justice: An Annual Review of Research*, 2 (Chicago: University of Chicago Press, 1980), pp. 211–268.

[25] David Sudnow, "Normal Crimes: Sociological Features of the Penal Code in a Public Defender Office," *Social Problems* 112 (1964–1965): 255–276.

faced with extremely dilapidated and unsanitary dwellings, tend to distinguish two types of violations, apart from the categories in the code: violations they can impute to the misdeeds or negligence of proprietors, and those they attribute to slovenly housekeeping, carelessness and destructiveness of residents.[26] In all these cases, the rough codes developed by enforcers set priorities among the violations encompassed in the formal rules and carry out justice according to some mixture of personal and social norms.

The rules of thumb of enforcers become the street wisdom of targets about what violations an agency considers minor and not worth prosecuting—in other words, what a person can "get away with." Drivers know that the police usually "give you ten miles an hour." Tax accountants know that the IRS gives everyone a $100 charitable deduction without documentation. Rules of thumb pass from enforcers to targets partly through direct hints and coaching, and partly indirectly as targets observe patterns of enforcement. Public housing officials, wanting to give an edge to elderly or white applicants in a formally "first-come, first-serve" system, coach them on how to qualify for an "emergency" placement.[27] Educating the targets about how to work the system can thus be a way for officials to enlarge their discretion.

Rules of thumb can become so widely known and accepted that they are considered more legitimate than the formal rules that spawned them. When officials suddenly stop observing informal rules and instead "go by the book," citizens feel their rights have been violated. In one city, a new police chief who started enforcing "no parking" rules in a zone previously ignored soon found himself out of a job.[28] The trucking industry virtually depends on the non-enforcement of load limits on some roads. The airline industry depends on non-enforcement of F.A.A. take-off and landing interval requirements. Under the unspoken airport operating rules, planes may take off and land more frequently than under the formal F.A.A. regulations. Air traffic controllers have occasionally used this disparity to great advantage.

---

[26] Pietro Nivola, *The Urban Service Problem* (Lexington, Mass: Lexington Books, 1979), chap. 5.

[27] Jon Pynoos, *Breaking the Rules: The Failure to Select and Assign Public Housing Tenants Equitably*, (Ph.D. dissertation, Harvard University, 1974); cited in Michael Lipsky, *Street Level Bureaucracy* (New York: Russell Sage Foundation, 1980), p. 21. For a general discussion of how agencies teach their clients the rules of the game see Lipsky, pp. 61–65.

[28] Murray Edelman, *The Symbolic Uses of Politics* (Urbana: University of Illinois Press, 1964), p. 45.

RULES IN THE POLIS

Rationality Model	*Polis Model*
A rule should have the optimum balance between covering all situations and allowing for discretion.	Deciding how much discretion is necessary entails balancing competing values.
A rule should be perfectly complete and precise; all exceptions should be stated explicitly.	Policy problems are too complex and varied to allow for perfectly detailed rules.
	Crisis moods and legislators' need to please different constituencies by writing ambiguous rules are important reasons why rules are often deliberately vague.
	It is almost impossible to write rules without perverse incentives—incentives to comply in ways that frustrate the rule's intent.
A rule should be perfectly flexible, so that it can be applied sensibly to all possible situations.	A rule that is flexible enough to accommodate all situations would have to be so vague that it would not be a rule.
A rule should be neutral, meaning it should not confer advantages or disadvantages on some people. It should affect everybody similarly.	All rules draw lines, include and exclude, and create differences. All rules benefit some people and harm others.
A rule, to be effective, should be perfectly enforced.	Enforcement is done by people who are subject to many influences and pressures besides their official responsibility for enforcing rules.

RULES IN THE POLIS (*Continued*)

Rationality Model	*Polis Model*
	Many rules have built-in perverse incentives for the rule enforcers.
	Because rules are never perfectly precise and because there are usually more violations than enforcers can handle, enforcers rely on rules of thumb.

Instead of going on strike—illegal for federal employees—they can simply "work to rule" and cause horrendous flight delays.

Common knowledge about rules of thumb can undermine an agency's effectiveness, especially if the rules it seeks to enforce are widely violated. The Securities and Exchange Commission, whose staff and resources have not kept pace with the enormous growth in financial instruments and brokers it is supposed to regulate, has all but given up monitoring certain types of small-scale fraud and broker abuses. One commissioner lamented: "Word gets out on the street: If you limit your greed to a $1 million Ponzi scheme, you aren't going to get any flak from the SEC."[29] The deterrent effect of sanctions is lost if targets can figure out exactly which violations will be prosecuted. Formal rules thus depend in part on secrecy of the rules of thumb. Rules of thumb are the shadow government behind the formal rules; each set of rules cannot exist without the other, but rules of thumb must stay in the shadows to be effective.

In the polis, the myths of perfectly precise, neutral, and enforced rules are essential to the legitimacy of laws. Our reigning image of fairness remains the idea that "likes are treated precisely alike," however little guidance the formula provides in practice. In liberal political theory, which values individual autonomy far more than collective

[29] Bruce Ingersoll, "Busy SEC Must Let Many Cases, Filings Go Uninvestigated," *Wall Street Journal*, December 16, 1985, pp. 1, 23.

power, the myths are necessary to justify why people should ever give up their autonomy and obey government. At the same time, the formula of treating likes alike implies a competing formula for justice: giving each person his or her due. This formula requires inquiry into the particular circumstances of each case—an inquiry that is necessarily personal and open to considering unique circumstances that don't fit the rules precisely. The "each person his or her due" formula suggests that more vague rules and more flexible enforcement would be the better part of justice. Informal rules mediate the tensions between these two contradictory aspects of formal rules.

13

Facts

> To be political, to be in a polis, meant that everything was decided
> through words and persuasion and not through force and violence.
> —Hannah Arendt, *The Human Condition*

THE TWO FACES OF PERSUASION

Of all the means of coordinating and controlling human behavior,
none is more pervasive, more complicated, or less well understood
than persuasion. Certainly none arouses such ambivalence. In political
theory, persuasion has two faces, one revered and the other feared.

On one side, persuasion evokes images of reasoned and informed
decision, what we can call the rational ideal. In this by now familiar
model, individual behavior is interpreted as rational decision: individuals consciously formulate goals, gather information about alternative
means to achieve them, evaluate the alternatives, and choose the ones
most likely to succeed. The rational ideal esteems those who act
according to reason, and denigrates those whose decisions are based
on raw emotion, unconscious biases, blind loyalty, or momentary passion. It cherishes argument by fact and logic, and canonizes the scientific method of discovery. It drives a search for neutral facts, unbiased
techniques, and disinterested conclusions.

The rational ideal offers reason as the basis for government. Groups,
organizations, and even whole societies can emulate the process of
rational deliberation by individuals. Democracy, many have said, is

"rational"

government by discussion. Rational persuasion is associated with voluntarism. If people can be educated, they will not need to be coerced or even induced to behave in harmony with their own and the common good. ("The facts will speak for themselves.")

Information and knowledge, in the rational ideal, obviate the need for force because they can resolve conflict. ("The pen is mightier than the sword.") Most conflict is seen to derive from ignorance, not from fundamental differences of character or interest. In the United States during the 1790s, when the first wave of almanacs and gazetteers appeared, these compilations of descriptive facts and figures were touted as the solution to differences of opinion and political disagreements. Diversity of opinion, claimed one editor, arises from indolence, dogmatism, and "a want of certain data." To correct this lack, academics, clergymen, and historians offered their collections of facts, always "authentic," "impartial," and "accurate."[1]

The dream of conflict resolution through facts is by no means a relic of history. Milton Friedman, who believes "positive economics is, or can be, an 'objective' science in precisely the same sense as any of the physical sciences," asserted more recently:

> ... differences about economic policy among disinterested citizens derive predominantly from different predictions about the economic consequences of taking action—differences that in principle can be eliminated by the progress of positive economics—rather than from fundamental differences in basic values, differences about which men can ultimately only fight.[2]

And a contemporary policy analysis textbook offers this hope to students:

> Policy disagreements would lessen—and perhaps vanish—if we could predict with certainty the safety consequences of the breeder reactor, or the

---

[1]Patricia Cline Cohen, *A Calculating People* (Chicago: University of Chicago Press, 1982), Chap. 5; the quotations are from p. 155. Compare the "almanac view" of political conflict with James Madison's theory, in *Federalist Papers* No. 10, that different sentiments, views, opinions, and interests arise from "different and unequal faculties of acquiring property [and] the possession of different degrees and kinds of property [that] immediately results." Alexander Hamilton, James Madison and John Jay, *The Federalist* (New York: Tudor Publishing Company, 1957), p. 64.

[2]Milton Friedman, *Essays in Positive Economics* (Chicago: University of Chicago Press, 1953), p. 5.

costs of annual upkeep of clay courts, or whether a special shuttle bus for the elderly would be heavily used.[3]

The rational ideal has spawned numerous policy ideas based on rational persuasion and voluntary behavior change. We have embarked on educational campaigns to get people to stop littering and smoking; to use seat belts and drive safely; to conserve energy and join car pools; to limit population growth, prevent forest fires, finish high school, exercise, recycle trash, and donate their organs. To aid individuals in making informed choices, we have imposed mandatory disclosure requirements on people and institutions who might otherwise conceal information. Thus, we have food labels, cigarette warnings, fiber content labels, financial disclosure rules for issuers of stock, "plain English" requirements for insurance policies, "truth-in-lending" requirements for banks and other lenders, fuel-economy ratings of cars, energy-efficiency ratings of appliances, tire grading, octane rating, and milk and meat grading.

The rational ideal, in sum, offers a vision of society where conflict is temporary and unnecessary, where force is replaced by discussion, and where individual actions are brought into harmony through the persuasive power of logic and evidence. Government by persuasion brings out the highest human quality—the capacity to deliberate.

Persuasion's ugly face is captured in the words "propaganda" and "indoctrination." Indoctrination has two elements that distinguish it from the processes of education or informing conceived in the rational ideal. First, it is intentionally manipulative, disguising the hidden motives of its perpetrator. It is designed to make its audience or subject serve someone else's interests, rather than to foster the subject's self-interest through increased knowledge. Second, indoctrination robs people of their capacity to think independently. If it relies on appeals to fear, insecurity, or anxiety, it drives out rational thought, and if it relies on rational appeals (for example, visions of a more prosperous future), it distorts and withholds information so that rational deliberation is truncated.

Indoctrination suggests images of Big Brother, *1984*, and thought control. This face of persuasion evokes abhorrence and condemnation among political scientists, and for the most part, they take the position

[3] Edith Stokey and Richard Zeckhauser, *A Primer for Policy Analysis* (New York: Norton, 1978), p. 261.

that "it doesn't happen here."[4] Thus, Charles Lindblom argues that persuasion as a means of social control plays a central role only in totalitarian political systems. His model of an extreme persuasion-based political system, what he calls a "preceptoral system," is defined as:

> . . . a system of social control through highly unilateral governmental persuasion addressed not to an elite or to a bureaucracy alone but to an entire population. . . . It is more an aspiration than an accomplishment, more often a disguise for coercion—even terror—than an independent system of control.[5]

While the individual in the rational ideal is autonomous, free to deliberate and choose on the basis of accurate information, in the preceptoral system the individual is a puppet whose mind has been invaded by others and who acts as though he or she chooses voluntarily but is in fact directed from without. The purpose of persuasion here is to elicit active responses, not passive obedience. It is applied to everyone—not just the masses but the governmental and party elites as well. And it is pervasive, to be found not only in government communiqués and schools, but also in the press, the radio, the subway, public celebrations, and ceremonies.[6]

Each view of persuasion has its own language. "Information" in one is "propaganda" in the other. Information "enlightens" and "liberates;" propaganda "benights" and "enslaves." "Education" in one view is "brainwashing" in the other. "Learning" in one is "compliance" in the other.

The central debate about persuasion as a form of control in public policy concerns which of these visions is "correct" and where we should draw the line between them. For any policy based on persuasion, such as public information campaigns, disclosure rules, or educa-

---

[4] Harold Lasswell and Abraham Kaplan, in *Power and Society* (New Haven: Yale University Press, 1950), define propaganda as "political symbols manipulated for the control of public opinion." They then go through intellectual contortions in clarifications and footnotes to refine the definition so that it does not include forms of indoctrination common, if not essential, in liberal democracies. They exclude: the "use of symbols to gain acceptance or rejection of a scientific hypothesis," even when illogicality and emotional appeal are involved; advertising; and matters on which "disagreement is excluded by the group," and there is no controversy (p. 111).

[5] Charles Lindblom, *Politics and Markets* (New York: Basic Books, 1977), chap. 4; the quotation is on p. 55.

[6] Ibid., pp. 57–58.

tion, how do we know whether it represents enhancement of rational deliberation or manipulation of behavior? When does information become propaganda and education brainwashing? What are the boundaries of legitimate persuasion in a democracy? To what extent are individuals reasoning creatures and to what extent are they motivated by emotion, loyalty, and other "nonrational" factors? Can groups operate by rational deliberation, or are they driven by mysterious collective forces such as the urge to conformity? Are ideas always rationalizations of self-interest?

The short answer is that the boundary between the two sides of persuasion is blurry. As with inducements and rules, underlying the abstract model of how persuasion works in either the light or dark version is a complex social reality. Between the two idealized models of persuasion lies the vast terrain of influence.

Making Facts in the Polis

To see how persuasion operates in the polis, it is useful to start with the two idealized versions, then examine them to show how neither can exist in such pure form and how they meet in the middle.

The rational ideal presupposes the existence of neutral facts—neutral in the sense that they only describe the world, but do not serve anybody's interest, promote any value judgments, or exert persuasive force beyond the weight of their correctness. Yet facts do not exist independent of interpretive lenses, and they come clothed in words and numbers. Even the simple act of naming an object places it in a class and suggests that it is like some things and unlike others. Naming, like counting and rule-making, is classification, and thus a political act.

News accounts of torture and killings in Latin America typically describe these acts as "terrorism" when carried out by left-wing rebels or peasant resistance movements, but as "security measures" or "police actions" when carried out by officials of right-wing regimes.[7] Is there a neutral way to describe such events? Even the words "torture" and "killing" are loaded. We could try to find even more sterile substitutes (how about "application of physical force to the body" and "bringing about cessation of cardiopulmonary functions?") but these

[7] Noam Chomsky and Edward S. Herman, *The Washington Connection and Third World Fascism: Vol. I, The Political Economy of Human Rights*, (Montreal: Black Rose Books, 1979), p. 6.

rather mechanical metaphors convey a certain set of values, too—perhaps disrespect for humanity and life.

Compare two different ways of describing a certain group of workers in the nuclear power industry. They are hired on a temporary basis to make repairs and clean up spills; in doing these tasks, they are exposed to very high doses of radiation for short periods. Permanent employees are not given these tasks because occupational health regulations limit their total lifetime exposure. In the *New York Times*, these workers are called "stand-ins" and "temporary employees" and described as having "part-time vocations" and "careers." In *Mother Jones* and *The Progressive*, they are called "jumpers" or "sponges" and described as being in the "meat market" and "dying for a living."[8] Embedded in those short phrases are very different stories about the social structure of the nuclear industry.

There is no escape: to name is to take a stand. And if naming is political, there can be no neutral facts, no pure description to convey to others as neutral information. This is not to say there is no such thing as accuracy and distortion, no yardstick by which to judge descriptions of events. Viewers of the video showing the Los Angeles police arresting Rodney King would probably agree that "beating" comes closer to describing the event than "handcuffing" or "friendly wrestling." ("Even a dog distinguishes between being stumbled over and being kicked," said the great jurist, Oliver Wendell Holmes.) Moral ideas and social conventions about behavior and language give us some standards for judging names as more or less close to the truth. But every name is a symbol, not the thing itself, and in the choice of names lies judgment, comparison, evaluation, and above all the potential for disagreement. The problem of neutrality and objectivity begins in naming.

The problem of distinguishing information from propaganda goes far deeper than naming. What we think of as facts—statements about the true state of the world—are produced in social processes. Most of our knowledge and ideas about the world come not from direct observation but from social knowledge, from the accumulation and presentation of observations and beliefs. We have numerous social institutions charged with finding facts (the very metaphor comes straight out of the rational ideal): legislatures conduct hearings; government agencies collect data; courts hold trials to establish the facts

---

[8] Chris Anne Raymond, "Risk in the Press: Conflicting Journalistic Ideologies," in Dorothy Nelkin (Ed.), *The Language of Risk* (Beverly Hills: Sage, 1985), pp. 100–104.

of a case; research centers and universities have as their primary mission the development of information.

These institutions, or rather the people within them, make numerous choices in developing information. There is nothing automatic about the process. Legislators decide whom to invite to testify at hearings and how much time to give each witness. Agencies decide what sort of data to collect, how vigorously to pursue nonrespondents or other missing information, and how to categorize the information they do receive. Courts attempt to determine the facts of a case in order to decide which rules of law apply. But, in the words of one prominent jurist, Jerome Frank, "facts are guesses":

> The actual events, the real objective acts and words of [the two parties to a suit] happened in the past. They do not walk into court. The court usually learns about these real, objective, past facts only through the oral testimony of fallible witnesses. . . . Judicially, the facts consist of the reaction of the judge or jury to the testimony.[9]

Maybe Frank exaggerates a bit. Courts also rely on physical evidence and written documents. They bring in expert witnesses as well as ordinary people. Still, the two parties present different versions of the past or they wouldn't be in court in the first place. They are engaged in a contest to provide the most convincing representation of reality to the judge and jury.

Think of the Rodney King trial again. In this trial, past events very nearly did walk into court, to use Frank's phrase, because a bystander had captured the whole arrest on videotape. Judge, jury, and the American public could all watch a replay of what actually happened. They could and did watch it over and over. Did that settle the question of whether the police had "beaten" Rodney King and used unnecessary force? Hardly. Prosecutors used slow motion and freeze frames to argue that Mr. King had tried to get up off the ground and fight with the police. Therefore (the prosecution story went), police had reason to feel threatened, and their actions (clobbering Mr. King with nightsticks and kicking him while he was down on the ground) should be understood as using force necessary and appropriate for self-defense and for performing their job. (The jury was persuaded. A large part of the Los Angeles community was not.)

Just because it is hard to draw a line between two things—say beat-

[9] Jerome Frank, *Courts on Trial* (Princeton, N.J.: Princeton University Press, 1949), pp. 15–16.

ing and necessary force—does not mean there are no significant differences between the two or that we should abandon trying to make distinctions. The point, rather, is two-fold. First, it *is* often hard to draw bright lines between social phenomena, especially bright lines about moral and value differences. It's much easier to draw lines about things that don't matter than things that do. And second, in political life, precisely because it is so hard to draw clear lines about things that matter, fights arise at the lines and are about the lines. In the life of the polis, facts are always under dispute.

What about scientific facts? In medicine, the scientific gold standard for evaluating new drugs and therapies is the randomized controlled trial or RCT. Patients with a disease are randomly assigned to an experimental group, which receives the treatment in question, and a control group, which receives a placebo. Random assignment is supposed to control for all the extraneous factors that could influence the effectiveness of the treatment, such as age, income, or education. These studies are usually very large, using hundreds and sometimes thousands of subjects, and they are often "double-blind," meaning neither the patients nor their treating physicians knows who receives the treatment or who receives the placebo. In the end, these studies are supposed to tell us the bare facts: the treatment does or does not help cure the disease.

In practice, RCTs have produced disappointingly mushy results. Their findings have been subject to much controversy, even within the medical profession. Clinicians have often refused to accept study results as a guide to their own prescribing and treatment choices.[10] Why? First, the researchers must choose among basic definitions and ways of counting that are already controversial among the medical profession—questions such as what are the criteria for diagnosis of the disease under study, and what are the appropriate measures of effectiveness of the treatment? If basic definitions and criteria of a study are controversial, the study cannot be very persuasive.

Second, no matter how much experimenters try to eliminate human influence, the experiments involve human beings who try to exert some

---

[10] See Harry Marks, "Medical Science and Clinical Ambiguity: The Role of Clinical Trials in Therapeutic Controversies," (Harvard School of Public Health, Center for Analysis of Health Practices, 1981); and Alvan R. Feinstein, "An Additional Basic Science for Clinical Medicine: II. The Limitations of Randomized Trials," *Annals of Internal Medicine* 99, no. 4 (October 1983): 544–550. Another excellent study of the production of scientific facts is B. Latour and S. Wolgar, *Laboratory Life: The Social Construction of Scientific Facts* (Beverly Hills: Sage, 1979).

control over their lives, and therefore over the experiment. Patients, who are usually desperately ill if they are enrolled in a therapeutic trial, may not be content to sit by passively and take a placebo drug. Some people with AIDS who were enrolled in the AZT drug trials investigated the contents of their medications to determine whether they had received a placebo and or an active medicine. Then people with the medicine shared it with friends who had been given placebos.[11] Physicians, who on the face of it would seem to be far less affected than patients by RCTs, also exert some control over the experiments. They choose which patients to recommend as subjects, and they influence whether a patient decides to participate by the way they characterize the trial. In a well-known national trial of different treatments for breast cancer, many physicians would not route eligible patients into the experiment. Some believed it was better to be safe with a radical mastectomy than to take a chance on some of the less radical treatments tested by the experiment. Many felt that entering patients into the trial would jeopardize their relationship with patients and undermine their authority.[12]

Physicians, finally, are sometimes reluctant to accept RCT findings because using RCTs to decide on therapies removes clinical judgment from the individual physician and gives it to hospital-based, research-oriented medical teams instead. Much of the power, autonomy, and indeed clinical effectiveness of practicing physicians rests on their claims to "personal knowledge" and "clinical wisdom." They base their livelihood and prestige on knowledge derived from assessing the unique combination of elements in the individual case. They believe in medical facts different from those produced by RCTs. The scientific process represented by RCTs incorporates only one kind of knowledge and favors one set of medical interests over another.[13]

[11] John Lauritsen, *Poison By Prescription: The AZT Story* (N.Y.: Asklepios, 1990), p. 30. Many gay patients, who were well organized in social and political networks, also pressured the FDA for non-randomized methods that would widen access to potentially lifesaving drugs. For a fascinating story about how the gay community revolutionized drug testing, see Patricia Siplon, "Action Equals Life: The Power of Community in AIDS Political Activism," P.h.D. diss., Brandeis University, 1996.

[12] K. M. Taylor, R. G. Margolese, and C. L. Soskolne, "Physicians' Reasons for Not Entering Patients in a Randomized Clinical Trial for Breast Cancer," *New England Journal of Medicine* 310, no. 21 (May 24, 1984): 1363–1387.

[13] Sandra J. Tanenbaum, "Knowing and Acting in Medical Practice: The Epistemological Politics of Outcomes Research," *J. of Health Politics, Policy and Law*, vol. 19, no. 1 (Spring 1994):27–44.

Randomized controlled trials in medicine are just one form of scientific fact-making. Yet because they are based on a highly developed theory of scientific method, one that respects all the conventions of good experimental design, they illustrate the kinds of difficulties that arise even in the seemingly most objective and factual of knowledge spheres. In the polis, most information is created from a point of view by real people with personal and institutional loyalties, cultural and social backgrounds, and enduring as well as more temporary interests.

The rational ideal not only overstates the purity of information, it also exaggerates the rationality of people in using information. That humans do not make decisions in purely rational fashion is a point that needs no belaboring. A voluminous social psychology literature tells us we rely on habit, stereotypes, and cultural norms for the vast majority of decisions. We are as much influenced by the source of information—the person's race, looks, social manners, reputation, and credentials, or whether the source is a person or some other medium—as by the content. We are subject to extremely strong influence by peers, co-workers, family, and other groups of which we are a part. The drive to conformity with important reference groups would seem to be at least as strong as the drive to select the best means to an end.[14] When we move from the experimental laboratory of social psychology to the real world, we find a similar story. In our various social and political roles, we act largely according to prior attitudes and beliefs rather than new information. This is true for voting decisions, for the decisions of judges, for teachers' assessment of student performance, and for mental health professionals' evaluation of their patients.[15]

One could argue that all these challenges to the image of man as a rational creature founder on the same criticism: relying on shortcuts—be they stereotypes, group norms, attitudes, or one's own previous decisions—is the most effective and least costly means of assessing

[14]On the importance of the source see Carl I. Hovland, Irving L. Janis, and Harold Kelley, *Communication and Persuasion*, (New Haven: Yale University Press, 1953), chap. 2; and J. S. Coleman, E. Katz, and H. Menzel, *Medical Innovation: A Diffusion Study* (Indianapolis: Bobbs Merrill, 1966). On conformity, see Hovland, Janis and Kelley, Chapter 5; and Irving L. Janis, *Victims of Groupthink* (Boston: Houghton Mifflin, 1972).

[15]On voting, see Angus Campbell et. al., *The American Voter* (New York: Wiley, 1964), especially chaps. 6 and 7. On judicial behavior, see David Rohde and Harold Spaeth, *Supreme Court Decision Making* (San Francisco: W. H. Freeman, 1976). On teachers, see Robert Rosenthal and Lenore Jacobson, *Pygmalian in the Classroom: Teacher Expectations and Pupils' Intellectual Development* (New York: Holt, Rinehart and Winston, 1968). On mental health professionals see David Rosenhan, "On Being Sane in Insane Places," *Science* 179 (January 19, 1973): 477–485.

alternative courses of action, and so it is rational decision making. But that argument stretches the concept of rationality so far that it only makes the point more sharply. It erases the line between autonomous, individual, reasoned decision and unreflective, conformist behavior.

Having examined the ideal of rational persuasion, we can come at the problem from the other side and ask whether indoctrination is really beyond the realm of the polis—even the liberal democratic polis. Indoctrination, recall, was defined as highly unilateral persuasive efforts that are intentionally manipulative, that are designed to secure the interests of the indoctrinator, and that deprive people of their capacity to make independent and reasoned decisions. Many political scientists have insisted heavily on the criterion of unilateralness—that is, indoctrination requires that the persuasive efforts be carried out by a single central governmental authority. In theory, if manipulative messages are thrown at a population by two or more competing groups, the effect of each is neutralized and people are protected from indoctrination.

Let us for the moment, however, not make totalitarian government a necessary condition for indoctrination and so not limit indoctrination to totalitarian regimes by definition. Instead, let's regard it as a relationship in which dominant elites control people's beliefs and knowledge in a manipulative and self-interested way. Then it is possible to see how indoctrination can happen in non-totalitarian societies.

First, indoctrination can be carried out outside the framework of a unilateral or centralized bureaucracy. Dominant groups in every society inculcate values and attitudes that help preserve their position, and they do this without obvious apparatus of centralized control. Schools in the United States perform this function without any centralized curriculum planning (as in France), without overt textbook censorship (as in the former Soviet Union), and without direct political control over the composition of school boards and the hiring of teachers. Schools are bureaucratic organizations that socialize their captive students, whatever else goes on in the process called education. They convey a "hidden curriculum" that teaches students about obedience to authority, about social stratification according to ascriptive ability characteristics, and about discipline, orderliness, and the subordination of self to central schedules.[16]

[16] See Philip Jackson, *Life in the Classrooms* (Chicago: University of Chicago Press, 1968); Richard Merelman, "Democratic Politics and the Culture of American Education," *American Political Science Review* 74, no. 2 (June 1980): 319–332; and Peter Woods, *The Divided School* (London: Routledge & Kegan Paul, 1979).

Lindblom, who makes unilateral governmental persuasion a criterion of his "preceptoral system," would be the first to argue that a powerful indoctrination of citizens by the business sector occurs in liberal
democracies, even though the business sector is neither a single actor
nor "the government." Business, he says, indoctrinates citizens to
accept its privileged position in making both economic and political
decisions, and to refrain from challenging the status quo on the "grand
issues" of political-economic organization—private property, private
enterprise, corporate autonomy, a vastly skewed distribution of income
and wealth, and the support of labor unions for business profitability.[17]

Business assures acceptance of its dominant position in controlling
the economy and government not through any central committee of
the business elite, but through its influence over public education and
mass media, and its superior organizational and financial resources.
For example, in the early part of the century, the newly emerging electric utility industry promoted itself by supplying schools and libraries
with materials on "the wonders of electricity and the romance of the
kilowatt," by offering stipends to teachers, and by pressuring textbook
companies.[18] After World War II, the nuclear industry embarked on a
similar public relations campaign on behalf of "Atoms for Peace." It
included the usual school materials; documentary films for television
(note again the rationalist metaphor of documenting pure facts); traveling exhibits; sponsorship of science fairs; aid to colleges in establishing nuclear engineering curricula; and development of a Boy Scout
merit badge in atomic energy.[19]

Business gets its message across indirectly, through news stories,
magazines, films, editorials, and speeches; all authored, initiated, and
funded by business leaders who share a similar outlook and interest.
Although liberal democracies do not share the "massive monolithic
processes" of communism and fascism, and do not silence their critics
entirely, they "fall [far] short of achieving a larger liberation of man's
minds to accomplish the degree of popular control" envisioned in
democratic aspirations.[20]

[17] Lindblom, op. cit. (note 5), especially chap. 15.

[18] Grant McConnell, *Private Power and American Democracy* (New York: Random
House, 1966), p. 19.

[19] Stephen Hilgartner, et al., *Nukespeak: The Selling of Nuclear Technology in America*
(New York: Penguin, 1983), pp. 72–82.

[20] Lindblom, op. cit. (note 5), p. 213.

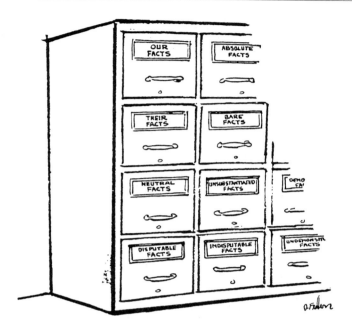

Indoctrination can happen, secondly, through ordinary government-citizen contact in daily life, perhaps more effectively than through blatant media campaigns. The preceptoral model suggests that indoctrination happens through direct provision of information in communications media—speeches, posters, books, newspapers, radio and TV broadcasts, films, exhibits and museums. But government agencies and services are another channel of influence quite apart from what is conventionally defined as "communication channels." In the modern democratic welfare state, government has face-to-face contact with citizens through an enormous number of street-level bureaucrats—people such as voting registrars, teachers, police, judges, parole officers, social workers, and eligibility determiners for the numerous health and income-maintenance programs. These people effectively dispense moral and political lessons, along with rewards and punishments.

The power of such low-key persuasion by petty officials is illustrated in V. O. Key's research on voting clerks and black voting in the South, before World War II:

> The registrar registers any qualified person, black or white, if he insists. When a Negro applies, however, she tells him that he will be registered if

he insists, but she gives him a quiet, maternal talk to the effect that the time has not yet come for Negroes to register in the county. The people are not ready for it now and it would only cause trouble for the Negro to register. Things move slowly, she tells the applicant, but the day will come. . . .[21]

No central bureaucrat wrote this registrar's lines and no state-controlled media broadcast her message. Yet, when Key examined records for her county in 1947, he found that only six people out of thirteen thousand eligible blacks were registered to vote. Of course, quiet talks were not the only influence on black voting behavior. Violence against blacks was a pervasive background threat. Nevertheless, this scenario must surely count as a dominant elite controlling other people's beliefs in a manipulative and self-interested way.

Government social service organizations have some very potent weapons with which to prod client behavior in the right directions. Social workers often hold the power to reduce or increase welfare benefits, to get clients into special housing and employment programs, or to remove children from families by pursuing claims of child abuse. Mental health professionals wield the power to institutionalize and release people. Judges hold the power to exact payments, send people to jail, or take away their children. Consider the power of a Texas judge who, in a routine child custody case, berated a bilingual Hispanic mother for speaking only Spanish so her daughter would become bilingual:

> You're abusing that child and you're relegating her to the position of housemaid. Now get this straight. You start speaking English to this child because if she doesn't do good in school, then I can remove her because it's not in her best interest to be ignorant."[22]

This kind of intimidation to force a naturalized American citizen to abandon her native culture may be infrequent. But when the intimidation is carried out by a government official in a state with a large Mexican and Mexican-American population and a law making English the only official language, it surely belongs near the indoctrination end of the persuasion spectrum.

Some service programs explicitly use the behavior modification

---

[21] V. O. Key, Jr. *Southern Politics* (New York: Knopf, 1949), pp. 566–567.

[22] State district court judge Samual C. Kiser, quoted in Sam Howe Verhovek, "Mother Scolded by Judge for Speaking in Spanish," *New York Times* August 30, 1995, p. A12.

techniques of deprivation and subsequent reward for good behavior. Prisons and juvenile detention homes offer cigarettes, special food, better accommodations, books and newspapers, and outdoor passes as incentives for cooperative behavior. Mental health institutions use the same things to reward socially acceptable or "normal" behavior such as neatness and cleanliness, and to reward work for which noninstitutionalized people would receive wages, such as janitorial work, laundry, and grounds-keeping.

This sort of behavior modification is hard to distinguish from the model of a preceptoral system in which persuasive efforts call for "active responses," not merely passive obedience. Communist regimes, with their efforts to make "a new man" suitable for participation in a socialist democracy, have served as the archetype of political indoctrination for American social scientists. But listen to some claims of American social scientists, who want to reform personal character and create virtuous citizens as a bulwark against what they call social pathology:

> If we wish to address the problems of family disruption, welfare dependency, crime in the streets, educational inadequacy, or even public finance properly understood, then government, by the mere fact that it defines these states of affairs as problems, acknowledges that *human character is, in some degree, defective and that it intends to alter it.* . . . The essential first step is to acknowledge that in almost every area of public concern we are seeking to induce persons to act virtuously, whether as schoolchildren, applicants for public assistance, would-be lawbreakers, or voters and public officials. . . . *Virtue . . . is learned by the regular repetition of right actions.* We are induced to do the right thing with respect to small matters, and in time we persist in doing the right thing because now we have come to take pleasure in it.[23]

Finally, indoctrination can happen as much through withholding of information as through the provision of information. The classic model of preceptoral systems neglects the importance of withholding information in influencing public opinion and decision making. It conceives of indoctrination as a concerted positive campaign to fill

[23] James Q. Wilson, "The Rediscovery of Character: Private Virtue and Public Policy," *The Public Interest*, no. 81 (Fall 1985): 3–16; the quotation is on p. 15, emphasis added. For other calls for government to engage in character training, see Gertrude Himmelfarb, *The De-moralization of Society* (New York: Knopf, 1995); Amitai Etzioni, *The Spirit of Community* (New York: Crown, 1993); and James Q. Wilson, *The Moral Sense* (New York: Free Press, 1993).

people's minds with slogans and propaganda. But secrecy and silence can be just as manipulative, and perhaps more so because they are less obvious.

Democratic political theory as well as the field of policy analysis rhetorically embrace the principles of unrestricted access to information and use of complete information in policy decision making. Rhetoric notwithstanding, withholding information is a fundamental and essential part of strategy in all aspects of human affairs, from the highest level of international negotiations down to the most intimate level of personal relationships. Secrecy is integral to both markets and government.

As we saw in Chapter 3 ("Efficiency"), withholding information from potential and actual consumers is crucial to sellers' power. Through withholding, sellers are able to maintain a stable base of consumers and thereby garner long-term stability and security for themselves. That is why producers of goods and services fight ferociously to preserve secrecy. Chemical manufacturing and processing companies resist disclosure of contents to workers, physicians, and local governments, using as their justification the need to protect trade secrets. And, indeed, in a competitive economy, trade secret protection is necessary for survival. Retailers frequently cooperate to withhold price information from consumers by not publishing price lists or by refusing to give price information over the telephone. Physicians, lawyers, funeral homes, pharmacies, opticians, banks, and credit companies have all engaged in this kind of withholding. On the other side, as we saw, consumers also withhold and disguise information, especially in the insurance and financial credit industries.

Secrecy is central to government, no less than to markets. It plays a role in elections, where candidates do their best to disguise sources of income and campaign support in order not to reveal loyalties to particular groups or deals made in exchange for promised votes. Those loyalties and deals, if made more public, would destroy the illusion that elected officials are responsible to "the voters" as a whole or that they decide policy issues entirely on the basis of reasoned judgment. Officials and legislators often draft new regulations or laws in semi-secret. Secrecy allows them to explore bargaining positions without committing themselves publicly, and so facilitates compromise.

Secrecy is the linchpin of defense policy. Military strategy is as much concerned with keeping our own capacities and plans secret as with developing actual military strength. The secrecy used to manipulate opponents can spill over into domestic politics. In 1994, former Reagan

Administration officials revealed that they had faked some weapons tests a decade earlier as part of the Strategic Defensive Initiative, popularly known as Star Wars. They rigged the tests to make a missile perform well in order to make the Soviet Union think the U.S. had developed an effective missile interceptor. Caspar Weinberger, who had been Secretary of Defense at the time, told the *New York Times:* "You're always trying to practice deception. You are obviously trying to mislead your opponents and to make sure that they don't know the actual facts." So far so good. But it seems that the faked test was also designed to fool Congress and persuade it to keep funding the program. A scientist on the project told the same *Times* reporter: "We would lose hundreds of millions of dollars if we didn't perform it [the test] successfully."[24] This was not the first or last time the Pentagon had deceived Congress with false test data,[25] nor the first time the executive branch had lied or falsified information for Congress. Where on the spectrum between democratic persuasion and indoctrination by "the government" should we place such politics—politics where the executive branch of government manipulates the legislature with falsified data?

Withholding of information from the general public occurs without formal censorship or classification. The nuclear and chemical industries conceal leakages and spills by simply not issuing press releases. The U.S. government nuclear installation at Hanford, Washington, made no public announcements of radioactive material leakages before a major one in 1973, and since then has used a very high threshold for deciding when to notify the media of probable leaks.[26] These decisions to withhold information from the public may be based on some obligation not to create needless alarm, but by withholding information, officials have appropriated for themselves the power to

[24] Quotations are from Tim Weiner, "Lies and Rigged 'Star Wars' Test Fooled the Kremlin, and Congress," *New York Times* August 18, 1993, p. A1; Tim Weiner, "Inquiry finds 'Star Wars' Tried Plan to Exaggerate Test Results," *New York Times*, July 23, 1994, p. A1.

[25] See Elinor Chelimsky, Assistant Comptroller General of the U.S. General Accounting Office, letter to Colonel William L. Capella, Office of Inspector General, Department of the Airforce, dated Aug. 16, 1993, documenting the Air Force's misrepresentation of its test data (available from U.S. General Accounting Office, Washington, D.C.); and U.S. General Accounting Office, "The U.S. Nuclear Triad: GAO's Evaluation of the Strategic Modernization Program," Statement of Elinor Chelimsky before the U.S. Senate, Committee on Governmental Affairs, June 10, 1993 (Washington, D.C., U.S. General Accounting Office, 1993, document no. GAO/T-PEMD-93-5).

[26] Hilgartner, el al., op. cit. (note 19), pp. 150–159. 28.

define "needless." The withholding of information blocks the formation of public sentiment against chemical plants and nuclear power.
Such blockage of opinion and preference formation must surely take
us away from rational persuasion toward the indoctrination end of the
persuasion spectrum.

Because secrecy is an integral part of strategy in the polis, policies
about revelation and withholding are a common object of struggle.
Many policy battles can only be understood as efforts by one side to
preserve its ability to conceal, and efforts by the other to gain access
to information. That is the issue behind all the mandatory disclosure
programs in consumer, safety, and health regulation. It underlies
much of the controversy in administrative rule-making procedures. To
take only one example, the federal administrative agencies are
required to publish draft regulations, give time for interested parties to
send written comments, and respond to all significant points raised in
the comments. This reform represents an effort by traditionally weak
groups such as consumers and environmentalists to make agency decision making more visible and less easily manipulable by traditionally
stronger client groups, especially the regulated industries.[27]

Persuasion as a policy instrument has often been viewed either as a
neutral instrument of science and the market, or as a dangerous
weapon of totalitarian governments. These ideal types obscure the
nature of influence in the polis. Shaping of information is an inevitable
part of communication and an integral part of strategic behavior. The
rational ideal is false in its pretense that information is neutral or that
people are primarily rational and independent creatures. But the preceptoral model is equally false in its presumption that indoctrination
occurs only where there is a single political authority dispensing propaganda through communications media and schools. Indoctrination,
defined as the intentional manipulation of opinions and preferences
and the destruction or prevention of independent judgment, occurs in
liberal democracies. It takes place as much through the withholding of
information as through the dispensing of it. And it happens in the
everyday relations between citizens and between the citizen and the
state.

[27] See Richard Stewart, "The Reformation of American Administrative Law," *Harvard
Law Review* 88, no. I (June 1975):1667–1813.

Persuasion in the Polis

Rational-democratic Model	Totalitarian Model	Polis Model
1. Reason is the basis for personal and government decisions.	People accept government propaganda, act like puppets, don't decide for themselves.	People use habit, simplifications, stereotypes, group norms, as well as reason, in making decisions.
2. Facts, data, and information are neutral, and can settle conflicts.	Information is slanted, limited, and highly controlled. It is used as means of social control, not democratic conflict resolution.	Facts and information (even names) are interpretive and usually contested. Information is used to influence and to manipulate.
3. The government uses information and education to bring individual actions into harmony with the public interest.	The government indoctrinates everyone via central control of communications apparatus.	Everyone tries to manipulate others' beliefs and preferences. The government and dominant groups have more resources to influence others, even without central apparatus.

14

Rights

Resolving policy problems with legal rights is a long-standing impulse in American politics. Well over a century ago, Alexis de Tocqueville noted:

> There is hardly a political question in the United States which does not sooner or later turn into a judicial one. . . . [L]egal language is pretty well adopted into common speech; the spirit of the law, born within schools and courts, spreads little by little beyond them; it infiltrates through society right down to the lowest ranks, till finally the whole people have contracted some of the ways and tastes of a magistrate.[1]

To appreciate how deeply rights are ingrained in our political culture, consider how many political demands are framed in terms of rights. The abortion issue is cast as a "right to life" on one side versus a "right to control one's body" on the other. The school integration issue is cast as a "right to equal education" versus a "right to attend neighborhood schools." The problem of plant closings and unemployment is fought as a battle between "enterprise rights" and the "right to work." Welfare policy pits the poor person's "right to subsistence" against the wealthier person's "right to dispose of one's property as one wishes." Consider, too, how many groups have mobilized around the concept of rights, following the example of the black civil rights movement: women, students, gays and lesbians, prisoners, consumers, Native

[1] Alexis de Tocqueville, *Democracy in America*, J. P. Mayer (Ed.), (New York: Doubleday Anchor, 1969), p. 270.

Americans, welfare recipients, the elderly, and the disabled, not to mention several organizing efforts on behalf of groups who cannot organize themselves, such as children, the mentally retarded, and the homeless.

Rights are yet another way of governing relationships and coordinating individual behavior to achieve collective purposes. Rights partake something of rules and sanctions, but as a policy strategy, rights are a more diffuse method of articulating standards of behavior in an ongoing system of conflict resolution.

The discourse of rights has two broad traditions, which I will label positive and normative. In the positive tradition, a right is a claim backed by the power of the state. It is an expectation about what one can do or receive or how one will be treated, but what distinguishes it from just any fantasy is the capacity to realize it by invoking the state's help if necessary. Oliver Wendell Holmes once defined law as "prophecies of what the courts will do in fact."[2] We can know whether a right exists only by seeing whether a government has backed similar claims in the past or by making a claim as a test case. Rights in this sense are thus specific to individual political systems.

In the normative tradition, it is harder to know whether a right exists (though it is not easy or cheap in the positive tradition), and there are many schools of thought about how we can define rights.[3] What holds the various normative schools together are two central beliefs: that people can have a right to something they do not actively claim or for which the state would not back them up; and that rights derive from some source other than the power of enforcement. In this tradition, one might claim that wives have a right not to be beaten by their husbands, even though many never seek help and much wife beating is ignored by law enforcement agencies. In the positive tradition, by contrast, wives have a right to be free of beating only if, when they protest beatings, the state takes their side and restrains the husbands.

In the realm of public policy, where there is a goal of changing people's relationships and social conditions, the positive tradition seems to offer levers to pull and a definitiveness that normative concepts lack. Yet advocates, reformers, and oppressed people often organize around the normative type of claim—namely, that people have rights yet

---

[2] Oliver Wendell Holmes, "The Path of Law," in *Collected Legal Papers* (New York: Harcourt, Brace and Howe, 1920), pp. 167–202; the quotation is on p. 173.

[3] I will offer a few more concepts of rights later on in this chapter, but for a good short review of the subject, I recommend Stanley Benn, "Rights," in *Encyclopedia of Philosophy* V. 7 (New York: Macmillan, 1967), pp. 195–199.

unrecognized legally. In the polis, the two sides of rights are inseparable. The main theme of this chapter is that the legal rights of real political systems are energized, constrained, and constantly challenged by normative meanings of rights.

A simple example will illustrate. When the founders of the United States decided to separate from Britain, they cast their Declaration of Independence in normative terms, invoking "the Laws of Nature and of Nature's God" to justify their action. They felt no need to point to human law, because, as they said, "We hold these truth to be self-evident, that all men are created equal, that they are endowed by their Creator with certain unalienable Rights, that among these are Life, Liberty and the pursuit of Happiness." Nevertheless, as they formed a new government, no one counted on Nature or God to guard the unalienable rights. Instead, they drew up a written constitution, appended a formal Bill of Rights, and provided for a judicial system to resolve the conflicts they knew would arise. Gradually, new meanings were read into the Constitution from the social controversies of the

CONCEPTS OF RIGHTS IN THE POLIS

Positive Rights	*Normative Rights*
1. A right is a claim backed by the power of the state.	A right is whatever people in a given society ought to be able to do, have, or expect from fellow citizens and the government.
2. Rights derive from the power of government.	Rights derive from some source other than power, such as morality, religion, rationality, or natural law.
3. People can have rights only to those things they claim and for which the state backs them up.	People can have rights to things they don't actively claim, and for which the state would not back them up.

times. For example, the Bill of Rights has been interpreted to include a right to "privacy," a word nowhere mentioned in it or the rest of the Constitution. Privacy, in turn, has meant different things in different eras. In the 1890s, constitutional scholars interpreted it to mean that the rich and famous should be protected from eager photographers and should have a right not to have unauthorized photos published.[4] To lawyers of more recent decades, a right to privacy has meant that no one could interfere with a person's using contraceptives, having an abortion, reading pornography at home, or engaging in homosexual practices.[5]

How Legal Rights Work: The Ways and Tastes of a Magistrate

What does it mean to call for a legal right to something as a policy solution? We can answer this question in two ways: first by describing what it is that people want or could possibly get when they call for a legal right, and second by describing what they must do to bring a right into existence or realize it.

People with disabilities often call for a "right to work," and there is now federal legislation that prohibits most employers from discriminating against a person on the basis of handicap. Many things prevent disabled people from working. Employers often refuse to hire them; some cannot drive or use public transportation to get to a job; some were not accepted in public schools as children, and so do not have the necessary education; or perhaps they cannot manage to perform all the tasks of an available job, as jobs are now defined. What might a right to work in this context mean?

It might mean that every time a disabled person applied for a job, he or she would receive individual consideration "on the merits." Employers would not be entitled to conclude that all blind people, say, are incapable of operating a machine. They would have to inquire into the capabilities of each applicant. This type of right is *procedural.* Pro- cedural rights spell out a process by which important decisions must

[4]See Samuel D. Warren and Louis D. Brandeis, "The Right to Privacy," *Harvard Law Review* 4 (1890): 193–220.

[5]On pornography, *Paris Adult Theater I v. Slayton*, 413 U.S. 49 (1973); on contraceptives, *Griswold v. Connecticut*, 381 U.S. 479 (1965); on abortion, *Roe v. Wade*, 410 U.S. 113 (1973); and on a failed attempt to include homosexual practices under the umbrella of a right to privacy, see *Bowers v. Hardwick* 478 U.S. 186 (1986).

you made in a certain way, but it does not include the right to an out-come of a certain kind (say, the employer must hire you).

Classic examples of procedural rights are the right to a fair hearing or a trial by a jury of one's peers. For the most part, the rights against discrimination demanded by blacks, women, the handicapped, and other minorities are procedural rights. They are claims to have deci-sions about employment or housing or schooling made on the basis of individual merit rather than ascriptive characteristics. Hence, there is a certain paradox in the civil rights strategy: in order to be treated as individuals, people first have to organize and make demands as a group.

A right to work might mean that no one can prevent you from work-ing—say, by making an outright rule against handicapped people in the workplace, or by erecting physical barriers to people in wheel-chairs. This would be a *substantive right.* Substantive rights go beyond procedure to specific actions and entitlements. In this case, we have provided a *negative substantive right*—the right to do something free of restraint. Negative rights are single-party rights in that no second party is necessary for an individual or group to assert them. Second parties can only prevent the assertion of negative rights (which they do illegitimately if the activity is indeed a right). The classic First Amend-ment freedoms are of this type—the right to free speech, assembly, religion—as are the right to organize collectively or to vote.

We could provide both a procedural right and a negative substantive right, and disabled people might still claim they don't have the right to work. A genuine right to work, they might say, means that someone has an obligation to create jobs that disabled people can do, and to hire them. The Americans with Disabilities Act of 1990, for example, requires employers to redesign jobs—tasks, equipment, schedules—to accommodate people with disabilities who are otherwise qualified. Government could also see to the provision of jobs for the disabled by organizing "sheltered workshops," or, as in West Germany, requiring all employers to hire the disabled as a certain portion of their work force.

This type of right would be a *positive substantive right*—an entitle-ment to have or receive something, such as a job, education, health care, or food. A positive substantive right implies the necessity of a second party to provide the "right-holder" with the entitlement. The assertion of a right to a job or to health care makes no sense if no one

---

[6]Negative substantive rights as I have defined them are the same as Isaiah Berlin's con-cept of negative liberty (see chap. 5 of this book), in "Two Concepts of liberty," in *Four Essays on Liberty* (New York: Oxford University Press, 1969), pp., 1969), pp., 118–172.

has a duty to provide it. Thus, positive substantive rights must always be coupled with positive duties or obligations of second parties.

All three types of rights are plausible claims about a right to work, so we can see how there might be a lot of political conflict over whether disabled people do or don't have a right to work and what is necessary to establish one. It is important to note, also, that all three types of rights define relationships. The relationships are most obvious in positive substantive rights, with their corresponding obligations. Procedural rights specify how one party must make decisions with respect to another. Negative substantive rights create relationships of noninterference. It is in this aspect—their *definition of relationships*—that rights can function as a social regulatory mechanism.

How do these ideas about relationships get translated into "real" rights or put into practice? What do people have to do to assert rights or claim new rights? Strictly speaking (the magistrate harrumphs), a legal right entails three elements. First, there must be an *official statement of the right*—a prior law, rule, decision, or contract that specifies or implies the right. Second, there must be a process for determining contested rights. And third, there must be a remedy, a way for rightholders to enforce the relationship defined in the right.

When groups seriously call for a right to something, they must go beyond slogan mongering and try to establish a formal legal rule to define the right. One route is statutory law—that is, either passing an entirely new statute or amending an old one. For example, amendments to the Urban Mass Transportation Act in 1970 declared that "elderly and handicapped persons have the same rights as other persons to utilize mass transportation facilities and services." The statute went on to assert a rather vague positive duty, saying that "special efforts shall be made in the planning and design of mass transportation facilities and services" to make them accessible. Federal transit programs were charged with implementing this requirement.[7]

Another route is administrative law. In fact, most statutes are fairly general and require administrative rules to implement them. In the public transportation example, the Department of Transportation issued regulations in 1976 defining what "special efforts" public transit agencies would have to make; in this case, the regulations merely offered illustrations rather than setting forth detailed requirements. (Armchair philosophers might enjoy speculating about what kind of

[7] Urban Mass Transportation Act of 1970, 49 U.S.C. 1612(a). This and the other examples of disputes over access to public transit are drawn from Susan Olsen, "The Political Evolution of Interest Group Litigation," in Richard Gambitta, Marilyn May, and James Foster (Eds.), *Governing Through Courts* (Beverly Hills: Sage, 1981), pp. 225–258.

right to public transportation, if any, was enjoyed by disabled people between 1970, when the statute was passed, and 1976, when the implementing regulations were passed.)

Formal statements of legal rights are also created in common law, the decisions of judges as they resolve disputes. In claiming rights, individuals and groups usually try to link their claim, through a lawsuit, to an existing constitutional phrase, statute, administrative rule, or to a prior court decision. For example, a disability rights group sued the Washington, D.C., transit authority under the Urban Mass Transit Act because the new subway system, with its steep escalators, was not accessible to people in wheelchairs. A federal judge enjoined the subway from opening until elevators were installed, and ordered that stations had to be constructed so that disabled people would have "ready access." Later, disabled people could point to the judge's decision as a statement of a right to accessible stations. In common law, judges thus articulate new standards of behavior in the course of resolving disputes about existing constitutional, statutory, administrative, or judicial standards.

If a group or individual does not succeed in getting a judge to interpret written law to include their demands, they may seek new legislation or a constitutional amendment. For a long time, many public and private employers offered disability insurance to their employees, but did not include pregnancy as a covered disability, even though they did

cover some conditions unique to men, such as baldness and vasectomies. Women's advocates tried litigation, but when the Supreme Court refused to read the Constitution's equal-protection clause as applying to the treatment of pregnant employees in disability plans, women's groups turned to Congress and got a legislative right to equal treatment in the Pregnancy Disability Act of 1978. Constitutional amendment is a more difficult route, as women found out with the Equal Rights Amendment, but difficulty doesn't stop many groups from trying.

Our decentralized federal system provides many levels of constitutions, statutes, regulations, and decisions that can serve as access points for claims of rights. The Constitution and federal laws are the most potent vehicles for establishing rights, because they apply to all citizens. But state and local governments are also key arenas for contests of rights. Many states have human rights laws that provide stronger protection against employment and housing discrimination than federal law, but only for the citizens of that state.

The second element of a legal right is a highly stylized *grievance process* through which individuals and groups channel their claims. This process, called litigation (from the disputing parties' point of view) or adjudication (from the judge's point of view), is associated with courts but can also take place in administrative agencies. For example, the Social Security Administration uses several hundred "administrative law judges" to hear claims of applicants who believe they have been unfairly denied disability insurance benefits. The essence of adjudication is that two parties—one claiming a right denied, the other alleged to have denied the right—air their dispute before a neutral third party. In theory, at least, they conduct their dispute through reasoned argument, rather than through force, exchange of money, or emotional appeals. And the third party or judge is constrained to make a decision by applying preexisting rules to the facts of the particular dispute.

Whether and how judges are constrained in making legal decisions is the central question of the field of jurisprudence. At one end of the spectrum of answers is the view that "the law is a seamless web" of logical relationships; judges' decisions, if they are good and honest judges, are entirely determined by preexisting legal rules. At the other end is the view that judges' decisions are mostly determined by factors outside the law—anything from their economic self-interest to their class interest to their political beliefs to what they ate for breakfast. Between these extremes is a range of views that sees judges' decisions

as the strategic interplay of ideas from the law and interests from outside the law.[8]

Still, it is the promise that disputes will be resolved neutrally,
according to preexisting rules rather than according to relative wealth
or power or charm, that gives rights their legitimacy as a mode of social
regulation. (Remember the ideal of the rule of law.) This abstract
model of adjudication is often at odds with reality, but it is nevertheless
the ideal that motivates political actors and it embodies key assumptions that must be tested in designing and evaluating a rights strategy
in public policy.

Finally, in order for rights to work as a policy strategy, there must be
an *enforcement mechanism.* With rules and inducements, the primary
responsibility for monitoring behavior lies with the government (or
rule maker). In practice, officials in enforcement and regulatory agencies rely heavily on citizen complaints to get their information about
rule violations, but we would consider a police department remiss if it
did nothing to stop crime other than answer the telephone. With
rights, by contrast, the primary responsibility for monitoring lies with
the right-holders. The assumption of our legal system is that violations
of rights will be discovered by right-holders themselves, as they are
harmed. This assumption points up another difference between rules
and rights. With rules, monitoring is meant to catch violations before
they cause much damage; with rights, an aggrieved party usually can
bring a claim only after an injury—physical or legal—has occurred.

Assuming that someone has discovered a violation and successfully
asserted a claim of right in an adjudicatory proceeding, there still
needs to be a way of ensuring that the right-withholder grants the right
to the right-holder. Systems of rights, like systems of rules, rely on
legitimacy to induce most people to comply voluntarily with laws and
judicial decisions. All that adjudication does, after all, is produce a
declaration. If one party doesn't heed the declaration, there is a need
for other remedies. Rights must be backed up by the threat of force.

Perhaps the most dramatic example of this principle was the case of
James Meredith, a black man who in 1963 obtained a federal court
order allowing him to enroll at the staunchly segregated University of
Mississippi. The governor of Mississippi announced he would defy the
order, declared Mississippi's courts "as high as the Supreme Court and
more capable," personally blocked Meredith's way into the university
buildings, and encouraged hundreds of angry citizens to come to the

---

[8]Two good places to explore this question are Edward Levi, *Legal Reasoning* (Chicago:
University of Chicago Press, 1949); and Leif Carter, *Reason in Law,* 2nd ed. (Boston:
Little, Brown, 1984).

campus to protest Meredith's registration. To back up the court order, President Kennedy federalized the Mississippi National Guard, dispatched several hundred troops to the campus to protect Meredith while he enrolled, and provided federal marshals to protect him until he graduated.[9]

The issue of school integration is often presented as a model of how legal rights are supposed to work. Legislatures and courts produce official declarations of rights; violations are discovered and protested in the process of litigation; adjudication explicates and clarifies rights by applying preexisting rules to new controversies; and, with proper enforcement, the whole process brings behavior into compliance with official policy. In this model, formal statements of rights become almost a magic wand that transforms society. Richard Kluger, assessing the impact of the Supreme Court's decision in *Brown v. Board of Education*,[10] said, "It meant that black rights had suddenly been redefined; black bodies had suddenly been reborn under a new law. Blacks' values as human beings had been changed overnight by the declaration of the nation's highest court."[11] Martin Luther King, Jr., called on President Kennedy to support a civil rights bill, and thereby "give segregation its death blow through the stroke of a pen."[12]

The magic-wand view has rightly been called "the myth of rights."[13] Rights rarely work as well as they did for James Meredith, and even if they sometimes work for one person or one situation, it is far harder for rights to alter the structures of institutional power and behavior that shape individual actions. A federal battalion may succeed in shepherding one man through college, but it cannot change attitudes and procedures that subtly discourage blacks from applying to most colleges or prevent them from succeeding as they pass through college and move into the job market. As Robert Dahl wrote in 1957, three years after *Brown v. Board*, "By itself, the Court is almost powerless to affect the course of national policy."[14]

Sometimes the rights strategy is envisioned as a top-down affair: a

[9] My account is drawn from Arthur M. Schlesinger, Jr., *A Thousand Days* (Boston: Houghton Mifflin, 1965; Fawcett paperback edition) pp. 858–867.

[10] *Brown v. Board of Education* 347 U.S. 483, 74 S.Ct. 686 (1954) is the case in which the Supreme Court first declared (in 1954) that "segregation is a denial of equal protection of the laws."

[11] Richard Kluger, *Simple Justice: The History of Brown v. Board of Education and Black America's Struggle for Equality* (New York: Vintage Books, 1977), p. 749.

[12] Quoted in Schlesinger, op. cit. (note 9), p. 849.

[13] Stuart Scheingold, *The Politics of Rights* (New Haven: Yale University Press, 1974).

[14] Robert Dahl, "Decision Making in a Democracy," *Journal of Public Law* 6 (1957): 279.

Rights as Policy Instruments

Types of Rights

Procedural Right	Defines a process by which decisions must be made
Substantive Right	Defines specific actions or entitlements people may claim
Negative	A right to be free of restraint; says no one can prevent you from doing something
Positive	An entitlement to have or receive something; specifies obligations of someone to provide whatever the entitlement is

Sources of Rights

Legislatures	Statutes passed by a legislative body at any level (federal, state, local)
Constitutions	Constitutions of the U.S. or any of its states
Administrative Agencies	Rules and regulations promulgated under agency authority
Courts	Past decisions and precedents of judges at any level of the court system

Mechanisms of Rights

Formal Statement	Given in one of the four sources above
Grievance Process	Adjudication between two (or more) parties to conflict by a neutral third party (judge)

Enforcement Process	Must be initiated by citizens who think their rights have been violated, or by corporations or assignees
	Adjudication process provided by government (though it helps to have private sources of funds to purchase legal advice)
	Compliance with courts' decisions; rests mostly on citizens' voluntary cooperation

legislature passes a new law or a court renders a decision incorporating a statement of right that forever after regulates a certain kind of relationship.[15] Sometimes the strategy is envisioned as bottom-up: the individual, relying on existing law, claims a right to a certain kind of relationship and, through litigation, succeeds in obtaining a new statement of rights.[16] But always in the myth of rights, formal, official statements of legal rights are the central animus, whether of claimants in their pursuit of grievances or of judges in their resolution of disputes.

ends up here, more vulnerable

Rights in the polis are not a matter of simple mechanism. Like rules, inducements, or any other policy strategy, they are fashioned in the strategic interplay among political actors, out of an amorphous and constantly changing set of ideas about right and wrong, good and bad, justice and injustice.

Making Rights in the Polis: The Normative Basis of Legal Rights

A willingness to bring grievances is absolutely essential to the function of a rights system. Cases do not and cannot come to court unless someone believes that his or her rights have been denied and decides to

[15] For example, see Kluger's interpretation quoted earlier (note 11).

[16] For example, after the James Meredith affair, an African delegate to the UN General Assembly praised the U.S. government for its handling of the race issue: "For one small Negro to go to school, it threatens governors and judges with prison sentences . . . It sends troops to occupy the University of Mississippi." Quoted in Schlesinger, op. cit. (note 9), p. 866.

bring a case. Courts can articulate as rights only those demands that individuals or organizations formulate as rights in the first place. The types of claimants and types of claims they bring determine the kinds of rights the adjudicative process produces. Rights as they appear in official statements, therefore, are defined by people's ideas about what rights are, by the forces that affect their willingness to claim rights, and by the power and resources they can bring to bear in the adjudicative contest.

Where do people get their ideas about rights? In part, to be sure, ideas come from official statements such as the Constitution and statutes, and from civic education about government and rights. In part, our ideas come from the broader intellectual currents of moral philosophy. In the United States, natural-rights philosophy has been an influential school, exemplified in the Declaration of Independence. In this tradition, rights derive from something higher than man-made law, and a just society should create laws that give form to already existing natural rights. If legal rights do not match natural rights, the natural rights still endure because they are "inalienable." Other strands of moral philosophy derive rights from principles of right and wrong, variously to be found in religious texts, rational argument, public opinion, or social practices and institutions.[17] Whatever the source of moral principles, the idea of moral rights allows for a discrepancy between legal rights and moral rights, so it is logically possible—and perhaps morally required—for people to claim rights that do not exist and that their government does not currently support.

This disjunction between moral rights and legal rights drives the whole system of rights-claiming. Not only do ideas and theories about moral rights provide the intellectual rationale for claims, they also provide the emotional impetus to action. People have many, many more conflicts than they bring into the legal arena through formal claims, and most conflicts are handled by putting up with the problem, ignoring it, or discussing it with the other party.[18] What propels people into courts is a feeling that there is a moral issue at stake. As one study

[17] For an overview, see Benn, op. cit. (note 3). For a sophisticated view of rights as deriving from rationality, see Bernard Gert, *The Moral Rules* (New York: Harper Torchbook, 1973); as deriving from social practices, see Michael Walzer, *Spheres of Justice* (New York: Basic Books, 1983), especially chap. 3.

[18] For an elaboration of this theory of legal disputes as the tip of the iceberg of social conflicts, see Marc Galanter, "Reading the Landscape of Disputes: What We Know and Don't Know (and Think We Know) About Our Allegedly Contentious and Litigious Society," *UCLA Law Review* 31 (1983): 4–71, especially, pp. 11–18.

concludes, people seek outside help in conflicts when they "conceptualize their problem as a principled grievance."[19]

How people come to conceptualize problems as legal grievances is one of the great mysteries of social science. Causal models surely play a role. People do not make claims against others if they understand a problem as an accident of fate. Only when they can identify a human agent as responsible for a problem does the prospect of claiming make any sense. This answer, though, only sends us on a different chase after the various social and political forces that push problems into the conceptual realm of human causation (see Chapter 8).

Formal laws, previous court decisions, and social movements certainly contribute to people's ideas about the kinds of problems for which they can legitimately feel aggrieved and expect a legal remedy. Some scholars think norms of justice emerge out of a society's changing technological capabilities and its attempts to manage new problems.[20] Others take a less benign view of the expansion of rights, seeing norms about rights as deliberately manufactured by a "rights industry" composed of civil rights organizations, law professors, political advocates, and media publicists.[21] Yet another theory finds the source of American reliance on rights in our early political culture, which emphasized protection of private property rights as the chief purpose of government.[22] For all their disagreement, these disparate theories agree that informal norms are powerful influences on the formal rights that develop in the legal system.

In the making of legal rights, it is not only claimants who are motivated by the normative meanings of rights. Judges, as well, appeal to moral ideals and norms. Nowhere are these visions more evident than in the area of tort law. Sometimes called the "law of accidents," or "liability law," tort is the branch of law that deals with activities of daily life that are not regulated by criminal prohibitions or formal

[19] Sally Engle Merry and Susan S. Silbey, "What Do Plaintiffs Want: Reexamining the Concept of Dispute," *The Justice System Journal* 9 (1984): 151–178; the quotation is on p. 154. Galanter (note 18, pp. 30–31) thinks the bulk of legal disputes are prompted by instrumental rather than moral concerns, however. See also William Felstiner, Richard Abel, and Austin Sarat, "The Emergence and Transformation of Disputes: Naming, Blaming, Claiming . . ." *Law and Society Review* 15 (1980–81): 631–654.

[20] See, for example, Lawrence Friedman, *Total Justice* (New York: Russell Sage, 1985), and Jethro K. Lieberman, *The Litigious Society*, 2nd ed. (New York: Basic Books, 1983).

[21] Richard Morgan, *Disabling America: The "Rights Industry" in Our Time* (New York: Basic Books, 1984).

[22] Mary Ann Glendon, *Rights Talk* (New York: Basic Books, 1991), esp. chaps. 1–2.

contracts. It is concerned with the myriad ways people can harm each other and with what kind of care and protections they owe each other; with determining what sorts of injuries we can reasonably expect people to prevent, and with arranging compensation for injuries when compensation seems just. Tort law regulates the harms that come from cars, pets and farm animals, building construction, consumer products, medical treatment, and simply carrying out one's job or business.

There is no official code of torts, as there is a criminal code. Instead, much of tort law relies on the idea of the "reasonable man," an image of what people in a community think ought to be the standards of behavior. Through this fictional device of projecting oneself into the character of the reasonable person, courts gradually articulate standards of behavior that change with times and express visions of community life and public interest. Late nineteenth-century tort law was solicitous of the needs of nascent industry. Judges often assumed that railroad and factory accidents were an inevitable or at least necessary cost of industrialization. They did not often find that industrialists had an obligation to prevent accidents, or that people injured by railroads, streetcars, automobiles, or machines had a right to be compensated. Contemporary tort law is far less protective of new technology, and views a far wider range of side-effects as being subject to human control. For example, courts have held vaccine manufacturers liable for the extremely rare cases in which vaccines cause serious injuries, even though liability may discourage drug companies from producing vaccines.

Judges' opinions in tort cases are full of language indicating their reliance on what they take to be community norms and expectations. They often justify their decisions by saying that they are only doing what "civilization" or "public interest" or "standards of decency" or "our complex modern society" requires. Here is just a sampling:

From 1931, a dispute concerning a bicyclist injured when he ran into the partly opened door of a parked car:

> We apply the standards which guide the great mass of mankind in determining what is proper conduct. . . .[23]

(Armchair philosophers, awake: How would the mass of mankind resolve this case?)

---

[23] *Osborne v. Montgomery*, 234 N.W. 372 (1931).

From 1872, a dispute concerning spitting in someone's face:

> ... the law ... should afford substantial protection against such out-
> rages ... that the public tranquillity may be preserved by saving the neces-
> sity of resort to personal violence as the only means of redress. .... The act
> was the very refinement of malice.[24]

And finally, from 1944, a suit against *Coca-Cola* over a Coke bottle
that exploded in a woman's face:

> *Public policy demands* that responsibility be fixed wherever it will most
> effectively reduce the hazards to life and health inherent in defective prod-
> ucts ... *It is to the public interest* to discourage the marketing of products
> having defects that are a menace to the public.[25]

Normative meanings are like the forces of gravity, pulling and pushing on all legal rights. Because tort law rests on no official code, judges'
reliance on normative visions for resolving disputes is perhaps brought
into sharper relief than in other areas of law. I use examples from tort
law because once you recognize its Sunday School voice, you will hear
it in judicial opinions everywhere. Here are two more examples, this
time from constitutional law.

In 1986, the Supreme Court had to decide whether a state can carry
out a death sentence on a convicted murderer who becomes insane
while on death row. The majority opinion called execution of the
insane "savage and inhuman." It cited as grounds for the decision "the
natural abhorrence civilized societies feel at killing one who has no
capacity to come to grips with his own conscience or Deity," and the
need "to protect the dignity of society itself from the barbarity of exact-
ing mindless vengeance." "Civilization" and "dignity" then became
the reasons for the majority's insistence on adequate procedural protections for the defendant. The nebulous "demands of public policy"
served as the basis for Justice Rehnquist's dissent: "Creating a constitutional right to a judicial determination of sanity [offers] an invitation
to those who have nothing to lose by accepting it to advance entirely
spurious claims of insanity."[26]

In 1954, in *Brown vs. Board of Education,* the Supreme Court held
that segregated public schools were no longer permissible. In its opin-

[24] *Alcorn v. Mitchell,* 63 Ill. 553 (1872).

[25] *Escola v. Coca-Cola Bottling Co.,* 150 Pa. 2d. 436 (1944), emphasis added.

[26] *Ford v. Wainwright,* 477 U.S. 399 (1986).

ion, the Court explicitly overruled one of its earlier decisions, *Plessy v. Ferguson*, in which it had held that "separate but equal" facilities for whites and blacks did not violate the equal protection clause of the 14th Amendment. Here is how the justices explained their decision to reverse themselves:

> In approaching this problem, we cannot turn the clock back to 1868 when the [Fourteenth] Amendment was adopted, or even to 1896 when *Plessy* was written. We must consider public education in the light of its full development and its present place in American life throughout the Nation. Only in this way can it be determined if segregation in public schools deprives these plaintiffs of the equal protection of the laws.[27]

Having thus defined the legal question as the place of education in "American life," the Court focused on how segregated schooling affects the place of blacks in communities:

> To separate [children] . . . solely because of their race generates a feeling of inferiority as to their status in the community that may affect their hearts and minds in a way unlikely ever to be undone.[28]

The *Brown* decision is often cited to show the impact of social science research on judicial policy, because the judges accepted evidence from psychologists about segregation's effect on children. The opinion, however, relegates social science to a footnote, and gains its persuasive power instead by evoking our compassion for black children.

Whenever judges are about to depart from precedent, either to create new rights and duties or to restrict old ones, they justify the decision (and prepare the audience) with rhetoric about changed social conditions. They conjure up pictures of society then and now, tell a story of how law has failed to keep pace with social change, and conclude that "the legal response we are about to give is our only choice." For an example of pictures in action, take the case of a college student who murdered a former girlfriend, shortly after telling his therapist in the university health service about his intent. The question arose whether the therapist should have warned his patient's girlfriend. Normally, a doctor must maintain strict confidentiality about anything a patient says. Creating a duty for therapists to warn other people would be a major change in the formerly sacrosanct doctor-patient relation-

[27] *Brown v. Board of Education*, 347 U.S. 483, 74S. Ct. 686 (1954).
[28] Ibid.

ship. The court reasoned by drawing the following picture:

> Our current crowded and computerized society compels the interdependence of its members. In this risk-infested society we can hardly tolerate the further exposure to danger that would result from a concealed knowledge of the therapist that his patient was lethal.[29]

These pictures of society in fact do much of the work of legal reasoning. The pictures, not logic, justify the decision. Consider two Supreme Court decisions about the Voting Rights Act, a law passed by Congress in 1965 to ensure that blacks have a meaningful right to vote. Since some southern white politicians proved so adept at making up election rules and drawing district boundaries to preclude black candidates from winning, Congress required them to get approval from the Justice Department before they changed their voting rules or districts. South Carolina challenged Congress' authority to supervise state and local voting rules, and in a major decision in 1966, the Supreme Court upheld the Voting Rights Act.[30] Chief Justice Warren began his opinion with a lengthy history of voting discrimination in the south. He described how the southern states used literacy tests to keep blacks from voting.

> "Typically they made ability to read and write a registration qualification. . . . White applicants for registration have often been excused altogether from the literacy and understanding tests or have been given easy versions, have received extensive help from voting officials, and have been registered despite serious errors in their answers. Negroes, on the other hand, have typically been required to pass difficult versions of all the tests, without any outside assistance and without the slightest error."

To the Warren Court, racial discrimination in voting was an "evil." When it looked at the behavior of white elites in southern states, it saw "stratgems" and "subterfuge" and "unremitting and ingenious defiance" of federal law. The rationale for supervision of these southern voting districts was that "jurisdictions which had resorted to the extraordinary strategem of contriving new rules of various kinds for the sole purpose of perpetuating voting discrimination . . . would be likely to engage in similar maneuvers" to evade the provisions of the Voting Rights Act.

In 1992, a much more conservative Supreme Court again consid-

[29] *Tarasoff v. Regents of University of California*, 131 Cal. Rptr. 14 (1976), p. 411.

[30] *South Carolina v. Katzenbach* 383 U.S. 301 (1966). All the quotations in this paragraph are from this opinion.

ered the scope of the Voting Rights Act. This time the case was brought by Laurence Presley, the first black person since Reconstruction to be elected to the six-member county commission of Etowah County, Alabama.[31] A new white commissioner was also elected in the same election. Before the two new commissioners even took office, the four incumbent white commissioners "reorganized" the duties of office. Instead of each commissioner controlling road funds and construction jobs for his district, as had been done in the past, road funds for the whole county were put into a pool and controlled by the four holdover commissioners. The newly elected white commissioner was given the job of overseeing the county department of engineering. Mr. Presley was assigned to oversee maintenance of the county courthouse—in effect, he was made chief janitor.

Mr. Presley thought the change of duties was the kind of significant and discriminatory change in voting rules that ought to require approval by the Justice Department. The Supreme Court ruled that the Voting Rights Act does not apply to changes in the duties of office, only to changes that directly concern the act of voting. Justice Anthony Kennedy's opinion for the majority was devoid of any historical picture of black disenfranchisement, in which stripping an office of its powers just when blacks finally got elected was part of a long pattern of maneuvers to keep blacks from holding power. Instead, Kennedy wrote, it is merely a "felicitous consequence of democracy, in which power derives from the people," that "every decision taken by government implicates voting." Therefore, the real problem raised by this case was how to draw a clear line between "changes in rules governing voting and changes in the routine functioning and organization of government." The main dangers he saw were not discrimination and black disenfranchisement, but "unconstrained expansion" of the Voting Rights Act, and federal suffocation of states and localities:

> "If federalism is to operate as a practical system of governance and not a mere poetic ideal, the States must be allowed both predictability and efficiency in structuring their governments."

Each of these decisions created a new definition of the rights of black citizens and the obligations of federal and state government. Each did so by invoking a picture of society, and each court could have rendered a different decision by drawing a different picture. These pic-

---

[31] *Presley v. Etowah County Commission* 112 S. Ct. 820 (1992). All the quotations in the following paragraph are from this opinion.

tures, not the wording of statutes or logical deduction, are the inspiration for legal decisions, and the element that compels—or fails to compel—our loyalty in accepting them.

These pictures of society enter into the implementation of rights at other points in the system besides the judges' decisions. As we saw in Chapter 12 ("Rules"), lawyers, prosecutors, inspectors, and other rule enforcers incorporate their own norms of justice in their rules of thumb. They compare the case at hand with their own picture of a "normal burglary" or a "well-meaning factory owner" or a "typical drunk." These "folk legal categories" give substance to the dry formulas of law.[32] To summarize, I can do no better than Oliver Wendell Holmes's description of the law in 1881:

> The life of the law has not been logic; it has been experience. The felt necessities of the time, the prevalent moral and political theories, intuitions of public policy, avowed or unconscious, even the prejudices which judges share with their fellow men, have had a good deal more to do than the syllogism in determining the rules by which men should be governed.[33]

MAKING RIGHTS IN THE POLIS: THE POLITICAL BASIS OF LEGAL RIGHTS

A central element of the myth of legal rights is the idea of "equality before the law." In theory, the identity of litigants should not affect the weight of their claims—the consideration they receive or the ability of their claims to gain acceptance by the judge, given equal merit. Nor should their identity affect their ability to reach a court in the first place. The legal system, so the theory goes, is structured to promote individual participation by even the weakest member of the community. According to one scholar, it "provides a uniquely democratic . . . mechanism for individual citizens to invoke public authority on their own and for their benefit, . . . without any requisite involvement by a collectivity or any necessity for a public consciousness."[34]

[32] See Chapter 12 of this book (Rules); also Lynn Mather and Barbara Yngvesson, "Language, Audience and the Transformation of Disputes," *Law and Society Review* 15, 1980–81: 775–821.

[33] Oliver Wendell Holmes, Jr. *The Common Law* (Boston: Little, Brown, 1881), p. 1.

[34] Frances Kahn Zemans, "Legal Mobilization: The Neglected Role of Law in the Political System," *American Political Science Review* 77 (1983): 690–703; quotation is on p. 692.

The imagery of the myth comes straight out of the market model, where the public interest emerges miraculously from individual pursuit of self-interest. Just as individual consumers in a competitive market help society achieve maximum social welfare through their own self-interested behavior, individual citizens in this model of legal rights help society create and defend the whole body of democratic law when they assert their own individual legal rights.

In the polis, however, litigants do not simply arrive before the court as interchangeable representatives of abstract issues. Disputes are contests between people who hold positions in society that give them more or less power in the courts. If, as the classic theory holds, legal disputes are contests between individuals who just happen to represent larger interests, they are also contests between large interests, who happen to be represented by particular people.

Using the conceptual framework of Chapter 9, we can describe these contests as involving concentrated and diffuse interests. Marc Galanter has written a very compelling description along these lines.[35] Concentrated interests in legal disputes are parties who use courts often in the course of running their everyday affairs; he calls these "repeat players." Diffuse interests are people who use courts rarely or sporadically—"one-shotters" in his terms. Landlords, insurance companies, banks, and of course lawyers and prosecutors are in court all the time; tenants, policyholders, debtors, and one-time delinquents find themselves in court only on rare occasions, and then, a suit is a major event in their lives. These different relationships to the judicial system give the different types of players not only different resources to use in legal contests, but also different goals in settling disputes.

Repeat players have many cases and know they will have more in the future. They have low stakes in the outcome of any one case, and greater stakes in maintaining an overall position of strength. They are more likely to care about obtaining a declaration of rights—a statement of a new rule that will be favorable to them in most of their cases—than in winning a particular case. And they are more likely to have resources to pursue their long-run interests, not only because they are often large businesses, but also because going to court is part of their business, so they plan to devote resources to litigation and they can achieve economies of scale.

One-shotters are by definition focused on the case at hand. They

---

[35] Marc Galanter, "Why the 'Haves' Come Out Ahead: Speculations on the Limits of Legal Change," *Law and Society Review* 9 (1974–75): 95–160.

probably have an intense interest in the case—the outcome will affect their lives profoundly—but the case itself isn't usually about their means of livelihood and they probably have few resources and little inclination to mount a legal battle. They have good reason to compromise, to settle the case quickly and stop feeding money to lawyers. They are more likely to care about the tangible outcome of the case (will they owe money or go to jail?) than about establishing a rule to govern future cases. Even an organized interest group may need the tangible victory of an immediate solution to a grievance in order to hold the group together. For example, in several suits over accessibility of public transit to the handicapped, disability rights groups have usually settled for agreements that the transit agencies would modify stations and vehicles, rather than holding out for a new legal mandate or statutory interpretation.[36]

The sharply drawn dichotomy here is really a continuum, as we saw in Chapter 9. What really matters is the relative concentration of competing interests in a single contest. Many disputes are between two repeat players, such as those between unions and employers or regulatory agencies and regulated firms. Many are between two one-shotters, such as divorce cases or neighborhood disputes. The vast bulk of legal contests, however, is between repeat players and one-shotters—landlords versus tenants, prosecutors versus criminal defendants, finance companies versus debtors, manufacturers versus consumers, the Social Security Administration versus Social Security claimants, or welfare agencies versus welfare clients.

This disparity means that the parties are not equal before the law. Not only is there a difference in financial resources and legal talent, but also a difference in bargaining resources. Repeat players can usually afford to wait longer than one-shotters; they have continuing contact with court personnel and so better access to information, if not favors. Since almost all cases are settled by bargaining before they reach formal adjudication, these differences in bargaining resources matter.[37]

The disparity between concentrated and diffuse interests also means that whether adjudication produces a new statement of rights (a rule change) or merely a divisible settlement between two immediate parties depends in large measure on the identity of the parties. Two repeat players, both of whom have a large stake in a rule, are more likely to

[36] Olsen, op. cit. (note 7), pp. 240–244.

[37] About 80 to 90 percent of criminal cases are plea-bargained, and around 90 percent of civil cases are settled by negotiation. See Galanter, "Reading the Landscape," (note 35 above), pp. 27–28.

fight it out to the end, forcing the court to produce a rule change as well as a tangible remedy. Whether adjudication produces a rule change is important, in turn, because legal rights derive their power as regulatory instruments from their ability to govern more than one case at a time, to set standards for large areas of behavior.

If the identity of disputants matters a great deal for both the type of outcome (rule change versus tangible remedy) and the winner, then, as one might guess, a great deal of political energy goes into "constructing" winning disputants. While Galanter is right—and powerfully insightful—in insisting on the significance of the two types of disputants and the prevalence of imbalanced contests, the appearance of disputants before tribunals is not entirely a random affair, untouched by strategic maneuvering.

The conscious structuring of disputants occurs in several ways. Interest groups deliberately use "test cases" as a strategy to redefine rights of their members, and in doing so they seek out plaintiffs with a high potential to win. The ideal plaintiff will have not only a factual situation that seems to compel the desired legal outcome, but also several other attributes: a good public image; personal qualities that the average American admires and identifies with; a situation that evokes broad sympathy; and a determination to litigate all the way to a rule change. The National Association for the Advancement of Colored People (NAACP) handpicked plaintiffs in most of the civil rights cases of the 1950s and 1960s—among them, James Meredith. Meredith, a nine-year veteran of the Air Force, was especially suited for the school desegregation case, both because his military service to the country created a corresponding public moral obligation to him, and because he presumably had the stomach to withstand the violence that assertion of his legal right would entail.[38] In this strategy, although the nominal plaintiff is an individual, he or she is supported by an organization that may have enormous legal and financial resources and a concentrated stake in the issue.[39]

[38] For a description of the NAACP's test case strategy, see Clement Vose, *Caucasians Only: The Supreme Court, The NAACP, and the Restrictive Covenant Cases* (Berkeley: University of California Press, 1967).

[39] No one really knows how much of litigation is motivated or coordinated by organizations instead of individuals, but there is vast disagreement about both the extent of the phenomenon and whether it is healthy or unhealthy for the legal system. On the numerical question, see Galanter, "Why the 'Haves'. . . ," (note 35), p. 136, note 101. On the evaluative question, see Zemans (note 34 above); Scheingold, (note 13), especially chap. 8; and Morgan (note 21).

Interest groups can also structure disputes so as to have an organization or several organizations as the named plaintiff or defendant. Trade unions, for example, play an active role as plaintiffs in disputes over occupational safety and health legislation. If a membership organization does not exist—which is likely in the situation of a diffuse interest—then with a bit of lawyerly leadership, the device of a class action suit can be used. In the case of silicone breast implants, as in most other consumer product liability suits, there was no membership organization of women who had implants, but class action rules allow lawyers to create a class of injured plaintiffs, through advertising and information alerts to both patients and doctors. Eventually about 400,000 of the one million women with breast implants joined the suit.[40]

When people are represented in court by an organization, the legal system becomes something less of a democratic institution where individuals "invoke public authority on their own and for their own benefit." Both judges and would-be disputants worry about whether an organization or class is truly representative of the plaintiffs it purports to represent. Judges scrutinize organizations for evidence that members have some control over their leaders, and they examine proposed classes to see whether all members share legally relevant characteristics and agree to be bound by the outcome of the case. The rules for determining when organizations and unorganized "classes" may be plaintiffs have been the subject of intense struggle, because they can potentially change the balance of power between concentrated and diffuse interests.

For their part, leaders of collective suits often mimic the strategies of legislative politics in constructing their plaintiffs. Susan Olsen identifies two such strategies. *Stacking the plaintiffs* involves choosing individuals with the right characteristics for success (as in test cases) and amassing a substantial number of plaintiffs, on the theory that numbers do influence a judge. As one disability rights advocate put it, "You can't sit up there [in front of a judge] and say you're going to make multi-million dollar modifications to this [transit] system and you're going to cost the taxpayers all that money just because three people say it's their legal and civil rights."[41] *Ticket balancing* involves combining as plaintiffs individuals or organizations who represent different con-

---

[40] Gina Kolata, "A Case of Justice, or Total Travesty?" *New York Times*, June 13, 1995, pp. D1, D5.

[41] Quoted in Olsen, op. cit. (note 7), p. 249.

stituencies within the larger interest group. For example, leaders in a California disability transit suit carefully solicited participation from the established, more conservative United Cerebral Palsy and the newer, more militant Berkeley Center for Independent Living.

These more legislative strategies in the judicial arena parallel the strategies of problem definition we saw in Chapter 8, where political actors consciously frame a problem to make interests appear concentrated or diffuse, selfish or public. Stacking the plaintiff and ticket balancing are both ways of broadening the normative appeal of a position. Symbolically, they convert the individual or organized plaintiff into an altruist, someone who is suing on behalf of others. These devices also convey an implicit message that "a lot" of people are affected by the dispute, and in a political culture where the principle of majority rule is supreme, the demonstration of large numbers counts.

Do Rights Work?

It all depends (the magistrate's favorite phrase) on what we mean by "work." Rights do not generally work in the mechanistic sense portrayed in the first part of this chapter: Someone notices a discrepancy between actual behavior and an official statement of rights and is moved to litigate; litigation evokes a new declaration of rights; the new declaration leads to the realization of rights; and the implementation of rights is equivalent to significant social change.[42] Rights, however, have other effects, less direct than simply enforcing compliance with legal norms in specific situations, and these effects are in fact the principal means by which rights gain their effectiveness as a policy strategy. Specifically, rights "work" by mobilizing new political alliances, transforming social institutions, and dramatizing the boundaries by which communities are constituted.

The permeability of legally defined rights to normative concepts of rights is the great impetus for political mobilization. Litigation offers an arena where people can play out their problems as conflicts between good guys and bad guys. The availability of that stage can change peo-

---

[42] This is also Scheingold's formulation of the "myth of rights" op. cit. (note 13), p. 5. Gerald Rosenberg, *The Hollow Hope: Can Courts Bring About Social Change?* (Chicago: University of Chicago Press, 1991) provides an excellent review of the literature on questions of judicial impact (whether judicial declarations lead to significant changes in social and political relations) and judicial capacity (whether the legal system, given its design, is even capable of handling complex policy problems).

ple's conceptions of cause and responsibility and their expectations about entitlement. Mere contact with a lawyer can "increase the client's capacity for indignation."[43]

By attempting to apply preexisting rules, adjudication converts conflicts from the nitty-gritty facts of particular disputes to the high-sounding principles of law. The individual dispute is generalized by being likened to others of a similar kind—which kind is for the judge to decide and the lawyers to fight about. In generalizing, the dispute is politicized, lifted out of the realm of personal problems. The *Brown* decision did not integrate the schools, but it did officially acknowledge a widespread practice of segregation and the wrongness of that practice, and so encouraged blacks to think of themselves as part of a large group entitled to a different kind of treatment. Activist lawyers help this process along when they strategically create organizational and class plaintiffs. Rights, thus, can create a new sense of collective identity and stimulate new alliances.

At the same time, the system of rights and litigation is criticized for fragmenting larger social conflicts into disputes between single parties—say, highlighting one person out of a mass who are injured and one corporation out of an entire industry that engages in a harmful practice. The criticism has a good deal of validity, but it would be a mistake to ignore the dramatic increase in strategic use of litigation to reform entire institutions. This type of public law litigation is explicitly aimed at transforming whole social institutions.[44]

The classic rights model of rights is indeed aimed at discrete actions of identifiable parties. Public law litigation is avowedly aimed at changing a whole systematic pattern of practice in a large area of public policy, such as the racial balance of public school systems, the treatment of patients in mental hospitals, the management of prisons, the design of electoral districts, or the concentration of firms in an industrial sector. The parties to such a suit are numerous and amorphous. The defendant is more likely an institution or large bureaucracy, such as a school system or a state mental hospital system, whose individual employees come and go; and the plaintiff is more likely a class of "similarly affected" individuals, pulled together for purposes of the suit but lacking any political organization of their own. What is at issue is not

[43] Scheingold, (note 13), p. 135.

[44] See Abram Chayes, "The Role of the Judge in Public Law Litigation," *Harvard Law Review* 89 (1976): 1281–1316. For my description of public law litigation in the next few paragraphs, I rely heavily on Chayes and on Lewis Sargentich, "Complex Enforcement." Cambridge, Harvard Law School, 1978. Photocopy.

a single, discrete action of the defendant but a web of related ongoing activities that make up the way the defendant manages its affairs.

The goal of these suits, therefore, is not merely to remedy a past injury, provide compensation, or even gain compliance with a specific standard of behavior, but to transform the way an institution operates. Judges in these cases go beyond their usual role of adjudication. They often retain jurisdiction over the case for a period of years and are involved in recurring negotiations between the parties. The remedies are not simple declarations prohibiting some action but decrees articulating complex and detailed standards. For example, in a suit over a "right to adequate treatment" in a mental hospital, the decree set forth standards for the physical facilities, the psychological environment, the quantity and quality of the staff, and the treatment plans for the patients. Judges, too, are likely to take an active role in monitoring. Rather than relying on the injured parties to monitor compliance, they establish new official roles with powers to monitor, such as citizens' committees or special masters.[45]

After a period of growth of this kind of judicial engagement in institutional management, there has been a great deal of resistance from institutions seeking to regain their autonomy, and more hesitancy on the part of judges to engage in large-scale institutional monitoring. Scholars and advocates debate whether these new types of suits are successful in bringing about major social change. According to one recent scholar, the courts are successful in bringing about major social change only when the important political actors are ready and willing to make changes themselves. Moreover, deliberate efforts to create major social reform through litigation only drains people, talent, and energy from political reform (such as legislative changes) that might really make a difference.[46]

A conservative critique of rights, prominent in the 1990s, holds that American society has been too generous with rights, giving all sorts of entitlements to citizens without requiring any obligations or duties in return. Entitlements to public assistance, food stamps, and other forms of material aid, in this view, undermine people's willingness to work and their drive to self-sufficiency, and ultimately lower the productive

[45] "Note: Implementation Problems in Institutional Reform Litigation," *Harvard Law Review* 91 (1977): 428–463.

[46] This is the argument of and Gerald Rosenberg, *The Hollow Hope*, (note 43 above). For the view that litigation and rights strategies can make a significant difference, see Sheingold, *Myth of Rights*; Joel Handler, *Social Movements and the Legal System* (New York: Academic Press, 1978).

RIGHTS IN THE POLIS

Rationality Model	*Polis Model*
People rely on official statements of rights found in constitutions, statutes, administrative rules, or court opinion (positive concept).	People get beliefs and ideas about rights from moral philosophy, media, and other people, as well as from official statements (both normative and positive concepts).
Official statements of rights are clear, and judges merely apply formal rules to facts of the case, using logic and reason.	Official statements of rights are never perfectly clear; judges must interpret formal rules and they use norms and beliefs, as well as logic and reason.
Judges are not influenced by power of disputants, money, or anything except reason and facts.	Judges are influenced by their own experiences, beliefs about justice, and understandings of society.
All citizens have equal access to the courts to claim their rights; identity of litigants does not influence outcome of litigation.	Parties who are "repeat players" in courts have more power than those who use courts once or sporadically. Money helps.
	Interest groups and organizations deliberately structure and manage disputes to increase their chances of winning.
Courts ordinarily rely on voluntary compliance; in extraordinary situations, can call on legislative and executive branches to help enforce contested decisions.	Judges actively use rhetoric to increase voluntary compliance with their decisions. Legislative and executive branches get involved often, both to enforce court decisions and to overrule judges.

potential of the nation.[47] Liberals look instead at European social democracies, and see rights in the United States as extremely underdeveloped. The U.S. government, in this view, has little if any obligation to provide for the welfare and security of its citizens. The 1996 welfare reform ending the entitlement to AFDC is evidence to liberal critics of the fragility of rights. Thus, the liberal critique of rights is that they are too fragile, and don't include affirmative rights to subsistence and security. If rights don't "work" to foster democracy, it is because they are not strong and secure enough to provide the poor and the powerless with enough security so they can participate in civic affairs at all.

In the end, rights are not tools or instruments, operating mechanically and consistently. Like all policy instruments, they are dependent on and subject to larger politics. Perhaps their most distinctive feature, as policy instruments, is that they provide occasions for dramatic rituals that reaffirm or redefine society's internal rules and its categories of membership. Disputes about whether immigrants have a right to public education or Medicaid coverage, for example, are about the differential rights of various types of residents and citizens. Legal arguments and disputes can offer compelling visions of society. They are a vehicle for telling stories about what society means and what it stands for. They define which kinds of troubles will be regarded as tough luck and which will elicit social aid. They moralize about what behavior is good or bad and dramatize societal values through contests between real people on a public stage. The can bring about significant social change, but they are not predestined to do so.

[47] Lawrence Mead, *Beyond Entitlement* (New York: Free Press, 1986) This argument is, of course, the contemporary American version of Malthus' eighteenth century tract, *An Essay on Population.*

15

Powers

When the space shuttle Challenger exploded, President Reagan appointed a commission to determine what went wrong. After months of investigation, the commission determined that the immediate cause of the accident was a faulty O-ring seal, the kind of rubber gasket in the bottom of your kitchen blender. Not a very dramatic explanation for a major tragedy, but fortunately the commission found a more interesting contributing cause: a "flawed decision-making process" within NASA, the space agency. Of course, the commission recommended changing the design of the seals, but the bulk of its report concerned reforming NASA's decision making: add an independent committee to oversee future rocket design, redefine and strengthen the program manager's authority, and represent astronauts in program management.[1]

This chapter is about policy solutions that entail reforming a decision-making process, or what might be called *constitutional engineering*. They are based on the idea that different types of collective decision-making processes yield different kinds of outcomes. Advocates of process reforms usually argue that a new process will produce better policies—ones that are more just, more efficient, more consistent with liberty, or, as in the case of NASA, more safe. These arguments are based on the metaphor of mechanism: the content of decisions is shaped by the structure of a process in a seemingly automatic fashion.

[1] Report of the Presidential Commission on the Space Shuttle Challenger Accident (Washington, D.C.: Superintendent of Documents, 1986).

The impulse to restructure authority in order to solve problems goes all the way back to the founding of the nation. The American constitutional debates were about how to prevent tyranny and oppression by designing a system for making political decisions. Perhaps because Americans had an open choice about how to structure our government, we perceive structure as something eminently changeable rather than fixed, and we debate continuously about the merits of different decision-making structures. From the Founding Fathers' constitution making to Vice President Gore's "reinvention" of government, Americans have shown a deep faith in the possibility of creating decision-making structures that will render good decisions.

These strategies are all ways of changing who makes the decision. Each is a call for empowering a different set of people to make decisions and to have jurisdiction over something. In that sense, each is about what H. L. Hart called power-conferring rules, or rules that confer legal powers on individuals, organizations, and public bodies enabling them to create "structures of rights and duties within the coercive framework of the law."[2]

What is at stake, then, in changes of decision-making structure is the power to control a sphere of policy. A call to restructure is always a bid to reallocate power. Thus, there is another way to read arguments about constitutional engineering. They are always attempts by someone who is not winning in the arena where policy is currently made to shift decision making to an arena where they might prevail. As a matter of strategy, losing interests will always argue for the shift in terms of logic and mechanics: the new decision-making structure, by the design of its mechanism, will produce decisions in the public interest. But underneath this public-spirited logic is another kind of calculus: a new configuration of participation and authority might enable a currently subordinate interest to become dominant.

Every choice about the structure of authority can be examined from these two perspectives. First, does it make the trains run on time? Does it "work" to solve the nominal problem? This is the level at which most policy evaluation is conducted. As this book has tried to show, however, the definition of the nominal problem is hardly uniform or fixed. Simply defining the nominal problem is a political process that yields a variety of contending definitions.

More importantly, the nominal problem always involves questions of a second kind: What is the nature of the community that is consti-

---

[2] H. L. A. Hart, *The Concept of Law* (Oxford: Clarendon Press, 1961), p. 27.

tuted by the type of authority structure used to "solve" the problem? Who is given the right to make decisions about the problem? Whose voice counts, both for choosing leaders and for choosing policies? Who is subordinated to whom? What kind of internal hierarchy is created? Who is allied with whom? How does the authority structure create loyalties and antagonisms among members of the community?

With these two levels of analysis in mind, we can now examine how the strategy of constitutional engineering works in some of its major variations. These variations are the recurrent refrains in American politics: (1) *Change the membership* of the decision-making body; (2) *change the size* of the decision-making body; (3) *shift the locus* of decision making among federal, state, and local governments.

Changing the Membership

The key premise of this strategy is that the qualities and interests of people who make decisions shape the kinds of decisions they make. Since we have a representative rather than a direct democracy in the United States, the strategy can be applied at two levels: changing the composition of the electorate that decides upon representatives, or changing the identity of representatives themselves. One involves changing the membership of the class of voters; the other involves changing the membership of the class of officeholders.

Although democracy is based on the principle that every citizen counts equally in policy-making, all democracies impose restrictions on who is allowed to vote. The classical Athenian democracy did not allow women or slaves to vote. Neither did the American democracy until relatively recently. In the United States we have always excluded children and youths up to age 18, and until 1971, those up to age 21. Many American states and many other countries made property ownership a requirement for voting. Such exclusions always permit the subjugation of one set of people to the decisions of another.

Exclusions are commonly called "voter qualifications" and they are justified in terms of competence. The criterion for exclusion (race, gender, age, property) is defended as a proxy measure of ability to understand public affairs and make intelligent voting decisions. Thus, when in 1966 the Supreme Court struck down Virginia's $1.50 poll tax as a precondition of voting, Justice Harlan dissented with a classic defense of voter qualifications. He thought it quite rational to suppose that payment of a poll tax "promotes civic responsibility, weeding out those who do not care enough about public affairs to pay $1.50." Likewise, he added, "people with some property have a deeper stake in community affairs, and are consequently more responsible, more educated, more knowledgeable, more worthy of confidence, than those without means" and *"the community and Nation would be better managed if the franchise were restricted to such citizens."*[3] Here, in a version applied to voting restrictions, is the more general argument that changing the membership of a decision-making body will improve the outcomes.

Even the majority opinion in the decision accepted without question that a state has a legitimate interest in fixing voter qualifications. The court simply held that wealth could not be one of them, because, "like race, creed, or color, [it] is not germane to one's ability to participate intelligently in the electoral process. . . . To introduce wealth or payment of a fee as a measure of a voter's qualifications is to introduce a capricious or irrelevant factor." Exactly what the majority *would* consider relevant factors it did not venture to say.[4]

Battles over the composition of the electorate are by no means confined to some original moment of a community's founding. Voter exclusions are a constant topic of policy conflict. Voting rights for the homeless are at issue in the 1990s, because most states impose residency requirements and use a mailing address as proof of residency. New Jersey became the first state to require election boards to register the homeless, even if a person did not have a permanent address.[5] The state of Texas, home to some large military bases, once excluded members of the armed forces who resided there from voting in state elections, on the theory that they might be more loyal to the army than

[3] *Harper v. Virginia Board of Elections*, 383 U.S. 663, 86 S.Ct. 1079 (1966).

[4] Ibid.

[5] See Joseph Sullivan, "Trenton Relaxes Rules for Voting by the Homeless," *New York Times* April 20, 1991, p. 26.

the state and so vote against the state's interests. The Supreme Court struck down the qualification in 1965, suggesting that a state cannot fairly expect its voters to have no other loyalties or memberships.[6] By Texas's logic, after all, a state might also deem it proper to exclude members of the Catholic Church, the American Civil Liberties Union, or the National Rifle Association.

Race and ethnicity as proxy criteria for citizen competence have been central to American conceptions of voting rights—sometimes quite explicitly, and often much more subtly.[7] In the late nineteenth century (and on into the twentieth), white male elites elaborated a "science" of racial categories and identities, and asserted that whole nationalities of immigrants were morally and intellectually deficient in various ways. One of the most famous and influential treatises of this sort was by Edward A. Ross, a founder and president of the American Sociological Association and an adviser to President Theodore Roosevelt. He argued that immigrants from everywhere but England and northern Europe were illiterate, immoral, and did not know how to exercise citizenship responsibly. They were needy and pliant, and would easily sell their votes to machine politicians who promised them favors or money. Thus, immigrants were to be blamed for the corruption of city politics. Trying to show how open-minded he was, Ross asked himself whether even those immigrants who were not "debauched" or "misled" by ward bosses might have something to contribute to American political life. No, he concluded, there was nothing to be gained by admitting "myriads of strangers who have not yet passed civic kindergarten" and giving them the right to vote:[8]

> "The plain truth is, that rarely does an immigrant bring in his intellectual baggage anything of use to us. . . . The clashings that arise from the presence among us of many voters with medieval minds are sheer waste of energy."[9]

Battles over the qualifications of officeholders are as intense as the ones over voters. Officeholders, be they legislators or administrators, theoretically represent the interests of their constituents. Therefore,

[6] *Carrington v. Rash* 380 U.S. 102 (1965).

[7] See Rogers Smith, "Beyond Tocqueville, Myrdal, and Hartz: The Multiple Traditions in America," *American Political Science Review* vol. 87, no. 3 (Sept. 193): 549–566.

[8] Edward A. Ross, *The Old World in the New* (New York: The Century Company, 1913). Quote on p. 276.

[9] Ibid., pp. 276, 279.

the theory goes, by changing either the identity of representatives or the ability of constituents to control them, we can change the kinds of decisions they will render. The Space Shuttle Commission's recommendation to include more astronauts in program management exemplifies this logic: astronauts, more than any other group of people, have an interest in shuttle safety and so will make decisions in a way that gives priority to safety.

But what does it mean to "represent" constituents? One concept, called *descriptive representation*, holds that representatives who share important demographic characteristics with their constituents can best represent their interests.[10] This concept of representation drives demands for ethnic and gender diversity on boards, committees, and other representative bodies. The logic here is that people who share demographic characteristics will "think, feel, and reason" like one another and consequently will have like policy sentiments.[11] An alternative concept, called *substantive representation*, holds that representatives who share important policy beliefs and goals with their constituents can best represent them. The key issue is "not what representatives look like but whom they look after, whose interests they pursue."[12]

In a sense, the very labels prejudice the debate, since of course representation on substantive matters is more important than superficial descriptive characteristics. The logic of descriptive representation is not as silly as it is sometimes made to sound, however, for the crucial thing about descriptive representation is that not just any demographic characteristic will do. Rather, when one or two demographic characteristics, such as race, religion, or gender, are important determinants of power and opportunity in a society, then those characteristics must form the basis of representation in order to ensure that people on the weak side of the dividing line are represented. In a society where race is an important political dividing line and a factor that deeply shapes people's political views, minorities may need representatives of their own race. Where gender is an important determinant of political power and policy attitudes, men may not adequately represent women.

[10] Hannah Pitkin formulated the concepts of descriptive and substantive representation in *The Concept of Representation* (Berkeley: University of California Press, 1967).

[11] James A. Morone and Theodore R. Marmor, "Representing Consumer Interests: The Case of American Health Planning," *Ethics* 91 (April 1981): 431–450.

[12] Morone and Marmor, ibid., p. 438. For a balanced and thoughtful discussion of whether descriptive representation can yield substantive representation, see Frank J. Thompson, "Minority Groups in Public Bureaucracies: Are Passive and Active Representation Linked?" *Administration and Society* 8 (August 1976): 201–226.

In the end, the central test of representation is not whether representatives share demographic characteristics with constituents, but whether they are *accountable* to their constituents. To see the difference, try a thought experiment. Imagine that instead of holding elections for Congressional representatives, we allowed state governors to appoint them. A governor handpicks six black men and four white men for the state's delegation to the House of Representatives, corresponding precisely to the proportion of blacks and whites in the state. The black representatives all believe that the distribution of wealth and income is entirely a reflection of what people deserve, that racism no longer exists, and that a woman's place is in the kitchen. They support policies to end all government aid to the poor, repeal the Civil Rights Act, suspend all anti-discrimination legislation, and discourage women from higher education and professional careers. Most black citizens of the state protest the appointments, saying their interests are not represented. The governor meets with their leaders and asks, innocently: "You've got your own kind, and more than a majority I might add. So what's the problem?" The problem is that under my hypothetical scheme, the black citizens have no influence over "their" representatives and no way to kick them out of office if they do not effectively represent the citizens' policy views.

The controversy over race-based districting is partly a dispute over these two views of representation.[13] In one view, blacks are better off being represented by liberal Democrats of any color than by Republicans of any color, because liberal Democrats tend to support policies such as affirmative action or urban economic development that benefit blacks. Blacks should work to elect as many liberal Democratic candidates as possible, rather than withdrawing into majority-black voting districts to elect a look-alike. Moreover, if black candidates run in "protected," mostly black districts, they may gain some seats but will not make the necessary alliances to enable them to win larger statewide offices.[14] On the other side, a representative who owes her seat to a solid majority of black voters is more likely to be responsive to that

---

[13] I say partly because creating black-majority voting districts for Congressional seats was a strategy of the Republican party under President Bush to create more safe Republican seats. Since black voters are traditionally strongly Democratic, redistricting to concentrate blacks in a few districts effectively removes Democratic voters from all the other white-majority districts. Thus, much of the motive for creating black-majority districts had nothing to do with how best to represent black citizens' interests.

[14] Carol Swain, "The Future of Black Representation," *American Prospect* no. 23 (Fall 1995): 78–83.

constituency than one who is beholden to a coalition of different groups. Moreover, no black has ever been elected to Congress from a white-majority district in the South, so without black-majority districts, blacks in southern states will never get the opportunity to gain the experience and power of Congressional office.[15]

The issue of race-based districting illustrates a generic dilemma of representation. Interests of any person or group are always multidimensional and a representative system established along one dimension will neglect interests defined along another. Even people who share a very important characteristic such as race or gender have conflicting interests on other dimensions. There are black homeowners and black renters, women employers and women employees, for example, whose various interests in housing or labor policies are substantially different.

One argument against descriptive representation is that the potential criteria for representation are open to almost infinite expansion. (Don't let that camel get even its nose into the tent.) Does every ethnic and linguistic group need special representation by one of its own? Should Latinos and Asians have "their" representatives? And where do we stop dividing people: do Mexican-Americans, Puerto Rican-Americans, Cuban-Americans, and Columbian-Americans all have the same interests? What about other aspects of identity that deeply affect people's political interests, such as sexual orientation, income, or level of education? (Senator Roman Hruska of Nebraska once proposed that the mediocre, no less than the brilliant, deserve representation on the United States Supreme Court.)

This is the kind of line-drawing argument Justice Kennedy made in the *Presley v. Etowah County Commission* case we saw in the last chapter. Every government decision implicates voting, so where do we stop applying the Voting Rights Act, which requires state legislatures to get prior approval from the Justice Department before they make policies that affect voting? Justice Stevens, in his dissent in that case, exemplified the counterargument. Look to historical experience, he said. "This is a case in which a few pages of history are far more illuminating than volumes of logic and hours of speculation about hypothetical line-drawing problems."[16] The central purpose of the Voting Rights Act

---

[15] See Chandler Davidson and Bernard Grofman, eds., *Quiet Revolution in the South: The Impact of the Voting Rights Act 1965–1990* (Princeton, N.J.: Princeton University Press, 1994).

[16] Dissent by Justice Stevens, in *Presley v. Etowah County Commission*, 112 S.Ct. 820 (1992).

was to end various devices that either excluded blacks from voting and registration in the south, or rendered their votes ineffective. The device used by whites in Etowah County—redefining the duties of office once a black man got elected—certainly renders black votes ineffective. It should require prior approval. End of problem.

In the issue of race-based districting, Stevens' reasoning would again have us look to historical experience. The original purpose of encouraging black-majority districts was to overcome a legacy of state redistricting policies that prevented most blacks from ever electing their favored candidate. Therefore, redistricting that provides a remedy for that problem ought to be permissible. We don't need to answer the line-drawing question in order to decide about race-based districting in the South. And when we do want to consider representation based on other groupings, we can inquire about each one whether its members have been the victims of the same kind of "unremitting and ingenious defiance" of federal law that triggered special protections for blacks.

There is another solution to the problem of representing excluded interests in decision-making, a solution that has often been tried in American politics. Instead of trying directly to achieve parity for weak political groups inside the dominant institutions, create alternative or parallel institutions to represent weak interests. This strategy was the basis of the War on Poverty of the 1960s. In order to give voice to poor and minority constituencies in the cities, the federal government set up "community action agencies" to administer federal grants for job training, preschool, and other antipoverty programs. The federal program rules stipulated that the agencies had to be independent of local government, and must be composed of members of the poor communities they served.

The strategy both works and it doesn't. Nobody would say that the War on Poverty succeeded in putting poor people in charge of government, or even giving them enough power to challenge established government agencies most of the time—much less that it succeeded in defeating poverty. But the community action agencies did mobilize poor and minority constituencies to participate in elections, did recruit a large number of blacks, Hispanics, women, and others who had never been a part of government, did give them experience in running an agency and negotiating with other parts of government, and did force established political participants to deal with them. In 1965, there were 70 elected black officials at all levels of government in the United States, and those mostly on the lower levels. There were no black mayors. By 1981, there were 5014 black officials, including may-

REDEFINING MEMBERSHIP IN THE POLIS

Electorate	Change voter qualifications
	Examples: property ownership, race, gender, residence, nationality
Officeholders	Change the system of representation
Descriptive	Representatives are selected according to demographic characteristics (such as race, gender) they share with constituents
Substantive	Representatives are selected according to policy beliefs and goals they share with constituents
Accountable	Representatives are accountable to constituents if constituents have ability to influence representatives and to remove them from office.

Understanding the Polis: Arguments about voter qualifications and systems of representation are strategies to change the distribution of power in policy making.

ors of 170 cities, many of whom had come up through the ranks of community action programs. The strategy of representing previously excluded groups in parallel institutions, then, does not cause a revolution, but it does integrate new groups into mainstream politics.[17]

CHANGING THE SIZE

One of the favorite pastimes of political theorists is debating the merits of different-sized decision-making units. James Madison staked out the classic position that "large is better" in his famous *Federalist Paper*

[17]This analysis of the functions of representation and the War on Poverty come from James Morone, *The Democratic Wish* (New York: Basic Books, 1990).

No. 10, arguing for adoption of the Constitution.[18] The question he posed was whether a small or large republic would be more favorable to "the election of proper guardians of the public weal." Which size would be more likely to prevent tyranny by factions of like-minded citizens whose interests are "adverse to the rights of other citizens or to the permanent and aggregate interests of the community?" He advanced three arguments in favor of the large republic.

First, since even a very small community needs a certain minimum number of representatives (and, we can suppose, officials), the number of representatives will be proportionately greater in a small community than in a large one. At the same time, the proportion of the general citizenry who are "fit characters" to hold office is the same in both small and large communities. Therefore, he concluded with apparent mathematical certainty, a large community offers more options of fit officials and "a greater probability of a fit choice." The smaller community would have to reach deeper into its pool of members, dredging up less qualified ones just to fill the same number of offices. The argument, of course, depends upon seeing "fitness to govern" as a fixed resource, one that exists in limited quantity among a population. If instead you believe that fitness to govern obeys the laws of passion—that it is created and increased by experience in public life, for instance, or that it inheres in the relationship between a representative and his or her constituency rather than in the representative's individual character—then you would have a hard time swallowing the argument.

Second, Madison thought it would be harder for "unworthy candidates" to win over a large number of people than a small number, or as he put it, "to practise with success the vicious arts, by which elections are too often carried." The point is at least debatable, as even Madison knew. It is certainly plausible that people in large groups, knowing their vote "counts for less," are less critical or attentive in their evaluation of candidates.

The third argument was the killer, and the one for which Madison is most often remembered: The larger the community, the greater the variety of parties and interests it will contain, and the less likely any majority of members will have a common interest or "motive to invade the rights of other citizens." In addition, a majority composed of a larger number of people would have a harder time acting in concert.

[18] James Madison, "Federalist Paper No. 10," in Alexander Hamilton, James Madison, and John Jay, *The Federalist* (New York: Tudor Publishing Co., 1937), pp. 62–70.

Using the same logic, one of my friends (who never took a political science course) advised me to choose a condominium in a building with a couple of hundred units rather than ten or twenty. He explained that with such a large number of members, the condo association "wouldn't always be voting to do things you don't want to do, especially to spend your money." True, I thought, but suppose I *wanted* to get the roof fixed or do some landscaping? The principle of inhibiting majority action might work for me if the only issue I cared about was spending versus not spending money on the building, and I were always anti-spending. But if I cared about other dimensions of policy— essential plumbing and heating services versus amenities, improvements that increase my resale value versus those that do not—the Madisonian principle would not benefit me.

With the *Federalist Paper No. 10*, Madison began a whole genre of American political theory: abstract arguments purporting to show that large or small units logically and inevitably lead to better public decisions. All of them rest on an implicit conception of a contest between good and bad interests (see Chapter 8), and all argue that their favorite size will strengthen the good interests. Here is Grant McConnell, a twentieth-century follower of Madison, and advocate of opening up agriculture, labor, and business regulation to larger spheres of decision making:

> Material values are much more characteristic of narrow than of broad constituencies; "altruistic," "sentimental," or "public" interests are more readily given expression and support in large constituencies.[19]

There is an equally strong tradition in American political culture of favoring small decision-making units.[20] The small community is revered as a repository of human values. It is based on personal, face-to-face relationships instead of bureaucratic, paper-record knowledge. Small units are said to make decisions with better knowledge of problems, knowledge gained from personal experience and intuitive understanding of intangible communal values. Small units can resolve conflict with flexible and informal solutions, whereas large units must rely on more formal, even rigid, rules. Small communities, being more homogeneous, can use the sense of loyalty and fellowship to smooth over differences. Finally, and quite the contrary of Madison's argu-

[19] Grant McConnell, *Private Power and American Democracy* (New York: Random House, 1966), p. 117.

[20] McConnell, ibid., chap. 4, is an excellent essay on the ideology of small units.

ment, small groups are more conducive to rational deliberation because a small number of people can really talk, listen, discuss, criticize, and argue. Here is a contemporary version of the argument that small units produce better policy decisions:

> Decisions on community problems made at the community level are potentially better than those made at the national level, because only at the community level can the community be seen as a whole . . . and only there can widespread citizen participation be organized and the contributions of the citizens blended with those of the professionals in the decision-making process."[21]

There is a different and I think more compelling line of argument in favor of small political jurisdictions. Small units are preferable not because they (supposedly) produce better substantive policy decisions, but because they provide greater opportunity for individual participation. Following Madison's logic, a smaller jurisdiction has a higher ratio of offices to citizens than a larger unit. Participation, in turn, is valued for the kind of experience it provides individuals and for the relationships it fosters. Where there is more participation, there is more dialogue and deliberation, more chances to develop bonds of personal trust and loyalty, and greater capacity to work out conflicts with maximal consideration of conflicting interests.[22]

No self-respecting political debate would be complete without a middle-of-the-road, it-all-depends proposition. Some social scientists claim to have found such a solution to the small-versus-big puzzle by asking, "better for what purpose?" A structure of power such as small or big units should not be thought of as good in itself, but only as a means to a desired end.[23] The test comes in action: smaller units might be better for delivering services such as police protection or garbage collection, while larger units might be better for providing national defense or developing space technology. The analytical question here is whether the trains run on time. In this view, each policy problem has "implicit scale characteristics," or inherent requirements for different

---

[21] James L. Sundquist and David W. Davis, *Making Federalism Work* (Washington, D.C.: Brookings Institution, 1969), p. 250.

[22] For thoughtful examples, see Jane Mansbridge, *Beyond Adversary Democracy* (New York: Basic Books, 1980), and Benjamin Barber, *Strong Democracy* (Berkeley: University of California Press, 1984).

[23] Aaron Wildavsky, "A Bias Towards Federalism," in *Speaking Truth to Power* (Boston: Little, Brown, 1979), p. 147.

levels of resources, political support, and compliance. Political authority must be designed to provide just the right size jurisdiction to compel the supply of resources, elicit the necessary cooperation, and mobilize political support.[24]

By this reasoning, policy problems arise because "governments and their citizenry come together under circumstances in which the legally defined spatial boundaries are increasingly out of alignment with the boundaries of the substantive public issues on which they interact."[25] The metaphor suggests taking our policy problems to a mechanic rather than fighting them out in a political contest. By focusing on ends (better for what?) rather than distribution (better for whom?), this approach conceals questions of power. Problems of authority are converted into a matter of technical requirements.

At issue in these debates is not whether small or big is more beautiful, but who is dominant in a given arena. As McConnell rightly says, "the fundamental error of the ideology of small units lies in its ignoring of questions of power within the unit of organization."[26] The same can be said, of course, for the ideology of large units. The hidden story in every small-versus-big debate is a contest between particular interests.

Madison's stated purpose in *Federalist Paper No. 10* was to prevent any faction from sacrificing the "public good" or the "interests of others" to its own passions and interests. A faction, according to him, might be either a minority or majority of citizens. For Madison, the public interest is not necessarily what the majority wants. The will of the majority can be adverse to community interests. (Hence the famous phrase "tyranny of the majority.") So Madison set about designing a system that would make it very difficult for any majority to accomplish its will. The argument for a large republic is precisely that a larger citizenry makes it hard for any majority to form and act in unison.

Madison's essay is nominally about majorities and minorities in the abstract, whatever the substance of the policy issue. American society at that time could have been divided into a majority and a minority on any number of significant dimensions: white versus nonwhite, female

[24]Paul R. Schulman, *Large-Scale Policy Making* (New York: Elsevier, 1980; distributed by Greenwood Press, Westport, Conn.). The phrase "implicit scale characteristics" is on p. 78.

[25]Eugene Smolensky et al., "An Operational Approach to an Efficient Federal System, Part 1, On the Specification of Horizontal Relationships." Mimeograph, quoted in Wildavsky, op. cit. (note 23); emphasis added.

[26]McConnell, op. cit. (note 19), p. 115.

CHANGING THE SIZE OF DECISION-MAKING UNITS

Small is Better	*Large is Better*
1. Small communities have face-to-face knowledge and people are more likely to have empathy for fellow citizens. Decisions will be based on better intimate knowledge of community.	A larger community offers a greater selection of possible representatives and a greater chance of finding more competent ones.
2. Small communities can use flexible and informal solutions, and use loyalty and empathy to smooth over conflict. Small communities are more conducive to rational deliberation.	It is harder for demogogues to persuade a large number of people than a small number. Decisions will be based more on reason than emotion.
3. It is easier to form a unified majority in a small community, so government action is more possible; less chance of deadlock.	The larger the community, the less likely there will be a unified majority on any issue. Policy is less likely to be dominated by a faction or special interest.
4. Small communities provide greater opportunities for participation in governance.	It is harder for a small elite to capture a larger government.

Understanding the Polis: Arguments about size are strategies to empower some people at the expense of others.

versus male, adults versus children, the healthy versus the sick, Anglicans versus non-Anglicans, the mediocre versus the brilliant. The only dimension Madison mentioned, however, is property: "The most common and durable source of factions has been the various and unequal distribution of property. Those who hold and those who are without property have ever formed distinct interests in society." His only concrete examples of the dangers of faction are "a rage for paper money, for an abolition of debts, [and] for an equal division of property." Madison's constitutional design can thus be read as an attempt to prevent the poor and propertyless majority from concerting to equalize wealth and property, or even more narrowly, as an effort to persuade economic elites to support the Constitution by reassuring them that their property would be safe under its regime.

The Madisonian arguments for large size and checks on majority power were really strategies for keeping power in the hands of a particular minority. General arguments about the "best size" for a jurisdiction must always be interpreted at this second level, as arguments supporting a particular configuration of power.

CHANGING FEDERALISM

Closely related to arguments about size are injunctions to change the number of decision-making units from few to many or many to few. In the American system of federalism, these are issues of centralization and decentralization. In a system with many units, each unit will generally encompass fewer people, and vice versa; a perfectly centralized system would have only one large decision-making unit for everyone. Hence, the theoretical arguments for decentralization and centralization often rest on the supposed virtues of smallness and largeness.

Like the theories about size, political arguments about federalism tend to be abstract and metaphorical. Decentralization puts authority in the hands of people who are "close to the problems" and "know the lay of the land." It allows for diversity of solutions to meet the range of local needs. States serve as "political laboratories" for experimentation with new ideas before they are applied to the nation as a whole.[27] Advocates of centralization tell a different story: Locating authority in many small jurisdictions leads to domination by local elites, policies that maintain the status quo, enactment of racial and other prejudices, and little or no redistribution of either power or wealth.

Welfare reform in the 1990s exemplifies how an issue of substance—in this case poverty and its relief—can be debated in terms of

---

[27]The laboratory metaphor was first used by Supreme Court Justice Louis Brandeis in *New State Ice Co. v. Liebman*, 285 U.S. 262 (1932) and later popularized by New York Governor Nelson A. Rockefeller in *The Future of Federalism* (Cambridge, Mass.: Harvard University Press, 1963), pp. 53–54.

constitutional engineering. Of course, there is lots of debate about specific program rules, such as who should be eligible for AFDC, how
long someone should be able to receive benefits, and whether beneficiaries should be required to work or to live with their parents. But the
more general issue of whether the program should be structured as an
entitlement or as block grants is a struggle over who gets to make these
kinds of program rules in the first place—one Congress or fifty state
legislatures. The entitlement program created in 1935 gave a wide
scope of authority to the federal government to set basic framework
rules, and required states to request permission from the federal government if they wanted to deviate from national rules and policies. A
block grant program is more than just a fiscal device; it shifts authority
to the states, giving them wide latitude in spending the grants, with
only a few restrictions stipulated by federal legislation.

On the surface, many politicians and advocates argue in terms of
the relative competence of federal and state government. Republicans
generally decry big (federal) government, claiming that states need
more flexibility, and that local officials should be empowered to set
program rules since they are more familiar with local labor markets
and economic conditions. Democrats and advocates of the poor generally argue for maintaining a federal entitlement program, because,
they say, state officials might turn a deaf ear to the poor in bad times,
while an entitlement program ensures an automatic increase in welfare rolls when economic conditions get worse. Beneath the surface,
however, the congressional politics of welfare reform in 1995 did not
follow the obvious lines of division on substance—on whether AFDC
should be smaller and more stringent, or larger and more liberal. Even
though Republican state governors (of whom there were 30 in 1995)
wanted the federal government to give more control over AFDC to the
states, even though most Republicans favored the big cuts in welfare
spending that block grants could accomplish, and even though Republicans controlled Congress, many Republican members of Congress,
along with Democrats, were reluctant to support the block grant proposal because it meant giving up some of *their* control over policy.
They wanted to be able to protect their favorite programs (or the favorite programs of their powerful constituents), and they wanted to be
able to stipulate program rules (such as prohibition on benefits for children born out of wedlock) that expressed their political beliefs.[28]

[28] See Jeffrey L. Katz, "Members Pushing to Retain Welfare System Control," *Congressional Quarterly* January 28, 1995, pp. 280–83; and Jeffrey L. Katz, "Governors Split on
Welfare: Funding Methods at Issue," *Congressional Quarterly*, February 4, 1995, p. 370.

Federalism, then, is more than a matter of the size and number of decision-making units. It is an issue of power. The real trouble comes in figuring out how the units should be related: which ones should have authority over others, on what kinds of issues, and with what enforcement powers? The very idea of federalism is something of a paradox. It combines autonomy of subunits with central authority of national institutions. This combination of contradictory principles can be made to work easily enough in words—Nelson Rockefeller celebrated federalism as "stability without rigidity," "security without inertia," and "diversity within unity"[29]—but poetry does not resolve the tensions of concrete situations.

Many have tried their hand at writing a workable formula for federalism. James Sundquist and David Davis, in *Making Federalism Work*, begin with the central premise that "the effectiveness of the execution of federal programs depends crucially upon the competence of community institutions to plan, initiate, and coordinate.[30] Federal agencies should therefore have a "policy of deference" toward local agencies in overseeing the expenditure of federal grants. Yet "the federal agencies cannot be bound absolutely by whatever the local planning process comes up with. They must guard not only against *waste and extravagance* but against proposals that may *distribute the benefits of federal programs unfairly* or [are] in other ways *inconsistent with the national purpose. . . .* [They] must guard against *proposals by one community that have adverse effects on others.*"[31] Having established these criteria (which any reader of this book will recognize as made of rubber), they offer the following formula for allocating authority between the federal government and local agencies:

> It is one thing for federal officials to draw the line against a local proposal on grounds of illegality, waste, inequity, discrimination, spillover effects, or unavailability of funds and quite another for them to substitute their judgment for that of local communities on matters that do not involve these considerations.[32]

Rhetorical formulas such as this can only serve as intellectual weaponry for contests over authority. The crucial issue in policy politics is not whether a particular allocation of power among federal, state, and local governments makes for punctual railroads, but how it distributes

[29] Op. cit. (note 27), p. 7.

[30] Sundquist and Davis, op. cit. (note 21), p. 243.

[31] Ibid., p. 249, emphasis added.

[32] Ibid.

both political authority and material outcomes. We can refine the question even further: Is there really a difference between the distributive results of centralized and decentralized systems? Do they consistently benefit different sets of people?

The federal government is often held to be more likely than smaller state and city governments to undertake redistribution. For one reason, it has a far larger and more progressive tax base than the states or cities (which tend to rely on sales and property taxes, rather than income tax) and so it has the sheer fiscal ability to engage in redistribution. By attaching strings to its numerous federal aid programs, it can effectively force cities and states to carry out national goals, such as directing money to poor neighborhoods or programs for otherwise powerless minorities.

Another reason the federal government is more likely to undertake redistributive policies is that cities and states have relatively more permeable boundaries. If they attempt to redistribute, businesses and individuals can leave their jurisdiction to avoid the high taxes; and if they provide a generous array of welfare, education, health, and housing benefits as compared to other cities and states, new residents will migrate in from other jurisdictions to take advantage of the benefits.[33] The federal government has relatively impenetrable boundaries, by contrast. People cannot (or at least probably will not) readily flee the country to escape national taxes (though they can move their money outside U.S. borders), and immigration restrictions control the influx of would-be benefit seekers.

It is worth noting that this structural argument cuts in precisely the opposite direction of Madison's argument for a large republic. Madison thought the forces for equalizing income and property were less likely to succeed in a large, national arena, where it would be hard to form a majority. The dominant contemporary view, by contrast, holds that redistribution is more likely to occur at the national level because that is the only jurisdiction with a captive population.

Growth policy offers an interesting example of the interaction of boundaries and policy.[34] Land use, zoning, and building regulations have traditionally been a prerogative of local governments, and growth, in turn, has been a widely accepted goal of local communities

---

[33] Paul Peterson, *City Limits* (Chicago: University of Chicago Press, 1981) makes this argument as applied to cities. Paul Peterson and Mark Rom, *Welfare Magnets* (Washington, D.C., Brookings Institution, 1990) makes the argument as applied to states.

[34] For the analysis of growth policy, I rely on Jeffrey R. Henig, *Public Policy and Federalism* (New York: St. Martin's, 1985), chap. 7.

as they exercise these powers. Growth, like the proverbial bigger pie, seems to provide more for everyone: more jobs, more homes, more customers, more new business opportunities, and more tax revenues for more services. But starting around the 1960s, people in some fast-growing communities began to perceive the negative consequences of growth: pollution, destruction of park and farmlands, increased cost of schools, overburdened road and water systems, crowding, rising crime rates, destruction of historic buildings, and strained public services. By the early 1970s, many communities began using their zoning and building codes to restrict growth by limiting the number and kinds of new housing stock.

The effect of many of these restrictions is to exclude minorities and the poor. Requirements for minimum lot size or prohibitions on apartments and multifamily dwellings raise the cost of housing, as does a limit on the total supply of housing units in the face of high demand. No-growth policies and "planned" development, some say, are a guise for discrimination. Advocates for minorities and the poor in and outside of these communities often try to bring the issue to the larger arena of state government. In some places, they have succeeded in getting state laws that prohibit communities from excluding low- and moderate-income housing, or in getting state courts to strike down exclusionary zoning ordinances. But the locus of decision-making itself, whether at the community, state, or federal level, does not determine whether policy will be exclusionary. Some communities use their powers for exclusionary purposes and others do not. Some states play a redistributive role, while others do not. What matters is the constellation of forces within any given unit.

The choice of locating powers to control growth at the local or state level does affect the way the benefits and burdens of growth will be distributed across communities, however. Growth is going to occur somehow and somewhere.[35] As long as local communities retain authority, they can displace the burdens of growth elsewhere. Those that enact exclusionary rules will push low-income, minority, and large-family home seekers into other communities. Very likely the first communities to enact exclusionary policies are the wealthiest and whitest already, so local control only solidifies the differences between communities. Moving growth-control authority to the higher level of state government increases the possibility that growth will be distrib-

[35] Even though the birth rate is falling, increased divorce rates, delayed marriages, and longer life expectancies create a higher rate of new household formation, and thus a pressure for new dwellings.

CHANGING THE DISTRIBUTION OF POWER AMONG
LEVELS OF GOVERNMENT

Arguments for Decentralization	*Arguments for Centralization*
1. Gives authority to local officials who have better knowledge of their communities.	Gives authority to national officials who are less parochial, less likely to share local prejudices, and more likely to have a broader view.
2. Allows for diversity of solutions to meet different local needs.	Stimulates policy decisions based more on technical issues and less on narrow local self-interests.
3. Allows localities and states to experiment with policy ideas and develop knowledge about what works.	Allows for standardization of policy in all jurisdictions, and enhances fairness (because all citizens are treated alike).
4. Gives communities more autonomy, thereby enhancing liberty of members.	Allows central officials to redistribute power and resources among smaller jurisdictions, thereby promoting equality.

Understanding the Polis: Arguments about allocating authority among different units within a nation are strategies to redistribute power and resources among competing interests.

uted more evenly across communities. The poor, minorities, and lower-income towns themselves have absolutely no representation inside exclusive wealthy communities. At the level of state government, they may be able to forge an alliance to obtain policies that require all communities to bear their share of growth. But the picture isn't all so rosy, either; wealthy communities are likely to carry more clout in state government, despite their lack of numbers.

The moral of the story is that higher levels of government always have the possibility of effecting redistribution among their subunits. They may even have some leverage over the distribution within subunits, particularly where they distribute financial aid and can attach strings to it. (You can have some housing money, but only if you agree to use a portion of it for low-income housing.) But whether higher levels of government in a federal system in fact produce redistributive policies and exactly what kind of redistribution they promote are not questions determined by their sheer size or the availability of coercive instruments. The outcomes are determined by the specific constellation of attitudes and interests that is able to dominate in the larger arena.

Arguments for a shift of authority to a higher or lower level in a federal system, or in any hierarchy for that matter, are usually couched in terms of efficiency, justice, or public interest. They assert that one level rather than another is inherently better able to make good decisions on an issue or more likely to produce better policy. In fact, behind such arguments is a hope that some particular interest is stronger in a particular arena.

All proposals for restructuring authority should be read at this second level. The debate might be about at-large voting districts versus single-member districts; about legislative versus judicial branch competence; or about private sector versus public sector efficiency. But underneath the seemingly technical argument that a different structure of authority necessarily produces better outcomes is a vision of competing interests and an effort to change the balance of power between them. The hope in proposals for structural change is to split up old or potential alliances, establish new ones, and so place a favored interest in a position of dominance.

Conclusion: Political Reason

Inspired by a vague sense that reason is clean and politics is dirty, Americans yearn to replace politics with rational decision making. Contemporary writings about politics, even those by political scientists, characterize it as "chaotic," "the ultimate maze," or "organized anarchy." Politics is "messy," "unpredictable," an "obstacle course" for policy, and "a hostile environment" for policy analysis. There is "an uneasy relationship between social scientists and public officials," because one group provides "disciplined research" while the other has "undisciplined problems." Policy is potentially a sphere of rational analysis, objectivity, allegiance to truth, and pursuit of the well-being of society as a whole. Politics is the sphere of emotion and passion, irrationality, self-interest, shortsightedness, and raw power.

The enterprise of extricating policy from politics assumes that analysis and politics, can be, and are in some essential way, separate and distinctive activities. Charles Lindblom, who does not believe the two spheres are separate very often, formulated the differences very clearly:

> When we say that policies are decided by analysis, we mean that an investigation of the merits of various possible actions has disclosed reasons for choosing one policy over others. When we say that politics rather than analysis determines policy, we mean that policy is set by the various ways in which people exert control, influence, or power over each other.[1]

[1] Charles Lindblom, *The Policy-Making Process* (Englewood Cliffs, N.J.: Prentice-Hall, 1980), p. 26.

Most social scientists, and indeed many practitioners and proponents of policy analysis, are uncomfortable with a strict dichotomy between reason and power, but their response has been to develop versions of a middle ground that combines elements of the different spheres, still assuming their distinctiveness.

From one side come visions of rational analysis that is a little more like politics. Lindblom offered a less ambitious form of rational analysis, known variously as "muddling through" or incrementalism, in which policymakers would formulate very small goals (incremental change) and consider only a very limited number of alternatives.[2] Amitai Etzioni proposed "mixed scanning" that would combine fundamental "rationalistic" decision making with incrementalism.[3] Charles Schultze suggested that policy analysts could be "rationality advocates" within politics, throwing their weight against presumably "political advocates."[4]

From the other side come models of politics that make it a little more like analysis. Policy making is portrayed as a sequential process that sometimes gets out of order. An issue is put on the agenda and defined. It moves down the conveyor belt of political institutions, from legislative committees to chambers of the whole, where it is converted into a "policy alternative" or program. The program moves on to the bureaucracy and out into the field, where it is implemented and perhaps evaluated. Even though no political scientist (so far as I know) thinks that the process actually happens this way, many use this framework as the norm or benchmark against which they describe what actually happens. The "real" policy-making process is seen as an approximation of the norm, with occasional or perhaps even frequent deviations. Thus, for example, David Robertson and Dennis Judd begin their book on American public policy with a definition and description of the policy process that follows this sequential model.

[2]Charles Lindblom, "The Science of Muddling Through," *Public Administration Review* 19 (1959): 79–88; and *The Intelligence of Democracy* (New York: Free Press, 1965).

[3]Amitai Etzioni, "Mixed-Scanning: A 'Third' Approach to Decision-Making," *Public Administration Review* 27 (1967): 385–392.

[4]Charles Schultze, *The Politics and Economics of Public Spending* (Washington D.C.: Brookings Institution, 1968), p. 96.

Then, they comment that actual policy making is more "untidy" than the model and go on describe actual policy making in American history without ever referring to the model again.[5]

This book challenges the dichotomy of analysis and politics from which such middle grounds are blended. The categories of thought behind reasoned analysis, I argue, are themselves constructed in political struggle, and nonviolent political conflict is conducted primarily through reasoned analysis. It is not simply, therefore, a matter that sometimes analysis is used in partisan fashion or for political purposes. *Reasoned analysis is necessarily political.* It always involves choices to include some things and exclude others and to view the world in a particular way when other visions are possible. Policy analysis is political argument, and vice versa.

Metaphoric versus Calculating Reason

The rational model of decision making is reasoning by calculation. It rests on estimating the consequences of actions, attaching values to the consequences, and calculating to figure out which actions yield the best results. But, as we have seen in Chapter 9 ("Numbers") and Chapter 10 ("Decisions"), calculation cannot occur until we already have categories in place. The definition of categories determines how a count will come out.

Categories are human mental constructs in a world that has only continua. They are intellectual boundaries we put on the world in order to help us apprehend it and live in an orderly way. That is the meaning of the phrase "social construction of reality" and the school of thought it denotes—not that there is no reality apart from social meanings, but that we can know reality only by categorizing it, naming it, and giving it meaning.[6]

That the world is composed of continua, not categories, is as true in the natural world as in social affairs. Stephen Jay Gould tells of controversies that racked the scientific community in earlier times: is (or are) a Siamese twin(s) with one head and two lower bodies one person or two people? Is a Portuguese man-of-war a single organism,

---

[5] David Robertson and Dennis Judd, *The Development of American Public Policy* (Glenview, Ill.: Scott Foresman, 1988).

[6] The phrase is the title of a book by Peter L. Berger and Thomas Luckmann (New York: Doubleday, 1966).

as it functions, or a colony, as it evolved?[7] A botanist wonders when a plant stem stops being soft tissue and becomes wood?[8] There are no objective answers to these questions, because <u>nature doesn't have categories; people do.</u>

We might be tempted to write off the problem of the Siamese twin(s) as an insignificant rarity, but the question it raises comes mighty close to ones we ask in contemporary policy debates: Is a fetus a person? Is a frozen fertilized ovum a person? When does life end? Is the person who shoots someone, sending him into irreversible coma and brain death, guilty of murder? Or is the person who pulls the respirator plug the one who ends the victim's life? Is the fighting in Bosnia a threat to American interests? Is our economy in a recession?

There are, to be sure, objective facts underlying all these situations. The fetus could probably be described as consisting of certain kinds of tissues, with a determinable weight, chemical composition, and anatomical formation. But these kinds of facts are simply not the ones that matter in politics. What people care about and fight about are interpretations of fetuses, shootings, wars, and economies. What communities decide about when they make policy is meaning, not matter. And science cannot settle questions of meaning.

Given a world of continua, there is infinite choice about how to classify. Legend has it that according to a certain Chinese encyclopedia, animals are divided into: (a) belonging to the emperor, (b) embalmed, (c) tame, (d) suckling pigs, (e) sirens, (f) fabulous, (g) stray dogs, (h) included in the present classification, (i) frenzied, (j) innumerable, (k) drawn with a very fine camel hair brush, (l) et cetera, (m) having just broken the water pitcher, (n) that from a long way off look like flies.[9] We take delight in this list because it liberates us from our own conceptual cages and reminds us how powerful a hold our categories have on our ways of looking at the world. Compare the Chinese taxonomy of animals with this list of the causes of poverty from a widely read American sociology textbook of the 1920s and 1930s: poor natural resources, adverse climate, adverse weather, insect pests, disasters,

[7] Stephen Jay Gould, "Living With Connections," and "A Most Ingenious Paradox," both essays in his *The Flamingo's Smile: Reflections in Natural History* (New York: Norton, 1985).

[8] Robert Greenleaf Leavitt, *The Forest Trees of New England* (Jamaica Plain, Mass.: Arnold Arboretum of Harvard University, 1932), pp. 113–115.

[9] I got this story from Laurence Tribe, "Policy Science: Analysis or Ideology?" *Philosophy and Public Affairs* 2, no. 1 (1972): 66–110. Tribe got it from Michel Foucault, who got it from Jorge Borges.

illness and diseases, physical inheritance, mental inheritance, adverse surroundings of children, death or disability of the earner, unemployment, lack of proper wages, traditions, customs, habits, advertising and installment buying, fluctuations between costs of living and income, inequitable distribution of wealth and income, family marital relations, political conditions, and unwise philanthropy.[10]

Policy is centrally about classification and differentiation, about how we do and should categorize in a world where categories are not given. The old saws about "treating likes alike" and "giving each person his due" tap into a powerful drive for order, even if they are indeterminate about what that order should be. Policy arguments are convincing to the extent that they give a satisfying account of the rightness of treating cases alike or differently.

Political reasoning, therefore, is primarily a reasoning of sameness and difference, and of good and bad or right and wrong. The reasoning of more or less is only secondary. Policy argument takes the general form of claiming that something should be included in or excluded from a category. A cake belongs in the category of "parts of meals" rather than "food item by itself." Demolition of a historic building belongs in the category of "harm to others" rather than "self-regarding action." Stripping an elected office of its powers just when a black man gets elected belongs in the category of "voting discrimination" rather than "government action indirectly related to voting." All the forms of problem definition discussed in Part III are techniques of classifying. Literary devices serve to make something look more like one thing than another. Numbers carry implicit categorizations of the things they measure. Causal stories divide events into those like accidents and those like willed or controlled actions, and within the realm of control they differentiate kinds of responsibility. Representations of interests divide political actors into strong and weak forces and good and evil characters. Representations of rational decisions divide human actions into the possible and impossible (the things left out), and within the realm of the possible, into larger and smaller outcomes.

Reasoning by calculation, the reasoning of more or less, becomes important in politics only once categories have been established. Then we can ask, will policy A or B lead to the least harm? Or, does library budget A or B give us more value for the money? We cannot even ask

[10] I derived this list from J. L. Gillin, *Poverty and Dependence* (1921, 1926, 1937), which C. Wright Mills reviewed in his essay on then-contemporary sociology texts: "The Professional Ideology of Social Pathologists," *American J. of Sociology* vol. 49, 1943, pp. 165–180; the list of poverty causes is on p. 172.

such questions until we have established what counts as a harm, what kinds of actions are possible, what a library is, and what counts as value.

POLITICAL REASONING AS STRATEGIC REPRESENTATION

If political reasoning is metaphoric, what makes it different from poetic metaphor? Political reasoning is always conducted as part of a struggle to control which images of the world govern policy. More precisely, three elements make metaphoric reasoning in politics different from pure poetic metaphor.

First, the stakes are higher. Poets try to persuade their audiences of the rightness of their metaphors, too, but political actors are struggling to control immediate and often very concrete policy results. Political reasoning frames issues for decision in politics.

Second, because political reasoning is part of a contest over policy, it is always addressed to a hostile audience. A political metaphor always faces a potential opponent, a competing metaphor. That opponent might simply be the status quo, the usual or dominant way of looking at things, or what a community takes for granted. Or it may be a specific opponent, a political actor who poses and defends an alternative metaphor. Sometimes no one challenges a reigning metaphor, but that doesn't mean it is secure forever.

Third, political reasoning is strategic. It is designed to build constituencies, to break up old alliances and forge new ones, and to galvanize
people into action, or alternatively, to maintain old power structures
and lull people into complacency. It seeks to evoke values and emotions by presenting something as good or evil, innocent or guilty,
responsible or not, possible or impossible, strong or weak, right or
wrong. Ultimately, political reasoning is a process of creating, changing, and defending boundaries.

POLICY PARADOXES AS BOUNDARY TENSIONS

In a world of continua, boundaries are inherently unstable. Whether they are conceptual, physical, or political, boundaries are border
wars waiting to happen. At every boundary, there is a dilemma of
classification: who or what belongs on each side? In policy politics,
these dilemmas evoke intense passions because the classifications confer advantages and disadvantages, rewards and penalties, permissions
and restrictions, or power and powerlessness.

Each type of policy solution presented in Part IV might be seen as a
mode of constructing and maintaining boundaries. With inducement
systems, people try to cast their behavior as "fitting" in the category
that draws reward or escapes penalty. They try to influence inducement givers to see behavior in one way or another, or to draw the categories of rewarded and penalized behavior differently. With rules,
people seek to continue doing something important to themselves
while still coming "within" the rules of what is permissible. And rule
enforcers interpret rules according to their own sense of the bounds of
normality or justice. Persuasion as a policy strategy is permanently
mired in a debate about the boundary between indoctrination and
education. The articulation and administration of rights is a continuous struggle over the boundary between what the state does—the positive concept of rights—and what people think it ought to do—the
normative concept of rights. Finally, the design of authority structures
is a battle for participation, for inclusion among the category of decision makers. These mechanisms are best understood as modes of
establishing boundaries and stylized rituals for the conduct of boundary disputes. Through them, policy boundaries are drawn and
redrawn.

THE VALUE OF POLITICAL REASON

The rationality project often leads to formulas for the "best way" that are, in turn, species of political reason. They are strategies for framing issues so as to benefit some interests at the expense others. That does not mean, however, that we should abandon political reason.

Because political reason is a process of persuasion, it is an enterprise of searching for criteria and justifying choices. Equity, efficiency, liberty, security, democracy, justice, and other such goals are only aspirations for a community, into which people read contradictory interpretations. But while the interpretations divide people, the aspirations unite us. The process of trying to imagine the meaning of a common goal and fitting one's own interpretation to that image is a centripetal force.

The search for criteria to justify classifications forces us to articulate our wishes, preferences, and visions. Save for that pressure, we could not communicate and would not be a community. Political reasoning may seem to lack constraints, but it still forces us to interact with an audience, to persuade others, and to look outside our own will for grounds for action. In the process of articulating reasons, we show each other how we see the world. We may not ever see eye to eye, yet there is a world of difference between a political process in which people honestly try to understand how the world looks from different vantage points, and one in which people claim from the start that their vantage point is the right one.

Boundary tensions may be the curse of our existence as thinking and communal beings. But political reason is our privilege. It allows us to conduct our border wars with imagination words instead of weapons.

Credits

p. 4, © United Feature Syndicate, Inc; p. 29, drawing by Dana Fradon, © 1976 The New Yorker Magazine, Inc.; p. 50, courtesy of Boris Drucker; p. 80, © 1994 Mark Stivers; p. 95, Dave Coverly, courtesy *Bloomington-Herald-Times*; p. 111, © Bill Watterson; p. 140–41, Copyright © 1985 by The New York Times Company. Reprinted by permission; p. 147, courtesy Carol*Simpson Productions; p. 171, drawing by Tom Toles, © Universal Press Syndicate; p. 196, © 1995 David Sipress; p. 230, drawing by Tom Toles, © Universal Press Syndicate; p. 244, drawing by Mort Gerberg, © 1995 The New Yorker Magazine, Inc.; p. 270, © Randy Glasbergen; p. 278, John Branch, courtesy *San Antonio Express-News*; p. 293, courtesy Michael D. Rhoda, Briargate/Cheyenne Editions; p. 315, drawing by Dana Fradon, © 1977 The New Yorker Magazine, Inc.; p. 328, courtesy Jeff Danziger and the *Christian Science Monitor*; p. 353, © United Feature Syndicate, Inc.; p. 378, reprinted by permission of Signe Wilkinson and the *Philadelphia Daily News*.

Index